W9-BNC-194

DATE DUE

| FEB 0 5 2009 | |

The Psychology of
Gifted Children

WILEY SERIES IN DEVELOPMENTAL PSYCHOLOGY AND ITS APPLICATIONS

Series Editor
Professor Kevin Connolly

The Development of Movement Control and Co-ordination
J. A. Scott Kelso and Jane E. Clark

Psychology of the Human Newborn
edited by Peter Stratton

Morality in the Making: Thought, Action and the Social Context
edited by Helen Weinreich-Haste and Don Locke

The Psychology of Written Language: Development and Educational Perspectives
edited by Margaret Martlew

Children's Single-Word Speech
edited by Martyn Barrett

The Psychology of Gifted Children: Perspectives on Development and Education
edited by Joan Freeman

Further titles in preparation

The Psychology of Gifted Children

Perspectives on Development and Education

Edited by
Joan Freeman

Theodore Lownik Library
Illinois Benedictine College
Lisle, Illinois 60532

JOHN WILEY & SONS
Chichester · New York · Brisbane · Toronto · Singapore

155
.455
P974

Copyright © 1985 by John Wiley & Sons Ltd.

All rights reserved.

No part of this book may be reproduced by any means,
nor transmitted, nor translated into a machine
language without the written permission of the
publisher.

Library of Congress Cataloging in Publication Data:
Main entry under title:

The Psychology of gifted children.
   (Wiley Series in Developmental Psychology and
   its Applications)
   Includes index.
   1. Gifted children—Psychology. 1. Freeman, Joan,
   II. Series.
   BF723.G5P79 1985   155.4'55   84 -17340
   ISBN 0 471 10255 5

British Library Cataloguing in Publication Data:

The Psychology of gifted children—(Wiley Series in
   Developmental Psychology and its Applications)
   1. Gifted children
   l. Freeman, Joan
   155.4'55   BF723.G5

   ISBN 0 471 10255 5

Printed in Great Britain by
St Edmundsbury Press, Bury St Edmunds, Suffolk

List of Contributors

KIPPY I. ABROMS, *Chairperson Special Programs, Department of Education, Tulane University, New Orleans, LA 70118, USA.*

ROBERT BROOKS, *Senior Lecturer in Education Studies, Faculty of Education, Brighton Polytechnic, Village Way, Falmer, Brighton, BN1 9PH, UK.*

NAVA BUTLER-POR, *Senior Lecturer, School of Education, University of Haifa, Mount Carmel, Haifa 31 999, Israel.*

HERMAN VAN BOXTEL, *Psychologogisch Laboratorium, Katholieke Universiteit, Montessorilaan 3, 6500 HE Nijmegen, Holland.*

JAMES R. DESLISLE, *Assistant Professor Special Education, Kent State University, Ohio 44242, USA.*

HANS J. EYSENCK, *Professor of Psychology, University of London Institute of Psychiatry, De Crespigny Park, Denmark Hill, London SE5 8AF, UK.*

LYNN H. FOX, *Professor of Education and Director, Intellectually Gifted Child Study Group, The Johns Hopkins University, Whitehead Hall, Baltimore, Maryland 21218, USA.*

JOAN FREEMAN, *Hon. Tutor, Department of Education, University of Manchester, Manchester M13 9PL, UK.*

JAMES J. GALLAGHER, *Kenan Professor and President of the World Council for Gifted and Talented Children, Frank Porter Graham Child Development Center, Highway 54 Bypass West 071 A, University of North Carolina at Chapel Hill, NC 27514, USA.*

JEAN-CLAUDE GRUBAR, *Professor Education Spécialisée, Laboratoire de Psychologie des Aquisitions Cognitives et Linguistiques, Université de Lille III, 9 rue August Angellier, F-59046 Lille Cédex, France.*

ERIKA LANDAU, *Director, The Young Person's Institute for the Promotion of Art and Science, Supervisor, Department of Psychotherapy, Tel Aviv*

University, Technical College, 32 University Street, POB 17074, Tel Aviv 61170, Israel.

MICHAEL LEWIS, Professor and Chief, Division of Child Development, Rutgers Medical School, Medical Education Building CN 19, New Brunswick, New Jersey 08903, USA.

D. T. E. MARJORAM, Divisional Inspector Metropolitan and South Midland Division, Her Majesty's Inspectorate, Department of Education and Science, William Blake House, 8 Marshall Street, London, W1V 1LP, UK.

LINDA MICHALSON, Assistant Professor of Pediatrics, Rutgers Medical School, Medical Education Building CN 19, New Brunswick, New Jersey 08903, USA.

FRANZ J. MÖNKS, Professor of Developmental Psychology, Psychologogisch Laboratorium, Katholieke Universiteit, Montessorilaan 3, 6500 HE Nijmegen, Holland.

R. D. NELSON, Lecturer in Mathematical Education, Department of Education, University of Manchester, Manchester M13 9PL, UK.

A. HARRY PASSOW, Jacob H. Schiff, Professor of Education, Teacher's College, Columbia University, New York, NY 10027, USA.

ROSAMUND SHUTER-DYSON, Editor, The Psychology of Music, Journal of the Society for Research in Psychology of Music and Music Education, 6 Rectory Close, Tadley, Basingstoke, Hampshire RG26 6PH, UK.

DIANA SHMUKLER, Senior Lecturer in Developmental and Clinical Psychology, University of the Witwatersrand, 1 Jan Smuts Avenue, Johannesburg, 2001 Republic of South Africa.

JEAN-CHARLES TERASSIER, Psychologue, President, Association Nationale pour les Enfants Surdoués, 26 Rue Paul Derouléde, 06000 Nice, France.

KLAUS K. URBAN, Akademischer Rat, Faculty of Education, Universität Hannover, Fachbereich Erziehungswissenschaften 1, Bismarckstrasse 2, D-3000, Hannover 1, West Germany.

BURTON WHITE, Director, Center for Parent Education, 55 Chapel Street, Newton, Massachusetts 02160, USA.

JOANNE WHITMORE, Assistant Dean for Teacher Education, College of Education, Kent State University, Kent, Ohio 44242, USA.

ZHA ZI-XIU, Lecturer, Institute of Psychology, Academica Sinica, Beijing, People's Republic of China.

WENDY ZIMMERMAN, Post-doctoral Intern, Intellectually Gifted Child Study Group, The Johns Hopkins University, Whitehead Hall, Baltimore, Maryland 21218, USA.

Contents

Foreword

By and large it is probably true that the most able and talented children in Europe and North America receive the poorest education. There are reasons why this is so, and of course there are exceptions. In Britain the educational system makes some special provision for those unfortunate individuals who suffer physical or mental disability. Such special provision is costly and also it has its drawbacks because it tends to segregate and isolate. These matters apart, there can be little doubt that concern for those exceptional children at the bottom of the scale has led to a focusing of research and hence to a better understanding of their problems and an improvement in their education and care. We know surprisingly little about exceptional children at the other end of the distribution and this despite the long-standing interest which our society claims to have in talent and creativity.

The very fact that gifted children are able tends to militate against them; they do not need special provision, it is argued, because they do well enough without it. This may be true, and certainly it may be the case that where we have to select which exceptional children shall receive special provision we choose, on various grounds, the handicapped rather than the gifted. However there are both theoretical and practical questions associated with the concept of giftedness. What do we know of creativity and how to develop it? Is giftedness a general or specific capacity? Does it arise at all ages; are there gifted babies and gifted grandparents? Does giftedness occur only in a cognitive dimension, or are there individuals who are gifted socially or in motor functions? .How shall we know a gifted child? How should the gifted be educated? Is giftedness really a statistical construct or does it relate to psychological processes? Dr Joan Freeman's long interest in gifted children and their education has enabled her to bring together a remarkably diverse set of essays which touches on these and other questions. Contributors from eight countries on four continents discuss a wide range of theoretical and practical issues. The discussions and arguments presented here should serve to chart not only our knowledge but also our ignorance of giftedness, and that is a fine beginning for further work.

KEVIN CONNOLLY

Preface

The aim of this volume of papers is to pull together the dominant strands of thought and work on the contentious subject of exceptionally high ability in children. It is less than clear-cut, for example, where the psychology of giftedness begins and ends, for though it is primarily concerned with a small minority of children, it also covers all aspects of child development and educational expertise. The more we find out about the gifted, the more it seems to highlight matters relating to all children, and indeed the overwhelming conclusion from this book is that concern for the gifted must be seen in the context of all children. If gifted children, for instance, are not always given the aesthetic and creative encouragement they need at school, this also applies to the others there. But in compiling this book, several assumptions have had to be made about gifted children—that they are somehow different from other children, that the differences are worthy of concern and investigation, and that some action can be taken on their behalf.

The authors' approaches and conclusions range widely, and though they may disagree on certain points, they are all keen to discover more about gifted children, and to make the knowledge available to people involved with them. Efforts have also been made here to open up some important new vantage points, such as the wider international one, which may give the reader a sense of the excitement involved in exploring this still fragile area of developmental psychology. Almost all the chapters were especially prepared for this volume; those based on already published material have been adapted, and were included both because they are important, and also to reach a wider audience than in the academic journals of the different nations in which they first appeared. Translating Chapter 18 from the original Chinese was editorially interesting, beginning with some unusual requests

to local Chinese restaurants (which were not able to be taken away), fruit-
less communication with the local Chinese Community Centre, and eventual
success, for which I am very grateful to Belinda Timlin at Oxford University.
It was also difficult to persuade Dr Zha Zi-Xiu to present her name as the
author, as she explained that she was part of a team, though she did finally
agree to be designated as the writer.

The text is arranged in three, somewhat overlapping, sections. The
first tackles the thorny problems of definition and identification of gifted
children, particularly those who do not show their gifts; the second focuses
on how it is to be gifted, and on the characteristics and behaviour of the children; while in the third section, consideration and suggestions are offered
about the education of the gifted. An overview of the whole subject, based
on these themes, is discussed in the first chapter. Reference in the book to
children and adults in terms of their sex is neutral, where it is possible, but
otherwise either 'he' or 'she' is used in random order, as in life.

My most sincere thanks go to all the contributors to this book for their
valuable work, most of which came in on time. I am truly grateful to
the Rockefeller Foundation of New York for the month's scholarship at the
Bellagio Study and Conference Centre, Italy, where great progress was made
on this book. Celia Bird, Michael Coombs and Wendy Hudlass at Wiley's
have given me constant encouragement; I thank them and Kevin Connolly,
the editor of this series, for their considerable help. But most of all I am
appreciative of the practical help and encouragement of my husband, Hugh.

JOAN FREEMAN

The Psychology of Gifted Children
Edited by Joan Freeman
©1985, John Wiley & Sons, Ltd.

CHAPTER 1

A Pedagogy for the Gifted

JOAN FREEMAN

Giftedness is not a description which is acceptable to everyone, particularly those who see all children as 'equal'; indeed, the very idea that some children have gifts while others have not seems unjust. The concept implies something extra, as is recognized in many languages, such as the Italian superdotado, the French surdoué, or (in translation) the Chinese supernormal. The term 'gifted' is often used as though it were a unitary syndrome, though gifted children have as many individual differences as any others, but (as with handicapping conditions) gifts often come in clusters. Sometimes children are highly able in a broad spread, such as verbally or aesthetically, but talent can also occur singly, such as for mathematics alone.

Perceptions of what is meant by gifted have changed considerably since the term was first used, around the beginning of this century. Initially, it referred to adults who had achieved outstandingly, and then, when it filtered down to children, was given to the top few per cent who had outstanding academic success. Since about the 1960s, it has been broadened to include, not only those of varying abilities, such as social and creative skills, but much more of the population—up to about 25 per cent of all children. The historical perceptions of the concept of giftedness are described by Passow (Chapter 2), particularly as it applies to the United States.

Attitudes towards the idea that some children are very much better at some things than other children are bound up with social and political outlooks, so that educational aims in different parts of the world affect the recognition of and provision for the gifted. The American attitude towards individual fulfillment, where toddlers can be called 'severely gifted' or 'geniuses' to draw attention to their needs, is actually closest in provision to the Russian concept of developing each according to his abilities for the good of the nation. In Western Europe, educational aims are less specifically designed to pull out the best abilities of the child, but aim to promote a more generally cultured adult. The distress caused by distinguishing some children as gifted often has 'elitism' at its root, the implication being that this somehow confers a form of 'unearned' privilege, but it is possibly a left-over from the old style of discrimination, in which money and social position rather than ability, brought genuine privilege. As even the idea of a 'meritocracy' has echoes of unwarranted power, it looks as though some new terminology is needed.

Whether they evolve through personal experience, by tradition, or by catching the zeitgeist, attitudes towards extra educational provision for any group of children are bound to affect the way these services function. For example, when mental and physical handicaps in children were viewed as unmanageable by teachers and unfair to other pupils in the normal classroom, such children in many countries were sent to special schools, but now that they are acceptable as children 'in their own right', most are being integrated into ordinary classes. The commonest attitudes to the gifted have been summed up by Tilsley (1982) as concerns with elitism, their value as a national asset, their capacity to develop without special help, the justice of allocating scarce resources to them (vis-á-vis the less able or handicapped), and the adequacy of existing educational provision to meet their needs.

Klaus Urban tackled this delicate matter of attitudes towards the gifted in his research in West Germany (Chapter 20) and has possibly found the vital key on which the opposition to special provision hangs. For his population, it was not so much the definition of the children as gifted which was resented, but spending money on their behalf. Teachers had no objection to the children receiving special education, but objected strongly to special equipment to help it along—illogical perhaps, but attitudes are not usually formed just to an equation.

Great strides have been made in providing for the gifted in many countries, and a common concern amongst them was shown by the formation of the World Council for the Gifted and Talented in 1975, an organization which has held several international conferences. Gallagher, the 1983 President of the Council, reviews provision across the world, relating it to different cultures and economies (Chapter 19). He explains how many countries have evolved ways appropriate to their culture of helping the gifted, and outlines the educational stategies which have been the most successful. Many countries are trying to stimulate the talents of their gifted children so as to find creative solutions to their particular needs from within their own human potential, though where tradition rules, there may be concern about a possible threat to the existing system in the development of giftedness and creativity, which may be avoided. The socialization of children in developing countries within their families is particularly important for understanding the development of giftedness there, since the family is much more influential than in the West. The Middle-Eastern family, for instance, embodies its strong authority in the father, which affects the outlooks and chances of girls. This aspect of gifted childrens' lives is neatly illustrated by the study from Israel by Butler-Por (Chapter 17), where three styles of living—Western, Kibbutz and Arab—were examined for their effects on children's self-concept and motivation for achievement.

It is of special interest in the international context to know what is going on in China, a classless society, where what one sees as the ethical problems of 'elitism' so prevalent in the West, have been accepted as a priority for the country's well being, and special provision has been made for her brightest children (Tittle, 1982). This began with Keypoint or Pivot schools which were set up in 1978 after the hiatus of the Cultural Revolution, and pedagogical research is now in full swing as part of the modernization programmes of the People's Republic; some of this is described by Zha Zi-xiu, on behalf of her team (Chapter 18). Similar systems exist in other communist countries, notably the Soviet Union (Dunstan, 1983), which practices more intensive selection for the gifted than any Western European nation, being keen for each child to fulfil his potential for the nation. There are at least 100 music schools in Russia, and about as many each for the different arts and for mathematics. Bright children are not segregated in normal schools, but provision is made for them via out-of-school activities, in special classes, and where necessary, in special boarding schools.

In practice, the term 'gifted' is always used in a comparative manner, indicating outstanding abilities, so that it is a relative judgement. Even in the same area of activity, children can be called gifted at different levels of achievement, depending on the basis used for the comparison. For example, children with the same intellectual ability who are attending different schools may be seen by their teachers as dull, average, or gifted, depending on the level of their classmates. A child is never termed gifted without reference to others, and this labelling is more than likely to affect the attitudes and behaviour of others, as well as the child's own self-concept (Cornell, 1983). Such relative and often subjective understanding of the meaning of giftedness emphasizes the importance of clear definition in the criteria for selection of research populations, in the interpretation of results, and in comparisons between studies. Generally, children are identified as gifted in terms of their precocity, so that in time, when they lose that edge, they are no longer recognized. Adults, however, in order to be termed gifted, have to show their mettle in the quality of their accomplishments.

DIFFERENT KINDS OF GIFTEDNESS

The expression of exceptional ability, especially of the not strictly intellectual kind, is very dependent on circumstances. It can never be assumed that gifted children will somehow rise to the top 'like cream', or that they will always be seen in Plato's term as 'golden children'. Such descriptions apply only to the manifest achievers. A variety of reasons why a gifted child may be failing to function at her true level of ability in any field is described by Joanne Whitmore (Chapter 6), who shows that the over-riding problem for the under-achieving gifted is the lack of provision for them to learn. Its causes are always socio-psychological: where neither tests nor teachers identify the children as potentially gifted, it is because they may belong to a minority culture, are physically handicapped, maladjusted, or simply because not enough has been found out about them. She details many ways in which such injustice can be righted, including the changes in perspective which teachers and administrators would have to make. But perhaps a more insidious and certainly more widespread problem in the identification of the gifted, discussed by Lynn Fox and Wendy Braverman (Chapter 12), concerns girls. A socio-psychological cause is again at the root of the problem, essentially one of teacher expectations, together with the girls' conformities to their perceived norm of female behaviour.

Although no chapter in this collection is specifically dedicated to physical talent, it is discussed by several authors, such as Gallagher (Chapter 19), who explains how in some countries, this may be encouraged in schools where a high level of intellect is given less attention; Passow (Chapter 2) suggests this is because performance gifts are seen as less 'elitist', and are therefore less controversial. But in general, sporting talent is given considerable help in most schools round the world, with extra tuition, provision of equipment, competitions, and peer and society approval—a situation in which children with a bent for chemistry or languages are unlikely to find themselves.

Aesthetic ability is particularly dependent for its encouragement on cultural mores. As with other performance abilities, the arts are not usually contentious areas, and extra provision exists in many countries in the form of special schools for dance and music, though talent for fine-art generally receives relatively little help. In her description of musical giftedness (Chapter 9), Rosamund Shuter-Dyson covers many points which apply to the other arts, such as their inter-relationships, home influences on them, and the special characteristics of the children who have these talents.

The most recent focus on giftedness is on the difficult area of social gifts. One problem, for example, is in the American search for leadership traits in children—a concept not much favoured in Europe for historical reasons. In the wholesome context of education, social awareness and leadership potential are generally considered to be beneficial, though there is no obvious reason why these same skills cannot be turned to other purposes, as Robert Brooks (Chapter 16) has shown in his discussion of gifted delinquents. The present state of this prickly area of social giftedness is overviewed by Kippy Abroms (Chapter 11), who describes research evidence which indicates that pro-social behaviour is probably related to high intelligence and overall high ability.

However, when most people think of giftedness, they think of exceptionally high intelligence, a theme which courses through most of the chapters in this book. But is is important, especially with regard to gifted children, to avoid giving overwhelming stress to the intellectual aspects of their development, to the detriment of their emotional and physical needs (see Chapter 13). In fact, Scarr (1982) has concluded that motivation and adjustment are equally vital determinants of intellectual competance; the poor learning histories of children, labelled culturally disadvantaged, being more heavily influenced by the insufficiency and poor development of these factors than by cognitive insufficiencies.

The understanding of intelligence and the ways it has been and is likely to be measured—such as by electrical activity in the brain—are described by Hans Eysenck (Chapter 7), who also includes its relationship with creativity, another concern which threads through the text. Although the question of how much intelligence is heritable and how much is environmentally influenced is unlikely ever to be resolved to everyone's satisfaction, the field of battle is fully described. The value of cortical measures of intelligence is still only in a state of exciting promise (Gale and Edwards, 1983), but understanding of it is extended by the still experimental French work on sleep by Grubar (Chapter 8), who has found a close relationship between high IQ and sleep rhythms, notably cerebral 'immaturity' and greater plasticity of function.

THE ASSESSEMENT OF GIFTEDNESS

When tests were cruder, or were merely observations, it seemed that children developed new modes of thinking as they became older. But as tests have become more refined, and psychologists less narrow-minded, it is becoming difficult to prove that there is such a thing as psychological development. Abilities which were thought to develop slowly during childhood have been shown to be there right from the start. Even tiny babies have been shown to perceive, remember and understand things considered to be impossible just a few years ago. To show that new forms of thought develop in stages, in the way that Luria or Piaget have described, implies that these psychological mechanisms did not exist before; this is a difficult feat, for in spite of the increasing subtlety and preciseness of new forms of testing, they cannot be observed directly. Lewis and Michalson (Chapter 3) have been in the forefront of investigation into the abilities of newborn babies' abilities. They describe how giftedness was found to be detectable in infants, not by an IQ test, but in a more complex way involving the environment and potential. Burton White (Chapter 4) has taken these considerations higher up the pre-school age range, describing the first three years of a child's life as being a vitally important learning time and the basis of any manifest giftedness.

It is now becoming generally recognized that talents and gifts are unlikely to develop to anything like their full potential unless the child has the psychological and physical means of developing them. This implies that resources for the development of any special ability are themselves somehow part of the giftedness, and so should be included in the measurement. Some American states, realizing the unfairness of nationally designed tests for culturally deprived children, have devised special ones for particular groups. Children who would have scored only average or below on a nationally standardized measure can now be selected as in the top few per cent of their cultural group, are termed gifted, and are offered special education (Mercer, 1975). However, any comparison between different tests of ability which incorporate such variables as local dialect or diet is clearly impossible.

As the conceptualization of giftedness has become broader, so the means of measuring it have had to change. It is not only achievement which counts today, but the potential for achievement, and this often includes personality factors such as perseverance and originality, so that tests for giftedness may include measures of self-concept as well as aptitude. However, tests are not in favour with everyone. The somewhat unreliable paper-and-pencil creativity test, for example, has largely been replaced by evidence of progress from a child's daily work, which is more meaningful to him.

In contrast with what they see as the limited nature of IQ tests, said to identify only a sub-section of the gifted, Postlethwaite and Denton (1983) used the criterion of aptitude tests for tapping high potential in specific areas of the academic curriculum. Thirteen year-olds who scored in the top 10 per cent of their peers, in secondary comprehensive schools in Oxford, were tested for their potentials in English, French, mathematics, and physics. Teachers were also asked to nominate their top 10 per cent pupils. The national examination results at 'O' level, taken at sixteen years, provided the reliability criterion of future achievement, and in most subjects, teachers' nominations were largely confirmed by the test results. The main reason the researchers offer for the discrepancies between teachers' judgements of IQ and their own results, lies in the artificiality of the IQ to a teacher and in the relevance of the subject being taught; they therefore suggest that teacher nomination within these terms is a valuable aid in the identification of the gifted. This research is still in progress, but may perhaps answer the question of teacher influence on pupils' achievements, so that any doubts about self-fulfilling prophesies can be resolved.

There is considerable evidence to suggest that when children are identified as gifted by IQ in both Britain and the United States (in spite of the wide spectrum of IQ cut-off points), less than 50 per cent of them had been recognized as such before measurement by their teachers (Pegnato and Birch, 1959; Pohl, 1970; Tempest, 1974; Painter, 1980). But the two approaches to giftedness of IQ and academic achievement are not incompatible. Working with high-ability university students, Vernon (1983) considered that their faster cognitive processing, especially of a small number of basic cognitive processes, allowed them to acquire more information, which in turn increased their IQ scores.

BEING GIFTED

Though children who merit the adjective 'gifted' are in a minority numerically, this does not imply that, apart from their recognized abilities, they are in any way different from other children. Any assumption that emotional problems are part of the characteristics of the gifted has yet to be clearly demonstrated—an area discussed in Chapter 13.

However, drawing on his extensive psychological practice with gifted children in France, Terassier (Chapter 14) has outlined his conclusions about the problems of uneven development, when the development of the children's gifts is not paralleled by that of their other abilities, causing confusion to everyone concerned. These problems in adolescents, especially when peer relationships are involved, are considered by Mönks and Boxtel (Chapter 15), who attempt to understand the gifted adolescent within his social environment.

The Gulbenkian Research Project on Gifted Children (described in Chapter 13) looked in detail at some often-quoted characteristics of gifted children; many of them are not uncommonly found in the lists by which teachers are expected to identify the gifted, and many were discovered to be invalid. The general characteristics of physical, emotional, and mental development which were studied in the project are outlined below (and given in more detail in Freeman, 1983b).

Physical development

Though, as Terman (1925–1929) discovered, children with high IQs are likely to be physically better developed than those with lower scores, this

statistical correlation was seen to be due to the common feature of the
brighter children's high socio-economic levels. The better physical and
intellectual nurturing which middle-class children usually receive affects
both their physical development (Tanner, 1978; Davie et al. 1972), and their
IQ scores, notably in respect of improved problem-solving and educational
content. When children who were gifted on non-verbal tests were compared
with the average-scoring child, there was no significant physical difference.
Nor did gifted children, identified by either measure have a different pattern
of health from other children.

Eyesight

For once, the stereotype of the gifted child as being more likely to wear
spectacles than other children seemed to be correct.

Co-ordination

As with non-gifted children, co-ordination was found to be related to general
psychological adjustment, though boys had more difficulty with fine motor
control than girls, which is most likely to show up in their handwriting.

Emotional development

Gifted children, however measured, seem to be more emotionally stable
than other children (Gallagher, 1975; and see Chapter 13), and to be as ill-
affected by life circumstances as any other child. A high IQ score cannot of
itself bring about emotional maladjustment.

Feeling different

Gifted children did feel themselves to be different from others, but they
were aware that this difference was due to their superior intellect. They
described themselves as having considerable empathy with others, and were
generally more sensitive. Their personalities were not significantly different
from those of children with lower intelligence test scores, and it is probable
that some personality characteristics, such as ambition or curiosity, are in
fact features of their cultural circumstances rather than of their intellectual
abilities.

Sleep

The alleged characteristic of poor or little sleep of gifted children has never
been validated, and was not found to be so in the Gulbenkian study. Sleep

problems seemed to be more a matter of parental expectations than a behaviour which was related to IQ.

Friendships

Gifted children were found to mingle as freely as any other children at school; their teachers did not describe them as loners. But at home, they did have less friends than other children, though this was to some extent due to the nature of their out-of-school activities, such as musical instrument practice, and to the intellectual style of their hobbies.

Boredom

The children measured as gifted by IQ in the study did not complain of boredom in their non-specialist English schools, though their parents sometimes said they thought the children were bored. It is hard to say whether gifted children are more or less bored than others in the classroom situation.

Mental development

Giftedness may be measured by IQ tests, IQ tests with supplementary tests, or by achievement and other measures. It is important to know what measures (if any) are used in selecting the gifted, as this will affect the characteristics of the children selected.

Intelligence quotient

All children's achievements, including their IQ scores, are affected by their home backgrounds. This effect was seen very clearly in the Gulbenkian research, in that the parents (and grandparents) of the IQ 140+ children had very much higher levels of educational achievement and cultural activities than the other parents, including those of the children measured at an equivalent level of giftedness on the non-verbal Raven's test. The effective home background variables which improved the scores of non-verbally measured gifted children on the IQ test were of:

1. material provision (you can't become Yehudi Menhuin without a violin, or a scholar without books)
2. the parent's cultural activities (by themselves and with the child).

In this research project, it was apparent that the brighter the child on a non-verbal test, the more contaminated the IQ measure became by the children's educational environments, especially from IQ 130 upwards, which would involve about 3 per cent of the child population (Freeman, 1984). In other words, the brighter the child, the more he seemed to be able to extract information from the environment. Thus the environment is not the same for all children, but is somewhat adapted by the child according to his ability and outlook. Taking a process view of development, Scarr and McCartney (1983) have concurred with this idea by concluding that though opportunity is essential for genetic development 'most differences among people arise from genetically determined differences in the experiences to which they are attracted and which they evoke from their environments' (p. 433). In other words, if the environment is rich and varied in opportunities, it is the person's responsiveness to it which bring about individual differences— a theory which they say accounts for many of the seemingly anomalous results from work on family and twin studies. It is suggested on the evidence from the Gulbenkian Project that where an IQ test is used as a measure of giftedness, then some other form of non-verbal or specific ability measure be used in parallel, and that IQ from 130 upwards be regarded as reflecting achievement as much as native intelligence.

Verbal development

Even the children measured as gifted on a non-verbal test were found to be verbally precocious in the three skills of talking, reading, and writing. This high verbal ability was apparent as early as three years-old, and as they became older, the gifted became wider and more avid readers than other children.

Leisure activities

There was no apparent pattern in the children's hobbies or preferences. They did not make collections of things more than other children, though they were perhaps more intense about them; however, they had a great variety of interests, which included watching television (though they were more discriminating than other children), and they read anything which came to hand.

Curiosity

It was the quality of their curiosity which distinguished the gifted, though obviously, whether children ask questions is a feature largely conditioned by their upbringing. Sometimes the children appeared to their teachers to be not so much curious as 'know all', which was possibly due to their having to live up to their label as clever.

Concentration

The ability to concentrate, and to derive great benefit from it is a notable feature of a fine intellect and shows itself from an early age. It does not seem to be dependent on environmental circumstances.

Memory

The gifted children were said by their parents to have had exceptionally good memories from a very early age.

Sense of humour

Gifted children are often described as being able to see and emphasize absurdities in everyday life, and to enjoy playing with words and making up nonsense rhymes. But in this respect, these English children did not fit in with previous (often American) descriptions. In fact their humour, when it did show itself, was rather wry.

EDUCATIONAL NEEDS OF THE GIFTED

It is arguable that if educational provision were to meet the needs of all children, then there would be no reason for special concern for any exceptional group. It is something of a chicken-and-egg situation; if gifted children were to enjoy a truly child-centred education, then in theory, they would develop their exceptional abilities to an extent where these would be obvious. Yet how is their education to be provided appropriately when their capacities are unknown? Looking for comparison at the lowest ability range of exceptional children, and at the great progress that has been made in their educational provision, it would clearly be wrong to say that they would have benefited as well had their special needs not been taken into consideration.

In his experimental teaching with previously unrecognized primary-school gifted children, it seemed to Callow (1982) that before they had been identified and given special teaching, the children had been on their way to developing poor work habits. He found that they had been failing to develop the strategies necessary to tackle difficult problems which did not yield to a superficial approach, so that much of their talent could have stagnated—a situation which is probably generalizable to other gifted children who are not specially provided for educationally.

TEACHING THE GIFTED

Children do not normally start school with the label 'gifted' attached to them, and their opportunities to show what they can do are in practice often dependent on their classroom teacher—the outstanding conclusion of the Banbury Report on ability grouping in secondary comprehensive schools (Newbold, 1977). Gallagher (Chapter 19) expresses concern about the shared international problems of the inadequate spread of information and resources, especially in the training of teachers, for the gifted. He outlines suggestions to help remedy the situation, covering the teaching and learning aspects of the gifted child in the classroom, as well as the need for continued in-service support for the teacher. However, in spite of the heavy responsibility placed on the teacher's discernment at the 'chalk face', she does not have independence of choice, but is in fact at the end of a chain of direction. Given that educational provision is somehow reflecting the wishes of the wider society to bring up its young in an appropriate way, there are consequent profound influences on each teacher's work and on each child's experiences, and though these relate to all children, their special significance for the gifted is outlined here.

The most comprehensive work on the effects of the school on pupil's achievement is that of Rutter *et al.* (1979), who concluded on the basis of both empirical data and the re-examination of published statistics that schools had very much more impact than had previously been realized. While accepting that children in the same school will have different experiences, it was still statistically clear that after adjusting for intake characteristics: 'children at the most successful secondary school got four times as many exam passes on average as children at the least successful school' (Rutter, 1983). Even intelligence is not necessarily correlated with achievement in some schools; each school has its own ethos which can be particularly important for a child of exceptionally high ability. This team's findings for the successful schools include:

1. Tracking does improve performance, when organized via test achievement rather than teacher perception, and given easy mobility for pupils between tracks. A positive group effect was found in the concentration of pupils with good cognitive performance.
2. Although balancing a school's intake either ethnically or economically made little difference to the pupil's achievements, not surprisingly, schools with more intellectually favourable intakes tended to have better outcomes, i.e. to produce more high achievers.
3. Schools with high pupil achievements used more praise for good work in their teaching and in public. This is important for the gifted, who can miss out on praise when expectations for them are high.
4. An academic emphasis, with a task-focused approach to defined goals and high expectations of the pupils, was a crucial component of effective teaching. This should include pupil participation in educational planning, something in which many gifted pupils are keen and able to participate (Freeman, 1979).

Probably the single greatest influence on all teaching is the cloud of examinations and tests, which though it may be no bigger than a man's hand for the reception-class teacher, soon begins to become dominant on a school's syllabus. American children are said to be the most tested in the world, such that Eisner (1979), making a plea for a more liberal educational provision, believes that 'test scores function as one of the most powerful controls in educational practice', by which teachers define their teaching priorities. It is seen in all forms of selective school, such as the gymnasia of many European countries, the French Lyce' and the remaining secondary grammar schools in Britain. It is especially seen at the end of the process of secondary education in Britain, where the relatively standardized national examinations at 16 and 18 years provide evidence for teachers, pupils, and researchers of children's uptake of their lessons. With very bright children in the class, it would not be unreasonable to expect teachers to try to make the most of their pupils' examination-passing potential, for the sake of all-round honour, but with relatively light regard for the children's aesthetic and creative potential. This focus on recognized achievement has a tendency to rub off on the pupils, who also take examination success as their priority, and often as the source of their self-esteem. For some high achievers, examinations may be merely an exciting hurdle in the school calender, but others seem to spend the rest of their lives proving their ability to do well in life 'tests', from conversations to business deals.

Schools which have a name for being 'the best' are often those which have the most examination passes, and which have chosen to emphasize what of their teaching the tests assess. The effect on education of this routine and these predetermined goals is often to diminish the sparkle and excitement of discovery in learning, which is so vital to creative endeavour. However, gifted children may well do either more than the teacher expects, or something quite different, and thus put paid to the best laid educational plans.

A further serious bias in the teaching of the intellectually gifted is the present stress in education on rationality and measurement, which Eisner (1979) refers to as 'scientism'. Here, cognition has been theoretically separated from affect, to the deficit of subjects (and children) which need both, such as art or drama and their forerunner—play (Chapter 5). The gifted are often dissuaded from being serious about these educationally low-status subjects, as Delisle (Chapter 21) found in his own career and subsequently as a school-teacher, because these children are said to be too bright for such intellectually 'unsatisfying' pursuits.

This urge to quantify and control has also made it difficult to fit an exceptional child into school curricula which have been statistically designed to suit most children, effectively excluding the child as a participant in designing his own learning. Bias towards measurement also sets the parameters of the finding and solving of problems, so that what is not measurable is seen as intellectually ill-conceived. There is a recognizable relationship between educational planning and the kind of teaching it produces. For example, the effects of curricular research incorporated into teaching involve breaking up the subject matter into tiny consequential parts, obliging the gifted to spend tedious, educationally negative time working through them, when they could easily jump a few stages.

Two chapters in this book are dedicated to the encouragement of creative teaching which is not examinable. Diana Shmukler (Chapter 5) describes its preschool environmental influences, and gives evidence to show how children need the psychological freedom which comes from security to enjoy exploration through play—something that may well be denied to those who are good at passing exams. Erika Landau (Chapter 23) takes the theme into school by suggesting that, whatever degree of psychological freedom has been given to the child at home, the teacher is in a position to improve on it in the atmosphere of the classroom, with an open, questioning style of teaching, which results in improved creative and effective thinking. The combination of psychological freedom, which assists the child to good self-concepts, and a teacher who is ready to listen and guide, rather than dictate, is the basis of the creative classroom, providing a safe haven in which the gifted might try out their intellectual wings. At best, a teacher should be the senior learner in a communal effort, at worst an instructor training children out of being autonomous learners. The open approach asks that the teacher should give minimum direction to help the child start thinking about the subject, and should inspire him to ask the questions which will enable the gifted to go beyond the work-sheet, the textbook, and the 'correct' answer to try out their ingenuity. A biology teacher, for example, tackling the subject of hygiene in the Middle Ages, would not tell the class how it was done, but would provide the basic information and let the pupils work this out for themselves. Problems are a diagnostic measure for the bright—their intelligence will show up in their answers.

Although the creative questioning attitude is extremely important, one of the problems of the intellectually gifted is that their thinking is at an advanced stage and quality, so that they often sail close to the risk of poor practical activites, especially in an academically orientated school. When they first learn to write, it can be seen that their thoughts run ahead of their pencils. High IQ children are notoriously bad at hand-writing (Freeman, 1979), the content of their work often being superficial and incomplete, compared with what is going on in their minds, because it is such a tiresome business getting it down on paper. This is confusing for teachers, since the children usually talk with considerable fluency, and often turn to the written word of books for relaxation in preference to more practical activites such as team games. Such children will derive more excitement and take their ideas further by discussing them, than by associating them with the boredom of writing them down. Some teachers have said that this problem is largely overcome by teaching the children to type, though perhaps even this has now been superseded by word-processing for the lucky ones.

A CURRICULUM FOR THE INTELLECTUALLY GIFTED

To put any form of education for the gifted into operation, it is essential to know how the children differ in their educational needs from other children. These differences can be summarized in brief—whatever their talents, those who are exceptionally good at learning will do it faster and at a greater depth and breadth than other children (Wallace, 1983a). But this simple statement brings about a host of problems for all educational personel.

They learn faster

When a child has the ability to grasp a concept quickly, it means that she will need minimum, if any, practice to retain what she has learned, and consequently little if any revision. As all classrooms are to some extent mixed-ability, this throws the timing of lessons and problem-posing and -solving strategies into disarray. The gifted pupil may not only need an accelerated pace, but may quite naturally skip over sequences in the learning, which the other children will have to master before they can move on. A gifted child may know the answer before the teacher has finished the question.

This problem of pace is particularly noticeable in the teaching of the mathematically able, which Marjoram and Nelson have described (Chapter 10). From his years of research with mathematically precocious youth, Stanley (1976) is strongly of the opinion that they need separate and accelerated mathematical education, though Evyatar's work (1973) has indicated that a change of subject, such as art, may be more beneficial to young mathematicians, than more of the same—a tendency which Passow (1981) has described as 'overteaching' the gifted in the area of their gift. In recommending a broad syllabus for the gifted, Marjoram (1983) points out that the halls of fame are peopled with many who achieved greatness in fields other than those for which they were intended.

The ability to grasp ideas and reach conclusions more quickly, can mean in practice that gifted pupils may complete a work-sheet so rapidly that they may do it several times to keep themselves occupied in the classroom—a boring, soul-destroying sampling of school life. It is not only teachers who complain of too much paper-work; the gifted child can share in their agony of death by a thousand work-sheets.

Pace is also a big problem in the use of language, especially in reading; the gifted child seems to absorb the written word almost on impact, without the need to practice, and often before the age of five. At school they speed through conventional reading schemes, absorbing complex ideas and word patterns, so that a reading diet more advanced in both content and skill is actually required. This is particularly notable in primary school project work, when the gifted child will need to seek reference from adult level source-books, having soon exhausted those considered suitable for his age.

Greater depth and breadth

To extend the 'core-curriculum' for the gifted, one can take a subject in greater depth or breadth, either poring over the same problem in finer and finer detail or relating it to other subjects outside the basics. Children who are exceptionally good learners need both. They often become so involved with what they are learning that detail, complexity, and their exceptional degree of understanding bring about a high conceptual level, which calls for the introduction of a wider field of study.

Wallace (1983) points out the possibly far-reaching consequences of educating the gifted child appropriately, describing how she will steadily increase the intellectual difference between herself and her chronological peers by her relatively faster progress. This growing disparity can be handled most easily in a class where every member is aware that he is valued, but in addition, gifted children benefit emotionally and intellectually by regular meetings with others of like calibre in out-of-school settings for chess, astrology, archaeology, or play. Gifted children often have a natural desire for detail, to get to know all there is about a subject, so that the teacher may have to press for the greater educational benefits of a broader perspective. It is also important to see that as children move from one teacher to another, this extension of the curriculum is continued; therefore, careful notes should be made (as they should be for all children) to see that the gifted child is not provided with a stimulating education one year, only to be told to conform the next.

THINKING SKILLS

The society in which today's children will become adults is already visible as one in which many human activities are likely to be done by mechanical means. An ideal education for the gifted would concentrate less on content, which they find relatively easy to accumulate, than skills. Particularly in the more academic schools, most teaching has been concerned with conveying a body of knowledge, rather than attempting to develop independent thinking; however, gifted children, who have the ability, should be assisted by thinking exercises towards concept formation. It is not so much a matter of introducing philosophy to the class-room, though there are many who would enjoy it, but of teaching children (especially those who are most capable of handling it), the basics of the creative processing of information.

For example, children should learn how to obtain information and put it into a form in which it may later be retrieved. This implies that they must have a full understanding of the material as well as the higher-level abilities to synthesize from it, and to follow through to novel understandings. Problem-solving skills should be built in to teaching in many subject areas, so that the pupils are obliged to think for themselves. The skills of communicating what they have found are as important as the discoveries themselves, and should be taught and practiced in schools.

Language is a vital aspect of intellectual skills—even in maths, it is important for concept formation, and of course for communication. However, it cannot be taken for granted that intellectually gifted children will have a wider or more complex vocabulary than other children. Butler-Adam (1982), investigating intellectually gifted white children in South Africa, found that their advanced speech development was limited to a circumscribed area, mainly of their personal interests, and that some of these young children's non-verbal skills were greater than their language skills. Her suggestions for language teaching for the gifted are summarized here:

1. Novel or unusual stimuli should be presented, to ignite the children's wish to talk, write, or draw their reactions.
2. A broad range and balance of both language activities and linguistic expertise should be available, particularly in the primary school, so that children can exercise their language.
3. Access to all the school's libraries, laboratories, practical rooms, audio-visual aids, and other equipment should be made freely available (if under supervision).

Although reading has been seen to be central to achievement and scholastic performance, mechanical ability to read is not more important than the other cognitive and linguistic skills of reading. High IQ children are capable of quick and easy mechanical reading, which means that they may sometimes miss out on meaning and expression. The teacher should look at the books to which the child has access—many are bromides rather than stimulants, information-givers rather than thinking skills. Gifted children's writing, often lagging behind their reading and speaking, can also be turgid. It should be a means of personal expression, which should be viewed with sympathy, and different types of writing such as reports, stories, and advertising should be practised, with some non-intrusive specialist help for spelling and grammar.

EXTRA-CURRICULAR ACTIVITIES

Every neighbourhood, no matter how culturally deprived, has its share of interesting things for pupils to see and do, and interesting people to meet. Although this statement applies equally to all children, the gifted have the problem of meeting people with whom they can identify. Delisle (Chapter 21) has found this to be pertinent to vocational choice, particularly for girls, and has outlined many ways of making use of the community as an arena in which the gifted can develop.

The familiar educational triangle of child, parents, and school is particularly important for out-of-school activities, especially where the school is not able to provide either the resources or the teacher time to give the gifted the extra they need. Numerous activities and ways of participating in the community for clever children are given in Freeman (1983a).

Many schools run clubs and societies for children's interests, which because they are for specialists, often reach a high standard of excellence, challenging the very bright. Where they do not exist, children could be encouraged to start such activities themselves, with help from teachers or parents; several schools could combine their efforts. Such groups often find that they can have access to different kinds of institutions which welcome keen pupils, such as radar stations, computer laboratories, and farms. These societies not only provide the gifted with the opportunity to learn more about their particular interest, but to mix with like-minded children, which can be a great relief to them.

CONCLUSIONS

It is the right of all children in a civilized society to be educated according to their abilities, and that includes the gifted. The provision of the special facilities and care that this group need is but one aspect in the greater context of better education for all children, and it does have a general beneficial effect. Assessment procedures and increased awareness for identifying the gifted can increase the teacher's sensitivity towards individual differences of all the children in the class. Changes in the curriculum on behalf of the gifted are usually conceptual and can increase the cognitive level in the classroom, not only raising the overall standard of all the children's work, but adding to the variety and excitement of their learning. However, almost all the research evidence reaches the same conclusions for the gifted—that in spite of considerable efforts on the part of psychologists and educators, their needs are not generally being met. Gifted children can be helped by:

1. Information for parents and teachers about how they could spot a gifted child, preferably without the use of psychological tests.

2. Some special provision in ordinary schools for children who are brighter than the others.
3. Understanding that giftedness is not a 'problem', so that the label does not create tensions.
4. Concern for the child, as a child, which is not overbalanced by over-expectation and exploitation.
5. Concern for gifted children who are not showing their abilities, such as the handicapped, the culturally deprived, and girls.
6. Initial teacher training, good in-service support, and posts of special responsibility to help teachers recognize and encourage special talents of all pupils.

REFERENCES

Butler-Adam, J. E. (1982). *Language Ability in Children of High Measured Intelligence* . Institute for Social and Economic Research, Durban, South Africa.

Callow, R. (1982). The Southport inquiry and after. In *The Gifted Child at School* (ed. D. H. W. Grubb), Oxford Society for Applied Studies in Education, Oxford.

Cornell, D. G. (1983). Gifted children: the impact of positive labelling on the family system. *Amer. J. Orthopsychiat.* **53**, 322–335.

Davie, R., Butler, N., and Goldstein, J. (1972). *From Birth to Seven.* Longman, London.

Dunstan, J. (1983). Attitudes for provision for gifted children: the case of the USSR. In *Face to Face with Giftedness* (eds B. M. Shore, F. Gagné, S. Larivée, R. H. Tali, and R. E. Tremblay), Trillium Press, New York.

Eisner, W. *The Educational Imagination.* Macmillan, London.

Evyatar, A. (1973). Enrichment therapy. *Educational Research,* **15**, 115–122.

Freeman, J. (1979). *Gifted Children: Their Identification and Development in a Social Context.* MTP Press, Lancaster and University Park Press, Baltimore.

Freeman, J. (1983a). *Clever Children: a Parents Guide,* Hamlyn Paperbacks, London.

Freeman, J. (1983b). Identifying the able child. In *Finding and Helping the Able Child* (ed. T. Kerry), Croom Helm, London.

Freeman, J. (1984). Gifted children. In *The Biology of Human Intelligence* (ed. C. Turner), Eugenics Society Symposia, Vol. 5, Oliver and Boyd, Edinburgh.

Gale, A., and Edwards, J. A. (1983). Cortical correlates of intelligence. In *Pysiological Correlates of Human Behaviour,* (eds A. Gale and J. A. Edwards), Academic Press, London.

Gallagher, J. J. (1975). Research summary of characteristics of the gifted. In *Psychology and Education of the Gifted* (eds W. B. Barbe and J. S. Renzulli), Wiley, New York.

Marjoram, D. T. E. (1983). The secondary school curriculum and the gifted child. In *Face to Face with Giftedness* (eds B. M. Shore, F. Gagné, S. Larivée, R. H. Tali and R. E. Tremblay), Trillium Press, New York.

Mercer, J. R. (1975). Psychological assessement and the rights of children. In *The Classification of Children,* Vol. 1, (ed. N. Hobbs), Jossey-Bass, San Francisco.

Newbold, D. (1977). *Ability Grouping.* NFER, Slough.

Painter, F. (1980). Gifted children at home and school. In *Educating the Gifted Child* (ed. R. Povey), Harper and Row, London.

Passow, H. A. (1981). Nurturing giftedness: ways and means. In *Gifted Children: Challenging their Potential* (Ed. H. A. Kramer), Trillium Press, New York.

Pegnato, S. W., and Birch J. W. (1959). Locating gifted children in Junior High Schools: a comparison of methods. *Exceptional Children*, **25**, 300–304.

Pohl, R. G. (1970). Teacher nomination of intellectually gifted children in the primary grades. *Dissertation Abstracts*, **31**, 2237A.

Postlethwaite, K. and Denton, C. (1983). Identifying more able pupils in secondary schools. *Gifted Education International*, **2**, 92–96.

Rutter, M., Maughan, B., Mortimore, P., and Ouston, J. (1979). *Fifteen Thousand Hours*. Open Books, London.

Rutter, M. (1983). School effects on pupil progress: research findings and policy implications. *Child Development*, **54**, 1–29.

Scarr, S. (1982). Testing for children: assessement and the many determinants of intellectual competance. In *Annual Progress in Child Psychiatry and Child Development* (eds.) S. Chess and A. Thomas), Brunner/Mazel, New York.

Scarr, S., and McCartney, K. (1983). How people make their own environments: a theory of genotype → environment effects. *Child Development*, **54**, 424–435.

Stanley, J. C. (1976). Youths who reason extremely well mathematically: SMPY's accelerative approach. *Gifted Child Quarterly*, **20**, 237–238.

Tanner, J. M. (1978). *Foetus Into Man*. Open Books, London.

Tempest, N. R. (1974). *Teaching Clever Children 7–11*. Routledge and Kegan Paul, London.

Terman, L. M. (ed.) (1925-1929). *Genetic Studies of Genius*, Vols I–V. Stanford University Press, Stanford.

Tittle, B. M. (1982). The brightest in China. *Gifted Education International*, **1**, 45–50.

Vernon, P. E. (1983). Speed of information processing and general intelligence, *Intelligence*, **7**, 53–70.

Wallace, B. (1983). *Teaching the Very Able Child*. Ward Lock Educational, London.

SECTION I

Identification

The Psychology of Gifted Children
Edited by Joan Freeman
©1985, John Wiley & Sons, Ltd.

CHAPTER 2

The Gifted Child as Exceptional

A. HARRY PASSOW

Any discussion of the nature of giftedness and talent is heavily dependent on the definition used. It is important to know what giftedness is and how it is manifested, so that children can be identified and suitably provided for.

THE BACKGROUND

Galton published his book *Hereditary Genius* in 1869, drawing attention to his concern with very high ability, though a year before, William T. Harris had made a more practical move by introducing flexible promotion, as a way of providing for abler pupils in the St Louis schools. Other American school systems followed suit by instituting various programmes to meet the needs of 'pupils of more than average capability', 'brilliant children', 'pupils of supernormal mentality', 'gifted', and a variety of other terms—referring to individuals with high intelligence quotients and possibly also high scholastic attainments. 'Rapid advancement classes' for exceptionally bright children were started in New York City in 1900. By 1915, what eventually became known as the 'SP' classes were designed to hasten the progress of bright children by enabling them to complete seventh, eighth, and ninth grades in two years. It was Guy M. Whipple who was credited with having established the term 'gifted' as the standard designation of children of supernormal ability in the USA, having used it in Monroe's *Cyclopedia of Education* (referred to in Henry, 1920).

The reviews of programmes and provisions for the gifted in the early years, which appeared in the National Society for the Study of Education

(NSSE) 19th and 23rd Yearbooks (1920 and 1924), were clear that it was the highly intelligent and high academic achievers who were considered to be gifted, and it was the traits and characteristics of such individuals which determined the recognized nature of giftedness.

Although there was a good deal of activity and some research before Terman's Genetic Studies of Genius in 1922 (Terman, 1925)—the bibliography in the 19th NSSE Yearbook contains 163 items, and the 23rd NSSE Yearbook includes an annotated bibliography of 453 items—it was his team which began the first large-scale longitudinal study of the nature of the gifted. The Stanford Study 'was designed to discover what physical, mental and personality traits are characteristic of gifted children as a class, and what sort of adult the typical gifted child becomes' (Terman and Oden, 1959). Terman's search was aimed at locating 'subjects with a degree of brightness that would rate them well within the top one per cent of the school population'. A score of 140 IQ on the Stanford-Binet test, and for high-school pupils one of 135 IQ on the Terman Group Intelligence Test was what Terman described as the 'arbitrary standard' set for children's inclusion in the study.

However, Terman did not view the task of adding to knowledge about the origin and physical and mental traits of gifted children as an end unto itself. As he pointed out in the first report:

> When the sources of our intellectual talent have been determined, it is conceivable that means may be found which would increase the supply. When the physical, mental, and character traits of gifted children are better understood it will be possible to set about their education with better hope of success ... In the gifted child, Nature has moved far back the usual limits of educability, but the realms thus thrown open to the educator are still *terra incognita*. It is time to move forward, explore, and consolidate. (Terman, 1926).

The initial Terman study and the subsequent follow-up studies (which are still continuing, although Terman died in 1956), have lent support to the hypothesis that the early promise of intellectually gifted children is likely to culminate in outstanding achievement during adulthood. When one of Terman's co-workers, Catherine Cox (1926), took a reverse path by studying biographical material on 300 of the greatest men in history in an attempt to estimate their IQs, she found that all her subjects were highly superior in general intelligence. Among Terman's many findings was that, contrary to popular beliefs of the time, intellectually gifted youngsters were also far superior to their less highly endowed age peers in general health and physique, mental health and adjustment, adult intelligence, occupational status and earned income, publications and patents and even 'contentment'. Later British studies of gifted children, including those of Pringle (1970) and Hitchfield (1973), using a national cohort of children, and more recently Freeman (1979), found evidence in accord with Terman's.

Increasingly, superior intelligence, defined in various ways such as a percentage of the population (e.g. highest 1 or 2 per cent in general intelligence), or a particular cut-off score on a test of intelligence (e.g. 125 IQ or 135 IQ), was considered to define the gifted, and further programmes and provisions were made in American schools for nurturing the intellectually superior child. Lists of the mental, emotional, social, and physical characteristics—most of them lengthy and detailed—of children who scored high on individual or group tests of intelligence, and possibly of high scholastic merit too, were drawn up by a number of writers (Durr, 1964; Hoyle and Wilks, 1975; Ward, 1975; Clark, 1979; Tuttle and Becker, 1980). Obviously, though, as descriptions of the gifted are composites of a considerable number of individuals, not all children who are identified as gifted will possess all the cognitive, affective, physical or intuitive talents which are ascribed to them as a group, and sometimes a single characteristic in a child can indicate a special gift or talent.

Leta S. Hollingworth (in Pritchard, 1951) was studying the nature and needs of the gifted in New York City at the same time as Terman was conducting his longitudinal studies in California. She defined gifted children as those 'who are in the top 1 per cent of the juvenile population in general intelligence' which, in her view, was the 'power to achieve literacy and to deal with its abstract knowledge and symbols'. Nevertheless, in 1931, she had written:

> By a gifted child, we mean one who is far more educable than the generality of children are. This greater educability may lie along the lines of one of the arts, as in music or drawing; it may lie in the sphere of mechanical aptitude; or it may consist in surpassing power to achieve literacy and abstract intelligence. It is the business of education to consider all forms of giftedness in pupils in reference to how unusual individuals may be trained for their own welfare and that of society at large. (p. 49)

Cyril Burt's work on highly able children began in 1915 in Britain (Burt, 1975). It was this initial work which finally resulted in the national division of children by ability for different kinds of secondary education in 1944, by an examination taken at 11-plus years of age. The top scoring 25 per cent were selected to go to academic grammar schools, while the other 75 per cent received a more practical education in a secondary modern school. Other English speaking researchers, such as Parkyn of New Zealand (1948) and Lovell and Shields in England (1967) continued in the tradition of using intelligence, as measured, as the indication of giftedness in children.

However, as early as the 1940s, writers had begun to point to the limitations of intelligence tests in defining and identifying the gifted. Pritchard wrote for instance:

If by gifted we mean those youngsters who give promise of creativity of a high order, it is doubtful if the typical intelligence test is suitable for use in identifying them. For creativity points to originality, and originality implies successful management, control, and organization of new materials or experiences. Intelligence tests contain overlearned materials ... The content of the intelligence is patently lacking in situations which disclose originality or creativity. (Pritchard, 1951).

Writing in the American Association for Gifted Children's (AAGC) publication, Lally and La Brant (1951) pointed out how, since schools had been traditionally concerned with academic subjects, 'the search for gifted children has usually discovered the brilliant student in such areas' and that identification procedures tended to parallel the school emphasis—excluding those pupils talented in the arts. They noted that far less was known about special gifts other than intellectual giftedness.

THE DEFINITION IS EXPANDED

Definitions of gifted and talented have become more inclusive, or as Renzulli (1978) put it, 'more liberal'. Passow et al. (1955) have defined talent as the capacity for superior achievement in any socially valuable area of human endeavour, but limited the areas at that time to 'such academic fields as languages, social sciences, natural sciences, and mathematics; such art fields as music, graphic and plastic arts, performing arts and mechanic arts; and the field of human relations'.

The programme for the gifted in the Portland (Oregon) Public Schools (1959), sponsored by the Ford Foundation, took the position 'that a definition of giftedness limited to academic aptitude was much too narrow, and that there is a variety of socially useful abilities in children which should be identified and developed'. Portland's definition of giftedness 'included approximately the upper ten percent of the most intellectually talented pupils and also the same proportion of the most talented in each of the seven special aptitudes ... art, music, creative writing, creative dramatics, creative dance, mechanical talent and social leadership' (p. 13). It was one of the few school systems which defined giftedness broadly and which attempted to identify and nurture a broad array of gifts and talents.

In the Yearbook of the National Society for the Study of Education, Witty (1957) recommended that the definition of giftedness be expanded and that we consider any child gifted whose performance, in a potentially valuable line of human activity, is consistently remarkable. His suggested definition advocated a broad conception of the nature of giftedness, though phrases such as 'potentially valuable line of human activity' and 'consistently remarkable' raised a good many problems of specificity and meaning.

Perhaps the most widely used definition in the United States these days—'used' in the sense that a good deal of the literature alludes to it, and a great many school systems accept it as the guide to their planning—is that of the US Office of Education. It was suggested by an advisory panel to the then Commissioner of Education, Sidney Marland, Jr., and presented in the Marland Report (1971). For the most part, it has been accepted quite uncritically, but as Renzulli (1978) has pointed out, 'has served the very useful purpose of calling attention to a wider variety of abilities that should be included in a definition of giftedness ...'. It is as follows:

Gifted and talented children are those identified by professionally qualified persons who by virtue of outstanding abilities, are capable of high performance. These are children who require differentiated educational programs and/or services beyond those normally provided by the regular school program in order to realize their contribution to self and society. Children capable of high performance may not have demonstrated it as high achievement, but can have potential in any of the following areas, singly or in combination.

1. general intellectual ability
2. specific academic aptitude
3. creative or productive thinking
4. leadership ability
5. visual and performing arts
6. psychomotor ability

Renzulli (1978) has analysed definitions of giftedness, reviewed studies of the characteristics of gifted individuals, and proposed a definition of giftedness which he believes is useful to school practitioners, and which is defencible in terms of research findings. His conception of giftedness includes three elements: above-average ability; task commitment—a focused form of energy; and creativity (see Chapter 15).

More recently, Tannenbaum (1983) has proposed a psychosocial definition of giftedness which sees outstanding performance or excellence as produced by an overlap of five factors.

1. General ability—the 'g' factor, or tested general intelligence.
2. Special ability—special aptitudes and capacities.

3. Non-intellective factors—eg: ego strength, dedication, willingness to make sacrifices, and other traits integral to the achieving personality.
4. Environmental factors—in the home, school and community settings, which provide stimulation and support.
5. Chance factors—unforseen circumstances in the opportunity structure and prevalent life-style which can affect outlets for gifted performance.

THE INCLUSION OF CREATIVITY

Getzels and Jackson's (1958) studies of highly creative and highly intelligent youth led them to speculate that if a precedent were to be set by 'allowing an exception to the practice of labelling only high IQ as "gifted", the possibility of expanding the concept to include other potentially productive groups becomes a genuine challenge to both educators and research workers'. By 1962, the Year Book of Education was concerned that the then current emphasis on creativity could cause the older notions of intelligence to become outmoded.

Creativity—a term with as many meanings as intelligence—has been viewed by researchers such as Torrance and Taylor, as both a necessary ingredient of intellectual giftedness, and as a type of giftedness, to be identified and nurtured. Gallagher and Weiss (1979) have described how

There have been numerous attempts to sort out the special characteristics of the creative child—that child who possesses superior ability to generate, visualize, dramatize, or illustrate a new idea, concept, or product. While there is a close relationship between high mental ability and creativity, it has become clear that there are particular intellectual skills and personality traits which predispose certain children and adults to creative activity.

According to Taylor (1975) creativity research has focused on at least seven areas: (a) the creative personality, (b) creative problem formulation, (c) the creative process, (d) creative products, (e) creative climates, (f) creativity and mental health, and (g) creativity and intelligence.

Many researchers during the past two decades, such as Parnes (Parnes and Harding, 1962), have concluded that creativity can be nurtured. In line with this idea, I. Taylor (1975) initiated a creative development programme which focused on: '1) transposing one's ideas into the environment; 2) formulating basic or generic problems; 3) transforming ideas through reversals and analogies; 4) generating outcomes with creative characteristics; and 5) facilitating these prowesses through exposure to direct sensory stimulation' (p. 26). In Calvin Taylor's view (Taylor and Ellison, 1975) research has shown 'that we have talents of many different types, not just of "general intelligence", including academic, creative, planning, communicating, forecasting, and decision making', and to tap this range he has proposed a Multiple Talent Teaching Approach.

Several countries are now adding creativity to their guiding concepts of identification of the gifted, though both in developed and less-developed countries, identification is still normally dominated by the criteria of intellectual or academic aptitude, even when facilities for psychological assessement are still at a relatively primitive stage. Some, lacking locally standardized tests, are obliged to use American or British ones, though none can claim as many as the United States where a recent national study examined no fewer than sixty-five instruments covering a wide variety of abilities (Richert *et al.*, 1982). This initial scholastic concern usually moves on to such 'non-academic' subjects as graphic and performing arts. It works the other way in some countries, however, where it is just because those subjects are viewed as less controversial than academic ones, those very areas of dance, drama or music receive special provision: to differentiate in the common curriculum can be viewed as elitist, while differentiation in performance gifts is often more generally acceptable (Passow, 1984).

Identification procedures in different cultures appear to be tied to their prevailing concept of giftedness. In some countries, it is a multi-step process—initial screening, selection and evaluation. In some, only tests are used, while in others informal approaches are also included. But evaluation and research on instruments and procedures for identification continue to be rare in almost all countries.

MANIFEST GIFTEDNESS

Several researchers since Cox (1926) have focused on the gifted performances of adults, rather than on the potential for outstanding achievement by children. A group headed by the Goertzels (Goertzels *et al.*, 1978), for example, has conducted two investigations of some 700 'eminent personalities', individuals who have achieved success in various areas—sciences, business, literature and drama, etc. They studied the family backgrounds in which their subjects' personalities were formed, their personal lives particularly as adults, and the work which brought them the fame which represents their impact on society. The Goertzels built composite portraits of the eminent, or of the gifted and talented, which provide insights into their nature.

Observations made by the Goertzels include the following.

> The eminent man or woman is likely to be the firstborn or only child in a middle-class family where the father is a businessman or professional man and the mother is a housewife. In these families there are rows of books on shelves, and parental expectations are high for all children ... Children

who become eminent love learning but dislike school and school teachers who try to confine them to a curriculum not designed for individual needs. They respond well to being tutored or to being left alone, and they like to go to special schools such as those that train actors, dancers, musicians, and artists ... they are more self-directed, less motivated in wanting to please than are their peers or siblings. They need and manage to find periods of isolation when they have freedom to think, to read, to write, to experiment, to paint, to play an instrument, or to explore the countryside. Sometimes this freedom can be obtained only by real or feigned illnesses; a sympathetic parent may respond to the child's need to have long free periods of concentrated effort ... They treasure their uniqueness and find it hard to be conforming, in dress, behavior, and other ways. (pp. 336–8).

Brandwein (1955) has hypothesized that three types of factors are related to academic success in the sciences. These include genetic factors for high-level verbal and mathematical ability; predisposing factors, such as persistence (willingness to spend extra time on the subject, ability to withstand discomfort, ability to face failure and continue working), questing, dissatisfaction with the present explanation and aspects of reality; and activating factors, opportunities for advanced training and contact with an inspirational teacher.

Tannenbaum (Passow and Tannenbaum, 1978) has argued that the gifted individual is characteristically a producer rather than a consumer of culture. He maintains that it is not sufficient for a pupil to get good grades, absorb information rapidly and excel in convergent thinking activities. Giftedness involves new conceptualizations, divergent approaches, creative problem solution and unusual problem solution. In his view, pupils who simply consume information, no matter how rapidly, represent only one kind of giftedness and that not the most significant.

Getzels and Csikszentmihalyi (1975) have turned the focus of study around from the gifted child's ability to tackle problem solving, on which there is a rich body of literature and an abundance of conceptual and empirical studies, to problem finding on which there has been relatively little systematic study. As they put it, 'the world is ... teeming with dilemmas. But problematic situations do not present themselves automatically as problems capable of solutions, to say nothing of creative solutions'. Studying adult fine artists, Getzels suggested altering the paradigm of the human as 'not only a stimulus-reducing or problem-solving organism but also a stimulus-seeking or problem-finding organism'. They hypothesize that problem finding seems to be a crucial component of creativity—one which has been relatively unstudied in understanding the nature of giftedness (see Chapter 23).

OVERVIEW

As giftedness is virtually always defined operationally, with some implied concept of its nature, how then can the nature of giftedness be discussed objectively? Clearly, there is no widespread accepted theory of giftedness, although a considerable body of knowledge exists about individual differences and their nurturance. Renzulli (1980b) has observed that:

> In spite of vast amounts of research on every conceivable aspect of the learning process, we still have difficulty pinpointing the reasons for the remarkable differences in learning efficiency and creativity among persons with similar genetic backgrounds and environmental experiences. We simply don't know what factors cause only a miniscule number of Thomas Edisons or Langston Hugheses or Isadora Duncans to emerge while millions with equal 'equipment' and educational advantages (or disadvantages) never rise above mediocrity. Why do some people who have not enjoyed the advantages of special educational opportunities achieve eminence while others who have gone through programs for the gifted fade into obscurity? (p. 601)

There are of course some things we do know. The gifted and the talented come in a tremendous variety of shapes, and sizes. Some gifted youngsters are only above average with respect to the criteria applied, while others are so unusual as to be extremely rare; some individuals are gifted or talented in one area, while others seem to be unusually able in practically any area. Some individuals, who seem to have outstanding ability, have relatively little motivation or interest for developing that potential, while others are both highly talented and highly motivated. Some are high achievers and quick absorbers of information, while others make use of knowledge in new and different ways. Some are basically consumers of knowledge while others are potentially outstanding producers as well as consumers. Some are especially precocious, manifesting unusual potential at early ages while others are 'late bloomers' who do not show unusual potential or performance until much later. There are cultural differences too, which affect the talent areas which are most likely to be rewarded and consequently nurtured. Reissman (1962) has even written about 'slow gifted children', individuals who may take a long time to learn basic concepts, but when they finally do so ... 'use these ideas in thoughtful, penetrating fashion'. The gifted are clearly not a homogeneous group.

There does seem to be consensus at present that identification procedures cannot be limited to tests of intelligence, even when those tests are given individually. A variety of techniques, procedures, and instruments, which can take into account their different educational and life experiences, must therefore be used to identify gifted and talented children, and with that aim, various kinds of rating and screening scales have already been developed and used. Some identification approaches rely heavily on performance, products and behaviours of individuals which are judged to be unusual, creative, or imaginative, as evidence of giftedness.

Passow and Tannenbaum (1978) have pointed out that the definition of gifted and talented provides the direction, not only for the identification procedures, but for the design of educational opportunities and differentiated curriculum which follow. This is a process which Freeman (1979) has described as the use of the 'medical model' in education in which a 'syndrome' is presupposed and the appropriate educational 'treatment' is offered. However, it works both ways—the procedures and techniques used for identification affect the kinds of differentiated experiences to be provided, and vice versa—the child's experiences affect his or her test results. They see identification as an integral part of differentiation, rather than as a two-step diagnostic model with educational differentiation, and suggest that prescribed enrichment becomes a vehicle for identification, as much as identification facilitates enrichment. For instance, standardized tests of language and cognition do not help identify a potential poet in the elementary school. Instead, a programme of instruction and practice in creative poetic expressions in different structural forms can enable children with poetic talent to reveal themselves. It is the creation of pupil products which contributes to self-identification and since product development is a continuous one, identification is also seen as a continuous process, rather than a single-event test administration. Identification of the gifted and talented is related not only to systematic observation and intelligent interpretation of test and observation data by educator, but to creating facilitating educational opportunities for gifted or talented behaviour and consequent self-identification.

Many questions still remain to be answered. Is precocity necessarily a manifestation of giftedness? Is giftedness potential alone or must it be made visible through actual performance? Are 'under-achievers' indeed gifted or should only achievers be considered gifted? Can an individual be outstanding in some very narrow area, only mediocre or even below average in most other areas, and still be considered gifted? Is creative or productive behaviour a component of all giftedness or is it a kind of giftedness in and of itself? Does an individual need to attain affective maturity to match his or her cognitive maturity to be considered gifted? Are there levels of affective maturity—personal, social, emotional maturity—which should be expected before identifying an individual as gifted?

Educational planners must be sensitive to the critical importance of clarification in their operational conception of the nature of giftedness, and of the many issues raised with respect to identification, curriculum differentiation, resource allocation and other aspects of education and development of gifted and talented children and youth. The conception of the nature of giftedness and talent is at the heart of all educational planning efforts.

ACKNOWLEDGEMENT

This is an expanded version of 'The nature of giftedness', which appeared in *Gifted Child Quarterly*, 1981, Volume 25, Number 1.

REFERENCES

Brandwein, P. F. (1955). *The Gifted Child as Future Scientist.* Harcourt Brace, New York.

Burt, C. (1975). *The Gifted Child.* Hodder and Stoughton, London.

Clark, B. (1979). *Growing up Gifted.* Charles E. Merrill, Ohio.

Cox, C. M. (1926). *The Early Mental Traits of Three Hundred Geniuses.*, Volume II, *Genetic Studies of Genius.* Stanford University Press, California.

Durr, W. K. (1964). *The Gifted Child.* Oxford University Press, New York.

Freeman, J. (1979). *Gifted Children: Their Identification and Development in a Social Context.* MTP Press , Lancaster and University Park Press, Baltimore.

Gallagher, J. J., and Weiss, P. (1979). *The Education of Gifted and Talented Students.* Council for Basic Education, Washington DC.

Getzels, J. W., and Csikszentmihalyi, M. (1975). From problem solving to problem finding. In *Perspectives in Creativity* (eds I. A. Taylor and J. W. Getzels), pp. 90–116. Aldine, Chicago.

Getzels, J. W., and Jackson, P. W. (1958). The meaning of 'Giftedness—an Examination of an Expanding Concept. *Phi Delta Kappan*, **40**, 275–277.

Goertzel, M. G., Goertzel, V., and Goertzel, T. G. (1978). *300 Eminent Personalities.* Jossey-Bass, San Francisco.

Henry, T. S. (1920). *Classroom Problems in the Education of Gifted Children. 19th Yearbook*, Part II. National Society for the Study of Education, University of Chicago Press, Chicago.

Hitchfield, E. M. (1973). *In Search of Promise.* Longman, London.

Hoyle, E., and Wilks, J. (1975). *Gifted Children and their Education.* Department of Education and Science, London.

Lally, A., and La Brant, L. (1951). Experiences with children talented in the arts. In *The Gifted Child* (ed P. Witty), D. C. Heath, New York, pp. 243–256.

Lovell, L., and Sheilds, J. B. (1967). Some aspects of a study of the gifted child. *Brit. J. Educ. Psychol.*, **37**, 201–208.

Marland, S. P., Jr. (1971). *Education of the Gifted and Talented*, Volume I. Report to the Congress of the United States by the US Commissioner of Education, US Government Printing Office, Washington DC.

Parkyn, G. W. (1948). *Children of High Intelligence.* New Zealand Council for Educational Research, Oxford University Press.

Parnes, S. J. (1962). Can creativity be increased? In *A Source Book for Creative Thinking* (eds S. J. Parnes and F. Harding). Scribners, New York.

Passow, A. H. (1984). Education of the gifted. *Prospects*, **14**, 177–187.

Passow, A. H., Goldberg, M. L., Tannenbaum, A. J., and French, W. (1955). *Planning for Talented Youth.* Teachers College Press, New York.

Passow, A. H., and Tannenbaum, A. J. (1978). Differentiated curriculum for the gifted and talented: a conceptual model. A paper prepared for the Office of Projects for the Gifted and Talented, Montgomery County (Maryland) Public Schools, New York, Teachers College, Columbia University.

Portland Public Schools (1959). *The Gifted Child in Portland*, Portland Public Schools, Oregon.

Pringle, M. L. K. (1970). *Able Misfits*. Longman, London.

Pritchard, M. C. (1951). The contribution of Leta S. Hollingworth to the study of gifted children. In *The Gifted Child*, (ed. P. Witty), D. C. Heath, New York, pp. 47–85.

Renzulli, J. S. (1978). What makes giftedness? Reexamining a definition. *Phi Delta Kappan*, **60**, 180–184.

Renzulli, J. S. (1980). What we don't know about programing for the gifted and talented. *Phi Delta Kappan*, **61**, 601–602.

Reissman, F. (1962). *The Culturally Deprived Child*, Harper, New York.

Richert, E. S. Alvino, J., and McDonnel, J. (1982). *National Report on Identification: Assessement and Recommendations for Comprehensive Identification of Gifted and Talented Youth*, Educational Information and Resource Center, Sewell, New Jersey.

Tannenbaum, A. J. (1983). *Gifted Children: Psychological and Educational Perspectives*, Macmillan, New York.

Taylor, C. W., and Ellison, R. L. (1975). Moving towards working models in creativity: Utah creativity experience and insights. In *Perspectives in Creativity* (eds I. A. Taylor and J. W. Getzels), Aldine, Chicago, pp. 191–233.

Taylor, I. A. (1975). A retrospective view of creativity investigation. In *Perspectives in Creativity* (eds I. A. Taylor and J. W. Getzels), Aldine, Chicago, pp. 1–36.

Terman, L. M. (ed.) (1925) *Mental and Physical Traits of a Thousand Gifted Children*, Vol. I, *Genetic Studies of Genius*, Stanford University Press, California.

Terman, L. M., and Oden, M. H. (1959). *The Gifted Group at Midlife*, Vol. V, Stanford University Press.

Tuttle, F. B., Jr. and Becker, L. A. (1980). *Characteristics and Indentification of Gifted and Talented Students*, National Education Association, Washington DC.

Ward, V. S. (1975). Basic concepts. In *Psychology and Education of the Gifted* (eds W. B. Barbe and J. S. Renzulli), Wiley, London.

Witty, P. (1957). Who are the gifted? In *Education for the Gifted*, 57th Yearbook of the National Society for the Study of Education, University of Chicago Press, Chicago, pp. 41–63.

The Psychology of Gifted Children
Edited by Joan Freeman
©1985, John Wiley & Sons, Ltd.

CHAPTER 3

The Gifted Infant

MICHAEL LEWIS AND LINDA MICHALSON

From a biological-evolutionary perspective, individual differences in ability imply that some members of a species will perform some tasks better than others, and that these differences are necessary for the process of natural selection and thus the survival of the species. Considering both the sizeable number of infants and children who might be identified as gifted in terms of their outstanding abilities, and their potential importance to the well-being of human society, one wonders why the study of giftedness has been so neglected in favour of studies of normal or handicapped children.

The resources which Western society devotes to identification, assessment and intervention projects for handicapped children of all kinds, and the minimal effort directed toward studying giftedness during infancy, indicate that a concern for the former far outweighs that for the gifted. In two leading psychology journals devoted to research in development—*Child Development* and *Developmental Psychology*—approximately 10 per cent of the articles within the last two years, in the field of infancy, were concerned with handicaps and developmental delay, while not a single study appeared on the identification or development of gifted infants. This asymmetry in our concern for exceptional children not only indicates a failure to appreciate the full range of developmental outcomes, but also has potentially harmful aspects. Although a society must have compassion, it also needs to find ways to identify those persons who can make substantial contributions to the general good.

The graph of the distribution of well-known human abilities, such as performance on an intelligence test, is bell-shaped (the normal curve), and whether in reality or by statistical artifact, most people fall within its normal measured range. At its lower end, however, there is a small bulge in the graph, reflecting abnormalities in normal development, and showing that the number of retarded individuals exceeds the number of gifted whose IQ scores fall smoothly within the upper limits of the normal pattern of the distribution of intelligence. This imbalance of identification is probably because our measures are better at detecting retardation than giftedness, and in addition we have access to a catalogued multitude of syndromes and symptoms to alert us to the likelihood that an infant is less than normal, for instance, with Down's syndrome. As yet, though, there are no reliable stigmata of giftedness.

How then can we identify the first signs of giftedness? One possibility is to look for it in the offspring of adults already identified as gifted. Although the genetic transmission of certain traits is a widely debated issue, most of those who believe in the heritability of IQ recognize that the heritability coefficient is less than 0.50 (Scarr-Salapatek, 1976). Consequently, the search for giftedness is not likely to be successful if we only look at the parents' gene pool, rather than including the interaction of genetic endowment with environmental factors. For instance, Mozart's early musical ability is often cited as evidence for the heritability of musical traits, yet examination of his social environment reveals that he was surrounded by a family of very talented musicians. We have only to consider the parents and family environments of gifted individuals, or to look at the children of gifted parents, to confirm that genius does not originate solely from genetic characteristics (e.g. Feldman, 1982).

MODELS OF DEVELOPMENT

To understand the problems both of identification and of the nature of gifted development, three major models of development are described:

1. The biological/status model: In this, the individual's early (known) characteristics are used to predict later status outcomes. Although some status theorists do acknowledge the role of environmental events in developmental outcomes, they belong more to the interaction tradition than to the 'pure' biological/status tradition.
2. The environmental model: In contrast, rather than trying to identify individual traits to be associated with future giftedness, this model posits that children's subsequent status can be predicted from knowledge of their early environmental experiences.
3. The interaction model: According to this model, individual characteristics are seen at any point in time, as interacting with environmental experiences. Giftedness does not then reside in either the individual or the environment as the critical aspect of its development, but it is their interaction which produces or predicts subsequent developmental

outcomes. If giftedness is indeed a genotype, whose phenotype depends on the environment to facilitate its emergence and growth, many potentially gifted children, raised in culturally impoverished families, may never be able to express their giftedness. Thus, Mozart's musical genius, which might have been an individual trait, might not have been actualized without the musical environment of his family.

These three models guide much of our remaining discussion of giftedness. For example, when we talk about identifying gifted infants, we need to consider whether to look at the innate characteristics of children, the nature of their environment, or the interaction between the child and environment. In this chapter, it will be argued that an analysis of giftedness must focus on individual skills or capacities, rather than on general intelligence. This approach may detect more gifted individuals than would normally be expected in a bell-shaped distribution, because the range of areas in which an individual might excel (e.g. verbal abilities, mathematics, music) is much broader than a composite measure of intelligence allows.

The first topic discussed is the early identification and development of giftedness, in particular the problems of identifying gifted infants, on which the current literature offers little guidance. The second major topic focuses on the development of skills in the gifted infant by considering the general nature of development and the different paths that a child's abilities may take over its course. Thirdly, some data will be presented which were collected as part of our on-going longitudinal study of a group of children between the ages of three months and six years. Because of the extensiveness of the data base, consisting of measures on a wide variety of social, emotional, and cognitive functions from infancy into middle childhood, we are capable of exploring the behaviours of infants who were subsequently characterized as gifted.

IDENTIFICATION OF THE GIFTED INFANT

Historically, the scientific attitude has been that giftedness does not begin or cannot be detected before age three; even today, this premise is incorporated into the US Government's Gifted and Talented Children's Education Act of 1978, which states that: 'the term "gifted and talented children" means children ... who are identified at the preschool, elementary, or secondary level as possessing demonstrated or potential abilities' (Thomason, 1981).

Although Terman's work (1925) provided a tremendous amount of empirical data on over 1000 elementary and high-school pupils, it contained little information about these children as infants. But once the identification of high-IQ children became reliable, a further desire to know about their non-intellectual abilities, traits, and accomplishments provided the impetus for further research. For the first time, on the publication of the follow-up studies of Terman's gifted children after sixteen years (Terman and Oden, 1947) the personality characteristics, school progress and life achievements of gifted children who became successful in their careers could be compared with those who did not. It then began to be recognized that a high IQ in childhood was not the sole criterion of giftedness or success. In fact, the distinguishing characteristics which could identify children who would subsequently develop superior abilities are yet to be defined (see Chapter 6).

Profile of Felicia

When a renewed interest in infancy appeared in the early 1960s, Janet Brown made some interesting observations about individual differences that pertained to giftedness in the newborn. In two papers (1964, 1970), she described the child Felicia from birth up to eight years, at which age she showed not only superior intelligence but also unusual artistic ability. What distinguished Felicia as a baby from others who did not develop into gifted children? What were the characteristics of her early behaviour which reflected her later intelligence and creative ability?

Felicia was the first-born child of a professional family. As a new-born:

> Felicia was very appealing to the observers ... because of her expressiveness, alertness and maturity. She seemed to possess an unusual amount of self-direction, maintaining her state in spite of impinging stimuli, and reacting negatively to restraint and imposed changes such as being pulled to sit. She showed selectivity in her oral behavior by refusing the finger cot (dummy) but nursing well on the breast. Maturity of her physiological systems was evidenced by her ability to remain awake without crying and to show a stable response to the EEG situation. Her distal receptors, vision and hearing, functioned more like those of an older infant and she displayed a wide range of affect which was well integrated with movement. She seemed to show a quality of active responsiveness to external stimuli and to be off to a headstart among our group of babies in terms of being available to environmental experiences. (Brown, 1970, p. 121)

In another observation:

> Felicia impressed the observers as highly 'interactive' with the environment. She was awake a great deal, but unlike Charles (another baby in the study), she was frequently in active, tense states. She was described as 'actively grappling' with external stimuli on several occasions. (Brown, 1964).

To understand the uniqueness of Felicia's early behaviour, consider Brown's (1964) observations of two other new-borns in the nursery:

The bulk of Ted's activity seemed directed toward his successful attempts to decrease tension and return to sleep. External stimuli were responded to with a decrease in tension rather than attention or arousal ... Daphne ... was awake a great deal, but the quality of her responses was quite different from Felicia's. She seemed literally 'kicked around' by the environment, responding to low intensity stimuli with major state changes and unable to adapt to repeated stimuli. She was reactive, rather than interactive or non-reactive.

These interactions of the children with their environment are characterized in three ways: Felicia was responsive to and interactive with her environment, Ted was non-reactive, and Daphne was reactive but not interactive.

There are four major characteristics of Felicia's behaviour which may point to her potential giftedness. The first is the breadth and richness of her sensory responsiveness; Felicia was the only baby who stopped crying to attend to a visual stimulus, the only one who actively explored a stationary stimulus by moving her eyes back and forth over it, the only one for whom visual stimuli seemed to facilitate hand–mouth contact, and the only one who showed a positive affective facial response to a visual stimulus. She was also the only neonate who quieted to the sound of a voice alone, without holding or other intervention. Her response to visual and auditory stimuli seemed to have an 'obligatory' quality, not seen until two or three weeks of age in other infants.

The second notable quality of Felicia's early behaviour was its low level of gross motor activity. Her body movements tended to be restricted and tense, and she resisted major changes imposed on her, such as being pulled to sit. When held, Felicia would arch away and was not cuddly.

Thirdly, as a newborn, Felicia possessed an 'inner directedness', which was reflected in an unusually expressive face and a wide-eyed gaze. Brown (1970) noted that her expressiveness and wide-eyed gaze, which made her appear quite mature for a newborn, were soon noticed by the nurses, who dubbed her the 'personality kid'.

The fourth characteristic of Felicia's behaviour was an ability to respond to stimuli independently of another person. Holding did not facilitate her response to distal stimuli, which were equally effective when she was lying in her crib. This relative independence was most obvious in its contrast with another baby, who showed many of the same mature characteristics, but whose responsiveness was considerably increased when held. That baby eventually developed an extremely rich and complex relationship with his mother; he became very intelligent and emotionally sensitive, but never showed the independent creativity of Felicia. These four characteristics give some clues to those infant qualities that may be related to subsequent giftedness, and which are predominantly social or affective in nature.

If one believes, as interactionists do, that giftedness cannot be identified solely from a set of personal traits at any age, but that it develops in a process that involves both personal traits and environmental factors, then to understand Felicia's development, one must consider not only her personal characteristics but also the nature of the environment in which she grew up as a gifted child. Brown (1970) indicated that Felicia was not an easy baby to mother because of her highly intense involvement and responsiveness. Although no temperament measures were taken, she may have been a temperamentally difficult infant. Despite the parenting difficulties created by this difficult nature, her parents provided a good environment for her, in as much as their personalities happened to mesh very well with Felicia's. Brown (1970) reports that the mother acted as the 'passive partner' in interactions with her, 'thereby avoiding any premature confrontations with Felicia's strong instinctual impulses'.

This discussion of the quality of Felicia's parenting underscores two major interactive issues. Firstly, as we have already stated, that in order to understand development in general, and the development of giftedness in particular, both environmental factors as well as personal characteristics must be taken into consideration. Secondly, that the nature of the environment cannot be specified in any absolute sense; i.e. although responsive environments have been shown to be critical to the growth of intelligence (Lewis and Coates, 1979), the specific characteristics of a 'good' environment depend upon the nature of the particular child in that environment. The discussion above has not implied that Felicia's innate capacities were unimportant to her development, but only that in the absence of a 'good fit' with the caregiving environment, her superior potential may not have been achieved.

The critical role of the environment in development is emphasised in the work of Thomas and Chess (1977) and of Lerner (1982). In their notion of 'goodness-of-fit', the critical component in development (whether normal, gifted, or retarded) is the interaction between the child's primary behavioural style and the environment's response to that behaviour. The child's primary behavioural style in interaction with parental responsivity is likely to account for much of the variance in growing up gifted. Indeed, in predicting gifted development, it probably accounts for more variance than either the child's natural endowment or environmental opportunities alone.

Descriptions of gifted infants are rare, and Brown's two papers afford us an excellent opportunity to look at factors related to giftedness. That Felicia showed both unique characteristics early in life and was raised in an environment which facilitated these characteristics, and which also might have prompted the formation of new ones, indicates that the identification of giftedness (at any age) may require an understanding of both child characteristics and environmental factors. Below, we consider some of the research literature dealing with infancy and early childhood with respect to the early identification of giftedness and to some of the distinctive characteristics of early gifted development.

Some practical considerations of early identification

The standard definition of giftedness, set forth by the US government, recognizes the gifted as 'individuals who display outstanding performance or potential in one or more of the following areas: general intellectual ability, specific academic aptitude, creative or productive thinking, visual or performing arts, or leadership'. However, we propose that the indices of giftedness in infancy extend beyond these domains into others such as sensory responsiveness, emotional expressivity, attention and memory capacity, and social and family relationships—among the many that may contribute to the development of giftedness. Some of the ways in which giftedness can be detected in infants are discussed below.

IQ scores

Though intellectual giftedness can be readily identified in children by their superior performances on a standardized IQ test, there are reasons why this procedure is unrewarding. From a theoretical point of view, the use of IQ scores to identify giftedness is not in accord with an interaction model of development, which is well illustrated by considering the 'Quiz Kids'. These were a group of gifted (i.e. intellectually precocious) children who appeared on national radio, in films, and later on television; wearing caps and gowns, they answered questions put to them by a panel of experts on various topics. As infants, the Quiz Kids were heavier than average at birth, walked and talked sooner, and read earlier and more widely without being taught (Feldman, 1984). As children, they again exhibited the usual indices of intellectual giftedness: high IQ, early and avid reading, large vocabularies, rapid educational progress, strong curiosity and concentration, multiple interests and talents, and phenomenal memories.

What were these children like as adults? One received a Nobel prize in biology, but most assumed ordinary middle-class lives, many of the women becoming housewives and teachers, the men becoming attorneys, business executives, college professors, and physicians. Some were less successful: at seven years, Gerard Darrow was the youngest of the original Quiz Kids; at nine, he made the cover of *Life*, but at 47, he died a man in broken health, having spent many of his final years on welfare (Feldman, 1982). What happened in Gerard's life that he did not fulfil his early promise of giftedness? Although one cannot generalize from a case study, there are valuable clues in individual stories; Gerard's life, for instance, was filled with much stress, his mother dying four months after he was born. His schoolmates viewed him as smug and pedantic; they ridiculed and avoided him. One school-mate recalled him as a 'child with strange eyes and a strange way of talking ... He had Betty Davis mannerisms that looked like someone portraying neuroticism' (Feldman, 1982). Despite Gerard's early high IQ, environmental events such as poor peer relations, family life stress, and psychopathological tendencies seemed to influence the developmental course of his life. Again it seems to reflect that superior intelligence is not a sufficient basis for predicting giftedness, and that one must consider the interaction between environmental factors and individual characteristics.

In addition to theoretical difficulties, another reason why IQ is unrewarding is that in general, early IQ scores are less standardized and therefore less reliable indicators of subsequent development than at older ages (Bayley, 1933), and there is little relationship between intelligence test scores and other aspects of the child's intellectual life (Lewis, 1983).

Many explanations have been offered for the problems associated with infant intelligence tests, notably that before the age of two to two-and-a-half years, children possess relatively few verbal skills, and also that intelligence in pre-verbal or non-verbal infants is both highly complex and not readily assessed by traditional IQ tests. In addition, studies looking at IQ in infancy in relation to later development, have considered general populations of children, and this lack of predictability may not apply in the same way to subsamples, such as the gifted. In contrast to the evidence of consistency in retarded development, there are few data on the ability of early IQ scores to predict later intelligence in gifted children. One exception is a study by Willerman and Fiedler (1974), who identified four-year-olds with IQs of 140 or more, and then looked retrospectively at their eight-month Bayley scores. The results showed that the superior children at four years had not generally been advanced as infants, and could not be distinguished from the total population of infants at eight months on this measure of IQ.

Other cognitive measures

Cognitive measures other than IQ scores may be better indicators of giftedness in infancy and early childhood, such as those of attention and memory, which are important indicators of subsequent intellectual status. In fact, Lewis (1975) and Fagan and McGrath (1981) among others, have shown that early measures of attention are actually better predictors of subsequent cognitive ability than standard IQ tests. In a series of studies, Lewis and Baldini (1979) demonstrated that the rate of disinterest that an infant shows in response to redundant visual information is an early and reliable measure of the child's cognitive functioning, i.e. an infant must be able to remember having seen the stimulus in order to become disinterested in it over time. Thus, memory and retrieval capacities are implicated in attention and development. Using this measure of attention with three-month-olds, Lewis and Brooks-Gunn (1981) found that infants who became disinterested in the redundant stimulus faster at three months of age also scored higher on an IQ test at two years.

From a literature review of case studies of gifted children, a particularly critical factor for gifted development in infants appears to be cognition, comprising curiosity, attention, and superior memory. For example, as a newborn, Felicia showed an exceptionally high level of attention to visual and auditory stimuli, even in the absence of another person (Brown, 1964, 1970). Feldman (1982) reported that the typical Quiz Kid had a near-photographic memory in addition to a large vocabulary, a vivid imagination, lots of hobbies and collections, and an insatiable curiosity.

Verbal or language measures

Verbal intelligence or advanced language development may be a particularly important marker of giftedness. Anecdotal evidence suggests that gifted children (i.e. later identified as gifted on an intelligence test) are earlier to utter sounds, first words, and speech than non-gifted children. They also read at an earlier age, usually without being taught; one mother reported to us that her two-year-old child could read words that he had never seen before.

Many educators cite linguistic ability as an index of giftedness, characterized by an advanced vocabulary for age; the use of language in a meaningful way; and a richness of expression, elaboration, and fluency (Kirk, 1962; Terman and Oden, 1947). Additional language characteristics among the gifted include a high frequency of questions (Guilford et al., 1981; Torrance, 1962). In pre-school children, good memory skills are cited as indicative of giftedness, while language ability is recognized as the primary determinant in identifying the gifted at that age. However, recent empirical data on receptive and expressive language skills in a sample of pre-school gifted children failed to detect any differences between them and non-gifted children in their use of expressive language (Guilford et al., 1981), though the gifted did show advanced receptive language functions of auditory memory and memory for linguistic information, and they also used more question forms than the normal sample.

Affective characteristics

Among the variables which are affective in nature are emotional responsivity, self-concept, and persistence/motivation. Affective characteristics of

children must be considered amongst the issues related to the early identification of giftedness, because cognitive-intellectual development is not independent of affective factors (Lewis and Michalson, 1983); indeed, many
measures of early intelligence are based on them (Haviland, 1983). Also,
Birns and Golden (1969) showed that the amount of pleasure infants showed
in taking a test reflected their later ability better than the test scores. In
looking for signs of giftedness in the first three years of life, therefore,
the quality of infants' affective responses to the task should be considered,
as well as their levels of performance; this variable can be referred to as
'pleasure in learning' or 'motivation'. In Felicia's case, one aspect of her
distinctiveness as an infant was an 'inner directedness', referred to earlier.
Of six babies, she was the only one who showed a positive affective response
to a visual stimulus, and her behaviours were notable for their richness of
expression.

The literature suggests that gifted children generally score higher on measures of self-concept than normal or handicapped children (O'Such, et al.,
1979), although their academic self-concept is likely to be better than their
social self-concept (Ross and Parker, 1980). Contrary to a popular stereotype, good socio-emotional adjustment at the pre-school stage is in fact characteristic of gifted children (Lehman and Erdwins, 1981), so that not only
a rich affective system but also a positive self-concept and good emotional
adjustment may be important in predicting giftedness. As measured by self-
recognition, self-concept begins to emerge during the first year of life, and
can be tested in children as young as fifteen to eighteen months (Lewis and
Brooks-Gunn, 1979).

Motivation combined with personal commitment to an area of talent
over and above natural ability represent a critical component of fulfilled
potential: 'There are two basic transformations in the achievement of eminence. The first is that of intellectual giftedness to creative giftedness ...;
the second, even more important, is the transformation of this intelligent
creativeness into a combination of talent, drive, and values that "succeed" '
(Albert, 1980). In a three-year study of the development of talent, Bloom
(1982) studied the special qualities of Olympic swimmers, pianists, and research mathematicians who attained world-class status in their fields prior
to the age of 35. Interviews with parents, teachers, and the subjects indicated that the important characteristics in most talent areas included: (a) an
unusual willingness to do great amounts of work (practice, time, and effort)
to achieve at a high level or standard; (b) great competitiveness with peers
in the talent field, and a determination to do one's best at all costs; and (c)
the ability to rapidly learn new techniques, ideas, or processes in the talent
field. In the case of the mathematicians, much of the child's time was spent
in solitary projects and play, as well as in solitary thinking. A great deal of
independent learning from books and observing others, in addition to much

question-asking of adults, were also characteristic of talented mathematicians at an early age.

Although in Bloom's sample these qualities were observed in children in their last stages of training and development (usually after age fifteen), it is not unreasonable to think that they might be manifested during infancy and early childhood in the form of persistence and task orientation. In a series of studies on simple instrumental learning in infants, Lewis, *et al.*, (1983) found large individual differences in persistence in infants as young as ten weeks. Moreover, persistence and affective pleasure in pursuing the task were found to be related to rate of learning; such a measure of individual consistency in infancy may be a valuable parameter in identifying giftedness in the first years of life.

Whether this focused behaviour actually produces giftedness or whether giftedness itself involves focused and directed behaviour remains undetermined. In either case, some motivational variable must play a crucial role in gifted development. In *The Eighth Day of Creation*, talking about Linus Pauling and James Watson, Judson (1979) indirectly considers this issue:

> To understand Pauling and Watson, you must remember that creativity is an ego drive, as much in science as anywhere else. I don't think there has ever been anybody doing great science whose ego has not been involved very, very deeply .... Only Linus showed the willingness to take the inductive leap. Then, once he had the idea, he pushed it. The history of science shows that that, in itself, is perfectly justified—yet it is the same egocentricity that led him to collect thousands of signatures of scientists on a petition to ban atomic testing.

While Pauling dismissed this intuitive difference, another contemporary scientist said: 'But didn't Linus also tell you that he has got more imagination than other people?' Whatever the processes, great creativity and giftedness, whether in science, art, or any other endeavour, may involve motivation and commitment in some way not found in our everyday actions and thoughts. One can think of no better example than that of Einstein, when asked what he wished to do with the remainder of his life; he replied that he could think of nothing more satisfactory than to spend the next 50 years thinking about light (Lewis, 1982).

Social knowledge and social relationships

An area of development intimately related to affective and intellectual domains is that of social knowledge and social relationships; the former of these refers to what individuals know about other people and the behaviours of those people, while the latter refers to the actual behaviours of individuals as they interact with others. Gifted pre-school children develop social knowledge earlier than other children (Austin and Draper, 1981), while many studies have shown that gifted children are as well or better adapted than normal ones (Miles, 1954, Chapter 20). Although as a group the gifted appear to have good socio-emotional adjustment, there are large individual differences within the group, and behaviour problems are not unusual (Nevill, 1937). Peer relationships may be tense at times and—as was the case with Quiz Kid Gerard Darrow—disruptive (Feldman, 1982). Within their own peer group, gifted children may be social isolates, interacting less with peers than with older children and adults.

Family interaction and environment

Another factor in gifted development represents the family's contribution; the development of eminent careers appears to involve a number of family variables. Most explanations for the differences between promise and fulfillment point to substantial differences in early facilitating environments, family factors, and educational-career opportunities (Albert, 1980). Families act to produce experiences for youngsters, and to select experiences in their development; parental experiences, behaviours, and personalities give form and substance to these basic family functions.

Both research studies and published personal accounts make clear that support from parents and teachers is critical in developing gifted talent in older children (Albert, 1980; Bloom, 1982; Torrance, 1981). Rejskind (1982) found that the amount of independence children experience in their relationships with teachers and parents influences their creative ability; there is probably an optimal amount of either freedom or pressure associated with particular tasks and types of talent area. Interviews with the Quiz Kids by Feldman (1982) contain many references to parental encouragement and support of intellectual and unusual talents:

> The families we Kids came from were solid, stable and affectionate; of the first 419 Quiz Kids, it was reported, only one ... came from what was then called a broken home. Quite a few Quiz Kids were the only children in their families and most ... had just one brother or sister ....
> An investigation of Quiz Kids' backgrounds showed that in each case there was at least one parent who shared enthusiasms with the child, who watched for areas of interest, who gave encouragement and praise for achievement, who made a game of searching out the answers to questions, who went out of his way to supply the tools of learning. At a time when adult and child worlds were sharply demarcated, Quiz Kids' moms and dads fed us generous helpings of attention with our oatmeal and spinach,

'exposed' us to the classics, played word games with us, and treated us like people, not pests.

During infancy, family interaction patterns are especially important determinants of later developmental status (Ainsworth *et al.*, Lewis *et al.*, in press). Not only do parental responses affect the infant's sense of security, but they also influence the child's motivation to learn and to explore the environment. Brown (1970) suggested that the quality of parenting Felicia received as an infant facilitated her gifted development; her parents were supportive of her individuality and of her personal expressions of intense needs.

These empirical findings and case reports suggest that we must examine parental attitudes toward education and infant development during the child's early years to determine the role of this factor in the development of giftedness.

Demographic variables

Finally, the role of demographic factors in gifted development must be examined; these characteristics, such as birth order, reflect in large part family interaction patterns or processes, and could very well have been considered under that rubric. Birth-order determines to some extent which family dynamics, interests, and values will be directed toward the child, for how long, and at what levels of intensity (Albert, 1980). For example, first-born children receive more direct stimulation from their mothers, and are responded to more frequently by their mothers, compared with later-borns (Lewis and Kreitzberg, 1979); first-borns also have higher IQs (Lewis and Jaskir, *in press*).

For many years, studies have shown consistent relationships between birth-order and various developmental outcomes (Lewis and Kreitzberg, 1979; Zajonc and Marcus, 1975). Studies of eminent persons indicate that as children, they are cognitively gifted, and often the first or only sons of better than average educated and socio-economically placed families (Albert, 1980). However, one must be cautious in interpreting the meaning of demographic variables such as birth order, since the effect of the variable is likely to be associated with a process (i.e. a particular pattern of interaction) rather than inherent in the variable *per se*.

No attempt has been made in this review to include all of the known facts about identifying giftedness and its development; for instance, the genetic studies which might have been considered under family influences have not been discussed, nor all of the major advances in the study of cognitive and affective development, as they might apply to gifted children. What must be emphasized is that:

1 Infant IQ scores alone are insufficient for identifying giftedness and for predicting the outcome of development at different points in the life cycle.
2 The developmental process and the identification of giftedness may be a function of the individual characteristics of the infant, environmental experiences, and their interaction.

In discussing giftedness, we have suggested that its identification requires multiple measures, some located in the child and some in the environment; this discussion implies that giftedness is a unitary quality. However, in any such discussion, it is extremely important that we consider giftedness not only as an entity unto itself, but also as a set of diverse and potentially unrelated skills. Once we go beyond conceiving of giftedness only in terms of general IQ, the problems of its identification and associated developmental issues become increasingly complex. That some children are gifted in one skill, such as mathematics, but not in other skills, such as language, forces us to recognize that the concept of giftedness is far from being merely a superior IQ. This recognition must lead to rejection of IQ as a means of identifying giftedness in infants; instead, we need to focus on individual skills and to devise measures to assess superior skills. Thus, if we want to identify a gifted musician, for example, we need to define the early precursors of musical ability, such as perfect pitch. This approach allows us to specify particular aspects of giftedness and to conceptualize the development of those aspects singly; although these skills may be considered in concert with other aspects, care must be taken in combining all aspects into a general notion of 'giftedness'.

SKILL DEVELOPMENT AND THE GIFTED INFANT

Intelligence has been conceptualized by some as a unitary attribute—'g'— whose growth is a continuous and stable function, reflecting quantitative rather than qualitative change (Burt et al., 1934; Spearman, 1927). Thurstone (1938), Cattell (1952, 1953), and Guilford (1956) challenged that general model and offered an alternative view of intelligence as a loosely related set of diverse skills. More recently, attention has been given to this same issue with respect to infants' and young children's intelligence, as measured by some of the available psychometric tests. Although the general 'g' model of intelligence is still commonly subscribed to (e.g. Wilson et al., 1971), questions about the validity of this concept have been raised, and during the last decade, research concerning the nature and development of infant intelligence has produced evidence incompatible with the notion of general intelligence.

First, the notion of a unitary and pervasive general mental ability implies that performance on a variety of intellectual tasks will be intimately related. Yet research on the relationship between performance on various tests of mental skills has provided little evidence that infant IQ performance, when considered as a total score, is highly related to other concurrent intellectual activities (King and Seegmiller, 1973; Lewis and McGurk, 1972; Uzgiris, 1976).

Secondly, given the expectation that 'g' is stable over the life-span of an individual, and that it grows quantitatively rather than qualitatively, one might expect high correlations in intelligence over age. However, as mentioned previously, infant intelligence test scores during the first two years of life correlate weakly or not at all with scores earned at age four or later (Bayley, 1970; Stott and Ball, 1965). Even within the infancy period, IQ scores do not predict future performance (Bayley, 1933; Lewis and McGurk, 1972; McCall, 1979).

Recognition of these problems led McCall et al., 1972, 1977 to propose an alternative approach to the study of infant development, based on a concept of intelligence as a set of separable skills: there is 'no such thing as "general intelligence" or "g" at any age, but there are skills which have functional utility at a given developmental level that may emerge, change, and/or disappear as development progresses' (McCall et al., 1972). To apply this concept of intelligence to development, they performed principal component analyses on items from the Gesell Developmental Schedules and from the California First Year and Preschool Scales, precursors of the contemporary Bayley Scales of Infant Development (McCall et al., 1972, 1977).

Stages or qualitative shifts in the nature of mental activity with age were identified by both changes in the item composition of the first principal component over age and by discontinuities in the pattern of correlations between the first principal components obtained at various ages. These stages of mental development were then described in terms of the first principal component; for example, the primary mental activity in the first two months of life was found to be attentiveness to environmental stimuli, while the period of three to seven months was characterized by the active exploration of objects. Though 'minor' skills associated with subsequent components were recognized, their role in McCall's model is minimal.

Although McCall et al. explicitly rejected the notion of 'g', by using principal component analysis, they did identify a single, general ability most characteristic of mental activity at a particular developmental stage. Essentially, McCall's position diverges from the 'g' model of intelligence only in that the nature of 'g' is seen to change from stage to stage.

Another approach to the issue involves a multi-dimensional view of intelligence (Lewis and Enright, 1983). According to this analysis, there is a set of separable abilities at each age, rather than a single, general one and a variety of paths through which development occurs. Although little stability in total IQ is evident over the first three years of life, specific abilities that characterize performance on the Bayley Scales of Mental Development at different ages can be isolated through factor analyses and rotation.

In addition to documenting changes in the nature and composition of skills over development, Lewis and Enright (1983) investigated the relationships among these skills over age. Testing over 150 infants across the first three years of life, the researchers found that crucial sets of skills could be identified at different age-points (Figure 3.1). Some skills showed continuity over time, while others appeared, and then diverged onto alternative courses. The various paths taken by the skills reflect three different developmental models. Homeotypic continuity is exhibited when the same behaviours represent different processes at different ages; e.g. motor behaviour may be related to manipulation ability at age one, and to the concept of means-end at age two. Heterotypic continuity represents the constancy in a particular trait over age, despite changes in the behaviours through which it is expressed; for instance, auditory production at three months and verbal skills at twelve months are both related to language ability. Finally, the lack of continuity in development is exhibited in terms of the late appearance of some skills (e.g. imitation), the disappearance of others (e.g. motor precociousness in manipulation), and the transformation of some skills into others (e.g. search behaviours at three months into lexical skills at twenty-four months).

Specifically, in the Lewis and Enright (1983) study, non-verbal abilities were expressed by means-end behaviours at twelve months (puts cubes in cup, attains toy with stick) and by spatial skills (completes form board) at twenty-four months. Furthermore, a number of different relationships between related skills over development could be observed. In some cases, early skills appeared to be primitive analogues of the later, more mature skills which replaced them; for example, twelve-month verbal-skill, which consisted of early vocalizations (jabbers expressively, imitates words) was a precursor of more sophisticated linguistic skills at twenty-four months. In other instances, earlier skills seemed to mediate the development of subsequent skills. Thus, social attention at three months may have been related to lexical abilities at twenty-four months in males because it facilitated social interaction and provided opportunities to learn language. Finally, some skills remained isomorphic over development: imitation at twelve months was related to imitation at twenty-four months.

These analyses, based on a large sample of infants, suggest that in order to understand the early development of either gifted, normal, or handicapped children, one must use a skills analysis rather than a general one, based solely on the concept of intelligence as 'g'. Even within this analysis, however, our data are incomplete, since social skills, affective characteristics, and family factors have not been included in the item pool of the test.

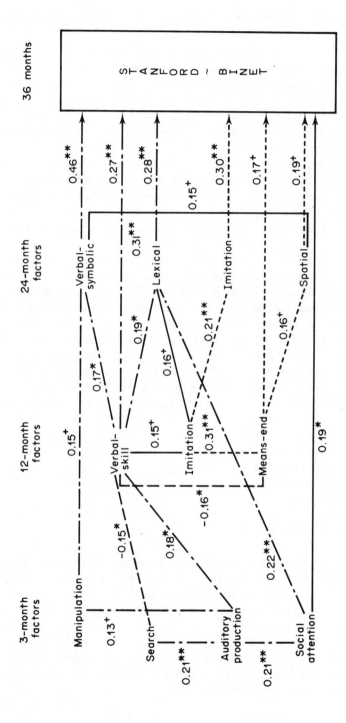

FIGURE 3.1 Path analysis of skill development from 3 to 36 months. (From Lewis and Enright, 1983)

AN EMPIRICAL ATTEMPT TO IDENTIFY GIFTED INFANTS

In the theoretical discussion above, it was concluded that the use of a full-scale IQ score, at least in infancy and early childhood, does not reflect the diversity of skills critical to developmental outcomes. Since many of these skills are unrelated to one another, a skills analysis is essential for identifying the early signs of giftedness. In the same way that a full-scale IQ score is inadequate for identifying giftedness in infancy, a full-scale IQ score is inadequate at later ages as the criterion variable in a retrospective analysis of giftedness during infancy. For example, an IQ score at age six years cannot be used to identify a sample of gifted children for the purpose of identifying differences in infancy that are related to subsequent gifted performance. A better approach is to construct a matrix in which specific skills in infancy are related to specific skills at a later age; we adopted this strategy in the following study.

Over 150 infants were tested at three, twelve, twenty-four, and thirty-six months of age (Lewis and Enright) and again at six years, when two cognitive tests were administered: the WPPSI and CIRCUS, a standardized test used to assess school-related skills in the pre-school child (Bogatz, 1979). For the purpose of skills analysis, each subject was given a Total Quantitative Score, comprised of scores on the arithmetic sub-scales of the WPPSI and the arithmetic abilities on CIRCUS. Each subject was also given a Total Verbal Score, consisting of the verbal sub-scales of the WPPSI and the vocabulary sub-scales of CIRCUS. On the basis of their scores for each skill—quantitative and verbal—the sample children were divided into the following groups:

1. Gifted—scoring in the top 5 per cent on the quantitative tests and in the top 5 per cent on the verbal tests.
2. Average—scoring in the middle 5 per cent on the quantitative tests and on the verbal tests.
3. Below average—scoring in the bottom 5 per cent on the quantitative tests and on the verbal tests.

The relationships between the performance of these children at six years and their abilities during the first three years of life are shown in Table 3.1. The infant skills are listed on the vertical axis of the figure; the criterion skills at six years are listed on the horizontal axis. The signs within the figure reflect whether or not the criterion measure at six years differentiated the gifted, average, and below-average groups on any of the skills during infancy. The Bayley Mental Development Index at three, twelve, and twenty-four months and the Stanford-Binet Intelligence Test score at thirty-six months are included at the bottom of the figure.

TABLE 3.1   Skills analysis of giftedness. The signs indicate whether 'gifted' children (quantitively or verbally) scored higher than (+), lower than (−), or no different from (0) other subjects during infancy

	Skills at 6 years	
Infant skills by age	Quantitative	Verbal
3 months		
Manip.	−	+
Social	0	+
Search	−	+
Audit.	+	−
Tot. MDI	−	+
12 months		
M-E	−	−
Imitation	−	+
Verbal	0	+
Tot. MDI	−	+
24 months		
Lexical	0	+*
Spatial	0	+
Imitation	+	+
Verbal-Symb.	0	+*
Tot. MDI	0	+*
36 months		
Stanford-Binet	+*	+*

* P   0.05

With the full-scale intelligence test scores, the verbally gifted six-year-olds obtained superior scores on the intelligence tests at three, twelve, and twenty-four months; the difference between the groups was statistically significant at twenty-four months. In contrast, the children who were quantitatively gifted at six years showed no differences from other infants on tests of general intelligence. Interestingly, both groups of gifted children showed superior performance on the Stanford-Binet intelligence test at three years.

These data underscore the need for a skills analysis approach to identifying gifted infants. Only the children who were gifted in verbal ability at six years could be differentiated from the other children in infancy; the children who were gifted in quantitative ability at six years were indistinguishable from other infants. From this finding, we can infer that different skills develop along different paths from infancy into early childhood;

therefore, in order to predict giftedness at a future point in time, we must answer the question: 'Gifted in what?'

In examining the relationship between specific infant skills and six-year performance (Table 3.1), it was found that compared to the quantitatively gifted children, the verbally gifted at six years could be differentiated from the total sample of infants on the verbal factor of the Bayley at twelve months, and on the lexical and verbal symbolic factors at twenty-four months. The difference between the groups was statistically significant at twenty-four months.

CONCLUSIONS FROM THE RESEARCH

These data again illustrate the importance of a skills approach in the analysis of giftedness. Not only must one specify gifted outcomes in terms of a particular kind of ability, but one must also delineate earlier development in terms of specific skills that might mark giftedness. Although our analyses are retrospective, the preliminary findings indicate that superior verbal ability at six years is related to verbal skills during infancy; superior quantitative ability is not.

Even though the results of this study point to some continuity between giftedness in early childhood and infant cognitive ability, many of the findings are not statistically significant. However, two firm conclusions are warranted:

1 The development of intellectual ability is best perceived as a transformational process in which early skills are not simply immature forms of later abilities.
2 Individual differences in early abilities are not maintained across developmental stages.

The findings confirm those of Willerman and Fiedler (1975) that, using a retrospective analysis, one cannot detect giftedness in infancy on the basis of general IQ scores. However, larger samples, a greater array of skills, and more refined measures are needed before we can conclude that early cognitive ability is not related to subsequent giftedness.

Furthermore, as emphasized above, domains other than cognitive must be considered in our search for the early precursors of giftedness, and regardless of which child characteristics one selects for analysis, they should not be studied apart from environmental factors. Thus, although the cognitive variables of our study showed only a moderate relationship to giftedness at six years, the relationship may be enhanced when we analyse the environmental effect on gifted performance, and consider the interaction between environmental and child variables.

The major conclusion of this work is that the development of giftedness, like all development, is a complex phenomenon, involving attributes of both the child and the environment, and overlaid with the possibility of a transformation of skills across age. One reason, though, for the difficulty in identifying gifted infants may be that the concept 'gifted infant' is unwarranted; the reality may be that during infancy there is only a potential for giftedness that requires some 'optimal' environment for development. In contrast to handicapping conditions, giftedness may not exist early in life, but emerge only as the product of an interaction between infants' genetic endowments and the environments in which they are raised.

ACKNOWLEDGEMENTS

Developed in part with a grant from Gifted Children Advocacy Association, PO Box 115, Sewell, New Jersey 08080, USA—Arthur Lipper III, Chairman. The authors are also grateful to the W. T. Grant Foundation for funding in part data collection and analyses.

REFERENCES

Ainsworth, M. D. S., Blehar, M. C., Waters, E., and Wall, S. (1978). *Patterns of Attachment.* Erlbaum, Hillsdale, New Jersey.

Albert, R. S. (1980). Family positions and the attainment of eminence: A study of special family positions and special family experiences. *Gifted Child Quarterly*, **24**, 87–95.

Austin, A. B., and Draper, D. (1981). Peer relationships of the academically gifted: A review. *Gifted Child Quarterly*, **25**, 129–133.

Bayley, N. (1933). Mental growth during the first three years. *Genetic Psychology Monographs*, **14**, 1–93.

Bayley, H. (1970). Development of mental abilities. In *Carmichael's Manual of Child Psychology* Vol. 1, 3rd edn, (ed. P. H. Mussen). Wiley, New York.

Birns, B., and Golden, M. (1972). Prediction of intellectual performance at three years from infant tests and personality measures. *Merrill-Palmer Quarterly*, **18**, 53–58.

Bloom, B. S. (1982). The role of gifts and markers in the development of talent. *Exceptional Children*, **48**, 510–522.

Bogatz, J. (1979). *Circus Manual and Technical Report.* Addison Wesley, California.

Brown, J. L. (1964). States in newborn infants. *Merrill-Palmer Quarterly*, **10**, 313–327.

Brown J. L. (1970). Precursors of intelligence and creativity: A longitudinal study of one child's development. *Merrill-Palmer Quarterly*, **16**, 117–137.

Burt, C., Jones, E., Miller, E., and Moodie, W. (1934). *How the Mind Works.* Appleton-Century-Crofts, New York.

Cattell, R. B. (1952). *Factor Analysis: An Introduction and Manual for the Psychologist and Social Scientist.* Harper, New York.

Cattell, R. B. (1953). Research designs in psychological genetics with special reference to multiple variance. *American Journal of Human Genetics*, **5**, 76–91.

Fagen, J. F., and McGrath, S. K. (1981). Infant recognition memory and later intelligence. *Intelligence*, **5**, 121–130.

Feldman, R. D. (1982). *Whatever Happened to the Quiz Kids.* Chicago Review Press, Chicago.

Guilford, J. P. (1956). The structure of intellect. *Psychological Bulletin*, **53**, 267–293.

Guilford, A. M., Scheuerle, J., and Shonburn, S. (1981). Aspects of language development in the gifted. *Gifted Child Quarterly*, **25**, 159–163.

Haviland, J. (1983). Looking smart: The relationship between affect and intelligence in infancy. In *Origins of Intelligence*, 2nd edn, (ed. M. Lewis), Plenum, New York.

Judson, H. F. (1979). *The Eighth Day of Creation*, Simon and Schuster, New York.

King, W., and Seegmiller, B. (1973). Performance of 14 22-month-old black, first-born male infants on two tests of cognitive development: The Bayley scales and the infant psychological development scale. *Developmental Psychology*, **8**, 317–326.

Kirk, S. A. (1962). *Educating Exceptional Children*, Houghton-Mifflin, Boston.

Lehman, E. B., and Erdwins, C.J. (1981). The social and emotional adjustment of young intellectually-gifted children. *Gifted Child Quarterly*, **25**, 134–137.

Lerner, R. (1982). Children and adolescents as producers of their own development. *Developmental Review*, **2**, 342–370.

Lewis, M. (1975). The development of attention and perception in the infant and young child. In *Perception and Learning Disabilities in Children* Vol. 2 (eds W. M. Cruickshank and D. P. Hallahan). Syracuse University Press, New York.

Lewis, M. (1982). Newton, Einstein, Piaget and the concept of self: The role of the self in the process of knowing. In *Piaget and the Foundation of Knowledge* (ed. L. S. Liben), Erlbaum, Hillsdale, New Jersey.

Lewis, M. (ed.) (1983). *The Origins of Intelligence*, 2nd edn. Plenum, New York.

Lewis, M., and Baldini, N. (1979). Attentional processes and individual differences. In *Attention and Cognitive Development* (eds G. Hale and M. Lewis). Plenum, New York.

Lewis, M., and Brooks-Gunn, J. (1979). *Social Cognition and the Acquisition of Self.* Plenum, New York.

Lewis, M., and Brooks-Gunn, J. (1981). Attention and intelligence. *Intelligence*, **5**, 231–238.

Lewis, M., and Coates, D. (1979). Mother–infant interaction and cognitive development in 12-week-old infants. *Infant Behavior and Development*, **3**, 95–105.

Lewis, M., and Enright, M. K. (1983). *The Development of Mental Abilities: A Multidimensional Model of Intelligence in Infancy.* (Unpublished manuscript).

Lewis, M., Feiring, C., McGuffog, C., and Jaskir, J. Predicting psychopathology in six-year-olds from early social relations. *Child Development* (in press).

Lewis, M., and Jaskir, J. Infant intelligence and its relationship to birth order and birth spacing, *Infant Behavior and Development* (in press).

Lewis, M., and Kreitzberg, V. S. (1979). Effects of birth order and spacing on mother–infant interactions. *Developmental Psychology*, **15**, 617–625.

Lewis, M., and McGurk, H. (1972). Evaluations of infant intelligence. *Science*, **178**, 1174–1177.

Lewis, M., and Michalson, L. (1983). *Children's Emotions and Moods: Developmental Theory and Measurement.* Plenum, New York.

Lewis, M., Sullivan, M. W., and Brooks-Gunn, J. (1984). Emotional concomitants of contingency experience in early infancy. (Unpublished manuscript).

McCall, R. B. (1979). The development of intellectual functioning in infancy and the prediction of later IQ. In *Handbook of Infant Development* (ed. J. D. Osofsky). Wiley, New York.

McCall, R. B. Eichorn, D. H., and Hogarty, P. S. (1977). Transitions in early mental development. *Monographs of the Society of Research in Child Development*, **42**, (3, Serial No. 171).

McCall, R. B., Hogarty, P. S., and Hurlburt, N. (1972). Transitions in infant sensori-motor development and the prediction of childhood IQ. *American Psychologist*, **27**, 728–748.

Miles, C. C. (1954). Gifted children. In *Manual of Child Psychology*, 2nd edn, (ed. L. Carmichael). Wiley, New York.

Nevill, E. M. (1937). Brilliant children: With special reference to their particular difficulties. *British Journal of Educational Psychology*, **7**, 247–258.

O'Such, K., Twyla, G., and Havertape, J. (1979). Group differences in self-concept among handicapped, normal, and gifted learners. *The Humanist Educator*, **18**, 15–22.

Rejskind, F. G. (1982). Autonomy and creativity in children. *Journal of Creative Behavior*, **16**, 58–67.

Ross, A., and Parker, M. (1980). Academic and social self concepts of the academically gifted. *Exceptional Children*, **47**, 6–10.

Scarr-Salapatek, S. (1976). An evolutionary perspective on infant intelligence: Species patterns and individual variations. In *Origins of Intelligence: Infancy and Early Childhood* (ed. M. Lewis). Plenum Press, New York.

Spearman, C. E. (1927). *The Abilities of Man*. Macmillan, London.

Stott, L. H., and Ball, R. S. (1965). Evaluation of infant and preschool mental tests. *Monographs of the Society for Research in Child Development*, **30**, Serial No. 101.

Terman, L. M. (ed.) (1925). Mental and physical traits of a thousand gifted children. In *Genetic Studies of Genius*, Vol. 1, Stanford University Press, California.

Terman, L. M., and Oden, M. (1947). *The Gifted Child Grows Up*. Stanford University Press, California.

Thomas, A., and Chess, S. (1977). *Temperament and Development*. Brunner/Mazel, New York.

Thomason, J. (1981). Education of the gifted: A challenge and a promise. *Exceptional Children*, **48**, 101–103.

Thurstone, L. L. (1938). Primary mental abilities. *Psychometric Monographs*, No. 1.

Torrance, E. P. (1962). *Guiding Creative Talent*. Prentice-Hall, Englewood Cliffs, New Jersey.

Torrance, E. P. (1981). Predicting the creativity of elementary school children (1958–1980), and the teacher who 'made a difference'. *Gifted Child Quarterly*, **25**, 55–62.

Uzgiris, I. C. (1976). Organization of sensorimotor intelligence. In *Origins of Intelligence: Infancy and Early Childhood* (ed. M. Lewis). Plenum, New York.

Willerman, L., and Fiedler, M. F. (1974). Infant performance and intellectual precocity. *Child Development*, **45**, 483–486.

Wilson, R. S., Brown, A. M., and Mathew, A. P., Jnr. (1971). Emergence and persistence of behavioral differences in twins. *Child Development*, **42**, 1381–1398.

Zajonc, R. B., and Markus, G. B. (1975). Birth order and intellectual development. *Psychological Review*, **82**, 74–88.

The Psychology of Gifted Children
Edited by Joan Freeman
©1985, John Wiley & Sons, Ltd.

CHAPTER 4

Competence and Giftedness

BURTON WHITE

In exploring the issue of competence and giftedness, it is important to ask: 'What is giftedness?' Webster's Dictionary appears to place emphasis on genes; 'gifted: having a natural ability or aptitude, or talented'; 'talent: any natural ability or power, natural endowment, or a special superior ability in art, mechanics, learning, etc.'; 'gift: suggests of a special ability that is bestowed upon one as by nature, and not acquired through effort', i.e. what you bring into the world, implying that the special talent involved will surface, no matter what. A psychological dictionary, however, gives the following definitions: 'possessing one or more special talents or abilities of a high order, for example, in music, painting, or maths'; 'possessing a very high degree of brightness, sometimes stated as an IQ of 140 or above'. This second definition, seems to avoid confrontation with the classical nature–nurture controversy, and indeed only talks about possession at some stage in life of a special ability. It says nothing about the issue of how it got there. But what is required for the development of human competence may perhaps not be compatible with what is required for development of the gifted or very talented.

Entering the field of psychology from a career in mechanical engineering, I soon discovered the work of Abraham Maslow (1950), who was very much interested in human potential and in self-actualization. The concept of human potential seems to be one that allows us to bridge whatever gap might exist between those of competence on the one hand and of giftedness and talent on the other. Yet it surely relates to both, and the degree to which human potential is simply not realized should be a matter of concern and regret.

59

This exposure to Maslow's work led me to begin a research career concerned exclusively with children between birth and six months of age, which focused on the role of early experience in the surfacing of the first human abilities; that work lasted from 1958 to 1968 (White, 1971). In 1965, the United States in particular (and other parts of the world to a lesser extent) began an unprecedented assault on the question of why some children get through the first six years of life well prepared to enter formal education, while many others are already headed for failure or gross underachievement. The key element in this was the Head Start Programme, which was primarily concerned with children between three and five years of age, from poor families. This was only one of many investigations that began, for the first time in psychological research, to look seriously at the forming of a human being in the pre-school years. The trend of research in the pre-school years (concerned both with early childhood education and child development) was to tackle the question of under-achievement of children from poor families and minority groups directly (Bronfenbrenner, 1974). Leading a study on the child's first six years of life for the School of Education at Harvard, I realized that this was an opportunity to widen the field of research beyond the boundaries of under-achievement and deprivation to the whole area of human potential. The real question to be asked was: 'How does one help any human being make the most of whatever potential he brings into the world?'

In this study, it soon became clear that the child who looked outstanding at six (coping with the everyday tasks of living better than 95 per cent of other children) had a pattern of special abilities which, under the best of circumstances, could be found in the three-year-old. Indeed, it was our consensually agreed judgement that in the case of a child who got off to a wonderful first three years, development between three and six was more a case of refinement of a collection of existing abilities than of the emergence of others. This led us to concentrate on the first three years of life.

The first five or six years of work of the Harvard Pre-school Project (White *et al.*, 1973, 1978), led to the following conclusions:

1. Very few people ever make the most of their innate potential; there is tremendous waste of human potential, all the time.
2. Experiences play a very significant role in the realization of innate potential.
3. The maximum development of abilities is much more likely during the first seven months of life than from then on.
4. Poor levels of achievement sometimes begin within the earliest first seven months, but are much more often first noticeable shortly after the first birthday. Children begin to show their potential between their first and third birth-days, whether they are falling back or leaping forward.

(With all due credit to the concept of 'the late bloomer', this still seems a valid generalization.)

SOURCES OF EVIDENCE ABOUT THE IMPORTANCE OF EARLY DEVELOPMENT

Four sources of evidence should be named in relation to these particular judgements. First is the worldwide testing of the development of abilities in the first years of life, especially those of language and intelligence, mastery over the body, and primitive social skills. This has been done on broad-gauge tests like the Gesell, Bühler, Cattell, Denver, and Bayley—general tests of human achievement whose principal application is for crude screening of general growth. Repeatedly, two groups emerge from work of this kind. One features children who either start life with pathology of a substantial kind or soon acquire it during the first year of life; by the end of the first year, these are consistently being scored below 85, on general tests with an average level of 100. Research such as that of Knobloch and Passamanick (1960) has particularly shown that for such children, infancy test scores are predictive. A child who repeatedly scores more than a standard deviation below the mean in the first year generally looks weak in the second year and beyond.

The general understanding within child development research that infancy tests are not predictive is therefore not true for this particular group. It is true, however, for most children, and this is hard for both practitioners and parents to accept. A child with a Bayley Mental Index score of 135 at the first birthday is no more likely to be above average at three on a Stanford-Binet (or some other language or intelligence test) than a child with a score of 95 at the first birthday. (However, a one-year-old who tests like a three-year-old would probably reflect a different developmental trend). For 85–90 per cent of all children, though, testing in the first year of life does not tell you in which direction they are heading; after that, predictability of later intellectual and linguistic skills most often begins to become possible with testing late in the second year of life. The situation is complicated by the fact that children get very 'testy' during the second half of the second year, and make very poor subjects. A report that says '35 two year-olds scored "x" and thus ...', without a warning that the data are dubious, should be treated with suspicion. But by the age of two, scores on the Bayley Mental Index will correlate well with those on the McCarthy, Binet, and WISC over the next three, four, or five years. That prediction never reaches a very high level, and rarely goes beyond $+0.4$, or $+0.45$, depending upon the population, etc., even in years to come, but it starts to become useful, especially for special groups of children and for those at the extreme of the range, late in the second year. By the third year, it is quite stable.

The second source of evidence is educational programming experiences. It has been found over and over again, at least in the United States, that the status of a child at six years with respect to school readiness is predictive of where that child is going in the next few years of schooling and, indeed, probably further on. The child of six who, confronting a formal curriculum, is enthusiastic about learning, talented in language and intelligence, and not socially crippled, is one whose learning rate is such that each year in school will result in the gap between her and the average getting larger.

The other side of the coin has also long been found to be true—the concept of 'a widening of the gap'. The child who looks unprepared at six, who only has the skills of a four to five year-old, has a lower learning rate, and tends to fall further behind. Since about 1968, a phenomenal amount of money and effort in the United States has been devoted to trying to remedy this relatively sad state of affairs. Special enrichment programmes have been tried for under-achieving six, seven, and eight year-olds, but their results have been very disappointing (Rivlin, 1975). Special remedial education for children between six and ten has not had marked success, and it seems as if the patterns that are established in the first years are not easily altered, though exactly why this should be so, remains unknown. Since 1965, similar efforts have also been devoted to the three- to six-year-old range, the age group on which the bulk of the Head Start activity has been focused. It has been learned that many of the children who do very poorly when they are ten years old are not only identifiable by their sixth birthdays, but are already identifiable at their third; the gap has already been established by then. It has also been found that it is extraordinarily difficult to do much about such problems subsequently. There has been extensive publicity in the popular media about occasional short-term successes, and a propaganda campaign by the United States Government to suggest that long-term gains from these early programmes were substantial. However, overall, their track record is really quite disappointing (Bronfenbrenner, 1974).

The third source of evidence lies in psychiatric studies in the mid-1940s by Spitz to examine the vulnerability of children in the first years of life, when the primary affectional bond between parent and child either did not get a chance to develop or was interrupted for varying periods of time. These went under the general label of 'maternal deprivation studies', and their results were generally quite consistent, even though the quality of the research at times left much to be desired (Spitz, 1945, Bowlby, 1951). They did yield several important findings, however, notably that from six months on, an interruption of three months or longer in the relationship between mother and child seems to lead to profound, lasting damage. Gaps of less than three months do not seem to cause anywhere near the same problem, and a week or two does not amount to anything, which should relieve many anxious parents and give them a chance to take a holiday. The finding to be emphasized here is that if a child is five-and-a-half months old, and has spent the whole of that period in a situation without any loving, one-to-one relationship (even in an institution), and was then placed into a good milieu with much personal attention, no lasting harm was ever detected.

Given our only partially effective ways of assessing development it is possible that some such harm did occur, and it is quite possible that some lasting deficits might eventually be found. But on the whole, there was a marked difference between the effects of what happened to interrupt normal experiences (and the bond in particular) between the ages of six months and three years, compared to the impact of this unusual experience in the first six months of life. Those who emphasize the vital importance and risk involved in unusual experiences in the first weeks of life have to incorporate such general findings, made on thousands of children, into their views. My personal opinion is that getting through the first six or seven months of age well has been basically worked through in the process of evolution; it is a relatively easier job to make the most of your learning then, than it is in the period that follows the first half year of life.

The fourth source of information comes from basic research on human developmental processes, especially language and intelligence. Detailed studies of the process of development of the normal, or indeed any human being between birth and the age of three are only very recent, with the conspicuous exception of the work of Piaget (1952), who has made an unique contribution to our understanding of human development. If Piaget had not been interested in the origins of intelligence, or had not had three children, or had never lived, where would knowledge of the development of intelligence be? No other comparable work has been done in explaining the origins of object permanence, causality, thinking ability, or memory. It is only since 1965, in the United States at least, that the learning process in the first three years of life has been seriously examined. Though a good deal has been written and proclaimed about this, serious scientific study of it has been remarkably rare.

The best sources of useful information that young parents had until 1965 were Drs. Spock (1976) and Gesell and Amatruda (1941). They had had information on babies because they were in medicine, and had the responsibility for, (a) seeing to it that a child was developing normally, and (b) calming the anxieties of young parents (which took up much more of their time). Psychologists, and in fact most people teaching child development, would not have recognized a normal two-year-old if they tripped over her.

Not only were detailed studies of the first three years very rare, but detailed longitudinal studies, where the same child was studied over a period of many months, were even more unusual. A few very expensive longitudinal studies (including Terman's of the gifted) were initiated in the 1920s and 1930s in the United States (Kagan, 1964), but the yield from them was eventually not considered worth the expense, and by the 1940s they had fallen out of favour. Nevertheless, it is most likely that the ontogenesis of any creature as complicated and changeable as a human being cannot properly be examined without repeated, intensive studies on the same subject over a long period of time. These have simply not been done more than a handful of times. In the case of gifted children, most records have been kept by a relative on one particular child. It is interesting that we have generally failed to take advantage of nature's successes. Out of any thousand children being born, only a fraction of them will get off to an exceptionally good start in life; some of these successes could be studied scientifically, and that is what we have tried to do.

THE HARVARD PROJECT

In this, the development of several hundred children was studied between 1965 and 1978. The first objective was the definition of a talented six-year-old, since such a definition could not be found in the child-development literature. There were many studies of children in trouble, and many others inspired by Freud's ideas about infantile sexuality, but not much work on a typical six-year-old. However, one study was a delightful exception—that by Lois Murphy at Sarah Lawrence College (1956). Her subject was Colin, a boy studied between the ages of two-and-a-half to five-and-a-half years, while he attended nursery school, but never in the home, which is typical of this field of work. Colin was no genius; his IQ was about 140, but he was free from any gross abnormalities. His favourite activity was engaging in role play—coming in to school with some new identity, and challenging the teachers to figure out who he was. His nickname for himself was 'Bob Important'.

In the Harvard Project, children were not invited by the hundreds into the laboratory at the university. Instead, seventeen or eighteen research workers went, one at a time, to nursery schools, kindergartens, day nurseries, and homes; we stood quietly, ten feet or so away, and carefully observed and recorded what children were doing as they went about their ordinary business. Extensive field observations were done to find that one child in twenty-five to thirty whom everybody agreed coped with life better than the average. In the area of sensory skills (e.g. vision and hearing), no appreciable differences were found between outstanding children and others, and no substantial differences in perceptual-motor abilities, such as tossing balls back and forth or hopping on one foot. Nor were appreciable differences found in general control over their bodies, or in their humour, or likability. These outstanding children were not different from their peers in all ways, but appeared to be most different in the following areas.

First of all, their whole approach to social interchanges was special. They were exceptionally able to get and hold the attention of adults in socially acceptable ways; they had a variety of mechanisms for this purpose, and chose appropriate ones for each situation. They were very good at using adults as resources, after first determining they could not do something for themselves, though many other children were observed who were not accustomed to use adults in this way to complete tasks, and yet others who tended to over-use them. During our studies, it has been possible to pinpoint when this talent first surfaces in human life—it is first seen in a child's behaviour at about ten months. As he crawls about, he may want a biscuit or a particular toy, and may utter an 'uh uh' noise, while gesturing towards the adult who is nearby. By this behaviour, he means to say 'Excuse me, I want another biscuit', or 'I want my toy, which I can't reach, and I understand you can help me ...' etc. These children were able to express affection or mild annoyance to adults quite spontaneously. They could say 'I like you', and give somebody a hug, or 'would you leave me alone ... you're bothering me now ...'. They were very proud of their achievements, and spontaneously remarked about them.

In one of the films we have made, a three-year-old, as he starts a new painting, says to no one in particular, 'I'm doing a good job'. This is characteristic of capable young children; they engaged in role play, make-believe behaviour, and pretend behaviours much more than the average child. The roles they adopted were generally those pointing to the future (adults), rather than to the past (babies or animals). At six, some children could lead other five- and six year-olds, but were uncomfortable when asked to follow; others could follow, but were uncomfortable when asked to lead, whereas outstanding children could do both.

A capacity and desire to compete was another distinguishing characteristic of the talented six-year-old—'I can do better than anybody else' was a typical boast by such children. They also showed the ability to express affection and mild annoyance to peers. However, it also has been found in subsequent work that certain cultural groups do not like this characteristic in their children.

Altogether, this collection of social abilities indicated a child who is comfortable with adults, and who does not treat them primarily as fear objects or purveyors of authority, but almost like peers. He has the expectation that they are anxious to help, that they are interested in what he is doing, and that they are more capable than himself.

In the realm of non-social abilities, the capacity for language of these children was obviously advanced. In intellectual areas, they were found to have an unusually well-developed capacity to sense discrepancies or differences. These ranged from perceptions of simple differences in appearance (like a new haircut on another child) to differences in temporally organized sequences (such as noticing when somebody went out of turn) and also to errors in logic, e.g. on the part of the teacher. They live in a longer slice of time than other children, anticipating events that might be coming in the future. They are, of course, very capable of dealing with abstractions, as compared to the average, and are capable of taking on the perspective of another. In Piaget's system, seven- to eight-year-old children become less egocentric in their thinking style. They start, for the first time, to want very much to make themselves understood to somebody else, and habitually begin to rehearse what they are going to say, in an attempt to make themselves understood. This is absent in the typical two- and three-year-old child, and present in the outstanding three-year-old, and well developed in the outstanding six-year-old.

These children also make very interesting associations, many of which appear to be original. They have the capacity to plan and carry out complicated activities, the capacity to use resources effectively, and an interesting perceptual style—the ability to concentrate closely and, at the same time, keep track of what was going on in a busy room. They could cope with more information per unit of time than most age-mates, and still know what was going on. Whereas at around six years most children still have occasional difficulties with distractability, these can focus their attention well, in spite of a busy scene. This particular collection of behavioural characteristics is one that experienced teachers of three- to six-year-olds recognize, and generally endorse. Our findings were that three-year-olds who were developing well exhibited all of the characteristics, not in a polished form, but in differing stages of development.

The day-to-day lives of one- to three- year-old children were then examined, in the hope that these behaviours would be seen to emerge. Experiences were being looked for that were regularly associated with the development of such styles. The homes of children identified as likely to be outstanding, either positively or negatively, were visited when they were aged one; this likelihood was determined by looking at the performance of the older children in the family. Up to fifty-two visits were made to individual homes, over a two-year span. One of the limitations of both university-based and paediatrically based research is that neither child rearing nor very early education can be studied without becoming thoroughly familiar with the child's normal environment. Even today, when there is increased use of substitute care, most children still live mostly in their own homes. Although this is an awkward place to do research, it is an unavoidable one, yet very few workers have ever done intensive research in homes, or seem likely to do.

The Harvard Study continued with experimental work with average families, to test hypotheses about effective child-rearing practices and about the development of competence (White, 1979). From this, it was concluded that a distinction had to be made between the first seven months and the time from seven months to three years. The human abilities acquired in the first seven months are primarily.

1. Partial body control: the newborn is basically inept with respect to his body, but the seven- month-old baby has head control, can turn over (stomach to back and so forth), can reach accurately for nearby objects to bring them close for exploration, and has some arm and leg strength. Usually, though, she cannot get up to a sitting posture on her own, nor can she walk or climb.
2. Sensory skills: the newborn is neither blind nor deaf, but does not have precise visual or hearing abilities; for all practical purposes the six- month-old is a mature creature with respect to sight and hearing.
3. Intelligence: the first problem-solving skill, according to the work of Piaget, is likely to have been acquired by six or seven months of age. It has nothing to do with thinking ability (the manipulation of ideas), but consists of the ability to move minor obstacle A to the side, in order to reach for and procure object B. That is one of the very first intentional behaviours of consequence; it constitutes the sum total of the problem-solving skills of the seven-month-old child.

In this and other studies, it has been found that the average expectable environment ordinarily seems to contain all that is needed for the achievement of all attainable human abilities (excluding perhaps the gifted infant?) during the first seven months of life. In spite of the wide range of ways that untutored people (as most parents are) structure the experiences of their babies, most children acquire these first achievements quite adequately, yet there is evidence that the rate of achievement of abilities in the first seven months of life can be substantially increased. Children can, for example, learn to use their hands as reaching tools by three and a half months, rather than by five months. In the future, such early development could lead children to other cumulative achievements, that might encourage higher levels of skill very early on; but so far, no serious attack on that question has been pursued.

What kind of a being are we dealing with at seven months of age? First of all, one whose body is vertically orientated much more often than that of a newborn. For the first three- and-a-half months of life, the child is a horizontal creature, unless she is being held upright, and when held upright, children less than three months old are not comfortable. However, a seven-month-old is comfortable when upright, can see and hear quite well, and has, more than any other animal, a tremendous urge to learn and explore, yet no locomobility. She cannot get anywhere on her own, and it is quite possible that most seven- month-olds are rather frustrated; some confirmation of that notion comes when a child learns to crawl, or is placed in a well-designed walker. You do not have to induce them to explore the world—they take off. At that stage of life, the child is generally a friendly creature, and is also socially uncomplicated. She is not a manipulator, but adventurous and persistent; that is the seven-month-old pupil.

What will she acquire by the third birthday? Complete body control, complete sensori-motor intelligence, and higher mental abilities, or thinking. Towards the end of the third year, a full array of the social skills listed above has been gained, as well as two-thirds to three-quarters of all the language she will ever use in ordinary conversation for the rest of her life, including a receptive vocabulary of about 1000 words and all the primary grammatical elements in her native language. There is substantial evidence that higher mental abilities—language, social skills, and intrinsic interest in learning—are all 'at risk' then. Furthermore, it is very likely that children rarely receive the input that would allow maximum fulfillment of potential during this unique time of life. Unlike the abilities acquired in the first seven months, these precious abilities that distinguish us from other animals—our special capacities in thinking, language, social skills, and lifelong intrinsic interest in learning—undergo critical development in this seven- to thirty-six-month period, and are remarkably sensitive to environmental differences. Given the fact that we do not prepare the people who shape the world of these children for this task, and given general circumstances, it is unlikely that more than one in ten of our children get the kind of learning opportunities at this important period that would allow them to move forward as well as they might. When this notion is combined with what was reported above about the degree of permanence, or fixity of patterns of the three-year-old child, the overwhelming importance becomes clear of getting children off to a good start in the first years of life, rather than to waiting until they get to be six or seven years old.

INPUT FAVOURABLE TO THE DEVELOPMENT
OF COMPETENCE

What is the kind of input that would help children really move ahead, fulfilling much more of their opportunity for growth during this period? What are the requirements for, and the impediments to the realization of full potential at this time? First, children need physical normality and good health. There are common impediments, aside from obvious pathology like Down's Syndrome or total deafness at birth, that interfere with optimal results.

One problem in particular that deserves special attention is undetected mild to moderate hearing loss. In the last fifteen years or so, it has become increasingly clear that one very simple and common problem that gets in the way of good development of children in great numbers during the first two years of life is mild to moderate hearing loss. This is not necessarily permanent, and indeed is more often intermittent, yet for an interesting set of reasons, it is very often not detected until the child is six or seven years of age. The deaf child is usually spotted at birth, because when there is a loud noise, everybody jumps except the baby; almost any doctor or parent will spot the child with a profound loss. But the mild to moderate loss—of ten to fifty decibels—is much more common statistically at birth (though still infrequent) and much more likely to develop in the course of infancy because of the young child's small respiratory passages, proneness to infection, and allergic susceptibilities. Runny noses and babies are synonymous. Repeated episodes of otitis media (infections of the middle ear and associated fluid) are very common during infancy, and when that occurs, even a naive parent will very often sense that the young infant does not respond in expected ways to sounds. This observation is likely to be mentioned to a medical person, with the comment that the parents are worried about the child— 'Perhaps she doesn't hear quite well.' More often than not, the doctor will respond with: 'Don't worry about it ... she'll grow out of it', but it turns out that even naive parents are usually correct when they sense small hearing losses.

Whilst there are ways of screening for these problems in the first five months of life, and ways of correcting them, the consequences for human learning of chronically neglecting them are profound. The child who does not hear terribly well at six or seven months of life, when he is about to enter major language learning, has less interest in language, and simply will not learn as well as he might. If you do not acquire language optimally within the first three years of life, it is not possible to acquire higher mental abilities optimally. If you do not acquire both optimally in the first three years, you will be a different kind of social animal, because we civilize our children through speech during the eight- to thirty-six-months period. We do not grunt and groan at them, we explain things, which is why the six-year-old with hearing loss is typically socially awkward as well.

Motor control is not at risk with most children in the first years of life, but plays an enormously important role in overall development of the best talents in very young children. Common impediments to the fullest development of body skills and fullest enjoyment of that development are both the restrictive practices of anxious parents and the objective dangers for infants which are present in most homes. The learning environment is generally suited to adults, but not to newly crawling, naive babies. There is rarely any effort on the part of society or of the educational establishment to conceive of the home as the baby's learning environment, yet more fractures occur in the ten- to twenty-month period than at any other time of life, and there are also more accidental poisonings then. Parents who are not concerned about safety when a child starts to crawl are oblivious—they should be concerned! On the other hand, guided by knowledgeable people, they can easily make the home a safe and interesting place for a newly crawling baby. For example, a gate can be put on the third step, rather than at the bottom or the top of the stairs; the result is learning and fun without danger.

During infancy, children characteristically move very rapidly through motor development, and conquering the body means a great deal to them. Watch them practice when they are starting to climb; they persist in the face of each new challenge, and get a thrill out of their successes, while nothing reinforces that thrill more than the enthusiasm of an older person, especially one who is crazy about that child. Such early achievement usually has a very powerful impact on parents and grandparents. Pride in achievement may well have its roots in the normal motor accomplishments that begin with pulling-to-sit and end with walking; for most children this is during the seven- to eleven-month age range. Every normal child has the capacity to experience that kind of learning. All it takes is a healthy baby, the opportunity to practice, and an especially interested adult observer.

Thirdly, appropriate linguistic input is needed. Apart from undetected hearing losses, a common impediment is lack of awareness by parents of the process of language learning and teaching. Some of our most delightful parents were poor language teachers, because they did not speak to their children until the child spoke. It is interesting that children who are bright may not do any speaking until they are a year- and-a-half to two years old. They are capable of learning enormous amounts of language from six to eight months on, but the normal adult does not ordinarily talk to creatures who do not answer. So, once again (as in the case of restrictiveness when the child begins to crawl and then climb), a natural tendency interferes with the best possible learning. Chatterboxes make better language teachers than quiet people.

A style of child rearing has been observed that is most conducive to superb language learning. First, the home is made as safe as possible for the newly crawling seven- or eight-month-old. Then, the child is encouraged to explore this marvellous new world, and inevitably gets into three kinds of situations that cause her to approach an adult. One involves discomfort—she pinches a finger or falls down, and wants to be comforted. The second situation is that she may become frustrated by something; maybe a door will not come unstuck, or two pieces of a toy fail to come apart. The third is that she finds something very exciting, like a discarded carton, and wants to share the discovery with somebody. Under those circumstances, children developing especially well, turn to the adult, and ask for attention. It is very easy at that point to read a baby's mind; they are not yet very complex creatures. The parent is potentially a teacher with a motivated pupil, and she knows that pupil's interest of the moment. This is a far more opportune situation for learning than chasing an eleven-month-old baby around a room with reading materials.

Another ingredient for the development of competence is clear, consistent guidelines for relating to other people. Typical impediments to good social development are a lack of awareness of the details of social development and a fear of losing some or all of the baby's love, with a resultant reluctance to control, to set limits, to say 'no'. However, it is very hard to 'turn off' a baby in her own home. They must acquire solid attachment to some older person; this is a fundamental need of all new humans during their first years. Even if you beat a baby regularly (though I am not advocating it), he will still love you—it is essential to his survival. He needs time and attention from totally committed adults. The Harvard research, like the work of many others, showed that the key ingredient for a baby's best possible development is a good deal of time during the course of the day with somebody who loves him, between the ages of seven and twenty-four months.

Time to devote to one child becomes difficult to find when children are closely spaced; probably a child needs a good two-and-a-half years with one person, who is doing a fine job teaching him, in order to get the best possible curriculum. If one is in the middle of the development of language and of a close attachment to another person, and an interloper arrives at the end of the year, who gets attention before one, it is unlikely that the most will be got out of those first years. Our studies showed that two-year-old children usually dislike their one-year-old siblings—and show it. A two- year-old's reactions may be regarded as similar to those of a young husband's whose wife one day announced: 'Honey, I have wonderful news for you. Next week I'm going to bring someone home to live with us. He's going to be a little younger than you, a little better looking than you, and naturally, I'm going to pay more attention to him than you because he's new and he needs to be shown around. But, you'll get used to him, and I want you to love him ... he's going to be OUR new husband.' This is precisely what is expected of a two- year-old when there is a one-year-old in the family; they cannot handle such a situation with grace. The best giveaway to the reality in a home with two such children is when you ask a parent how the two-year-old girl likes her younger brother, and the parent pauses and then says, 'she loves her brother ... but there are times when she doesn't seem to know her own strength'.

Generally speaking, three teaching functions can be identified. The first is providing learning opportunities that are appropriate for the child's emerging interests and skills. Children change so rapidly in these first years that adults need detailed knowledge of the process, if they are to do that job well. The second is serving as a personal consultant for the child: facilitating learning, encouraging it, sharing enthusiasms, and comforting when she does not feel well. The third function (and one which is important if you desire a child whom you can enjoy as well as admire) is maintaining firm control and guidance with respect to social relations—teaching the child that she is extremely special, but no more so than anybody else in the world is to other people.

The primary hazards to the proper performance of these roles are, first of all, lack of knowledge. The teachers of young children (usually their parents) are not prepared for the job, and the notion that all you need in order to be an effective child rearer is to be a solid, normal woman is preposterous. Very few people can with ease handle two children under three, the younger one being aged over seven months; it is a very difficult job. In addition to lack of knowledge, and stress of this sort, there is also lack of support. We leave child-rearing to the nuclear family, and in most homes it is still the case that the man leaves it to the woman. That is neither fair nor promising for the outcome of the process. What is needed is systematic professional guidance of development from birth, with the family treated as the first and probably the most important educational system to which the child will ever be exposed.

Special talent in very young children is a topic of enduring interest, and will most likely continue to be so. For example, there is much enthusiasm about the Suzuki method in early music training, about maths and reading precocities, as advocated by Doman and the Montessori school, as well as the inevitable precocities in such sports as tennis, ice skating, and swimming. However, the question arises whether the development of a special talent, often referred to as giftedness, is compatible with the full development of all important human attributes?

The full array of human attributes includes motor skills, humour, imagination, intelligence, social skills, and intrinsic interest in learning. When questions are asked whether one or another programme to nurture special development is worth pursuing, the possibility cannot be denied of resultant precocity. In the first years of life, children can acquire skills that they ordinarily do not; anybody who denies that fact is simply not aware of the literature. However, adults should take care in the choice of methods they follow for this purpose, and especially the people in whose care they put their children. The likely costs should be evaluated, in regard to the child's total development, before any practices are adopted that promise precocity. Sometimes, the costs are just too great.

For the future, a much clearer picture of early human development is likely to develop slowly, especially concerning the relationships between innate potential and early experiences. Secondly, much higher levels of human achievement may well occur from three months on, with our current norms becoming gradually outmoded. Thirdly, I anticipate better decisions on whether or not to aspire to 'giftedness' for a child, and on how to help each new child develop into the most fully developed human being that her innate potential will allow.

REFERENCES

Bowlby, J. (1951). *Maternal Care and Mental Health.* Monograph 2, World Health Organisation, Geneva.

Bronfenbrenner, U. (1974). *Is Early Intervention Effective?* Vol. II, *A Report on Longitudinal Evaluations of Preschool Programs.* DHEW Publication No. (OHD), pp. 14–25.

Gesell, A., and Amatruda, D. S. (1941). *Developmental Diagnosis.* Hoeber, New York.

Kagan, J. (1964). American longitudinal research on psychological development. *Child Development,* **35**, 1–32.

Knobloch, H., and Pasamanick, B. (1960). Environmental factors affecting human development, before and after birth. *Pediatrics,* **26**, 2.

Maslow, A. H. (1950). Self-actualising people: A study of psychological health. *Personality Symposia,* No. 11–34, Grune & Stratton, New York.

Murphy, L. B. (1956). *Personality in Young Children* Vol. II. Basic Books, New York.

Piaget, J. (1952). *The Origins of Intelligence in Children,* 2nd edn. International Universities Press, New York.

Rivlin, A. M., and Timpane, P. M. (1975). *Planned Variation in Education. Should We Give Up or Try Harder?* Brookings, Washington, DC.

Spitz, R. A. (1945). Hospitalism: an inquiry into the genesis of psychiatric conditions in early childhood. In *The Psychoanalytic Study of the Child.* (eds A. Freud, H. Hartmann, and E. Kris), Vol. 1, International Universities Press, New York, pp. 53–74.

Spock, Dr B. (1976). *Baby and Child Care.* Pocket Books, New York.

White, B. L. (1971). *Human Infants: Experience and Psychological Development.* Prentice-Hall, Englewood Cliffs, New Jersey.

White, B. L., Watts, J. C. Itty Chan, B., Taylor Kaban, B., Rosen Marmor, J., and Boyde Shapiro, B. (1973). *Experience and Environment: Major Influences on the Development of the Young Child,* Vol 1, Prentice-Hall, Englewood Cliffs, New Jersey.

White, B. L., Taylor Kaban, B., Attanucci, J., Broyde Shapiro, B. (1978). *Experience and Environment: Major Influences on the Development of the Young Child,* Vol. 2. Prentice-Hall, Englewood Cliffs, New Jersey.

White, B. L., Kaban B. T., and Attanucci, J. (1979). *The Origins of Human Competence: The Final Report of the Harvard Preschool Project,* Lexington Books, Massachusetts.

The Psychology of Gifted Children
Edited by Joan Freeman
©1985, John Wiley & Sons, Ltd.

CHAPTER 5

Foundations of Creativity:
The Facilitating Environment

DIANA SHMUKLER

This century has seen a growing appreciation of childhood among psychologists, along with a move to understand and develop children's abilities, especially that of the intellect. As the limitations of the earlier fixed concept of intelligence have become recognized, it is no longer generally accepted as the total explanation of, for example, how a child deals with new situations. Over the last few decades there has been a noticeable focusing on creativity as a flexible aspect of the development of intellectual behaviour. Creativity, however, is an elusive notion, which does not lend itself easily to either assessment or even definition.

A child's natural reaction to a new experience is not, of course purely intellectual; it is one of play—an activity which is not obviously goal-directed, such as recreating and acting-out what the child has observed. Imaginative play refers to the introduction by the child of settings, times, and characters which are not immediately present in the environment and, since it makes something out of nothing, can be seen as creative expression with important developmental implications.

In good educational circumstances, when children are recognized as intellectually gifted, they may receive the great benefits of extra cognitive and academic stimulation, though sometimes their creative, expressive, and emotional development may be relatively neglected. The reasons for this imbalance are probably due to adult attitudes about what is considered appropriate for the education of the gifted, which tend to neglect the child as a child. Even very young gifted children are often unconsciously perceived as quasi-adults, with little if any need for play, so that suggested learning experiences for the gifted are relatively sophisticated and often 'bookish'. But play is an age-related activity, needed by all children; it is an important means of achieving learning for all levels of intellect, even though the ends may be different for each child.

It cannot be assumed that all children play imaginatively; cross-cultural studies indicate that in some cultures, it hardly ever occurs (Whiting, 1963; Ebbeck, 1973). Similarly, culturally disadvantaged children are rarely found to play freely and imaginatively (Feitelson and Ross, 1973; Freyberg, 1973). Even among middle-class children who have facilities and encouragement, very different levels of the frequency, amount, and quality of this type of play can be seen (Shmukler, 1983). It is often the case, too, that gifted children can need some help to develop the more imaginative aspects of their intelligence in play. In a study of seventy-three gifted primary-school children (mean IQ 159) compared with sixty-four bright-average children (mean IQ 115), Painter (1980) found that when the gifted played the usual children's games, it was often in a way which was more complex and mature. But they also spent more of their time on adult pursuits, such as scientific, technical and debating activites, and they tended to be rather 'bookish' and less imaginative.

The imbalance between the emotional and cognitive aspects of develop-ment can sometimes result in adjustment problems (Pringle, 1970; Gold, 1978) (see also Chapter 14). However, this chapter suggests that the value of play be recognized and included in educational provision for intellectually gifted children, so that their mental development may be healthier and bet-ter balanced. It describes early home environmental conditions which appear to enhance children's ability to play imaginatively, places emphasis on the roles of teachers and parents in implementing these findings, and provides some guidelines and practical suggestions.

THEORIES OF PLAY

Though it is a frequently used theoretical convenience, to approach the more flexible aspects of children's intellectual life, such as imagination, creativity and play, from either a cognitive or affective perspective, they are really two aspects of the same function. Cognitive theory, derived from Piaget, sees play as vital to the developing intellect, in the process of assimilating information into previously held knowledge. Play is thus both an intellectual pursuit and an experience. Affective theory which is psychoanalytically based (Bettlelheim, 1972), sees play as a cathartic activity allowing the child to cope with roles, feelings and eventually reality in achieving or mastering his goal.

But cognitive-affective overlaps have been recognized, for example in the link between Erikson's 'sense of trust' and Piaget's notion of 'ob-ject permanence', where a sense of trust in the outside world cannot be developed unless the infant also has a sense of permanent objects. Renzulli *et al.* (1981) have produced evidence that creativity is linked to affect as well as to intellect, which they have used as the base for the 'Three-ring' explanation of giftedness (examined in Chapter 15). The relationship between positive self-concept and creative endeavour has been described by Sisk (1980), and also by Torrance (1980), who has suggested that it is continuous through life, and capable of development; he has provided guidelines for its development.

However, it is not sufficient merely to recognize these links; a satisfactorily integrated theory of cognitive and affective effects should also describe how they interact with one another in specific circumstances. A good example is Singer's (1978) application of Tomkins' (1962) theory of the relationship of affect to speed of information processing. Singer suggests that it is only when information comes in at a rate which the child can control, and in such a way that it fits in with his understanding of the world, that it is accompanied by the positive experiences of surprise, interest, joy, and liveliness which enhance the learning. When information comes in too quickly for the child to assimilate into his existing understanding, it is accompanied by a feeling of anxiety, but when it comes in too slowly or repetitively, it produces feelings of boredom, possibly giving way to irritation, frustration, and anger. This cognitive-affective perspective provides a workable, comprehensive definition of the development of play as a pleasurable form of exploration, and as a controlled examination and assimilation of novelty; the rate of assimilation of information is implicitly that which makes integration easy and which keeps the arousal level optimal.

IMAGINATIVE PLAY AND CREATIVITY

While the psychometricians struggle for an operational understanding of creativity, tackling such difficult issues as the identification of its identifying criteria, others are examining the influences on it of personality and emotional characteristics. Qualities of personality, such as tolerance of ambiguity and willingness to risk have consistently emerged as salient features in describing the creative personality (see Chapter 23). Creative adults and adolescents often report a lonely, imaginative childhood, and describe having imaginary friends—a feature associated with a predisposition to imaginative play (Helson, 1965; Anastasi and Schafer, 1969; Manosevitz *et al.*, 1973). Indeed, the connection between imaginative play and creativity has been recognized since Freud's 1908 (in Freud, 1959) 'Creative Writers and Daydreaming' by, among others, Piaget (1962), Sutton-Smith (1967), Almy (1968), Klinger (1969) and Bruner (1972).

Creativity is usually described in one of three ways: in terms of the product of creative endeavour, of the process of creativity, or of the creative person. Its most popular conception is the first—as something which results in a novel product. In attempts to tie it down to formal assessment, this focus on production has brought attention to the cognitive aspects of creativity such as originality, ideational fluency, flexibility, and sensitivity to problems. This has led to much useful research and many intervention strategies; the latter include Guilford's (1959) factorial approach and Torrance's (1976) many techniques, suggestions and training programmes. The other two influential approaches, which concern the processes and persons involved, have been most influenced by the existential theories of Rogers (1962) and Maslow (1968). These 'humanistic' approaches are concerned less with end-products and more with the experiences of creativity; they have linked the enhancement of creative expression with the conception of an increased inner freedom.

Several investigations have provided evidence that an improved ability to play increases scores on measures of creativity such as those obtained from tests of divergent thinking. Smilansky's (1968) extensive research with disadvantaged children showed how socio-dramatic play increased their creative, intellectual, and social skills. Gottlieb (1973), examining the effects of modelling play on verbal fantasy production, found—as did Singer (1973)—that more imaginative children wrote more complex, well-developed stories of a divergent character than those whose play was shown to have a less-imaginative quality. Kindergarten children, who were trained in make-believe play showed stronger associative fluency than children in a free-play situation (Dansky and Silverman, 1975; Li, 1978).

In a study to find out whether the measured quality of a child's play could provide clues to divergent thinking abilities as an aspect of creativity, Liebermann (1977) identified a major factor which she defined as 'playfulness'; this was operationalized and measured by ratings of physical, social, and cognitive spontaneity, manifest joy, and sense of humour. It was positively related to measured ideational fluency, spontaneous flexibility, and originality. A follow-up study of forty-eight six-year-old children, whose playing styles had been registered five years earlier, was made by Hutt and Bhavnani (1972). They found that the children who had been seen as playing more imaginatively in the earlier study achieved higher originality scores on a creativity test. However, it cannot be said that early imaginative play is the cause of later creative originality; both may be the direct outcome of the children being more creative.

Familiarity with the means of creativity also seems to make a difference to its quality. Dansky and Silverman (1973) showed that an increased opportunity to play with objects led to greater variety in the way the children played with them. Similarly, Sutton-Smith's (1967) pre-school sample gave more alternative uses for familiar than for unfamiliar toys. Exploration is associated with inventiveness and play: Hutt (1971) found that the more exploratory children were, the higher their level of originality, and she described how the initial exploration develops into full-blown play.

In developing a model of creativity, a sample of play in 114 middle-class, pre-school children was rated for its multi-dimensional imaginative quality by independent observers (Shmukler, 1982). A factor-analytic interpretation of the data produced three factors. The first was heavily loaded on tests of imagination and creativity (the Rorschach inkblot and Singer's 'Imaginative Play Disposition Inventory') and appeared to be one of originality. Both the second—an expressive or behavioural factor, and the third—a social competence factor, were linked to the child's developing drive for mastery of his environment and to his striving sense of competence in the way that Erikson (1950) and White (1959) have described. Two further studies, one in the first grade and the second in the third grade, provided validation data for the long-term implications of these factors. The first two factors of originality and expressiveness were consistently found to be related to tests of divergent thinking and other assessements of imagination and creativity, but the third factor of social competance was related to its assessement by the teacher (Shmukler, 1983). The information-processing model shown below is offered as an integrated way of linking these three factors for their possible use in research and child care.

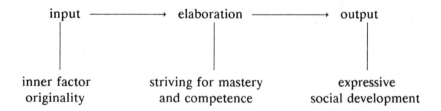

The input of new information and ideas could be in the form of stories, games, and materials, which lend themselves to the expression of the child's own originality via his unique elaborative and interpretive capacity in the assimilation process. The elaboration stage, which cannot be observed, assumes that motivation/arousal takes place with accompanying neurological activity. The output phase which depends on the right environmental support from parents and teachers, seemed to be the best place for the other two factors of expression and social development.

The empirical evidence (outlined above) indicates a relationship between an early predisposition to imaginative play and the capacity for divergent production. But more definitive and longitudinal investigations are needed to answer the question of whether this early predisposition provides a reliable indication of what is later to become recognizable as creative ability.

CREATIVITY, IMAGINATION AND MENTAL HEALTH

An important issue which needs to be raised in the context of giftedness is the relationship of mental health to imagination and play. Parents and teachers who are ambitious for a gifted child can place too much emphasis on measurable achievement, assumed heightened maturity, and a negation of play as a 'waste' of time (Gold, 1978; Freeman, 1979). They may relegate play to the category of 'indulgence', limited to when the real business of the day—formal work—is finished. This insistence that the only worthwhile activity is that approved of by adults, inhibits the development of the child's own way of learning.

It is popularly held by parents and teachers that a high level of fantasy could encourage children to become withdrawn, and that it may be detrimental to mental health by causing confusion between reality and fantasy. But the evidence is to the contrary: an imaginative predisposition helps children to integrate the two states of mind more effectively, enabling them to think more clearly and to build up a more realistic view of themselves and the world. A study by Tucker (1975), for example, disclosed that the more imaginative children were, the more accurately they could recall stories. Saltz and Johnson (1974) showed that children trained in imaginative play were better at detecting absurdities, and displayed an increased ability to distinguish fantasy from reality. By playing at acting what they have seen others do, children learn to comprehend ways of social behaviour, as well as coping with their own fears and fantasies. The child who lacks a well-developed inner life seems to be more susceptible to acting-out, with poor impulse control.

A number of studies have indicated that severely disturbed children find it difficult to play (Nahme-Huang et al., 1977). In fact, the failure to develop the capacity for play can be taken as a sign of serious pathology, since play may be seen as critical to the normal developmental process, and part of its function is that of working through problems (Gould, 1972). Psychotherapy often tries to recreate or capture the circumstances of early childhood (Pope and Singer, 1978); imagination and imagery are its valuable tools, providing powerful access to emotional experiences. Even when the treatment is brief (Hartley et al., 1952), imaginative play is an important, if under-used therapy for troubled youngsters, at any stage of their development.

THE ORIGINS OF PLAY AND CREATIVITY

The child's first human relationship is with his mother, who in early childhood also provides his main environment. Despite the recognition of Freud's emphasis on this relationship, as well as the emphasis of others such as Bowlby (1958) and Spitz (1965), many developmentalists have largely ignored the mother's function; for instance Piaget described the child's mental growth as though it were proceeding in a human vacuum. But since his detailed observations, many clinicians and research workers (e.g. Winnicott, 1970; Mahler et al., 1975; Kaplan, 1978) have built up a steadily increasing amount of data on these early months, highlighting the importance of the mother–child relationship and of interaction in early development (see Chapter 3).

Winnicott's (1970) brilliant analysis has provided important concepts of the origins of play and creativity, which seem to be related to later developmental sequences. However, his perspective is essentially clinical and, as Lewis and Rosenblum (1978) have pointed out, it is virtually impossible in practice to distinguish between cognition and affect in the very young. Therefore much infant research has been obliged to use one as evidence of the other; so that conclusions often seem to depend on where one wishes to start, and on what one wishes to stress.

In Winnicott's terms, the primary task of the 'ordinary good enough' mother is to create a 'holding' environment, which means that she should start at birth by adapting herself closely to the baby's needs in a form of developing dialogue. This begins as a set of shared idiosyncratic signals, through which the mother gradually moves closer to the shared, agreed reality (Riegel, 1976). It is both synchronistic, in relation to their body movements and eye contact, and assymetrical, in that since the mother has far more information about the world, she has to simplify her communication. Then, as the infant's cognitive/affective skills increase, she can and should gently start to make the adaptation less perfect. 'Disillusioning' the baby is a necessary process to help him learn to meet and deal with external reality, giving him some sense of self and not-self, though it needs to be carried out carefully and against a secure background (Mahler et al., 1975; Kaplan, 1978).

Imaginative play begins in the first year of life, when the baby makes use of an object, such as a toy or the corner of a blanket, which seems to represent his mother, and in which he invests some emotion. It is his first ceative act. Although this 'transitional object' is part of the outer world, it also stands for an inner need, establishing the boundaries of the emerging vital area between the self and the not-self, which is termed the 'transitional zone'—the play space. But it is only when the baby's needs are satisfied and he appears to feel sufficiently secure, that he is able to play and learn freely; at first, usually only when the mother is present. Without undue concern for external demands or pressing inner drives, he can express his experiences, be himself, and create something unique in the outside world. In normal circumstances, the original mother–infant play space later becomes replicated between child–family, individual–society, and individual–world. Thus, as the young child comes to abandon the developmental illusion of omnipotence, his most important transitional compensation comes through the area of play. This provides life-long relief from the constant need to meet the demands of reality in cultural experiences such as literature, art, music, and dancing.

The baby's play soon becomes more complex and less dependent on objects, so that by eighteen months, he is largely free of many of the features of the immediate environment, can act out stories (Fein, 1975), and becomes more social and co-operative. In this second year, as he becomes more adept at co-ordinating his senses, images, and movements, he starts to show the earliest signs of real pretence activity, using already developed schemata outside their normal context, such as drinking from a 'pretend' cup or pretending to go to sleep (Nicolich, 1977). His play develops to include more and more elements of pretending and representation, during which he needs good emotional support to quell any anxiety, which may come if the move from reality is too far or too fast. By three or four, the child's play has become truly transcending of time and space, involving role changes, acting, and imaginative sequences. By this stage, the child can not only distinguish between self and not-self, but also between pretend and non-pretend.

THE OPTIMAL BALANCE

Based on studies of early home lives of creative adults and adolescents, Weisberg and Springer (1961) identified certain home circumstances which are possibly crucial to the development of the creative personality. They described in each retrospective case, how the relationship between parent and child was seen to be non-possessive though not unaffectionate encouraging self-reliance and independence. Research has generally reaffirmed this relationship between non-intrusive, non-authoritarian attitudes of parents (Holland, 1961; Drevdahl, 1964) and creativity in children, while uncreative children have more vigilant, intrusive, and demanding mothers (Getzels and Jackson, 1962). Singer (1973) suggested that this optimal balance for imaginative disposition involves a close, secure relationship of 'holding' with a parent, as well as time and space for the child to be alone.

Against this background, the interactions of five-year-old, pre-school children and their mothers in unstructured play sessions were rated (Shmukler, 1981). The children's imaginative predispositions were measured by tests of their imaginations, observations of play at nursery school and teacher's ratings. The mothers of the more imaginative children seemed to be able to provide their children with some structure in this unstructured situation. This took the form of providing ideas and suggestions, such as setting the scene or providing the game place, but they were then able to withdraw from involvement, allowing the children to develop their play according to their own needs. These mothers seemed able to tolerate ambiguity, had little need to interfere, and endorsed fantasy and imaginative responses, staying in contact with their children either by verbal 'mm' responses or non-verbal eye contact.

In contrast, the mothers of the less-creative children seemed to have a much greater need to impose their ideas of structure, conventional responses, and correct behaviour on their children's play; their directive, instructive approach seemed likely to encourage convergent thinking. Complete disinterest was also observed on the part of some mothers; the children of such mothers roamed around the playroom, with little idea of how to organize the situation or to entertain themselves.

It was clear from these observations that creativity did flourish in the opportunity or psychological 'space' which the facilitating mothers provided for their children. Not only did they encourage and sustain creativity, but by being sensitive to their children's inner world, they also seemed to create it; they tolerated ambiguity and regression when necessary, and allowed them to express their inner products without fear of ridicule or censure. Within this security, the personality characteristics designated as creative were seen to be allowed to grow and develop.

IMPLICATIONS AND PRACTICAL INDICATIONS

The pre-school period seems to be the most fertile for the enhancement of imaginative play. These years are crucial to language, concept formation, creativity, and the development of awareness of the self and others. Play is a powerful tool in aiding the young child's ability to absorb and assimilate experiences in meaningful ways, i.e. to learn. Intervention with groups of children, such as in a pre-school playgroup, is possibly the most effective and efficient way of achieving this help. Many adults, however, feel that they will inhibit children's play if they intervene or participate. Though this may be true for clumsy interference such as dogmatic redirection, which does not take its clues from the child's activities, there is indicative evidence that careful adult guidance and suggestion can enhance the quality and inventiveness of play (Tamburrini, 1982).

Studies on play training make the following implicit or explicit assumptions—that imaginative play is, (a) important to the 'development of social and intellectual ability', (b) trainable, and (c) often underdeveloped in children. Researchers have used a variety of methods, such as adult models who present dramatic situations, plots, and role-taking with dolls (Marshall and Hahn, 1967), pipe cleaner figures acting roles which the children then take over, using toys as props (Freyberg, 1973), thematic fantasy play (Saltz and Johnson, 1974), play tutoring (Feitelson and Ross, 1973; Smith and Syddall, 1978), and a combination of play tutoring and excursions (Smilansky,

1968). Tizard (1977) showed that in nursery schools, when adults participated in the children's play it was more elaborate and had greater variety,
and as Dunn and Wooding (1977) also found, it went on for longer periods.

Most of such studies have been undertaken with deprived or disadvantaged children as part of the general concern with the development of these
children since the 1960s, and under the assumption that the middle-class environment is more encouraging of imaginative expression. Specific benefits
include originality, conservation of social role, concentration, complexity of
play, verbalization, group constructs and co-operation, perceptual, cognitive
and affective tasks (reflected in increased scores on WPPI, IPAT, PPVT),
improved understanding of conservation of mass and liquid, and also mathematical readiness (Marshall and Hahn, 1967; Feitelson and Ross, 1973;
Freyberg, 1973; Rosen, 1974; Saltz and Johnson, 1974; Smith and Syddall,
1978).

Despite positive results, however, there is some evidence which casts
doubt on the view that all the benefits of intervention can be explained
by play training, and suggests that it could be due, at least in part, to the
involvement of a warm, concerned adult (Smith and Syddall, 1978). None
the less, the general conclusion holds that imaginative play does not develop
automatically, and that intervention is an efficient and enjoyable way of
enhancing the cognitive, emotional, and particularly social skills of young
children. Play intervention stresses the active intervention of the adult in
teaching skills and techniques. It is a significant advance on previous non-
interaction and therapeutic approaches, notably in its joint emphasis on both
cognitive and affective processes, which encourages the synthesising and integration of their respective social skills.

THE ROLE OF THE ADULT

For play to develop well, environments outside the home, such as school,
have to be as facilitating as the mother in providing structure, support, the
relevant learning materials, and a living cultural tradition from which to
draw and on which to build. Without them, children cannot practice and
develop their talents; mathematicians need teachers, and musicians need
instruments. They must also provide the sense of freedom in which the child
feels that it is alright to make mistakes—a feature which can be lost when
achievement is over-emphasized. The adult's role is as a guide rather than a
director, within and as part of the child's environment, which neither implies
complete loss of control nor complete freedom, but helping to maintain
a balance between structure and freedom in the psychological 'space'. It
implies sufficient sensitivity to recognize and adapt the circumstances to the
times in which children are receptive to new materials and stimulation.

A problem which could face the concerned adult is that of the child who persists in one kind of play—mental inflexibility which is likely to have been brought about by anxiety and which the adult can try to identify. It might, for example, be the result of the parents insisting that the child 'learn' at school, so that by merely 'playing' there, he could experience some anxiety about returning home. The child could have been restricted at home in his choice of playthings, or perhaps not have been allowed to touch, so that he may find it difficult to cope with the new playthings at school, and will need some introduction to ways of playing with them, to take the edge off their unknown and fearful quality. The teacher has to create a new 'holding' environment, sufficiently secure to enable the child to risk doing what is disapproved of at home, and thus give him a 'licence' to play. At first, she may have to encourage the child to play with simpler, more babyish toys like those at home, to underpin his security, playing with him until she has bridged the home–school gap, and can then move on to more advanced material.

Novelty is not of itself creative, especially when many of the novel ideas are redundant because they are inappropriate in context. During play, the child experiments to find out what the environment can do, and assimilates these empirical results within that context, but where the environment or social conditions are hostile, they can block the process of creativity. The concerned adult should be able to recognize and to some extent manipulate the play environment appropriately, such as by controlling the rate of stimulation. Too much direction leads to an unwelcome atmosphere, which saps any child's self-confidence, though absence of guidance means that the child flounders, and still cannot learn how to cope effectively; the middle road is the best. However, there is evidence that certain conditions in the classroom can enhance creativity (Torrance, 1976; Jones, 1968); most of these studies have focused on techniques, but it seems that the teacher's attitudes and personality are equally important in facilitating creativity.

Provision for play involves the questions of 'what' and 'how'. The value of fantasy and imaginative material has been argued vociferously, and the educational community seems split down the middle on this issue. In South Africa, for example, fairy stories are taboo in state-run nursery programmes. From a clinical perspective, however, the 'relevant material' and 'living cultural tradition' should include the great tales and myths of our civilization. Bettelheim (1976) argued for the emotional significance of fairy tales, in that they provide a symbolic presentation of and solution to the child's existential dilemmas, such as sibling rivalry and separation. In addition to the reading and telling of stories, imaginative games are assisted by the provision of dressing-up clothes, unstructured boxes, packing cases, etc. which lend themselves for use as a variety of props.

The holistic or humanist approach to education conceptualizes creativity as a process which calls for the integration of cognition and affect in the classroom. By focusing on process, rather than content, the teacher could provide the balance between input in the form of ideas, know-how in terms of techniques, and security through good emotional support. It also allows the teacher to avoid dealing with psychodynamic content in emotionally charged situations, and to deal with skills instead (Shmukler *et al.*, 1983; Shmukler, 1984).

GIFTED CHILDREN'S PLAY

The principles of helping children to play imaginatively do not only apply to the disadvantaged, but to children who are better provided for, particularly the gifted. Bernstein (1972), in his researches into the effects of social class, has noted that many middle-class parents push their children towards achievement, and emphasize the mechanical skills of examinations rather than educational relevance. He termed such homes 'pseudo-educational pressure cookers'. There is also more specific evidence (Gold, 1978; Freeman, 1979) that ambitious parents of gifted children prohibit their children from playful activities, which they regard as a 'waste of time', and schools press for achievement in this way, for instance through their disproportionate emphasis on competition, even in play (games). However there is also evidence that the lower social classes coerce their children into more conforming modes of behaviour, preferring a more formal style of teaching at school, which militates against creativity (Anderson and Cropley, 1966; Rejkind, 1982). Perhaps it is not so much their economic level as the personal outlooks of parents which affects their attitudes to their children's creativity.

Gifted children sometimes have difficulty in integrating their high-level cognitive processes with their emotional maturity; a feature which can be further hindered by undue adult emphasis on intellectual expression (Kohn, 1977; Freeman, 1983). The gifted and creative in our society have as much need as other children to develop well-integrated personalities and the facility to rely on their emotional as well as their cognitive resources. In this sense, then, a plea should be made for allowing the gifted child the opportunity to daydream, fantasize, and engage in seemingly non-directed activities as a means of developing his mental resources.

The very able child is also likely to venture into intellectual territory, such as making suggestions about the subject matter of the lesson, with which the teacher is either not familiar or feels to be inappropriate. This move may deny him some or all of the essential approval and affection which he might have found in accepting more conventional paths of learning. It places quite a burden on the gifted creative child, for at the same time, he must persevere in the way he feels is right, sometimes in spite of adult and peer disapproval. In fact, the gifted need genuine emotional support in their adventures with concepts. When the adult can discuss the value of a child's ideas, postponing any final judgements on her efforts, and is not insistent that adult mores must rule, the child will have more courage to explore. It is particularly important for gifted children's development that they should be party to planning and judging their own endeavours, since the gift of high intelligence enables them to make more effective use of such feedback.

But the adult can give particular help to the gifted in the development of their play by encouraging them to use both their imaginative and conceptual abilities in harness. Kaplan (1980) suggests how the play of the young gifted child can be enhanced by the adult in the following areas.

Content

Concepts can be extended from or introduced to the play experience, and the adult can suggest generalizations and principles from there. For example, a child may be playing at imagining herself as a robot, from which the adult could guide the child into considering the broader-based issue of changes in goods and services as a consequence of technological advances.

Processes

Higher level thinking and research skills can be introduced and reinforced during play. For example, a gifted pre-school child might be building a tall shaky tower of wooden blocks. The adult could then discuss the problems of constructing the tower with him, as a way of teaching problem-solving and thinking skills.

Product

This may be the formation of new constructs to express what has been learned from the play experience. It occurs for example, when a young child is asked to devise a game which can be played with others, or to share information he has chosen to find out for himself.

Affect

Children can learn more about themselves from their play experiences, discovering their own abilities, interests, and needs, as well as finding out about the others they play with and their relationships with them. Play is something the young gifted child can share with all children, its special value being in providing social links between them in the practice of communication and of social skills. It is also valuable for the teacher as a means of assessing and evaluating the young gifted child, providing some evidence of the child's readiness for entry into other forms of curriculum provision. It should be the frequent alternative to the textual learning which is so often the basic medium of instruction for the gifted child.

CONCLUSION

Imaginative play, being both affective and cognitive, has an essential developmental function, helping the child to achieve a balance between inner and outer experience, and developing a reservoir of resourcefulness, liveliness, and self-esteem, encouraging both curiosity and the capacity for exploration. By its very nature, play demands that children use their potential to combine experiences into organized, yet flexible conceptual schemes. It is a thus a powerful adjunct to early educational, preventive, and remedial procedures, and should be paramount in any pre-school activity.

The process approach, described here, places stress on the realization of potential. It offers a worthwhile base for intervention, particularly with gifted children, whose social and emotional development may not be in accord with that of their intellects. Such children may also suffer from too great an emphasis on intellectual achievement, an impoverishment of imagination, and a tendency to regard play as irrelevant to their lives. The products of creative expression come from individuals who possess a combination of reason and intuition, imagination and discipline. The play of the gifted, at any stage of their development, is of special concern because of the creative potential which it holds.

REFERENCES

Almy, M. (1968). Spontaneous play: an avenue for intellectual development. In *Early Childhood Education Rediscovered* (ed. J. L. Frost). Holt, Rinehart and Winston, New York.

Anastasi, A., and Schaefer, C. E. (1969). Biographical correlates of artistic and literary creativity in adolescent girls. *Journal of Applied Psychology*, **53**, 4, 267–273.

Bernstein, B. (1972). *Class, Codes and Control.* Routledge and Kegan Paul, London.

Bettelheim, B. (1972). *School Review.* November, 1–13.

Bettelheim, B. (1976). *The Uses of Enchantment: The Meaning and Importance of Fairy Tales.* Thames and Hudson, London.

Bowlby, J. (1958). The nature of the child's tie to the mother. *International Journal of Psychoanalysis*, **39**, 211–221.

Bruner, J. S. (1972). Nature and uses of immaturity. *American Psychologist*, **27**, 678–708.

Dansky, J. L., and Silverman, I. W. (1973). Effects of play on associative fluency in preschool-aged children. *Developmental Psychology*, **9**, 1, 38–43.

Dansky, J. L., and Silverman, I.W. (1975). Play: a general facilitator of associative fluency. *Developmental Psychology*, **11**, 104–113.

Drevdahl, J. E. (1964). Some developmental and environmental factors in creativity. In *Widening Horizons in Creativity* (ed. C. W. Taylor). Wiley, New York.

Dunn, J,. and Wooding, C. (1977). Play in the home and its implications for learning. In *Biology of Play* (eds B. Tizard and D. Harvey). Heinneman, London.

Ebbeck, F. N. (1973). Learning from play in other cultures. In *Revisiting Early Childhood Education* ed. J. L. Frost). Holt, Rinehart and Winston, New York.

Erikson, E. H. (1950). *Childhood and Society*. Pelican Books, London.

Fein, G. G. (1975). A transformational analysis of pretending. *Developmental Psychology*, **11**, 3, 291–223.

Feitelson, D., and Ross, G. S. (1973). The neglected factor—play. *Human Development*, **16**, 202–223.

Freeman, J. (1979). *Gifted Children: Their Identification and Development in a Social Context*. MTP Press, Lancaster; University Park Press, Baltimore.

Freeman, J. (1983). Emotional problems of the gifted child. *J. Child Psychol. Psychiat.* **24**, 481–485.

Freud, S. (1959). Creative writers and day-dreaming, 1908. In *The Complete Psychological Works of Sigmund Freud* (translated by James Strackey in collaboration with Anna Freud), Vol. IX (1906–1908), *Jensen's 'Gradiva' and other works*. Hogarth, London.

Freyberg, J. T. (1973). Increasing the imaginative play of urban disadvantaged kindergarten children through systematic training. In *The Child's World of Make-Believe* (ed. J. Singer). Academic Press, New York.

Getzels, J. W., and Jackson, P. W. (1962). *Creativity and Intelligence*. Wiley, New York.

Gold, D. (1978). A study of attitudes, expectations and abilities within a NAGC branch. In *Looking to Their Future*. NAGC, 1 South Audley St, London.

Gottlieb, S. (1973). Modelling effects upon fantasy. In *The Child's World of Make-Believe* (ed. J. Singer). Academic Press, New York.

Gould, R. (1972). *Child Studies Through Fantasy*. Quadrangle Books, New York.

Guilford, J. P. (1959). Traits of creativity. In *Creativity and its Cultivation* (ed. H. H. Anderson). Harper and Row, Chicago.

Hartley, R. E., Frank, L. K., and Goldenson, R. M. (1952). *Understanding Children's Play*. Columbia University Press, New York.

Helson, R. (1965). Childhood interest clusters related to creativity in women. *Journal of Consulting Psychology*, **29**, 4, 352–361.

Holland, J. L. (1961). Achievement syndromes among high aptitude students. *Psychological Reports*, **8**, 384.

Hutt, C. (1971). Exploration and play in children. In **Child's Play** (eds R. E. Herran and B. Sutton-Smith). Wiley, New York. Originally published in *Symposium of Zoological Society of London*, **18**, 61–81, 1966.

Hutt, C., and Bhavnani, R. (1972). Predictions from play. *Nature*, 237.

Jones, R. M. (1968). *Fantasy and Feeling in Education*. Penguin, London.

Kaplan, L. J. (1978). *Oneness and Separateness: From Infant to Individual*. Simon and Schuster, New York.

Kaplan, S. N. (1980). The role of play in a differentiated curriculum for the young gifted child. *Roeper Review*, **3**, 12–13.

Klein, M. (1955). The psychoanalytic play technique. *American Journal of Orthopsychiatry*, **25**, 223–237.

Klinger, E. (1969). Development of imaginative behavior: Implications of play for a theory of fantasy. *Psychological Bulletin*, **72**, 4, 277–298.

Kohn, M. (1977). *Social Competence, Symptoms and Underachievement in Childhood: A Longitudinal Perspective.* Winston and Sons, Washington.

Lewis, M., and Rosenblum, L. A. (1978). *The Development of Affect.* Plenum Press, New York.

Li, A. K. F. (1978). Effects of play on novel responses on kindergarten children. *Alberta J. of Educ. Research*, **24**, 31–36.

Liebermann, J. N. (1977). *Playfulness: Its Relationship to Imagination and Creativity.* Academic Press, New York.

Mahler, M.S., Pine, F., and Bergman, A. (1975). *The Psychological Birth of the Human Infant.* Basic Books, New York.

Manosevitz, M., Prentice, N. M., and Wilson, F. (1973). Individual and family correlates of imaginary companions in preschool children. *Developmental Psychology*, **8**, 72–79.

Marshall, H. R., and Hahn, S. C. (1967). Experimental modification of dramatic play. *Journal of Personality and Social Psychology*, **5**, 1, 119–122.

Maslow, A. H. (1968). *Toward a Psychology of Being.* Van Nostrand, New York.

Nahme-Huang, L., Singer, D. G., Singer, J. L., and Wheaton, A. (1977). Imaginative play training and perceptual-motor interventions with emotionally-disturbed hospitalized children. *American Journal of Orthopsychiatry*, **47**, 2, 238–249.

Nicolich, L. M. (1977). Beyond sensorimotor intelligence: assessment of symbolic maturity through analysis of pretend play. *Merrill-Palmer Quarterly*, **23**, 2, 89–99.

Painter, F. (1980). Gifted children at home and school. In *Educating the Gifted Child* (ed. R.Povey). Harper and Row, London.

Piaget, J. (1962). *Play, Dreams and Imitation in Childhood.* W. W. Norton, New York.

Pope, K. S., and Singer, J. L. (1978). *The Stream of Consciousness: Scientific Investigations into the Flow of Human Experience.* Wiley and Sons, New York.

Pringle, M. K. (1970). *Able Misfits.* Longman, London.

Renzulli, J. S., Reis, S. M., and Smith, L. H. (1981). *The Revolving Door Identification Model.* Creative Learning Press, Connecticut.

Riegel, K. F. (1976). The dialectics of human development. *American Psychologist*, October, 689–700.

Rogers, C. R. (1962). Toward a theory of creativity. In *A Sourcebook for Creative Thinking* (eds S. J. Parnes and H. F. Harding). Scribner's, New York.

Rosen, C. E. (1974). The effects of sociodramatic play on problem-solving behaviour among culturally disadvantaged preschool children. *Child Development*, **45**, 920–927.

Saltz, E., and Johnson, J. (1974). Training for thematic-fantasy play in culturally disadvantaged children: preliminary results. *Journal of Educational Psychology*, **66**, 4, 623–630.

Shmukler, D. (1981). Mother–child interaction and its relationship to the predisposition to imaginative play. *Genetic Psychology Monographs*, **104**, 215–235.

Shmukler, D. (1982). A factor analytic model of elements of creativity in preschool children. *Genetic Psychology Monographs*, **105**, 25–39.

Shmukler, D. (1983). Preschool imaginative play predisposition and its relationship to subsequent third grade assessment. *Imagination, Cognition and Personality*, **2**, 3, 230–231.

Shmukler, D. (1984). *The Implications of Imaginative Play for the Process of Education.* Baywood Press, Farmingdale, New York, (in press).

Shmukler, D., Skuy, M., and Clark, L. (1983). A brief note on the relationship between imaginative play predisposition and early learning indicators. Unpublished manuscript in preparation for publication.

Singer, J. L. (1973). *The Child's World of Make-Believe.* Academic Press, New York.

Singer, J. L. (1978). The constructive potential of imagery and fantasy process: implications for child development, psychotherapy, and personal growth. In *Interpersonal Psychoanalysis* (ed. E. G. Witenberg). J. Wiley, New York.

Sisk, D. A. (1980). The relationship between self concept and creative thinking of elementary school children: an experimental investigation. Gate, 2, 47–59.

Smilansky, S. (1968). *The Effects of Socio-dramatic Play on Disadvantaged Preschool Children.* Wiley, New York.

Smith, P. K., and Syddall, S. (1978). Play and non-play tutoring in preschool children: is it play or tutoring which matters? *British Journal of Educational Psychology,* **48**, 315–325.

Spitz, R. A. (1965). *The First Year of Life: A Psychoanalytic Study of Normal and Deviant Development of Object Relations.* International Universities Press, New York.

Sutton-Smith, B. (1967). The role of play in cognitive development. *Young Children,* **6**, 202–214.

Tamburrini, J. (1982). Play and the role of the teacher. *Early Child Development and Care,* **8**, 209–217.

Tomkins, S. S. (1962–3). *Affect, Imagery and Consciousness,* Vols. I and II. Springer, New York.

Tizard, B. (1977). Play: the child's way of learning? In *Biology of Play* (eds B. Tizard and D. Harvey). Heinneman, London.

Torrance, E. P. (1976). Can we teach children to think creatively? In *Assessing Creative Growth: Measured Changes—Book Two* (eds A. M. Beondi and S. S. Parnes). Creative Synergetics, Great Neck, New York.

Torrance, E. P. (1980). Educating the gifted in the 1980s: removing limits on learning. *Journal for the Education of the Gifted,* **4**, 43–48.

Tucker, J. (1975). The role of fantasy in cognitive-affective functioning: Does reality make a difference in remembering? Unpublished Doctoral Dissertation, Teachers' College, Columbia University.

White, R. W. (1959). Motivation reconsidered: the concept of competence. *Psychological Review,* **66**, 297–333.

Whiting, B. B. (ed.) (1963). *Six Cultures: Studies of Child-rearing.* Wiley & Sons, New York.

Weisberg, P. A., and Springer, K. J. (1961). Environmental factors in creative function. *Archives of General Psychiatry,* **5**, 64–74.

Winnicott, D. W. (1970). *Playing and Reality.* Pelican Books, England.

The Psychology of Gifted Children
Edited by Joan Freeman
©1985, John Wiley & Sons, Ltd.

CHAPTER 6

New Challenges to Common Identification Practices

JOANNE WHITMORE

The 1980s appear to be an internationally critical period for gifted children, following a decade of sustained and growing concern about their relative neglect within formal systems of education. This neglect has resulted from a mixture of ambivalent attitudes, incomplete or inaccurate information about exceptional learners, and a failure to train school personnel to identify and provide for their special needs (Newland, 1976; Whitmore, 1980). Its effects can be seen in educational reports of gifted pupils as school drop-outs, having behaviour problems, lacking achievement motivation, and feeling indifferent or hostile towards school experiences.

Professional response has been to direct more and more attention and effort towards identifying the intellectually gifted high achiever for special education. However, if our aim in attempting to identify the gifted is not only to reduce neglect, but to preserve and fully develop children's potentials, identification practices need to be re-examined to include those who do not achieve outstandingly, and hence redirected in the light of new and challenging conceptions of giftedness. Only then can gifted education at last become established as an integral part of educational systems—no longer episodic, or a pawn of socio-political currents.

The purpose of this chapter is to set forth new challenges to common identification practices. That purpose cannot be accomplished without first discussing the fundamental questions or issues of, (a) who it is we want to identify, (b) when, and (c) for what purpose. It has been through challenges to definitions of giftedness that the need to re-examine identification practices has become evident; in a real sense, identification practices have defined giftedness for us.

After those fundamental questions have been addressed, identification practices will be re-examined in the second section of the chapter with guidelines offered for their improvement. The third part of the chapter will apply the recommended guidelines to specific groups of the gifted population who frequently have not been identified as gifted and therefore have not been provided with an appropriate educational programme. These groups are, (a) non-handicapped under-achievers, (b) handicapped pupils receiving special services, and (c) culturally different gifted pupils. The final section of the chapter will discuss the professional responses needed to meet the challenges set forth in the preceding sections; responses relating to changes in school policies and practices, the preparation of professionals at the pre- and in-service levels, and educational and psychological research.

THE FUNDAMENTAL ISSUES

The first question that must be raised in considering identification practices is: Why should we identify gifted pupils? Some individuals resist the establishment of identification procedures and deny the need for special educational provision. Supporters of gifted education argue that we must identify gifted pupils so that the appropriate modifications in curriculum and instruction can occur to guide each pupil toward more complete development of his/her potential for exceptional achievement and, ultimately, contribution to society. Implicit in their position is a belief that intellectual giftedness is a dynamic characteristic, the full development of which depends upon appropriate stimulation and guidance in school experiences. Professionals tend to agree that there is no justification or defensible rationale for identifying pupils as gifted unless the consequence of identification is more appropriate educational programming. If one endorses the position that we need to identify gifted pupils in order to provide them with optimal educational programming, the next question is whom will we identify by virtue of the definition implicit in our practices.

In the United States, nearly all gifted education has been designed to serve pupils of 'high academic ability' who are usually identified on standardized tests of aptitude by scores of IQ 130 or more, or on scholastic performances in the top 10–20 per cent. Typically, the pupils are recommended by teachers for gifted education because they give consistently high academic performances, are socially and emotionally mature, and are highly motivated to achieve in school. The operational definition of giftedness behind this approach is practical; only those who are already exceptionally advanced within specific subject areas of the curriculum are given special educational provision to allow them to progress further. In this practicality, there is also some implicit concern for the relief of the classroom teacher, who finds it difficult to keep the advanced pupil 'busy' or challenged.

However, recent attention given to potential, as in the use of the phrase 'demonstrated achievement and/or potential ability' in the 1972 US Office of Education definition of giftedness (Marland, 1972), demonstrates a change of perspective which must in time have a significant effect on identification procedures. If school personnel were to accept a simple definition of giftedness—as exceptional potential for learning and academic achievement—then identification procedures would have to be restructured. The sole use of achievements as criteria would have to be modified, and strategies developed to discern native intellect and potential so that a broader, more inclusive net would be cast. The change would be helpful to educators who are concerned about what they see as the 'exclusive' nature of special gifted provision, as well as to those who are aware that a significant number of youngsters have not been stimulated to show their giftedness in regular school lessons, yet have exceptional potential for learning and high achievement.

Any definition of children's abilities which stresses potential, as well as the expansion of identification practices, implies an educational philosophy which emphasizes the role of environmental nurturance. Research has provided evidence of the importance of early education (Bloom, 1964; Clark, 1979; White, 1975), and the longer-term role of schools in the development of human potential (Rutter *et al.*, 1979). This educational philosophy is based on the premise that, without appropriate 'gifted education', the child's exceptional intellectual abilities will not develop as fully as they could.

This concern for the nurturance of human potential undergirded the philosophy and values which generated America's Public Law 94-142, The Education for All Handicapped Children Act, which requires educational authorities to provide appropriate and free special services for the maximum development of every handicapped child's potential for learning. It also calls for a team of professionals to integrate their information about the child with parents so that they may co-operate in designing the best ways to meet the child's special needs. The same principles are valid for gifted pupils who are not high achievers, since excluding children who have not yet demonstrated their exceptional potential for learning from gifted education is likely to deny them the opportunity for stimulation and challenge, which would elicit a behaviour pattern of high achievement and motivation.

The study of gifted children who also have handicapping conditions suggests that educators have tended to provide specifically for the handicap(s) while neglecting, if not thwarting, the child's intellectual growth (Maker, 1977; Maker *et al.*, 1978). This issue has become prominent through the efforts of parents and teachers to acquire special services for those with specific learning disabilities (LD/Gifted). Many parental grievances in America have occurred because state or school district policies often do not permit a child to receive more than one type of special education service. That policy, however, directly contradicts the intent of Public Law 94-142 to guarantee a child an educational plan to accommodate both strengths and weaknesses.

These fundamental issues challenge the present operational definition of giftedness. Although existing practices are adequate and straightforward in seeking to serve gifted high achievers, if the definition includes pupil potential for exceptional achievement, the identification task will be much more complex and challenging, and future identification procedures will have to change radically. The remainder of this chapter will describe means by which those changes may be brought about.

OBSERVABLE CHARACTERISTICS OF INTELLECTUAL GIFTEDNESS

In defining intellectual giftedness as exceptional potential for learning and academic achievement, there are several observable key characteristics in children which, even in the absence of high scholastic achievement, can indicate its presence. Though this would normally require an analysis of the components of intelligence, the method suggested here is a simpler and more practical method than, for example, Guilford's theorized 120 mental abilities.

Essentially, the characteristics are derived from the principal categories of intelligent behaviour which distinguish human beings from other animals, including the ability to use assimilated information in effective problem solving. The intellectually gifted are those who manifest notable ease and speed in the development of cognitive behaviour, producing outcomes which are readily described as exceptional in quality and quantity. Characteristics which merely reflect socialization, such as leadership behaviour, emotional maturity, motivational and competitive characteristics, and various other personality characteristics or values, can mislead one searching for intellectual characteristics of giftedness.

Table 6.1 below suggests some observable characteristics of intellectual giftedness. It is divided into two parts, (a) Primary Identifiers, which are most reliable when accurately recognized, and (b) Secondary Identifiers, which often lead to identification but are more selective in the gifted population.

It should be noted that a child may exhibit all the characteristics in Table 6.1, yet still be neither a high scholastic achiever nor highly motivated by the basic school curriculum; neither mature nor a social leader. Furthermore, giftedness may exist in only one area of intellectual activity, such as mathematics, or creative writing; or alternatively, the child may excel in all curriculum areas.

TABLE 6.1 Observable characteristics of gifted children

Primary identifiers

Learns quickly and easily when interested

Exceptional cognitive power for learning, retaining, and using knowledge/ information

Advanced problem-solving skill—challenged by problems to solve; uses acquired knowledge and superior reasoning skills to attack, and often solve complex practical and theoretical problems

Oral language incorporates an advanced vocabulary used appropriately and complex language structure

Unusual comprehension of complex, abstract ideas—develops or elaborates ideas at a level not expected

High level of inquiry—the qualitative nature of questions raised and the subjects that arouse interest and sustained curiosity

Exceptional quality of thought as revealed through language and problem solving— remarkable manipulation of abstract symbols and ideas, including perceiving and manipulating relationship between ideas, events, people; formulates principles and generalizations through transfer of learning across settings or events; reflects and reasons to gain insights and to generate solutions

Secondary identifiers

Highly creative behaviour in production of ideas, things, solutions; can be noticeably creative and inventive (originality); fascinated by 'idea play'

A wide interest range; basically very curious

A profound, sometimes consuming interest in one or more areas of intellectual investigation

An intense desire to know and understand, to master skills and problems of interest

Shows initiative in pursuing 'outside projects' and may have elaborate hobbies of his/her own choice; manifests resourcefulness and an unusual capacity for self-directed learning, though possibly only in out-of-school activities

Enjoys self-expression, especially through discussion but also often through the arts

Exhibits independence in thought, a tendency toward non-conformity

Demands a reason or explanation for requirements, limits, undesired events

Tends to be perfectionist, severely self-critical, and aspiring to high standards of achievement; desire to excel and produce

Shows greater sensitivity and awareness regarding self, others, world problems, moral issues; may be intolerant of human weakness.

IMPROVING IDENTIFICATION PROCEDURES

In the search for potential giftedness, two basic changes are needed in the identification process. First, one should begin assessment at the time of the child's entry into the school system; it is particularly important to find such children early, since recent evidence has shown that early identification and provision can reverse patterns of severe and chronic underachievement in gifted children (Whitmore, 1980). Early identification can help the teacher provide more appropriate educational experiences and so stimulate the child's motivation to learn through participation in classroom learning (Clark, 1979; Robinson, et al., 1981; Whitmore, 1979, 1980). The second basic change required is a shift in purpose from relieving the needs of the classroom teacher to focusing on providing for the needs of the child.

Identification and provision should not be available only as a reward for the good, well-behaved children who strive to excel. Under the definition and philosophy suggested here, they would be an integral part of educational diagnostic and planning activities in a school system. Thus, in the course of studying the characteristics of each child, exceptional potential for learning would be recognized and planned for. Such a scheme would have to involve all the professional staff in the school, who, along with parents, would share the responsibility for nurturing the child's intellectual development.

OBSTACLES TO THE RECOGNITION OF POTENTIAL GIFTEDNESS

The first step in recognizing and subsequently removing any obstacles which could interfere with the identification of potential intellectual giftedness, is to consider them in five categories, (a) undue reliance on testing, (b) stereotypic expectations, (c) developmental delays or handicapping conditions, (d) classroom behaviour, and (e) lack of information about the child.

Reliance on testing

Although the use of intelligence tests has become the target of much critical review in recent years (Anderson, 1961; Garcia, 1981; Sternberg, 1982), parents and teachers still frequently regard the IQ score as ultimate, objective proof of the child's ability. Somehow we seem to have lost sight of the fact that intelligence tests were constructed to measure only samples of behaviour to help teachers understand classroom performance. Though group aptitude testing certainly identifies high achievers and good test takers, it does yield more information about school achievement and test-taking skills than about intellectual potential. An individual test of intelligence is more likely to evidence pupil potential for learning. Unfortunately, such a test is administered only once to a child because of the cost involved, and if, due to the influence of one or more possible sources of significant error, a gifted child scores lower than the cut-off point required to be labelled 'gifted', he or she may never be regarded as 'truly' gifted. The coupling of a moderate IQ score with average or below average school achievement almost guarantees that giftedness will be denied.

Unfortunately, there is a tendency to determine the educational needs of a child by examining an array of test scores with too much respect for their presumed objectivity, while perceptions and observations of parents and teachers are regarded as too subjective to be acceptable in decision-making. But keen observations by teachers of signs of superior intellectual abilities in a child should not be diminished in significance because of relatively low test scores. Rather, evaluation should be continued to assess the child's potential for learning, relative to the norms, until it is felt that the child's ability has been accurately assessed.

Stereotypic expectations

The most serious and pervasive obstacles to the recognition of giftedness are the stereotypic expectations which have developed among both professional staff and the public in response to Terman's (1925) classical work. In his time, Terman sought to dispel prevalent and negative myths about individuals with superior intellect by the longitudinal study of the social, emotional, physical, and intellectual development of gifted children. However, his sampling of the gifted population has been recognized as culturally biased, which has thrown some doubt on the universal applicability of the findings (Hughes and Converse, 1962; Jacobs, 1970; Whitmore, 1980). Terman's work provided excellent information about high achievers who were predominately white and socio-economically advantaged. It was not Terman, but rather the public and professionals, who formulated a stereotypic profile of gifted children based on his sample. As a result, the difficulty of recognizing intellectual giftedness in other less-advantaged groups of the population was increased.

The first problem presented by the dominant stereotype is that, in spite of more recent research literature, teachers still tend to expect a gifted child to excel, or to exceed the norms, in all areas of their development. The intellectually gifted are often expected to be more emotionally mature, that is more adaptable, self-controlled, independent, and responsible, and to cope more constructively with pressures, to respond more dependably to self-directed learning activities, and to strive more to please the teacher. This means that teachers often have reservations about referring a child for testing, or for consideration for placement in gifted education, if he or she exhibits immaturity in social and emotional characteristics. Many gifted pupils do undoubtedly possess characteristics of exceptional maturity, but acceptance of the stereotype can bias teachers to overlook intellectual giftedness in emotionally and/or socially immature children, or in those who seem consistently inattentive and careless in following directions. This problem is particularly pertinent when a gifted child is in a class of older pupils and his or her normal physical development results in perceived 'immaturity'. It then appears to limit the child's ability to perform tasks, such as handwriting, at an average class level, and teachers may then reject the notion of intellectual giftedness. However, public recognition of gifted individuals with physical handicaps (e.g. Franklin D. Roosevelt, Helen Keller, Thomas Edison, Ray Charles) has encouraged the recognition that intellectually gifted children may not always be physically superior.

The second stereotypic expectation is that a truly gifted child will excel in most, if not all, areas of the academic school curriculum. This is in spite of extensive debate on the nature of intelligence over the last quarter-century. In practice, teachers often assume that when a child is failing to do 'good work' in a major area of the curriculum, then his or her superior performance in other subjects is probably a case of 'over-achievement'.

As increasing numbers of gifted children enter American schools with relatively advanced reading skills—possibly the effect of early educational television programmes—so the expectations of teachers rise, and the gifted child with less than exceptionally advanced reading and writing abilities has a diminished chance of being recognized. Even though the child may have outstanding qualities in other subjects, such as science and social studies, those abilities can be rationalized as merely artefacts of high motivation or enriched home experiences. Teachers expect that 'bright', 'gifted' children will have reasonably uniform achievement behaviour, at least producing no less than 'average' work in any subject. The reverse also holds that when a child who has been identified as gifted fails to do well in specific subject areas, the teacher may reason that the difficulty is caused only by lack of motivation, effort, and disciplined behaviour.

The third major expectation, often rigidly held for gifted children, is that they have a high motivation to excel in school, shown by their striving behaviour, conscientious effort, and a very positive attitude towards school and the standard curriculum. This stereotype has been reinforced by Renzulli's (1978) popular approach to identification: his triad of identifying characteristics includes above-average intellectual ability, creativity, and task commitment. However, studies of young, gifted under-achievers suggest that some of the most highly gifted and creative children in American schools may become distressfully negative toward school and the curriculum, thus providing no evidence of task commitment in the classroom (Whitmore, 1979, 1980). Although high task commitment can lead to the identification of a high-achiever as gifted, its absence should never result in the automatic dismissal of the possibility of potential giftedness or in failure to test for superior intellectual potential.

Developmental delays or handicapping conditions

Because of teacher expectations that gifted pupils exhibit all-round high classroom performance, those gifted children with developmental delays or mild handicapping conditions, who perform at the average or below-average level on tasks involving basic skills, are additionally handicapped in their likelihood of being recognized as intellectually gifted. Developmental problems contribute, for example, to difficulties in writing, particularly in the early years of school; impaired eye-hand or perceptual-motor co-ordination can interfere considerably with achievement on tasks involving copying, reading, writing, and drawing. Similarly, giftedness tends to go unrecognized in children with average or below-average oral language skills, such as in the hearing-impaired or cerebral-palsy child with delayed language acquisition.

Educators tend to hold rigidly to timetables for the accomplishment of major developmental milestones, and when gifted children fail to meet these, their exceptional higher mental abilities are not recognized. As a consequence, their educational programme tends to deny them the needed intellectual satisfaction and feeling of reward in the functioning of their creativity, analytical reasoning, and problem solving that can increase their scholastic motivation. The curriculum most often offered to these gifted children emphasizes basic skill development through learning activities which are more appropriate for those of lesser mental ability.

Classroom behaviour

Again because of stereotypic expectations, gifted children who are not striving to achieve may be overlooked. Examples include the child who is passive or average in the class, with no obvious evidence of a spark of stimulating intellect, burning curiosity, or drive to know; or the one who is non-communicative, withdrawn, or extremely shy, lacking verbalization with which to display advanced intellectual abilities and knowledge. The disruptive 'problem' child, however, has a greater chance of being identified as gifted through the teacher's observations of his or her exceptional language and manipulative, problem-solving skills, or sometimes incidentally via the school psychologist's efforts to ameliorate an emotional/behavioural disorder. When a child neither completes assigned work nor participates fully in class activities, the probable recognition of giftedness by teachers is very low.

Most unidentified gifted children have been described as socially and emotionally immature, and many have exhibited very uneven levels of development across different areas of academic performance. In the Cupertino Underachieving Gifted Program (Whitmore, 1980), developmental delay in motor skills was the most common cause of children's frustration in learning activities, with reading difficulties the second most frequent cause. Children's emotional responses to the intense frustration created by the significant differences between mental and performance levels, e.g. frequent tears, 'tantrums', and distractibility, had led many teachers to the conclusion that the pupils were emotionally immature. Teachers, tending to expect gifted children to exhibit advanced maturity in all areas of development, found it difficult to consider a child as possibly mentally gifted if he or she could not even follow simple directions, control the impulse to talk, concentrate on work, or complete tasks on schedule.

When frustration and perceived failure to meet expectations reach a critical level with gifted under-achievers, they usually give up trying to do the assigned class work and develop ways of coping, often not constructively, with the conflict they are experiencing between their personal desires to excel and the messages they are receiving that convey failure (Whitmore, 1980). In coping with this personal conflict, some withdraw into their own safe world of fantasy or escape through interaction with peers. Others become very hostile and disruptive as they rebel uncontrollably against constraining and unrewarding school experiences. If an under-achiever is able to control his or her reaction and behaviour to 'get by' in class, giftedness will not be recognized in what appears to be more 'average' behaviour. Giftedness is usually considered 'real' only when manifested in high productivity and a quality of products attributed to academic high achievers (Dowdall and Colangelo, 1982; Renzulli, 1978).

Lack of information about the child

Frequently children are not recognized as gifted because the teacher does not have enough information about them, beyond their learning activities in the classroom. This is particularly true in the more formal classrooms, where the curriculum contains mostly factual knowledge to be memorized and comprehended, with little opportunity for self-expression, and where the daily schedule does not provide for the sharing of ideas, knowledge, and interests among pupils. Teachers who have a more interactive and personal teaching style will know more about their pupils, especially those who seek more information from parents and the children.

THE IDENTIFICATION OF HIDDEN GIFTEDNESS

The three principal avenues of identification are teacher observations, parent concern, and referral for special education services.

Teachers often make excellent identifiers of giftedness in under-achievers if they are trained to recognize critical indicators in an environment which is structured to elicit these revealing characteristics, as in the Cupertino Underchieving Gifted Program (Whitmore, 1979, 1980). Teachers sometimes recognize giftedness in low-performance children by a qualitative difference in features such as their language, general knowledge, reasoning and problem-solving skills, interests and hobbies, or critical and creative thinking, while others who show only moderate performance in everyday school achievement can sometimes be found to be gifted through their exceptionally high performances on standardized achievement tests.

Parents' astute observations have often provided the route to the identification of gifted under-achievers. For instance, parents may report they have noticed a gradual or sudden drop in school achievement and the development of a more negative attitude toward school, which also causes concern about their child's mental health and social behaviour. On the other hand, many parents become aware of their child's advanced mental abilities during conversations, projects, and problem-solving activities at home, which indicate that the child can learn exceptionally easily and can produce some surprisingly complex products; yet, the parents are puzzled when the child appears to hate school and is not performing well there.

Exceptional intellectual abilities are often revealed via an aptitude or intelligence test, such as the Stanford-Binet or WISC, which may contradict low scores on group-administered standardized aptitude tests. But sometimes exceptional intellectual abilities are noticed beforehand, during the 'warm-up' phase of a testing session. In that informal, one-to-one exchange, the skilled examiner can be alerted by the child's exceptional vocabulary and comprehension, knowledge, analytical reasoning, or interests and hobbies—sometimes more than through test scores. Test data are only part of the composite picture; observations made in a variety of settings, on a variety of tasks, in and out of school are at least equally important.

Ideally, to gain a complete picture of the child's ability, parents, previous teachers, all school professional staff currently working with the child, and relevant professional personnel within the community, should be consulted. This should be supplemented by the child's self-report. The profile provided by the test data would then complete the picture so that all concerned, including the child, could be involved in discussing and planning for the child's educational needs.

Specific sub-groups of gifted children, who are particularly vulnerable to being missed by teachers, parents and psychologists, are described below.

NON-HANDICAPPED UNDER-ACHIEVERS

There are children without physical or learning handicaps whose average, below-average, or failing academic performance in school impedes the recognition of their exceptional potential for learning. The nature and patterns of behaviour of under-achievers vary considerably; however, the performance of each child can be placed along several continua which describe discrepancies between:

1. Potential and actual performance.
2. The effects of under-achievement on the child and relationships with others.
3. The time-scale, whether temporary (e.g. due to transient family circumstances) or chronic.
4. The scope of the under-achievement, whether specific or generalized.

Children with the greatest discrepancies between estimated potential and actual performance come to the attention of educators much more readily than those with milder ones. The recognized children may then be recommended for special education services, in the course of which high IQ or aptitude is apt to be revealed, and the others remain unrecognized as gifted.

The keys to discovering the giftedness in under-achieving pupils reside in two teacher activities. First, listen to the child. If a teacher genuinely invites

TABLE 6.2 Gifted under-achievers

Obstacles to identification	Observations
Average or poor performance in reading and language arts	Complex oral language, vocabulary, comprehension
Passive or negative attitudes toward school, 'unmotivated'	Communication about child's interests, knowledge, hobbies levels of curiosity, questioning, enquiry/investigation
Immaturity in some or all areas of development	Problem-solving skills
Classroom behaviour—passive, withdrawn, or aggressive, disruptive	Originality and creativity evidence of cognitive processing, thinking
Insufficient information about the child's general knowledge, interests, language and thought	

communication from the child, and listens carefully, giftedness can often be detected in under-achievers. The teacher should encourage the child to share his or her ideas, interests, knowledge, and questions, which may reveal exceptionally advanced language and comprehension of abstract ideas, as well as advanced out-of-school activities. Second, involve the child in problem-solving tasks requiring higher levels of thinking. This provides an opportunity for the teacher to see how the pupil uses information in the processes of synthesis and analysis, and in deductive or inductive reasoning. In problem-solving activities the teacher also can observe characteristics of originality, creativity, and effectiveness in manipulating facts, events, and people, i.e. in other words, exceptional organizational abilities, and the capacity for independent, self-directed learning.

Table 6.2 summarizes the obstacles and keys to recognizing superior intellectual abilities in under-achieving, perhaps non-achieving, children at any age level. The characteristics are most easily identified in young children before self-expression becomes repressed and attitudes influencing behaviour are firmly set.

GIFTED CHILDREN WITH SPECIFIC HANDICAPS

This group includes all children with a sufficient degree of handicap to require special educational services, except the mentally handicapped who, by definition, cannot be intellectually gifted, and the emotionally or behaviourally disordered, who were included, more appropriately for our purposes, in the category of gifted under-achievers. Study of gifted handicapped children has concentrated so far on the aurally and visually impaired, the learning disabled, the cerebral palsied, and those with severe neurological impairment or brain damage. Orthopaedically handicapped children have been included only when the condition has interfered significantly with interaction with the environment, and consequently with learning.

There are four interrelated types of obstacles to the identification of gifted handicapped children:

1. As a consequence of parental and teacher expectations which limit opportunities by focusing attention on strengthening areas of deficit skill, most handicapped children have received significantly less, or virtually no stimulation of their higher cognitive abilities.
2. The content of the curriculum and the instructional mode typically found in special educational programmes are often inappropriate for the development of these children's intellects. In regular elementary classrooms, for example, they are often placed in the low-ability groups, and taught in a style appropriate for slower learners. On the other hand, in special education classes, children are trained in self-help

skills, but are not given encouragement or guidance in learning to develop their higher mental abilities. As a consequence, it has not been uncommon for handicapped pupils to be overlooked as gifted because of the lack of opportunity to observe their higher intellectual abilities.

3. There is a general lack of high academic achievement among these children due to limitations in their ability to learn and to produce the quantity of work at the pace typical of high achievers.

4. These children have a relative degree of dependence on others, often due to the nature of the handicap, resulting in an apparent lower level of emotional maturity, not usually associated with giftedness. Equally important, most teachers of the handicapped have not been trained to look for, stimulate, or develop the children's intellectual independence.

Some specific handicapping conditions bear additional, very serious impediments to identification. Those created by handicaps which impair communication skills are very troublesome because language, as a revelation of thought, has become our most reliable, informal indicator of giftedness. When the development of oral language is impossible or substantially delayed, there is a tendency for professionals and parents to behave as though the absence of language indicates an absence of intelligence, but one must seek for evidence of intellectual abilities without the aid of oral language in such cases. A similar problem exists with learning disabled children when their inability to read and write fluently, and at advanced levels of competence, suggests poor intelligence to teachers.

Less serious than the absence of language, but still having a significant impact on identification, is the relatively poor comprehension and abstract thinking of blind or visually impaired children. In them, conceptual development and abstract thinking seem to be delayed by the absence of visual stimulation or images; cognitive development occurs more slowly, and norms for chronological age-groups are invalid (Maker, 1977).

Indeed, Maker has suggested that gifted handicapped pupils ought to be compared with other similarly handicapped pupils in judging their mental abilities. Standardized tests must be appropriately adapted for the handicapping condition, as it affects the administration of the tests, and again for the relevant norms. However, tests are of limited value in determining intellectual giftedness among most handicapped pupils; a more careful case-study approach is required, with skilled professional judgement about an individual's response behaviour, in comparison with others possessing similar handicaps.

Intellectual giftedness may be revealed in handicapped children through observations of cognitive processes and learning behaviour. Memory is

TABLE 6.3 Gifted children with specific handicaps

Obstacles to identification	Key observations
Little or no productivity in school	Superiority in oral language — vocabulary, fluency, structure
Cannot read, write, spell easily or accurately ('learning disabled')	Memory for facts and events
Poor motor skills, co-ordination, writing; often child is easily distracted from tasks and described as inattentive (neurologically impaired, minimal cerebral dysfunction, developmental delay in motor area)	Exceptional comprehension Analytical and creative problem-solving abilities Markedly advanced interests, impressive knowledge Keen perception and humour
Absence of oral communication skills (e.g. cerebral)	Drive to communicate through alternative modes — palsy, deaf, visual, non-verbal, body language Superior memory and problem-solving ability Exceptional interest and drive in response to challenge
Behaviour is 'disordered' — aggressive, disruptive, off-task frequently	Superior verbal skill, oral language Exceptional capacity to devise ways to manipulate people and to solve 'problems' Superior memory, general knowledge
Extremely withdrawn, non-communicative	The most difficult to identify — the only key is response to stimulation of higher mental abilities unless superior written work is produced
Sensory deficits producing developmental delay — specifically, does not show evidence of superior language and thought, has difficulty conceptualizing and dealing with abstractions (blind, deaf and children with mild to moderate hearing and visual impairments	Exceptionally rapid response to stimulation and special education compared to others with similar handicaps Superior memory, knowledge, problem-solving skills Noteable drive to know or master

Modified from J. R. Whitmore (1981) Gifted Children with Handicapping Conditions: A New Frontier. *Exceptional Children*, **48**, 106–114.

perhaps the most revealing of these characteristics, and is relatively easy to observe in any handicapped pupil. Superior reasoning powers and exceptional skills in problem solving can be observed over time, if only in how to communicate without oral language or writing skill. A drive to master or to know and understand often produces exceptional perseverance, which with the manifested curiosity of an intensely enquiring mind are reliable indicators of intellectual giftedness. With non-language-impaired children, it is often possible to judge their mental abilities through their analytical, evaluative thought processes expressed verbally. Techniques of observation are summarized in Table 6.3.

CULTURALLY DIFFERENT CHILDREN

Culturally different children are defined here as those who, by virtue of the cultural group to which they belong, are unprepared to meet the expectations held for gifted pupils in the educational system. In American schools, this group includes all those who would not identify themselves as white, middle-class, and English-speaking. They could be, for example, American blacks, Mexicans, Oriental groups, all bilingual immigrant groups, and poor whites such as those found in Appalachia.

Obstacles exist for members of this group because teachers, mostly white and middle-class, often have stereotypic expectations of gifted children and are, therefore, misled by differences in language, general knowledge, and social behaviour. Though it varies among teachers and communities, it is possible to find teachers who presuppose laziness, slowness, lack of diligence, or a tendency toward delinquency within specific cultural groups and, consequently, assume those children are not intellectually gifted.

Culturally different children rarely have superior quality of oral language and self-expression in the dominant language of the community, which is generally expected of the gifted. This consideration applies not only to bilingual children, but also to American inner-city blacks using 'street language', and southern whites speaking 'hill-billy English'. The children's sensitivity to their differentness and to the norms for acceptable performance in school also exacerbates their difficulties with self-expression, causing them to be relatively non-communicative in the classroom.

Because they have been exposed to a different body of general knowledge and have developed different interests, children from minority cultural backgrounds may be handicapped when assessed for their mental ability by either tests or teachers. Then, on the assumption that they have received similar exposure to life experiences, deficits in 'middle-class white' knowledge can be interpreted as deficits in mental abilities, and differences in test scores taken as reflecting differences in the ability to comprehend and to store information for retrieval.

Another obstacle lies in the patterns of these children's classroom behaviour, where it is different from what is expected. Class participation may be minimal for a gifted but culturally different pupil due to break social discomfort; alternatively such children may find that their only school rewards come through social interaction and so they neglect their academic work. In American schools, the Mexican and Oriental children often are seen as shy, quiet and non-interacting, while the inner-city 'street kids' are expected to exhibit highly social and minimally academic behaviour in many classrooms.

TABLE 6.4 Culturally different gifted children

Obstacles to identification	Observations
Lack of frequent self-expression, fluent language	Problem-solving skills, including social behaviour
Stereotyped expectations for the sub-group	Memory for facts and events
	Thinking skills—analysis, synthesis, evaluation
Different background resulting in a different body of general knowledge and perhaps in different interests and values	Skills for organizing and manipulating his/her world, including people
Behaviour patterns of relatively low or quiet participation, or possibly higher social and disruptive behaviour	Qualitative differences in products of work—e.g. art detail
	Higher level of questioning manifested curiosity, responses to motivation techniques of the teacher

There is no defensible reason for the extensive and continuing failure to identify giftedness in culturally different children. But their recognition depends on finding some way of destroying the inappropriate stereotypic expectations about them, and a willingness to look for more reliable indicators. For these, we must look to language-independent cognitive characteristics such as skilful problem solving, even if only of a social nature, such as exceptional ability to organize and manipulate his or her world, especially people, which is often accompanied by remarkable independence. Children of this kind may be identified through their exceptional memories, thought processes, or advanced questioning reflecting intense curiosity and high-level responsiveness to the teacher's encouragement. Table 6.4 summarizes the obstacles and keys to discovering giftedness in culturally different children.

NEEDED PROFESSIONAL RESPONSES TO THE CHALLENGE

To increase our accuracy in identifying gifted pupils other than the easily recognized outstanding high achievers, specific responses are needed from educational leaders at both government and local levels, from teacher educators who instruct at both the pre- and in-service levels, and from researchers. Proposed changes in existing practices for each of these groups are discussed below.

GOVERNMENT AND LOCAL SCHOOL SYSTEMS LEADERS

Responses needed from this group of professionals fall into two categories: policies and practices. Policies should be revised, where necessary, to reflect an explicit commitment to the rights of gifted children to an appropriate education, with both curriculum and instruction modified to meet their individually diagnosed needs; this should begin on entrance and continue throughout children's school years. Some practices of governing bodies and school administrators need to be altered, too. The first practical need is for adequate financial resources for personnel to guide and monitor the identification process, and to design appropriate educational plans for these children. The funding should not be based on a fixed percentage identified as gifted (e.g. 3–5 per cent of the total school population, participation qualified by a score over 130 on an intelligence test), but be determined by the make-up of the total school population and by the proposed educational design. The second practical need is to provide incentives for school personnel to identify and help their gifted pupils, including those not recognized as high achievers.

Time should be set aside for professionals to meet, for conducting observations, and for testing pupils, so that assessments can be more complete and efficient, and can be shared by the professional team. At appropriate stages the parents should become involved in providing information and in responding to alternative plans. For this to occur successfully, educational leaders may have to cultivate a more positive attitude among teachers towards using parents' information and involvement. This could be done via structured one-to-one interviews with the parents or, if necessary, with questionnaires which would provide information to improve assessment and educational planning.

THE PREPARATION OF PROFESSIONALS

Children who do not fall into the category of average, including both the handicapped and the gifted, need special attention and provision in schools if they are to fulfill their potentials. However, though American teacher education has been restructured to include the recognition of handicapped children, most teachers still finish their training without any substantial knowledge about the gifted. Classroom teachers especially ought to be able to pick up clues of potential giftedness in their pupils, and to participate effectively in the professional team, contributing to the design of an appropriate education, and adapting the curriculum and their teaching methods to accommodate such children's special needs in the classroom.

Special educators of the handicapped have not usually received more than a brief, limited introduction to the concept of giftedness, while those educated to teach gifted children have minimal knowledge of handicapping conditions. There is a need for greater collaboration and sharing of information among special educators so that all handicapped pupils will be examined for their intellectual potential and their education will be designed to develop giftedness where it exists in handicapped pupils.

The training of educational psychologists is in equal need of improvement, with more attention given to the characteristics of giftedness, including alternative ways of assessing and developing intellectual potential in children who are regarded as average or low achievers. With this understanding, educational psychologists could provide leadership to the professional team, and would be more skilled in adapting standardized tests for use with gifted children who have specific handicaps. Educational psychologists should also have demonstrable expertise in alternative types of testing and in ways of eliciting optimal performance from children who come from sub-groups of the population who may not test well.

The support of the school administrator is vital to the improvement of methods of identifying gifted children since factors of school climate, the standards of teaching practices, and staff deployment have a critical influence on all educational provision. Administrators should be more aware of the individual needs of all pupils and should encourage the maximum development of teaching talents through experimentation and variety in teaching methods and curricula.

RESEARCHERS

There is an immediate need for sustained, systematic inquiry into the issues related to the identification and development of intellectually gifted children, particularly in their early years. Encouragement should be provided to expand basic research (investigating the nature of intelligence, learning styles, the function of the brain, etc.) which would examine issues related to policies and practices in the education of the gifted. There is also a need to develop and validate assessment techniques, attention being given to culture-free and non-academic tests for use with gifted handicapped children.

CONCLUSIONS

Some facts are clear.

1. Though we speak of giftedness as exceptional potential or demonstrated ability, in truth it is only those who have made their exceptional ability obvious through high scholastic achievement who are generally identified and provided with special educational opportunities.
2. In schools, more gifted pupils remain unidentified than recognized and appropriately educated.
3. The world cannot afford to lose the exceptional intellectual ability of one person, much less of the hundreds of thousands, that have been estimated (Gearheart and Weishahn, 1976; Whitmore, 1981).
4. School experiences do profoundly affect the development of a child's potential, as measured by intellectual accomplishments and academic achievement.
5. Specific groups of children with exceptional potential for learning and high scholastic achievement are often denied appropriate educational opportunities to develop their potential due to their possession of other unrelated characteristics, such as being of a minority race, low social class, different cultural background, or having handicapping conditions, developmental delays, and discomfort or personal conflict in the classroom environment.
6. Most teachers and other school professional staff have not been prepared to identify accurately the gifted children who are not high achievers and to provide for their special needs.

These facts pose challenges to existing practices; challenges which, if met, could establish gifted education as a permanent integral part of educational systems serving all children. Concern about the serious neglect of gifted pupils in past years, and the persistent failure to provide appropriate educational opportunities for them, must be coupled with a commitment to the rights of all children to receive an education structured to fit their needs and to develop fully their potential for growth of intellect and skills. We must accept responsibility for the fact that, through our treatment of children in our communities and schools, we shape their futures as 'drop-outs' or eminent successes. And what we choose to do with the world's human potential substantially influences the future course of humankind.

REFERENCES

Anderson, K. E. (ed.) (1961). *Research on the Academically Talented Student.* National Education Association Project on the Academically Talented Student, Washington, DC.

Bloom, B. S. (1964). *Stability and Change in Human Characteristics.* Wiley, New York.

Clark, B (1979). *Growing Up Gifted.* Charles E. Merrill, Columbus, Ohio.

Dowdall, D. B., and Colangelo, N. (1982). Underachieving gifted students: Review and implications. *Gifted Child Quarterly,* **26**, 179–184.

Garcia, J. (1981). The logic and limits of mental aptitude testing. *American Psychologist,* **36**, 1172–1180.

Gearheart, B. R., and Weishahn, M. W. (1976). *The Handicapped Child in the Regular Classroom.* C. V. Mosby, St. Louis, Missouri.

Hughes, H., and Converse, H. (1962). Characteristics of the gifted: A case for a sequel to Terman's study. *Exceptional Children,* **39**, 179–183.

Jacobs, J. (1970). Are we being misled by fifty years of research on our gifted children? *Gifted Child Quarterly,* **14**, 120–123.

Maker, C. J. (1977). *Providing Programs for the Gifted Handicapped.* The Council for Exceptional Children, Reston, Virginia.

Maker, C. J., Redden, M. R., Tonelson, S., and Howell, R. D. (1978). *Self-Perceptions of Successful Handicapped Scientists.* Unpublished manuscript, Department of Special Education, University of New Mexico.

Marland, S., Jnr. (1972). *Education of the Gifted and Talented.* Report to the Congress of the United States by the US Commissioner of Education, US Government Printing Office, Washington, DC.

Newland, T. W. (1976). *The Gifted in Socio-educational Perspective.* Prentice-Hall, Englewood Cliffs, New Jersey.

Renzulli, J. S. (1978). What makes giftedness? Re-examining a definition. *Phi Delta Kappan,* **59**, 211–216.

Robinson, H. B., Roedell, W. C., and Jackson, N. E. (1981). Early identification and intervention. In *Psychology and Education of the Gifted* (3rd edn) (eds W. B. Barbe and J. S. Renzulli), Irvington Publishers, New York, pp. 128–141.

Rutter, M., Maughan, N., Mortimer, P., and Ouston, J. (1979). *Fifteen Thousand Hours.* Open Books, London.

Sternberg, R. J. (1982). Lies we live by: Misapplication of tests in identifying the gifted. *Gifted Child Quarterly,* **26**, 157–161.

Terman, L. M. (ed.) (1925). *Mental and Physical Traits of a Thousand Gifted Children,* Genetic Studies of Genius Vol.1. Stanford University Press.

White, B. (1975). *The First Three Years of Life.* Prentice-Hall, Englewood Cliffs, New Jersey.

Whitmore, J. R. (1979). The etiology of underachievement in highly gifted young children. *Journal for the Education of the Gifted.* **3**, 38–51.

Whitmore, J. R. (1980). *Giftedness, Conflict, and Underachievement.* Allyn and Bacon, Boston.

Whitmore, J. R. (1981). Gifted children with handicapping conditions: A new frontier. *Exceptional Children,* **48**, 106–114.

The Psychology of Gifted Children
Edited by Joan Freeman
©1985, John Wiley & Sons, Ltd.

CHAPTER 7

The Nature and Measurement of Intelligence

H. J. EYSENCK

Whatever else may characterize gifted children, there is no doubt that the feature they have most in common is a high degree of intelligence; so much so, that it is difficult to conceive of one who is not highly intelligent. Though some musical, artistic, or other specifically gifted children may be an exception to this rule, it has usually been found that an above-average, if not a superior intelligence, is necessary for their talents to find social acceptance and fruitful application. The famous 'Idiots Savants' are psychologically interesting because of the contrast between their low intelligence and high specific achievement, such as the ability to perform certain types of mental arithmetic, but this facility has little social use or relevance to other children. But though intelligence is a necessary part of the equipment of the gifted child, we cannot also say that it is sufficient, and some of the evidence concerning this point will be considered presently.

THE NATURE OF INTELLIGENCE

Although the measurement of intelligence is one of the major achievements of modern psychology, many people (including some psychologists) neither recognize it as such, nor even accept the existence of 'general intelligence'. For the man in the street, it can seem extraordinary that a mental quality as immaterial and evanescent as 'intelligence' could be measurable, and he often sees an incompatibility between the measurement of psychological and physical variables, such as heat or gravitation. But this apparent contrast is very difficult to justify on either philosophical or scientific grounds because heat, gravitation, and intelligence are all concepts, not 'things', like tables, submarines, or pigs. Concepts do not exist in the same sense as 'things' exist; they are human structures imposed to bring order to the shifting sands of natural phenomena, making them amenable to scientific measurement and experimentation. The proper question to be asked is not whether 'intelligence' exists, but whether the concept, as it stands, is useful in bringing some degree of coherence to a large assembly of variegated facts, events, and behaviours.

An argument often presented is that the concept of intelligence cannot be taken very seriously because psychologists are not agreed on a theory about its nature, development and measurement. But in all science, such agreement comes late in the development of a concept, if it arrives at all. Even now, for example, there is no agreed theory of gravitation; starting with Newton's notion of 'action at a distance', which even its author conceded to be nonsensical, we have two major competing theories. One is Einstein's relativistic theory of attraction between objects in terms of a warping of space–time geometry, and the other is the quantum mechanics theory of particle interaction, i.e. by exchange of 'gravitons'. If after 300 years of study, the most outstanding scientists in the world have failed to agree on a theory of gravitation, it would surely be unrealistic to demand a unified theory of intelligence from psychologists, who have only been working with this concept for about 100 years.

There are, in fact, close similarities between the definition and measurement of the two concepts of intelligence and 'heat'. Both constructs start with everyday observations; for heat, people notice the different sensations produced by putting their hands in snow, or in front of the fire, and agree that there is a dimension of heat and cold, though these subjective impressions are not in perfect agreement with measurements made by a fluid-in-glass thermometer. Objectively measured temperature is but one factor in impressions of heat, which is also affected by, for instance, the 'chill factor', air movements which make us feel colder, or humidity, which makes us feel hotter than the thermometer's reading. The same is true of intelligence. We start out with impressions that some people are able to solve problems which continue to puzzle others; that some people learn quickly and others very slowly; that some people habitually make correct decisions in difficult situations, while others habitually make mistakes. In the same way as the concept of heat is postulated to account for differences in temperature, so we postulate an ability called 'intelligence' to account for differences in intellectual behaviour, such as problem-solving, etc. Tests (of IQ) are developed to measure this ability, the scores of which are highly correlated with the various intellectual behaviours which originally gave rise to the concept. If the correlation were poor, we would doubt the value of our IQ tests, though we would not expect the correlations to be perfect because, as in the case of heat, extraneous factors influence our everyday subjective judgements. One obvious interference is acquired knowledge, while another is personality, which may, for instance, interfere with problem-solving and sound judgement in neurotics (Eysenck, 1973; Freeman, 1983b).

The measurements of both IQ, and heat share many difficulties. To take but one comparable example; water is not suitable for liquid-in-glass thermometers because it contracts from the ice point (0 °C) to the temperature of maximum density (4 °C), thus showing a false decline in temperature when it is actually increasing. The liquids most widely used (mercury and alcohol) were partly chosen because they fit in best with the predictions made by the kinetic theory of heat. This choice of a physical measuring instrument being thus influenced by the theory is a procedure which is often criticized when used in psychological measurement.

It is also sometimes pointed out that intelligence tests are restricted to certain populations, because of language difficulties, educational deficits, etc., and that even with the same people, different IQ test give different results. But these difficulties, which have caused many people to doubt the scientific status of intelligence, can also be found in the apparently much simpler measurement of heat by thermometers, which are also restricted to certain ranges of temperature, and record differently in the same temperature. For example, as mercury freezes at -39 °C and boils under atmospheric pressure at 357 °C, temperatures above and below those have to be measured by other types of thermometers. Also, if a mercury-in-glass thermometer reads 300 °C, a platinum-resistant thermometer, at the same place and at the same time, would read 291 °C. No meaning attaches to the question as to which of these two readings is 'correct'—just as little as it does with differing scores from different IQ tests. When we add the fact that there are two kinds theory about heat—the thermodynamic and the kinetic—involving different concepts, the problems and difficulties with IQ measurement are clearly not dissimilar to those found in measurement of physical concepts and entities.

DIFFERENT VIEWS OF INTELLIGENCE

There are three important distinctions within the concept of intelligence— intelligence A, intelligence B, and intelligence C.

Intelligence A is the biological substratum of all cognitive behaviour, giving rise to individual differences of a largely or entirely genetic nature.

Intelligence B is the application of this ability in everyday life, and is very strongly influenced by cultural, educational, and social factors, by personality and the multitude of accidental events which befall everyone in life. It is the mixture which most people mean when they discuss 'intelligence', in the same way as the 'heat' people talk about subjectively is the mixture of temperature, chill factor, humidity, barometric pressure, etc. which they encounter in everyday life.

Intelligence C is defined as the IQ measurement of intelligence, which attempts to come as close as possible to intelligence A and to predict intelligence B as successfully as possible (Vernon, 1979).

Intelligence C may again be subdivided into two closely related but nonidentical concepts, which Cattell (1982) has called fluid and crystallized intelligence. The measurement of fluid intelligence comes as close as possible to intelligence A by means of culture-fair IQ tests, i.e. tests which aim to test the problem-solving abilities of an individual in as pure a form as possible, often with pattern tests. Crystallized ability is measured by means of tests which involve much more clearly educational and cultural learning; for instance, a vocabulary test in which the words are defined, or selected correctly from several alternatives. Such tests are based on the hypothesis that the more intelligent will learn more rapidly, and acquire a wider vocabulary than the dull, so that the result of the vocabulary test can be used as a yardstick of learning capacity. Typically, fluid and crystallized ability correlate around 0.6 in British or American population. However, Freeman (1983a) found that when children who had been measured as gifted in fluid intelligence (within the top 1 per cent), were compared for their crystallized intelligence, educational and environmental influences, uncontaminated by personality or emotional factors, did indeed distance the scores between these types of intelligence. At this very high level of ability, the correlation between the two types of tests dropped to 0.26. It seemed that the children's crystallized intelligence scores, which are very dependent on aquired information, were higher than would have been expected for average ability children. In other words, gifted children take more from their environments.

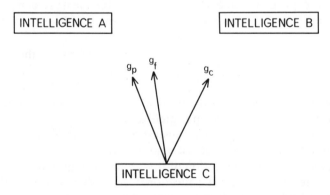

FIGURE 7.1 Intelligence A, B and C, and different types of IQ measures

Figure 7.1 shows the relations between Intelligence A, B, and C, and different measures of intelligence. A third type of test, using physiological measures, will be discussed presently. There have always been two rather divergent views, still contentious today, of the nature and measurement of intelligence, which have given rise to different conceptions, theories and types of tests. They began around the turn of the century with Sir Francis Galton in England, and with Alfred Binet a psychologist in France. Their disagreements centred on three points—definition, the effects of genetics and environment, and consequently how to measure intelligence.

Galton conceived it as a general ability entering into all types of cognitive activities to a greater or lesser extent, differing from person to person, and hence determining each person's general level of performance. But for Binet, intelligence was merely a kind of average of a number of different abilities— verbal, numerical, memory, suggestibility, etc. In Binet's theory we should not, strictly speaking, talk about 'intelligence' at all, but he was not consistent in his approach, and continued to use the overall term, rather than referring to and testing the separate abilities.

Modern research, using correlational and factor analytic methods, has demonstrated conclusively that there is a general factor of intelligence which runs through all cognitive types of tasks and problems, very much as Galton predicted, but that in addition, there are a number of special abilities, like verbal, numerical, memory etc., which are very much as Binet described (Eysenck, 1979; Vernon, 1979). Among modern psychologists only Guilford (1967) and Guilford and Hoepfner (1971) still dismiss the idea of general intelligence entirely, insisting instead on a very large number of separate abilities, though Guilford's system is difficult to accept on psychometric and other grounds. General intelligence is much the most important variable for the gifted child, though in addition giftedness in the various special abilities is very important in determining the direction of its development in terms of the child's interests and achievements.

The second area of disagreement is about the determination of individual differences in intelligence by genetic and environmental factors. Galton suggested a strictly genetic theory, and the use of twins for the quantitative evaluation of its influence. Binet was far more concerned with educational and environmental factors, and with ways and means of improving the abilities of retarded children. Again, one should not attribute too clear-cut a view to Binet, who tended to vacillate, but as an educational psychologist, he certainly believed in the modification of cognitive abilities.

The third great difference between these two approaches is concerned with methods of measurement. Galton favoured strictly biological and physiological methods, and suggested that reaction times would be the most appropriate method of investigation. Binet, though, preferred problem-solving and various other types of activity heavily dependent on educational, cultural and social background factors. It was his work which gave rise to the concept of the IQ, and practically all modern tests of intelligence are modelled on his original one.

Do Binet-type tests have any validity? If they do, in terms of our scheme of intelligence A, B, and C, we should expect C (Binet-type tests) to correlate with B (everyday-life evidence of intellectual achievement). Having reviewed this question in detail (Eysenck, 1979), the answer is undoubtedly yes. To take the question of prediction of school success first (which was the starting point of Binet's work), from a very large number of studies carried out in many different countries, IQ tests given at any stage of children's school life, or even previous to it, predict their final scholastic status with considerable accuracy.

Consider a study by Yule *et al* . (1982), in which a group of children were tested at 5-and-a-half years, and again at sixteen-and-a-half years, when their educational attainments were also assessed. The correlation between the two IQ tests, separated by eleven years, was 0.86, indicating that the children had hardly changed at all in their relative positions on the scale. As the authors said

> Perhaps the most striking of the findings in the present paper are those relating to Wechsler (WPPSI) IQ and scores for scholastic attainment at the end of compulsory schooling. The correlation between full scale IQ and reading (0.61) was as high as found in contemporaneously administered tests, while that between IQ and mathematics was a staggering 0.72, accounting for 50 per cent of the variance ... As remarkable is the degree of the association between IQ at entry and public examination results at school leaving.

These results are particularly impressive because they were achieved in comprehensive (non-selective) schools throughout the time the children were of secondary-school age, i.e. they could not be accounted for by the children's pre-selection, on the basis of test scores, to different types of schools.

Correlations between IQ and university success are lower, simply because, through selection, the range of intellectual ability in universities is normally very restricted, but they vary widely, depending on the degree of selection. They are much lower in Europe, where university admission is very limited, than in the United States; and in some American universities compared with others. Nevertheless, all correlations between success and IQ are positive, particularly where selection is less effective.

Other instances of great achievement in life, in business, in the army, or elsewhere have always given positive correlations with intelligence, although the size of the observed correlations differs widely between groups, countries and occupations. The reasons for this are fairly obvious, for worldly success is not dependent only on intelligence, but also on personality, nepotism, luck, and many other factors. Furthermore, in some countries, trade union and other egalitarian pressures can restrict the range of measureable remuneration, making differentiation difficult. However, comparisons between different occupations do often show a very clear-cut relationship between IQ and worldly success, the observed correlations ranging from the 80s to the 90s, largely due to the fact that the better-paid occupations require educational standards that can only be reached by people of relatively high intelligence. Thus, on these and many other criteria, there is an undoubted relationship between IQ and success in education, occupations and life generally, which is what would be expected if IQ tests measure intelligence as generally understood.

Terman (1959), in his famous study of gifted children, followed the careers of large numbers of Californian school children with IQs above 140, for many years. They showed a very high degree of worldly success, most achieving university degrees, many going on to post-graduate study and over 90 per cent ending up in prestigious, well-paid occupations. This applied particularly to the males, but also to a large proportion of the females, and the relatively small number of unsuccessful cases seemed to be accountable for in terms of personality and family disorders, which effectively made it difficult for them to use their high intelligence in a practical manner.

THE INHERITANCE OF INTELLIGENCE

The problems of behavioural genetics are highly complex and technical, and it is only possible to give a relatively dogmatic and simplified account here of some of the methods and major findings. First, however, it is important to emphasize a number of fundamental points of behavioural genetics, which are commonly misunderstood (Cattell, 1982).

Heritability

The heritability of a given trait, is defined as that portion of the total variance which is due to genetic causes. Though there is considerable disagreement about methodology, research data along many different lines suggest that something like 80 per cent of the total variance may be due to genetic causes and 20 per cent to environmental factors. However, Freeman (1983a) has suggested that there is a 'sliding scale' of these influences which varies with the initial intellectual genetic make-up. Because children who are born with considerable ability are better able to extract intellectual benefit from the environment, it takes up a higher percentage in the gifted individual's make-up, than for children less-well-intellectually endowed. It is important, though, to emphasize the precise meaning of these statements and some of the qualifications attaching to them.

First, estimates of this kind are estimates of population parameters, i.e. they apply to a given population, at a given time, and cannot be generalized beyond that population. Though it is a fact that heredity contributes 80 per cent to the total variance of differences in intelligence, as measured by IQ tests—at the present time—in typical British, European, or North American populations, it cannot be asserted that the same figure would be forthcoming were we to study present-day populations in India, or China, or Africa. Neither can it be assumed that a similar figure would be found were it possible to study British or European populations 300 years ago, or in 300 years' time. Changing environmental conditions make it more or less important, and thus change the estimated heritability. Recent studies in Russia came up with a heritability of 78 per cent, and similar studies in Poland and East Germany suggest similar heritabilities, but this does not mean that other communist countries, like Albania or China, would show similar heritabilities (Eysenck, 1982b).

Secondly, as heritability is a population statistic, its estimates only apply to populations, and not to individuals. It is wrong and indeed meaningless to say that because heritability is 80 per cent for a given population, this proportion applies equally to an individual. Indeed, it should indeed be obvious that for different individuals, the environment may have quite different importance.

Thirdly, there is the question whether a person's intelligence is laid down once and for all, or 'fixed', with no possibility of change. Again, we can only speak of a given population, at a given time, but at the moment, we simply do not know how to improve genetic intelligence in any way, although we do know to some extent how we can prevent it from developing! However, new discoveries, possibly of a physiological, biochemical, or hormonal nature, may alter the situation completely in the future.

The fundamental model underlying all the formulae of behavioural genetics, is that the functioning of any given trait will be determined by the effects of both the individual's genetic make-up and environmental circumstances. In laboratory animals, we can measure their effects by rearing animals from a number of strains in a range of environments and observing their mean performances, but the task is more difficult in humans because we have only limited control over them. In practice, the behavioural geneticist adopts approximate or quasi-experimental designs (Campbell and Stanley, 1963), in which balance and control is achieved not by randomization, as in true designs, but by exploiting natural situations (such as twinning) in a systematic manner. Such designs, of course, require greater caution than truly randomized ones, particularly in the use of independent checks on the validity of their underlying assumptions.

Twin studies

The logic of twin studies is quite straightforward. Twins are divided into identical (monozygotic) and non-identical (dizygotic) on the basis of similarity or dissimilarity of obvious physical characteristics which are known to be genetically determined, such as finger-prints or a variety of blood-group factors. Individuals are then measured on the trait in question, and the extent to which identical twins are found to resemble each other more than non-identical is taken as an indication of the relative importance of genetic influences. There are three methods of analysis used in the study of twins.

Identical twins, brought up together

Table 7.1 reports results from a study of IQ carried out by Herman and Hogben (1932), which show:

1. That there is no difference between like-sexed and unlike-sexed non-identical twins, suggesting that genes and environment operate on both sexes in the same way.
2. These subjects are no more alike than full siblings, indicating that twins are not treated differently from ordinary brothers and sisters in this respect.
3. Most importantly, identical twins are much more alike than non-identical twins or siblings; their average differences in IQ being less by a factor of almost 2.

TABLE 7.1   The differences in IQ of 4 groups of twins and siblings. (Herrman & Hodben, 1933)

Groups	N pairs	Mean IQ differences
MZ twins	65	9.2 ± 1.0
DZ twins of like sex	96	17.7 ± 1.5
DZ twins of unlike sex	138	17.9 ± 1.2
Siblings	103	16.8 ± 2.3

Since identical pairs share the same genetic inheritance, and non-identical twins do not, it is plausible to ascribe their greater IQ resemblance to genetics. Doubt has sometimes been expressed on this point because identical twins are treated more alike by their parents, but Loehlin and Nichols (1976) have shown that these influences had absolutely no effect on IQ; in fact twins who were treated more alike were no closer in intellectual ability than twins who were treated differently.

Identical twins brought up separately

Here, their identical heredities should ensure identical scores, if different environments do not have an effect; but it is not so. Studies have shown very similar results, namely very high correlations, usually between 0.7 and 0.8, but falling short of unity. The data are compatible with the notion of 80 per cent heritability when the observed correlations are corrected for unreliability of the tests used. It has been objected that many of the twins were separated at a rather late age, but this cannot be very important because comparing twins separated very early and those separated later in life disclosed, if anything, a greater similarity for those separated early in life!

Another criticism which is often made is that because twins are often farmed out to relatives or people of a similar socio-economic status, the separation of the twins is not entirely chance, and their backgrounds will still be correlated. This is true, but we can easily make a correction for this factor by looking at the observed correlation between cousins. Here too, the socio-economic status of the two families involved is rather similar, but the correlation between cousins is very low, usually between 0.1 and 0.2. In any case, recent and as yet unpublished work by Bouchard and others on identical twins brought up in very dissimilar environments, and separated very early in life, gives similar results to those obtained in earlier studies.

Adopted children

The IQs of these children are compared with both those of their true and adoptive parents. The usual finding has been that the children's IQs correlated much more highly with those of the true rather than the adoptive parents, although the latter provided the home environment. Oddly enough, though it might be expected that the environmental influence of the foster parents would grow stronger over time, in fact it works in the opposite way; correlations between the child's and his true parents' IQs increase during the time he is being brought up by others, and that between the child's IQ and his adoptive parents goes down!

Intra-familial relationships

Genetic theory predicts that the greater the degree of consanguinity, the greater should be the correlation between the IQs of different members of the family, and indeed the precise correlation which should occur with different degrees of consanguinity. Large numbers of studies have been done along these lines, and on the whole the data agree very well with genetic predictions, thus also reinforcing the findings from other data.

Regression effects

Data on both animals and humans do confirm the genetic principle that for any trait which is inherited less than 100 per cent, there is a regression to the mean in children's inheritance of their parents' characteristics, traits or abilities. This can be either upwards (from low-scoring parents), or downwards (from high-scoring parents). Figure 7.2 shows what most lay people consider the relationship between parents and children to be when there is a strong genetic influence; that bright parents have bright children, dull parents have dull children and average parents have average children.

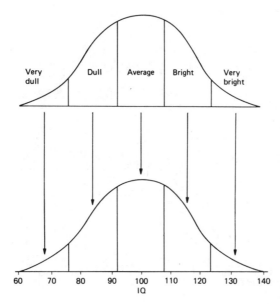

FIGURE 7.2 Erroneous view of hereditary determination of IQ of children (bottom diagram) according to intelligence of parents (top of diagram). (From Eysenck, 1979)

However, this picture is quite erroneous, and the true one is shown in Figure 7.3, which shows the regression to the mean. On it, the very bright parents have four children: one of them is very bright, two are bright, and one is average. Of the very dull parents' four children, one is very dull, two dull, and one average. Thus, we have two average children—one with parents who are very bright and one with parents who are very dull. This will illustrate the degree to which regression is a genetic factor, mixing up the offspring of high and low intelligence, high and low social class, high and low educational groups.

The degree of regression can be predicted by means of a genetic formula, which takes the degree of heritability of the trait in question into account, and when 80 per cent is entered as an estimate of heritability, the degree of regression actually observed in human populations is predicted with great accuracy (Eysenck, 1979). Social mobility is largely based on this factor, which seems to be effective in keeping the average IQ of different social classes constant, by enabling the bright working-class child to go up in the world, and the dull middle-class child to slip down. It can be illustrated within one family, where different intelligence levels in the children often result in changing socio-economic status along predictable lines.

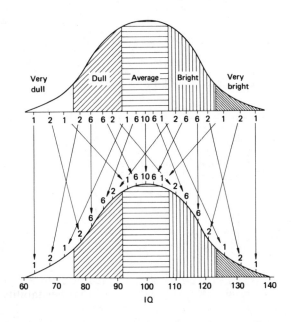

FIGURE 7.3 Correct picture of inheritance of intelligence, with parents at the top of the diagram and children at the bottom. (From Eysenck, 1979)

Though there are many other ways of demonstrating the importance of genetic factors (Eysenck, 1979), it is only possible to mention one here. It seems that intelligence is demonstrably dominant over dullness (in a technical sense), which means that there are dominant and recessive genes for high and low intelligence respectively. The proof consists in looking at the effects of so-called 'inbreeding depression', i.e. the tendency for the offspring of parents who are related (brother–sister, father–daughter) to have significantly lower IQs than children from unrelated parents of similar intelligence. This is due to the fact that related parents tend to have similar recessive genes, making for dullness, and thus lowering the IQ of their off-spring. Exactly the opposite occurs in heterosis, i.e. marriage of two people of different racial origin. This leads to the so-called 'hybrid vigour' type of effect, i.e. such parents tend to have children who are brighter than would be those of two parents of comparable IQ but the same race. The reason is that the recessive genes of such parents are less likely to be similar, because of their racial dissimilarity.

Though IQ is determined by both genetic and environmental factors, the former are much more influential than the latter in the ratio of about two to one. Galton again seems to have been nearer the truth than Binet. The 80 per cent and 20 per cent estimates mentioned here refer to variance, but to calculate their respective influences, we would have to take the square root of the ratio, i.e. $\sqrt{4/1} = 2$. Different heritablity estimates, however, are often given by different experts, ranging from as low as 50 per cent to as high as 90 per cent.

There are several reasons for this, one of the most important being the existence of differently defined types of heritability. Some are narrow in scope, only including basic (additive) variance, others add to that such influences as dominance and assortative mating—that high-IQ men tend to marry high-IQ women, and low-IQ men to marry low-IQ women, leading to an increase in the variation of IQ in the next generation. Also some geneticists correct their data for attenuation, i.e. the fact that most tests are lacking in perfect reliability, while others do not. Thus, for the same study, an un-corrected estimate of narrow heritability might be 60 per cent, a corrected estimate of narrow heritability 70 per cent, an uncorrected estimate of broad heritability 70 per cent, and a corrected estimate of broad heritability 80 per cent! These differences refer to different concepts, rather than indicat-ing disagreement on factual matters, but there are also chance errors which push some estimates up and others down, depending on the samples chosen, tests given, etc. It should also be remembered that heritability estimates are population estimates, and since different researchers deal with different pop-ulations, usually in different countries, the differences found are only to be expected.

THE PHYSIOLOGICAL MEASUREMENT OF INTELLIGENCE

All the work discussed so far has been in terms of Binet-type IQ tests, and one may justifiably ask why there have been no attempts to follow-up on Galton's suggestion. The answer must be that the Zeitgeist was op-posed to biological and genetic interpretations of intelligence, but favoured educational and cultural approaches, which held out the possibilities of helping the retarded—though not the gifted—aiming to achieve some kind of equality.

Wissler (1901), an American psychologist working at the turn of the century, did try out the Galton approach, but could not find a correlation between intelligence and reaction time, and this negative result dominated the field for the next sixty years or more. Yet in spite of the great influence it had, his work must be one of the worst-designed and most misleading experimental studies ever carried out. His measurements were very unreliable, his sample was a very restricted range of highly intelligent university students, and he did not actually measure intelligence, but used a university grades average, which in such a population are known to have very little correlation with measured IQ. Each of these three criticisms alone would be fatal to the validity of the experiment.

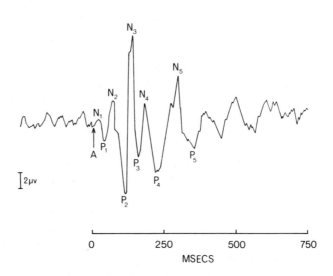

FIGURE 7.4 Simplified picture of evoked potentials. Wave to the left of point A indicates the ordinary EEG activity. At A a sudden stimulus (auditorial visual) is introduced, producing a flurry of negatives (capital N) and positive (capital P) waves, gradually dying away

In recent years, interest has again grown in the application of Galton's precepts, and it can now be said that quite high correlations can be found between reaction time measures and intelligence. Simple reaction times show a correlation with IQ scores of about 0.45, but much higher correlations can be obtained when more complex reaction time measures are used, i.e. having the subject react not to a single light, but being required to make a choice between four or eight separate targets (Jensen, 1982).

Even higher correlations can be obtained from a measure of the variability of a person's performance. When reaction times are measured over, say, 100 trials, they tend to vary, and the degree of variation is less in intelligent people than in dull ones, giving correlations of about -0.7 between variability and IQ. It is truly astounding that such a simple measure as reaction time and its variability can correlate to the extent of 0.7 to 0.8 with Binet-type IQ measures, which are a mixture of learning (e.g. vocabulary tests) and problem-solving of a fairly complex nature. Such a correlation would certainly not be predicted in terms of the usual theories regarding intelligence, such as Binet's, yet since these results have now been replicated many times, and in many different countries; they firmly support Galton's theory of a general factor of intelligence. On the other hand, theories which regard intelligence as merely the average of a number of different abilities are not capable of being reconciled with the data on reaction-time measurement.

Even more interesting and potentially important are recent attempts to measure physiological events which are hypothesized to lie at the basis of intellectual achievement. What has been used here is the evoked potential, a technique measuring with the electro-encephalograph a series of waves, produced by the imposition of a sudden stimulus, which might be auditory or visual, i.e. a noise delivered over earphones, or a flash of light (D. E. Hendrickson, 1982). Figure 7.4 shows the ordinary run of EEG waves on the left; at point A, there is a sudden imposition of the signal, and the figure shows a series of waves resulting from this. These waves can be analysed, and they do show very important differences between bright and dull (Eysenck, 1982c).

Figure 7.5 shows a typical set of six bright and six dull children's evoked potential waves; in each case, the actual IQ of the child is given. It will be seen that the two sets of waves are very different, those of the bright children being much more complex than those of the dull ones. For a sample of well over 200 school children, constituting a fairly random sample of the population, a correlation of 0.83 was found between Wechsler IQ and the complexity of the trace. Similar correlations have been observed for adult groups, using other tests of intelligence (Blinkhorn and Hendrickson, 1982).

The Hendrickson paradigm is not the only one which has given positive results. Schafer (1982) based his work on experiments concerned with the influence on the evoked potential of selective attention, expectancy, and how well children can deal with information. This could be seen in cognitive changes of EEG activity, when unexpected stimuli tended to produce larger evoked potentials than those whose nature and timing were known by the individual. Schafer has extended the scope of this demonstration by hypothesizing that individual differences in amplitude (cognitive neural adaptability) will relate to individual differences in intelligence. The physiological basis mediating this relationship is considered to be neural energy, as defined by the number of neurons firing in response to a stimulus. The functionally efficient brain will use fewer neurons to process a fore-known stimulus, whereas for a novel, unexpected stimulus, the brain will commit large numbers of neurons.

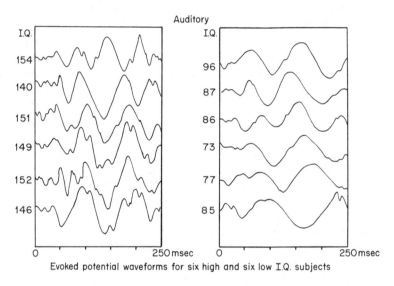

FIGURE 7.5 Evoked potential waveforms for 6 high and 6 low IQ subjects.
(Eysenck, 1982c)

Given the relationship between individual neuron-firing patterns and observed cortical-evoked potentials, the commitment of neuro-energy will be observed as amplitude differences between evoked potentials which have been elicited from various stimulus-presentation conditions. Schafer has been successful in demonstrating that high-IQ subjects showed much larger amplitude differences between expected and unexpected stimuli than did low-IQ subjects, correlations in excess of 0.8 being obtained. Clearly, this is another interesting area of measurement and theorizing, which casts new light on the concept of intelligence and on the possible differences between gifted and normal children.

We may actually be nearing the point where enough is understood about the physiological basis of intelligence to use physiological measurements as relatively pure, genotypic measures of IQ, very much in the way that Galton suggested. The theory underlying all these measures (Hendrickson, 1982) essentially centres on the conception of errors in transmission during information processing through the cortex; the more errors, the less complex the recorded trace, and the lower will be the IQ of the person in question (Eysenck, 1982a).

On this point, Galton again seems to have been right, and it is unfortunate that his approach was so completely neglected by psychologists for such a long time. From the practical point of view, Binet's methods of testing are obviously much simpler and cheaper, since they can be applied to groups, and used by relatively untrained people, whereas the EEG measurement requires a highly trained person, as well as apparatus and computers, and can only be done by one person at a time. However, from the scientific point of view, these results are far more interesting and important than the sum total of the millions of Binet-type tests which have been applied over the past seventy or eighty years.

THEORY OF INTELLIGENCE AND GIFTEDNESS

The construction of a theory encompassing all this diverse new information begins with a reconsideration of the old distinction, already apparent in Thorndike's work (1927), of power versus speed in IQ tests—a dichotomy closely related to that between untimed and timed tests. A timed test consists of items, each of which could readily be solved by practically all subjects given enough time, but since it is in fact timed, the number solved depends on the subject's speed, high IQ being identified with speedy solution. An untimed test is made up of items varying in difficulty level, many of them too difficult to be solved by most subjects. Although these two rather different types of test might be expected to tap quite divergent mental abilities, it has usually been observed that their results correlate highly, suggesting that mental power is simply a function of speed (Berger, 1982). Based on Hick (1952), Furneaux (1960) described a logarithmic relation between time taken to solve a problem, and its difficulty; for slow solvers, the time needed for a difficult problem can increase so much that the problem becomes for all practical purposes insoluble, though depending in part on the subject's persistence. He suggested that problem-solving could perhaps be regarded as a special case of a multiple-choice reaction, and developed a theory of intelligence involving a search process, which brought a relevant set of elements (perceptual or memory) into association with the solution. He also postulated a 'comparator'—a device which examines the results of this search, bringing together the neural representations of the perceptual material embodying the problem, the rules according to which the problem has to be solved and the particular organization of elements whose validity as a solution has to be examined.

This search hypothesis is, in fact, a fore-runner of many similar hypotheses later developed in the field of artificial intelligence (Newell and Simon, 1972, 1976; Newell, 1982), while the similarity between brain processes and computers is already apparent in Hick's hypothesis depending on the throwing of mental 'switches', which find a precise analogue in modern computers.

Jensen (1982) has further developed these hypotheses by pointing out that the conscious brain acts as a one-channel information processing system (a theory widely accepted in experimental psychology), which can deal simultaneously with only a very limited amount of information. Thus, it restricts the number of operations which can be performed simultaneously on the information that enters the system, either from external stimuli or from retrieval in short-term or long-term memory. It follows that speediness of mental operations is advantageous, in that more operations per unit of time can be executed without overloading the system.

His second important point is that there is rapid decay of stimulus traces and information, so that speediness of any operations that must be performed on the information while it is still available is advantageous. Also the individual compensates for limited capacity and rapid decay of incoming information by rehearsal and storage of the information into intermediate or long-term memory, which has relatively unlimited capacity compared with very limited short-term memory. However, the process of storing information in long-term memory itself takes time, and therefore uses up channel capacity, so that there is a trade-off between the storage and the processing of incoming information.

Jensen goes on to say that

The more complex the information and the operations required on it, the more time that is required, and consequently the greater the advantage of speediness in all the elemental processes involved. Loss of information due to overload interference and decay of traces that were inadequately encoded or rehearsed for storage or retrieval from long term memory results in breakdown and failure to grasp all the essential relationships among the elements of a complex problem needed for its solution. Speediness of information processing, therefore, should be increasingly related to success in dealing with cognitive tasks to the extent that the information load strains the individual's limited channel capacity. The most discriminating test items thus would be those that threaten the information processing system at the threshold of breakdown. In a series of items of greater complexity, this breakdown would occur at different points for various individuals, so that if individual differences in the speed of elemental components of information processing could be measured in tasks that are so simple as to rule out breakdown failure, as in the several reaction-time paradigms previously described, it should be possible to predict the individual differences in the point of breakdown for more complex tasks.

In this way, Jensen attempts to explain the observed correlations between reaction-time variables and scores on complex g-loaded tests, and simultaneously the high correlations between speed and power tests.

Attractive as these theories may be, and although they undoubtedly encompass a good deal of relevant information and factual material, a further step must be taken to explain these apparent differences in 'speediness' of mental processes. It seems unlikely, for physiological reasons, that mental speed is anchored in differential rates of propagation of nervous impulses, and although there may be a possibility of differential speed of processing through the synapses, an alternative hypothesis seems more likely, and better supported by experimental data. Such a model would lead to an integration of speed and the Hendrickson's 'error hypothesis', along the following lines.

It is well-known that messages which pass through the nervous system are transmitted repeatedly, rather than in isolation; this suggests that the nervous system must contain a comparator, which looks at these repeated messages and decides whether they are identical (and hence acceptable as representational of reality) or not (Sokolov, 1960, 1963, has advanced a similar hypothesis). If it is supposed that any particular 'message' is transmitted ten times, and that the comparator will accept it provided eight of the messages it receives are identical, in a person making few errors, the first eight messages received will very likely be identical, and hence acceptable. However, in a person making many errors, it may take twenty, thirty or more messages before the criterion is reached; hence, he will be very much slower in mental reactions, having to wait such a long time for the acceptance of the messages as 'correct'. Thus, correct processing of information is a fundamental variable, while speed of mental processing is a secondary one, depending on error-less information processing. Given this relationship, all the comments made about mental speed will apply also to error-less transmission, and would explain why this latter is so important in solving mental problems.

Fundamental to any such theory is the notion of a search process, which may be total and exhaustive, or heuristic (Newell and Simon, 1976). Much information has been acquired about the nature of such search processes by scientists interested in artificial intelligence, and computer programmes are available to demonstrate not only that these processes work, but also that they are similar in important ways to the events which occur during human problem-solving (Newell and Simon, 1972). If it is possible to devise a computer program for problem-solving which depends on heuristic search and a comparator, then the similarity of this arrangement and that suggested by Furneaux for a human problem-solver does seem to argue that we may now be on the threshold of a theory, not only of the solution of problems but also of differences in ability to solve these problems. Given that intelligence is a vital ingredient distinguishing gifted children from others, the development of these theories must be vital for proper understanding of giftedness.

INTELLIGENCE AND CREATIVITY

Originality and creativity are often taken to be cognitive traits, i.e. aspects or parts of intelligence. Thus, intelligence tests are often divided into measures of convergent and divergent thinking, the latter being more closely associated with originality and creativity. An alternative view, which is taken here, is that originality and creativity are not by themselves aspects of intelligence, but are rather traits of personality, i.e. non-cognitive, so that great achievement would be due to a combination of high intelligence and the appropriate personality configuration. This view, originally put forward by Spearman (1927), requires empirical support, which has recently been forthcoming in a series of studies, mostly by British psychologists.

Some of this work took its origin from the widely held hypothesis that genius and madness may be closely allied (Prentky, 1980). Common observation suggests that people who are highly original and creative may differ from the ordinary run, in showing personality qualities often associated with schizophrenics and other psychotics, and a number of genetic studies have indeed supported such a view. Heston (1966) studied offspring of schizophrenic mothers raised by foster-parents, and found that although about half showed psychosocial disability, the remaining half were notably successful adults, possessing artistic talents and demonstrating imaginative adaptations to life, to a degree not found in the control group. Karlsson (1968, 1970) found that among relatives of schizophrenics in Iceland, there was a high incidence of individuals of great creative achievement. McNeil (1971) studied the occurrence of mental illness in highly creative adopted children and their biological parents, discovering that the mental illness rates in the adoptees and in the parents were positively and significantly related to the creativity level of the adoptees. These and other findings support speculations, such as those by Hammers and Zubin (1968) and by Jarvik and Chadwick (1973) to the effect that there is a common genetic basis for great potential and for psychopathological deviation.

Eysenck and Eysenck (1976) have published an account of their investigation into the personality trait of 'psychoticism', based on the hypothesis of a continuum between normality and psychosis (Eysenck, 1950, 1952) and of the possibility of measuring this dimension by means of a questionnaire. Over a long period, this concept was clarified, and a psychoticism inventory produced, which was found to correlate minimally with other major dimensions of personality such as extraversion–introversion and stability–neuroticism. The Eysenck Personality Questionnaire (Eysenck and Eysenck,

1975) has been experimented with and validated in many different countries, and it has been found that three major personality dimensions of P (psychoticism), E (extraversion–introversion), and N (neuroticism–stability) emerge very strongly from an analysis of inter-correlations of questionnaire items everywhere (Eysenck and Eysenck, 1982).

Assuming that the P scale does measure, at least to some extent, the essence of the continuum from normality to psychosis, and assuming that the hypothesis linking creativity and originality with mental abnormality possesses some virtue, then we should be able to test this hypothesis in a variety of ways.

It was first tested, in an unpublished study by D. W. Kidner (in Eysenck and Eysenck, 1976). He administered several of the Wallach and Kogan (1965) tests of originality to male and female students, nurses and teachers, and found significant relationships between originality and creativity, on the one hand, and high P scores on the other. He also found that 'acceptance of culture', i.e. agreement with cultural norms, was negatively correlated with P, and also with creativity and originality.

Woody and Claridge (1977) made a particularly impressive study in Oxford of 100 university students , both undergraduate and graduate, in a wide variety of fields of specialization. They chose students as their subjects because of evidence that creativity is significantly related to IQ up to about 120, but that it becomes independent of it above this level (Canter, 1973). The tests they used were the Eysenck Personality Questionnaire (Eysenck and Eysenck, 1975) and the Wallach-Kogan Creativity Tests, somewhat modified and making up four different tasks (instance, pattern meanings, uses similarities, and line meanings). Each task was evaluated in terms of two related variables—the number of unique responses, and the total number of responses produced by the subject.

Correlation coefficients between psychoticism (P) and creativity scores for the five tests were all positive and significant, and those with the uniqueness score (which is of course the more relevant of the two) were all between 0.6 and 0.7. These values are quite exceptionally high for correlations between what is supposed to be a cognitive measure, and a test of a personality trait, particularly when general intelligence has effectively been partialled out from the correlations, through the selection of subjects.

It might be said in criticism of the studies so far reviewed, that they have dealt with psychological tests of creativity and originality in not very distinguished people, and that what is generally understood by originality and creativity demands something more than that. The objection is a reasonable one, although it should not be taken to question the remarkable success achieved by Woody and Claridge's empirical testing of the hypothesis linking P and creativity. The only study of what most lay people would consider genuine creativity has been reported by Götz and Götz (1979a, b).

Their work significantly extends that of other investigators who tried to link creativity in the arts with personality (e.g. Csikszentmihalyi and Getzels, 1973; Barron, 1972; Eysenck and Castle, 1970; and Drevdahl, 1956). Some of these studies are difficult to interpret, but we may note that Eysenck (1972) and Eysenck and Castle (1970) found that art students were significantly more introverted and neurotic than non-art students. Götz and Götz (1973) pointed out in criticism of this finding that art students in general may not be particularly creative, but when a group of highly gifted art students was compared with less-gifted and ungifted subjects, they found that the highly gifted students also had low scores on extraversion and high scores on neuroticism.

In the study under review, Götz and Götz (1979a, b) administered the Eysenck Personality Questionnaire to 337 professional artists living in West Germany, of whom 147 male and 110 female artists returned the questionnaire; their mean age was forty-seven years. One outstanding finding was that male artists were significantly more introverted and neurotic than non-artists, while for females, there was no difference on either of these dimensions. The authors suggest that in our Western world, it is mainly women with average or higher scores on extraversion who have the courage to become artists, while the more introverted and possibly more artistically gifted women do not dare to enter the precarious career. For scores on psychoticism, the results are very clear: male artists have much higher P scores than male non-artists, and female artists have much higher P scores than female non-artists. As Götz and Götz point out, these results suggest that many artists may well be more tough-minded than non-artists.

The work of Götz and Götz (1979a, b) thus offers important support for the results of Woody and Claridge, and the other authors cited above, in that it used actual artistic achievement as a criterion for the measurement of creativity and originality. In doing so, they give credence to the validity of divergent thinking tests as measures of creativity and originality. The fact that significant correlations are found between psychoticism on the one hand, and creativity and originality on the other, both in the artistic and in the non-artistic populations studied by other investigators, very much strengthens the hypothetical link between the personality trait and the behavioural pattern. We may thus be justified in concluding that originality and creativity are the outcome of certain personality traits, rather than being cognitive variables or abilities.

The Götz and Götz study is the only one which actually used the P scale, but other studies implicated traits in creative people which are clearly part of the P syndrome. Thus, work of the Institute for Personality Assessment and Research at Berkeley, under the direction of MacKinnon (1962), was concerned with creativity in architects, writers, and mathematicians. As described by MacKinnon et al. (1961) and Barron (1969), creative people showed traits of individualism and independence, lack of social conformity, unconventionality, and lack of suggestibility (Crutchfield, 1962); they were also below par in sociability and self-control. Responses on tests like word association were odd and unusual, almost like those of schizophrenics!

Most importantly, the creative subjects studied by the IPAR group consistently showed greater psychopathology on the Minnesota Multiphasic Personality Inventory depression, hypochondriasis, hysteria, psychopathy, and paranoia scales than did the controls. Lytton (1971) concludes that: 'It is difficult ... to deny that there is more than a chance association between psychiatric difficulties and creative powers.' This psychopathology is countered, however, by greater 'ego-strength', as also shown on the Minnesota Multiphasic Inventory scales.

So far as the position of Introversion and Neuroticism in the creativity field is concerned, introversion seems to be implicated both for artists and for scientists (Götz and Götz, 1979a, b; Cattell and Drevdahl, 1955; Roe, 1952, 1953; Andreani and Orio, 1972), although perhaps more for scientists than for artists (Hudson, 1966). Neuroticism, however, is clearly more strongly associated with the arts than the sciences (Wankowski, 1973; Eysenck, 1978). It is unfortunate that most empirical studies have used interviewing techniques and tests which do not always enable the reader to make clear distinctions between P, E and N; the use of standard tests like the Eysenck Personality Inventory would seem to make strict comparisons between studies possible, in a way that the random use of different inventories does not. Nevertheless, the major trends are unmistakable.

Obviously, personality by itself cannot produce original work of consequence; a reasonably high amount of intelligence and/or artistic abilities is required in order to enable a person possessing high creativity and originality to produce anything worthwhile. Nevertheless, for creative and original work in both science and the arts, intelligence by itself, even if allied with special abilities, may not be enough; personality may play a very important part indeed.

REFERENCES

Andreani, O., and Orio, S. (1972). *Le Radici Psicologiche del Talento*. Societ Editrice il Mulino, Bologna.

Barron, F. (1969). *The Creative Person and the Creative Process*. Holt, New York.

Barron, F. (1972). *Artists in the Making*. Seminar Press, New York.

Berger, M. (1982). The 'scientific approach' to intelligence: An overview of its history with special reference to mental speed. In *A Model for Intelligence* (ed. H. J. Eysenck). Springer, New York.

Blinkhorn, S. F., and Hendrickson, D. E. (1982). Averaged evoked responses and psychometric intelligence. *Nature*, **295**, 596–597.

Campbell, D. T., and Stanley, J. C. (1963). *Experimental and Quasi-experimental Designs for Research*. Rand McNally, Chicago.

Canter, S. (1973). Some aspects of cognitive function in twins. In *Personality Differences and Biological Variation: A Study of Twins* (eds G. S. Claridge, S. Canter, and W. I. Hume), Pergamon, Oxford.

Cattell, R. B. (1982). *The Inheritance of Personality and Ability.* Academic Press, New York.

Cattell, R. B., and Drevdahl, J. G. A. (1955). Comparison of the personality profile (16PF) of eminent researchers with that of eminent teachers and administrators and of the general public. *British Journal of Psychology*, **46**, 248–261.

Crutchfield, R. S. (1962). Conformity and creative thinking. In *Contemporary Approaches to Creative Thinking* (eds H. E. Gruber, G. Terrell and M. Werkheimer). Etherton Press, New York.

Csikszentmihalyi, M., and Getzels, J. W. (1973). The personality of young artists: an empirical and theoretical exploration. *British Journal of Psychology*, **64**, 91–104.

Drevdahl, J. E. (1956). Factors of importance for creativity. *Journal of Clinical Psychology*, **12**, 21–26.

Eysenck, H. J. (1950). Criterion analysis: An application of the hypothetico-deductive method to factor analysis. *Psychological Review*, **57**, 38–53.

Eysenck, H. J. (1952). Cyclothymia and schizothymia as a dimension of personality. II. Experimental. *Journal of Personality*, **20**, 345–384.

Eysenck, H. J. (1972). Personal preferences, aesthetic sensitivity and personality in trained and untrained subjects. *Journal of Personality*, **40**, 544–557.

Eysenck, H. J. (1973). *The Measurement of Intelligence.* MTP, Lancaster.

Eysenck, H. J. (1978). Personality and learning. In *Melbourne Studies in Education* (ed. S. Murray-Smith). University Press, Melbourne, pp. 134–181.

Eysenck, H. J. (1979). *The Structure and Measurement of Intelligence.* Springer, New York.

Eysenck, H. J. (1982a). *A Model for Intelligence.* Springer, New York.

Eysenck, H. J. (1982b). The sociology of psychological knowledge, the genetic interpretation of the IQ, and Marxist–Leninist ideology. *Bulletin of the British Psychological Society*, **35**, 449–451.

Eysenck, H. J. (1982c). The psychophysiology of intelligence. In *Advances in Personality Assessment*, Vol. 1, (eds C. D. Spielberger and J. N. Butcher), Lawrence Erlbaum, Hillsdale, New Jersey.

Eysenck, H. J., and Castle, M. (1970). Training in art as a factor in the determination of preference judgements for polygons. *British Journal of Psychology*, **61**, 65–81.

Eysenck, H. J., and Eysenck, S. B. G. (1975). *Manual of the Eysenck Personality Questionnaire.* Edits, San Diego.

Eysenck, H. J., and Eysenck, S. B. G. (1976). *Psychoticism as a Dimension of Personality*, Hodder and Stoughton, London.

Eysenck, H. J., and Eysenck, S. B. G. (1982). Recent advances in the cross-cultural study of personality. In *Advances in Personality Assessment* (eds C. Spielberger and J. Butcher), Lawrence Erlbaum, Hillsdale, New Jersey.

Freeman, J. (1983a). Environment and high IQ—a consideration of fluid and crystallised intelligence. *Personality and Individual Differences*, **4**, 307–313.

Freeman, J. (1983b). Intelligence. In *The Scientific Basis of Psychiatry*, (ed. Malcolm Weller). Bailliere Tindall, London.

Furneaux, W. D. (1960). Intellectual abilities and problem-solving behaviour. In *Handbook of Abnormal Psychology* (ed. H. J. Eysenck), Pitman, London.

Götz, K. O., and Götz, K. (1973). Introversion–extraversion and neuroticism in gifted and ungifted art students. *Perceptual and Motor Skills*, **36**, 675–678.

Götz, K. O., and Götz, K. (1979a). Personality characteristics of professional artists. *Perceptual and Motor Skills*, **49**, 327–334.
Götz, K. O., and Götz, K. (1979b). Personality characteristics of successful artists. *Perceptual and Motor Skills*, **49**, 919–924.
Guilford, J. P. (1967). *The Nature of Human Intelligence*. McGraw-Hill, New York.
Guilford, J. P., and Hoepfner, R. (1971). *The Analysis of Intelligence*. McGraw-Hill, New York.
Hammer, M., and Zubin, J. (1968). Evolution, culture and psychopathology. *Journal of General Psychology*, **78**, 154–175.
Hendrickson, D. E. (1982). The biological basis of intelligence. Part 2: Measurement. In *A Model for Intelligence* (ed. H. J. Eysenck). Springer, New York.
Herman, L., and Hogben, L. (1932). The intellectual resemblance of twins. *Proceedings of the Royal Society of Edinburgh*, **53**, 105–129.
Heston, L. L. (1966). Psychiatric disorders in foster home reared children of schizophrenic mothers. *British Journal of Psychiatry*, **112**, 819–825.
Hick, W. (1952). On the rate of gain of information. *Quarterly Journal of Experimental Psychology*, **4**, 11–26.
Hudson, L. (1966). *Contrary Imaginations*. Methuen, London.
Jarvik, L. F., and Chadwick, S. B. (1973). Schizophrenia and survival. In *Psychopathology* (eds. M. Hammer, K. Salzinger and S. Sutton). Wiley, New York.
Jensen, A. R. (1982). Reaction time and psychometric g. In *A Model for Intelligence* (ed. H. J. Eysenck). Springer, New York.
Karlsson, J. L. (1968). Generalogic studies of schizophrenia. In *The Transmission of Schizophrenia* (eds D. Rosenthal and S. S. Kety), Pergamon, Oxford.
Karlsson, J. L. (1970). Genetic association of giftedness and creativity with schizophrenia. *Heredity*, **66**, 177–182.
Loehlin, J. C., and Nichols, R. C. (1976). *Heredity, Environment, and Personality*. University of Texas Press, London.
Lytton, H. (1971). *Creativity and Education*. Routledge and Kegan Paul, London.
MacKinnon, D. W. (1962). The nature and nurture of creative talent. *American Psychologist*, **17**, 484–495.
MacKinnon, D. W., et al. (1961). *Proceedings of the Conference on 'The Creative Person*. University of California Alumni Centre, Lake Tahoe.
McNeil, T. F. (1971). Prebirth and postbirth influence on the relationship between creative ability and recorded mental illness. *Journal of Personality*, **39**, 391–406.
Newell, A. (1982). The knowledge level. In *Artificial Intelligence*, **18**, 87–127.
Newell, A., and Simon, H. A. (1972). *Human Problem Solving*. Prentice-Hall, Englewood Cliffs.
Newell, A., and Simon, H. A. (1976). Computer science as empirical enquiry: symbols and search. In *Communications of the ACM*, **19**, 113–126.
Prentky, R. A. (1980). *Creativity and Psychopathology*. Praeger, New York.
Roe, A. (1952). A psychologist examines sixty-four eminent scientists. *Scientific American*, **187**, 21–25.
Roe, A. (1953). A psychological study of eminent psychologists and anthropologists and a comparison with biological and physical scientists. *Psychological Monographs*, **67**, No. 352.
Schafer, E. W. P. (1982). Neural adaptability: a biological determinant of behavioural intelligence. In *International Journal of Neurosciences*, **17**, 183–191.
Sokolov, E. N. (1960). Neuronal models and the orienting reflex. In *The Central Nervous System and Behaviour* (ed. M. A. Brazier), J. Macy, New York.

Sokolov, E. N. (1963). *Perception and the Conditioned Reflex.* Pergamon Press, Oxford.

Spearman, C. (1927). *The Abilities of Man.* Macmillan, London.

Terman, L. M., and Oden, M. H. (1959). *The Gifted Group in Middle Life.* Stanford University Press, Stanford.

Thorndike, E. L. (1927). *The Measurement of Intelligence.* Columbia University Press, New York.

Vernon, P. E. (1979). *Intelligence: Heredity and Environment.* W. H. Freeman, San Francisco.

Wallach, M. A., and Kogan, N. (1965). *Modes of Thinking in Young Children.* Holt, Rinehart and Winston, New York.

Wankowski, J. A. (1973). *Temperament, Motivation and Academic Achievement.* University of Birmingham Educational Survey and Counselling Unit, Birmingham.

Wissler, C. (1901). The correlation of mental and physical tests. *Psychological Revue Monograph,* No. 3.

Woody, E., and Claridge, G. (1977). Psychoticism and thinking. *British Journal of Social and Clinical Psychology,* **16**, 241–248.

Yule, W., Gold, R. D., and Busch, C. (1982). Long-term predictive validity of the WPPSI: an 11 year follow-up study. *Personality and Individual Differences,* **3**, 65–71.

The Psychology of Gifted Children
Edited by Joan Freeman
©1985, John Wiley & Sons, Ltd.

CHAPTER 8

Sleep and Mental Efficiency

JEAN-CLAUDE GRUBAR

The simultaneous advance of both physiology and biochemistry has opened up a new conceptual approach to the study of intelligence. Old ideas of body–mind dualism are being questioned, especially that of physical processes in their relationship with superior cognitive abilities, which do, in fact, have a physiological substratum, since the mind originates in the brain. Indeed, this approach has been a favourite one for many years with research workers, who have studied cognitive deficits in relation to brain dysfunctions and have found levels of cognition directly related to the level and quality of brain activity (Berkson, 1963; Clausen, 1978; Ionescu, 1979; Ionescu and Grubar, 1981). It has been considered for a long time that among the various brain states, sleep is one directly associated in some way with cognitive abilities (Jenkins and Dallenbach, 1924; Van Ormer, 1932)—a relationship which Jackson (1932) formulated as the 'sleep cognition hypothesis'.

A brief review of the electrophysiological approach to sleep is given below, for the benefit of those who are not already familiar with it.

THE ELECTROPHYSIOLOGY OF SLEEP

Sleep stages

With the development and improvement of polygraphic techniques, the study of sleep has become both physiological and objective. Previously, the recognition of sleep was made merely by the absence, or at least reduction of overt interactive behaviour of the sleeper with his environment, and by the sleeper's subjective interpretation of his sleep. Even the traditional mythological and interpretive status of dreams has had to be reconsidered in this new light.

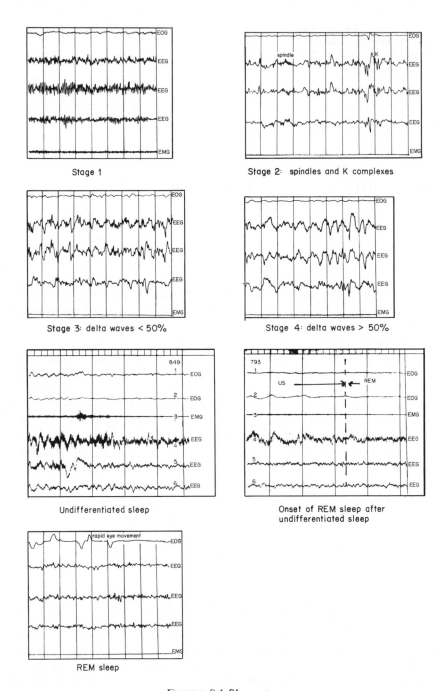

FIGURE 8.1 Sleep stages

Loomis *et al.* (1935) were the first to use electroencephalography (EEG) for the study of sleep. They found that during nocturnal sleep, the EEG waveforms fluctuated, with alternating rapid and slow waves. The parallel relationship between the kinds of waves and the intensity of stimuli required to wake the sleeper led Loomis and his co-workers to conclude that deep sleep was associated with low-frequency waves. It was they also, in 1936, who provided the first objective classification of sleep stages. This consisted of five sequential stages—A, B, C, D, E—each with its characteristic wave pattern. The later investigation by EEG of other physiological indices, which also varied during the night, provided a still better understanding of sleep.

TABLE 8.1   Polygraphic sleep characteristics

Sleep stages	EEG	EOG	EMG
Stage 1	Synchronous alpha waves are becoming discontinuous and are replaced by mixed frequencies waves in the 2–7 cps range	Some slow eye movements	Muscle tone slightly diminished compared with wakefulness
Stage 2	Presence of spindles: waves in the 12–14 cps range and of K complexes	Absence of eye movements	Muscle tone still visible
Stage 3	Decrease in EEG frequency but increase in amplitude; presence of 20 to 50 % delta waves (2 cps or lower)	Absence of eye movements	Muscle tone slightly more diminished
Stage 4	More than 50 % delta waves	Absence of eye movements	Muscle tone slightly more diminished
Undifferen-tiated sleep	Desynchronized EEG with low amplitude waves, delta waves and K complexes	Some eye movements	Short periods of muscle tone abolition
REM sleep	Desynchronized EEG with low voltage activity of high frequency	Occurrence of rapid eye movements, mainly in bursts	Complete muscle tone abolition

With the introduction of electro-oculography (EOG), Aserinski and Kleitman (1953) were able to discover a desynchronized, yet cyclical, sleep stage, associated with rapid eye movements, which always followed a slow-wave stage. It has been termed 'rapid eye movement' (REM) sleep by Dement and Kleitman (1957) and 'paradoxical sleep' (PS) by Jouvet *et al.* (1959) (see note

1). Then, with the help of electromyography (EMG), Berger (1961) finally completed the characterization of sleep stages. He described how EMG activity gradually decreases as sleep gets sounder, then disappears completely with the onset of EEG desynchronization and rapid eye movements.

By using a combined analysis of EEG, EOG, and EMG in periods of 30 seconds, Rechtschaffen and Kales (1968) proposed a standard classification of sleep stages which is commonly used by sleep investigators. Rechtschaffen and Kales' criteria are given and shown in Table 8.1 and Figure 8.1.

There is, however, a short transitional period between slow-wave sleep and REM sleep, consisting of a stage in which both slow-wave sleep and REM sleep indices co-exist. This transition period, which is generally observed before and after REM sleep, has been called 'intermediate sleep' by Lairy (1966) and 'undifferentiated sleep' (US) by Parmelee and Wenner (1967). It can be considered both as a primitive sleep state and as the period of REM sleep release (see note 2).

THE ONTOGENESIS OF SLEEP

The course of adult sleep shows several general characteristics. It is composed of four or five cycles (from stage 1 to stage REM), each lasting from one-and-a-half to two hours. Slow-wave sleep (stages 3 and 4) is prevalent during the first half of the night, while the duration of REM sleep periods increases as the night goes on. Usually, the first stage 4 is followed by a short period of US, which is itself followed by REM sleep. In normal conditions, individual sleepers present similar sleep patterns on consecutive nights (Webb, 1965).

Most sleep specialists agree on the relative lengths of the sleep stages for a normal adult: stage 1, 5–10 per cent; stage 2, 40–50 per cent; stage 3, 5–10 per cent; stage 4, 15–20 per cent; REM sleep, 20–25 per cent (Davies and Horne, 1975). The rate of undifferentiated sleep is scarcely 1 per cent for a normal adult.

The course and the relative lengths of the different stages change with chronological age. Roffwarg et al.'s (1966) work, corroborated by Feinberg and Carlson (1968) and by Williams et al. (1974), remains a constant source of reference. Parmelee and Wenner (1967) demonstrated that the REM sleep rate is higher in premature than in full-term neonates, and that it decreases with gestational age. Moreover, the latency of the first period of REM sleep, short in neonates, increases with chronological age. The very high REM sleep rate at birth could account for the plasticity of the nervous system at this crucial period for learning, and it remains particularly significant during the first year of life. It is not until the age of fifteen that sleep takes on its adult characteristics; as the individual grows older, he sleeps less and his REM sleep rate drops astonishingly.

FEATURES DESCRIBING SLEEP

Perhaps because of its paradoxicality, the REM sleep stage has been investigated more than any other. Even when sleep is very sound, most of its polygraphic characteristics still show similarities with those observed during wakefulness. Moruzzi (1965) divided the physiological concomitants of REM sleep into 'tonic' and 'phasic' components: events lasting all over the REM sleep period such as cortical desynchronization, muscle-tone abolition, and hippocampic theta waves are called 'tonic'; events which appear intermittently, in bursts, such as rapid eye movements, short rapid jerks and variations in vegetative phenomena, are called 'phasic'. These phenomena testify that REM sleep is a more active state than slow-wave sleep.

The quality of sleep can be ascertained via a variety of parameters, but the main features describing sleep may be classified in three categories: behavioural, electrophysiological, and mixed:

1. Behavioural features: time spent in bed, number of body movements, duration of periods with movements.
2. Electrophysiological features: number of each different stage (1, 2, 3, 4, US and REM), duration of each stage, rate of each stage, latency of each stage from the onset of sleep, number of eye movements during REM sleep, length of intervals between two consecutive eye movements, number of intervals between two consecutive eye movements of a given duration, eye movements density, duration of intervals between two consecutive identical sleep stages.
3. Mixed features: total sleep time, sleep latency (latency of the first spindle) and sleep efficacy. (A spindle is an EEG wave form which is spindle shaped, has twelve to fourteen spikes, and occurs during stage 2).

Most of these features are said to be static; only a few of them suggest the cyclical nature of sleep.

THE SLEEP OF THE MENTALLY RETARDED

The considerable research completed since the 1930s has provided more detailed evidence of the relationship between sleep patterns and mental efficiency which Jackson had originally proposed. For example, the sleep of normal and mentally retarded subjects was compared by Pètre-Quadens and Jouvet (1966), who found that for the retarded, both their REM sleep rates and density of their REM eye movements were lower, and phasic events during their REM sleep were dissociated. Comparisons of the sleep of normal and Down's Syndrome subjects have shown the latter to have characteristically more frequent and longer awakenings, a higher number of body movements, and shorter REM sleep durations (Schmidt *et al.*, 1968; Castaldo, 1969; Fukuma *et al.*, 1974).

Mentally retarded subjects have also been found to have a lower duration of paradoxical sleep (PS) than normal subjects (Fukuma *et al.*, 1974; Clausen *et al.*, 1977). Feinberg and his co-workers (1969) found a correlation of 0.74 between the rate of PS and IQ, as measured by the WPPSI, though the relationship between PS and sleep is probably not organic, but more general (Castaldo and Krynicki, 1974).

Three recent studies by Grubar (1975, 1978, 1983) and a study by Colognola *et al.* (1984) have demonstrated the specific sleep patterns of mentally retarded subjects of various aetiologies. For these children, the REM sleep rate is lengthened, the undifferentiated sleep rate is increased, the latency of the first REM sleep period is shortened, and the REM sleep phases reduced in number, to an extent which is significantly different from that of normal subjects of a similar chronological age. Moreover, comparing the intervals between consecutive eye movements of REM sleep has shown that short intervals (I 1 s) are significantly fewer with mental retardates (Grubar, 1983). These results show that for mental retardates, there is a real abortion of REM sleep, shown in Table 8.2.

TABLE 8.2   Comparison of 5 sleep indices in mental deficients and normal subjects of same chronological age

Parameters	Mental deficients $n = 54$*		Normal subjects $n = 17$		Significance level
	m	sd	m	sd	
REM sleep (%)	12.15	3.42	21.83	1.54	$p<.001$
First REM sleep phase latency (mn)	151	47	88	17	$p<.001$
Number of REM sleep phases	2.72	1.42	4.21	0.75	$p<.001$
Undifferentiated sleep (%)	4.71	1.54	1.19	0.38	$p<.001$
Number of undifferentiated sleep phases	7.71	2.86	7.35	1.61	NS

* 2 subjects with undetermined aetiology have been eliminated from statistical treatments.

THE SLEEP OF GIFTED CHILDREN

As the relationship between sleep patterns and cognitive ability had so often been found to be different for mentally retarded and normal children, there was the possibility that the sleep patterns of children at the other end of the ability spectrum—gifted children—might also be different from that of normal children. This study actually investigated their sleep patterns.

Methodology

There were five gifted and seventeen normal children of both sexes and of the same chronological age in the sample. The normal children had a mean IQ of 104 (SD 5), and a mean age of 9;0 (SD 2.1) the characteristics of the gifted children are given in Table 8.3.

TABLE 8.3   Gifted children characteristics

Subject	Sex	Age	IQ	Observations
S1	M	10;8*	171 (Terman–Stanford)	Institutionalized
S2	M	9;9	137 (Terman–Stanford)	Institutionalized
S3	F	13;1	142(WISC)	In her family
S4	M	13;8	145(WISC)	In his family
S5	F	10;9	152(WISC)	In her family
Mean		11;6	149	

* 10;8 means 10 years and 8 months old.

After dietetic and medical control, the children's sleep patterns were recorded in their usual life environments, which was an institution for two of them and their families for the three others. To control for the 'first night effect', every child was allowed one night for habituation, wearing all the electrode equipment, and the recordings were started at their usual bedtime on the following night. The subjects slept in their own beds, and generally woke up spontaneously.

The EEG was obtained from three bipolar settings; two from the dominant hemisphere and one from the non-dominant hemisphere. As all the gifted subjects were predominantly right-handed, the EEG derivations were: F8-T4, T4-02, T3-01, according to Jasper's 10–20 system (1958). The cups of the ETEP electrodes (see note 3), filled with 'Redux Paste' (Hewlett-Packard) were fixed directly on to the scalp with collodion.

Two types of oblique eye movements were recorded, according to the arrangement shown below:

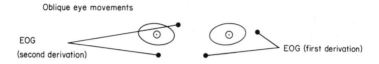

The EMG was obtained from electrodes fixed on to the chin (mental muscle tone), according to the recommendations of Rechtschaffen and Kales (1968) (see Figure 8.2-A).

The EEG, EOG, and EMG were first recorded on a pre-set magnetic tape recorder (Multiplex Cassette Recorder ETEP 816M ETEP) (see Figure 8.2-B). Afterwards, the magnetic recordings were read on an eight-channel polygraph (Mingograph Siemens-Elema) for visual interpretation.

The children's nocturnal sleep was analysed according to the criteria of Rechtschaffen and Kales (1968), adding the undifferentiated sleep stage. The sleep indices were collected on special analysis sheets (see copy in annex 1) for statistical treatment.

Results

The comparison between gifted and normal children concerned twenty-three sleep parameters—behavioural, electrophysiological, and mixed. There were no significant differences between gifted and normal children in respect of behavioural and mixed features; nor were time spent in bed, total sleep time, sleep latency, or sleep efficacy different for gifted and normal children. Considerable differences appeared, however, in electrophysiological parameters, which were dichotomized both in sleep indices and in the eye movements of REM sleep indices, which are described below.

SLEEP INDICES

Though the total sleep time and sleep latency of gifted and normal children were very similar, the course of their sleep, i.e. the divisions of the stages and cycles, was completely different. The number of complete sleep cycles (analogous to the number of REM sleep phases) was significantly higher in gifted children (see Table 8.4), though their duration was shortened.

For gifted children, the number of undifferentiated sleep stages was similar to the number of REM sleep stages, each of the first being followed by one of the second (see Table 8.5). The efficacy index (ratio between the number of REM-sleep periods and the number of undifferentiated sleep periods) was 1.18 in gifted children, whereas in normal children, the number

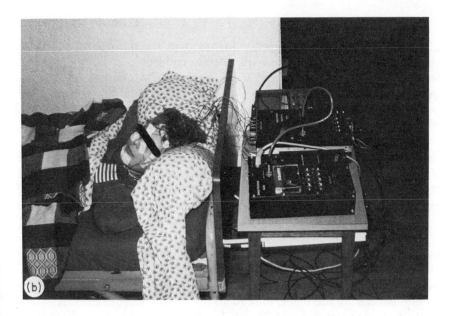

FIGURE 8.2 (a) A subject with the complete electrode equipment
(b) A subject in his bed

TABLE 8.4   Comparison of 5 sleep indices in gifted and normal children of same chronological age

Parameters	Gifted children $n = 5$		Normal children $n = 17$		Significance level Mann–Whitney 'U'
	Mean	Range	Mean	Range	
Latency of the first REM sleep phase (mn)	74	53–93	88	53–122	$p<.05$
REM sleep (%)	26.39	23.23–29.70	21.83	17.00–24.82	$p<.02$
Number of REM sleep phases	6.40	6–7	4.21	3–6	$p<.05$
Undifferentiated sleep (%)	1.34	0.30–2.07	1.19	0.67–2.22	$p<.025$
Number of undifferentiated sleep phases	5.40	2–7	7.35	5–11	$p<.002$

of undifferentiated sleep stages is higher than the number of REM-sleep stages (efficacy index: 0.57). With normal children, very often the undifferentiated sleep stages do not interlock with REM sleep at all. There are therefore more incomplete sleep cycles in normal children (and even more in the mentally retarded, who have a real lack of REM sleep, efficacy index: 0.35) than in the gifted (see Tables 8.2 and 8.4).

The number, duration, and rate of stages 1, 3, and 4 were similar in gifted and normal children, but the rate of stage 2 was slightly, though not significantly smaller in gifted children. Generally, the sequence of stage 1, stage 2, stage 3, stage 4, is fairly regular in gifted, compared with that of normal children: in the latter, there are often arousals in sleep cycles: stage 1, stage 2, stage 3, stage 2, stage 3, stage 4, stage 3, stage 4.

In normal children, as the night goes on, REM sleep periods become longer and longer, whereas slow-wave sleep gets less and less sound, i.e. absence of stages 3 and 4 in the course of the last sleep cycles. The picture was different for the gifted children, whose REM sleep periods grew longer and longer during the night, though stages 3 and 4 were often still observed in the last sleep cycles (see Figure 8.3).

The last sleep cycles of the gifted children were more similar to their first sleep cycles than was the case in the normal children. In short, the

TABLE 8.5   Sleep cycles and stages in 5 gifted children

Subjects	Effective sleep duration (mn)	Number of complete cycles	Number of periods of each stage					
			1	2	3	4	US	REM sleep
S1	515	6	2	7	6	5	6	6
S2	517	6	2	15	8	4	2	6
S3	481	7	2	9	8	6	7	7
S4	437	6	3	10	8	7	6	6
S5	498	7	2	10	8	5	6	7

sleep course of these gifted children contained more complete sleep cycles of shorter duration, and their last sleep cycles had more slow-wave sleep. However, the most striking difference between the gifted and normal children was in their desynchronized sleep, REM and undifferentiated sleep (see Table 8.4).

The latency of the first REM sleep period was shorter in gifted than in normal children (74 mn vs 88 mn, $p < .05$). The number of REM sleep phases, as well as their duration and rate, was higher for gifted children (respectively 6.40 vs 4.21, $p < .05$) for the number and (26.39 vs 21.83, $p < .02$) for the rate. The undifferentiated sleep rate was slightly higher for gifted than normal children (1.34 vs 1.19, $p < .025$), though the number of undifferentiated sleep periods was higher in normal children (7.35 vs 5.40, $p < .002$).

EYE MOVEMENTS OF REM SLEEP INDICES

The number of rapid eye movements during REM sleep was roughly similar for both gifted and normal children, but the density of eye movements (ratio between the total number of rapid eye movements and the total duration of REM sleep) was higher for the gifted.

A more refined approach—the analysis of the patterns of eye movements—produced interesting results. This technique, advocated by Pètre-Quadens (1969, 1972), is based on the study of the intervals between consecutive rapid eye movements, which are classified into short (I > 1 s) and long (I > 2 s) intervals. Short intervals are associated with high-frequency eye movements and long intervals with low-frequency eye movements. In this respect, the high-frequency movements were found to be significantly more numerous in gifted children (282.25 vs 168.11, $p < .002$) (see Table 8.6); correspondingly, low-frequency eye movements were significantly more numerous in normal children (239.94 vs 199.75, $p < .05$).

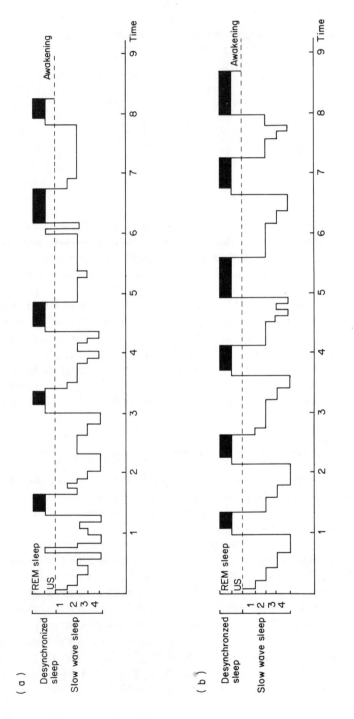

FIGURE 8.3   Hypnograms of normal (a) and gifted (b) children

TABLE 8.6   Eye movement activity during REM sleep in gifted and normal children of similar chronological age

Parameters	Gifted children $n = 4^*$		Normal children $n = 17$		Significance level Mann–Whitney 'U'
	Mean	Range	Mean	Range	
Intervals<1s	282.25	247–311	168.11	98–227	$p<.002$
Intervals>2s	199.75	160–255	239.94	87–411	$p<.05$
$R = \dfrac{I<1s}{I>2s}$	1.44	1.21–1.64	0.82	0.42–1.54	$p<.02$

* The EOG of one gifted child was unanalysable.

The ratio, R, between high and low frequency was significantly higher in the gifted children (1.44 vs 0.82, $p < .02$), and it was thus found that the patterns of rapid eye movements in sleep differed significantly between the gifted and normal children respectively.

DISCUSSION

More than enough convergent data have now been gathered to confirm Jackson's 'sleep cognition hypothesis' of an association between different types of cognitive deficit and sleep patterns. The recent data presented here, which were derived from gifted children, complement the earlier information to show that high-level cognition is also clearly associated with special sleep patterns, and as with mental retardation, the peculiarities involve REM sleep. All the data on sleep, which now span retarded, normal, and gifted children are consistent, and can be considered as tools with which to take an objective approach to intelligence.

Even where the amount of sleep is the same, both the cycles and lengths of the stages of children's sleep are quite different, and appear to be linked with IQ. The rate of REM sleep is positively correlated with the IQ ($r = 0.744$, $p < 0.01$) and is particularly high in gifted children. However, the latency of the first REM period is negatively correlated with the IQ ($r = -0.457$, $p < 0.01$), and this latency is shortest in gifted children.

Slow-wave sleep (particularly stage 4) is often present in the last sleep cycles in gifted children, and though its rate (13,20) is analogous to that of normal children, its pattern is different. Huon (1981) found that in adults with IQs of over 140, there is also an abundance of stage 4.

For gifted children, each period of REM sleep is preceded by one of undifferentiated sleep, which is usually considered to be both transitional and archaic. In the case of these children, however, it is really only transitional, as their brain mechanisms underlying sleep are more effective, compared with those of other children. Paradoxically, though, gifted children's relatively high rates of undifferentiated sleep indicate some immaturity of development. The high rates of REM sleep observed in gifted children can also be interpreted as a sign of immaturity, being similar to those of normal children whose chronological age is about one year-old (Roffwarg et al., 1966).

The persistence of juvenile characteristics in older persons was named 'neoteny' by Kollman (1884), and the existence of such features in gifted children as high rates of REM and undifferentiated sleep can be interpreted in these terms. It is a useful factor, though, and can be linked to higher brain plasticity, resulting in greater receptitivity and responsiveness towards the environment.

The ratio between high- and low-frequency eye movements in sleep is positively correlated with IQ ($r = 0.670$; $p < 0.01$). Pètre-Quadens (1978) and with Hoffman (1981) have shown that this ratio increases with chronological age, and considers it to reflect the organization of information—'order over noise'—as it has also been found to increase sequentially in a learning session (Spreux et al., 1982). It would appear that the high occulomotor rates observed in gifted children (1.44 vs 8.22; $p < 0.02$), which are similar to those seen in adults, may indicate a superior ability to organize information, and thus an advanced maturity of processing.

Indices of maturity therefore co-exist unexpectedly in gifted children; both immaturity—high rates of REM and undifferentiated sleep—and advanced maturity—high ratio of eye movement frequencies. This is in accord with Terrassier's (1979, 1981 and Chapter 14), description of 'dyssynchrony', the uneven development of psychological characteristics in gifted children, which can now be reconsidered in psychophysiological terms. Fortunately, this psychophysiological dys-synchrony appears to be beneficial in terms of brain plasticity and of organizational abilities.

CONCLUSIONS

Gifted children seem to have the potential to benefit from the paired advantages of greater brain plasticity associated with superior organizational abilities. This advance in the understanding of very-high-level cognition makes it clear that concern for the development of gifted children falls within the legitimate province of educational psychology.

Brain plasticity is worthless, however, if the environment is not stimulating, and organizational abilities are superfluous if the environment does not provide the right amount of material to be organized. Thus, if the potentials of gifted children are not exercised, they may remain latent, but in certain circumstances, they may even disappear altogether.

ACKNOWLEDGEMENT

I particularly wish to thank Dr G. Prat (Institut Beaulieu, Salies de Beárn, France) who allowed me to begin the study of gifted children in her institution and for her judicious advice. I also wish to thank the families who allowed their children to be recorded for their hospitality. Many thanks to Mrs Thilliez (IUT 'B', Université de Lille III) for her help and advice in English.

NOTES

(1) REM sleep is the term used in Anglo-American, PS in French studies.
(2) Some sleep specialists do not accept that undifferentiated sleep really exists.
(3) This decrease has been observed for all studied species; the REM sleep rate is always higher in neonates and young animals.
(4) ETEP: 214A, ancien chemin de La Valette, Toulon, France.

REFERENCES

Aserinski, E., and Kleitman, N. (1953). Regularly occurring periods of eye motility and concomitant phenomena during sleep. *Science*, **118**, 273–274.
Berger, R. (1961). Tonus of extrinsic laryngeal muscles during sleep and dreaming. *Science*, **134**, 840.
Berkson, G. (1963). Psychophysiological studies in mental deficiency. In *Handbook of Mental Deficiency* (ed. N. E. Ellis). McGraw Hill, New York, pp. 556–573.
Castaldo, V. (1969). Down's syndrome: a study of sleep patterns related to level of mental retardation. *Amer. J. Ment. Defic.*, **74**, 187–190.
Castaldo, V., and Krynicki, V. (1974). Sleep and eye movement patterns in two groups of retardates. *Biol. Psychiat.*, **6**, 295–299.
Clausen, J. (1978). Psychophysiology in mental retardation. *Internat. Rev. of Res. Ment. Retard.*, **9**, 85–125.
Clausen, J., Sersen, E., and Lidsky, A. (1977). Sleep patterns in mental retardation, Down's syndrome. *Electroenceph. Clin. Neurophysiol*, **43**, 183–191.
Colognola, R. H., Grubar, J. C., Gigli, G. L., Ferri, R., Musumect, S. A., and Bergonzi, P. (1984). Sleep in children with Down's syndrome. *Communications of the 7th Congress of the European Sleep Research Society, Munich.*
Davies, D., and Horne, J. (1975). Human sleep: measurement, characteristics and individual differences. In *Sleep Disturbance and Hypnotic Drug Depend* (ed. A. D. Chift). Excerpta Medica American Elsevier, Amsterdam, pp. 42–68.
Dement, W., and Kleitman, N. (1957). The relation of eye movements during sleep to dream activity: an objective method for the study of dreaming. *J. Exp. Psychol.* **53**, 339–346.

Feinberg, I., and Carlson, V. (1968). Sleep variables as a function of age in man. *Arch. Gen. Psychiat.* **18**, 239–250.

Feinberg, I., Braun, M., and Schulman, E. (1969). EEG sleep patterns in mental retardation. *Electroenceph. Clin. Neurophysiol.* **27**, 128–141.

Fukuma, E., Umezawa, Y., Kobayashi, K., and Motoike, M. (1974). Polygraphic study on the nocturnal sleep of children with Down's syndrome and endogenous mental retardation. *Folia Psychiat. Neurol. Jpn.* **28**, 333–345.

Grubar, J.-C. (1975). Debilite mentale et sommeil paradoxal. *Enfance*, **3-4**, 387–393.

Grubar, J.-C. (1978). Le sommeil paradoxal des debiles mentaux. *Enfance*, **2-3**, 165–172.

Grubar, J.-C. (1983). Sleep and mental deficiency. *Rev. EEG Neurophysiol.*, **13**, 107–114.

Huon, J. (1981). Le sommeil des sujets à quotient intellectuel élevé. *Electroenceph. Clin. Neurophysiol.* **52**, S128.

Ionescu, S. (1979). Approche Psychophysiologique de la déficience mentale. In *Les Débilites Mentales* (ed. R. Zazzo). A. Colin, Paris, pp. 383–420.

Ionescu, S., and Grubar, J.-C. (1981). Approche psychophysiologique de la déficience mentale. *Neuropsychiatrie de l'Enfance et de L'Adolescence*, **12**, 117–122.

Jackson, J. (1932). *Selected Writings of John Hughlings Jackson* (ed. J. Taylor). Hodder and Stoughton, London.

Jasper, H. (1958). The ten twenty electrode system of the International Federation. *Electroenceph. Clin. Neurophysiol.* **10**, 371–375.

Jenkins, J., and Dallenbach, K. (1924). Obliviscence during sleep and waking. *Amer. J. Psychol.* **s5**, 605–612.

Jouvet, M., Michel, F., and Courjon, J. (1959). Sur un stade d'activité électrique cérébrale rapide au cours du sommeil physiologique. *C. R. Soc. Biol. Paris.* **153**, Paris, 1024–1028.

Kollman (1884). Referenced in *Encyclopaedia Britannica, Micropaedia*, Tome VII, p. 257.

Lairy, G. (1966). Données récentes sur la physiologie et la physio-pathologie de l'activité onirique. *Excerpta Medica Internat. Congr. Ser.* **117**, 8–9.

Loomis, A., Harvey, E., and Hobart, G. (1935). Further observations on the potential of the cerebral cortex during sleep. *Science*, **82**, 198–200.

Moruzzi, G. (1965). General discussion. In *Aspects Anatomo Fonctionnels de la Physiologie du Sommeil* (ed. M. Jouvet), CNRS, Paris, pp. 638–640.

Parmelee, A., and Wenner, W. (1967). Sleep states in premature and full term newborn infants. *Develop. Med. Child Neurol.* **9**, 70–77.

Pètre-Quadens, O. (1969). Contribution à l'étude de la phase dite paradoxale du sommeil. *Acta Neurol. Psychiat. Belgica*, **69**, 769–898.

Pètre-Quadens, O. (1972). Sleep in mental retardation. In *Sleep and the Maturing Nervous System* (eds D. P. Purpura and F. E. Mayer), Academic Press, New York, pp. 229–249.

Pètre-Quadens, O. (1978). Logic and ontogenesis of some sleep patterns. *Totus Homo*, **8**, 60–72.

Pètre-Quadens, O., and Hoffman, G. (1981). Maturation of the REM sleep patterns from child through adulthood. In *Brain and Behaviour Adv. Physiol. Sci.*, Vol. 17 (eds. G. Adam, I. Meszaros and E. I. Banyai). Pergamon Press, New York, pp. 55–59.

Pètre-Quadens, O., and Jouvet, M. (1966). Paradoxical sleep in mental retardation. *J. Neurol. Sci.* **3**, 608–612.

Rechtschaffen, A., and Kales, A. (1968). A manual of standard terminology, techniques and scoring system for sleep stages of human subjects. *Public Health Service US Government Printing Office*, Washington.

Roffwarg, H., Muzio, J., and Dement, W. (1966). Ontogenic development of human dream cycle. *Science*, **152**, 604–619.

Schmidt, J., Kaelbling, R., and Alexander, J. (1968). Sleep patterns in mental retardation: mongoloids and monozygotic twins. *Psychophysiology*, **5**, 212.

Spreux, F., Lambert, C., Chevalier, B., Meriaux, H., Freixa, I., Baque, E., Grubar, J.-C., Lancry, A., and Leconte, P. (1982). Modification des caracteristiques du sommeil paradoxal consecutif a un apprentissage chez l'homme. *Cahiers de Psychologie Cognitive*, **3**, 327–334.

Terrassier, J.-C. (1979). Le syndôme de dyssynchronie. *Neuropsychiatrie de l'Enfance et de l'Adolescence*, **10-11**, 445–450.

Terrassier, J.-C. (1981). *Les Enfants Surdoués*. ESF, Paris.

Van Ormer, E. (1932). Retention after intervals of sleep and waking. *Arch. Psychol.* **21**, 137.

Webb, W. (1965). Sleep characteristics of human subjects. *Bull. Brit. Psychol. Soc.* **18**, 1–10.

Williams, R., Karacan, I., and Hursch, C. (1974). *Electroencephalography (EEG) of Human Sleep: Clinical Applications*. Wiley, London.

The Psychology of Gifted Children
Edited by Joan Freeman
©1985, John Wiley & Sons, Ltd.

CHAPTER 9

Musical Giftedness

ROSAMUND SHUTER-DYSON

In the Calouste Gulbenkian Foundation's Report on the training of professional musicians (1978), it was noted that many children study an instrument with great enjoyment and educational benefit, without getting beyond
a limited level of achievement. The working definition of 'gifted'—as having
the potential to become professional performers—was adopted; it was also
recognized that among such children, there is a very small group of 'high
flyers', and these were termed 'outstandingly gifted'. It does seem useful,
in fact, to draw a distinction between the talent of the child who might become an excellent violinist in a regional orchestra and that of the potential
international soloist or famous composer.

The first part of this chapter is concerned with the characteristics of musical giftedness, as seen in: (a) the development of outstanding musicians,
where the characteristics may appear 'writ large', (b) a discussion of the nature of musical talent and its relationship to other intellectual abilities, and
(c) the personality structure of musicians. Then, the identification of talent
by audition and by testing will be considered, and finally, provision for the
education of talented children, (a) in the home, and (b) in school.

CHARACTERISTICS OF MUSICAL TALENT

Outstanding musicians

Musical talents tend to appear relatively early in life; Revesz (1953) suggested that this may be partly due to music depending less than other arts on
general mental development. The early emergence of musical talent is strik-
ingly true in the case of 'musical prodigies'. Among thirty-seven outstanding

instrumentalists studied by Scheinfeld (1956), musical talent appeared at an average age of four years nine months, and in the case of students at the Juilliard School of Music at five years six months. Manturzewska (1979) compared forty-one entrants to an international Chopin piano competition with piano students of the Warsaw Academy of Music; they did not differ on age of beginning music lessons, which was between the ages of five and seven years for both groups. Jazz musicians also show precocity; Duke Ellington, for example, began serious study of piano at the age of seven.

Biographies of famous musicians are liable to contain errors, but there would seem to be enough reliable information to enable a pattern of 'typical' development of musical talent to be outlined. (For a detailed account of the development of musical abilities in general, see Shuter-Dyson and Gabriel, 1981.)

In a tentative interpretation of a general factor of musical ability, Wing (1936) surmised that 'it might be the capacity to attend specifically to abstract auditory stimuli—as distinct from the capacity to attend, say, to concrete auditory stimuli such as spoken words'. Highly talented children certainly seem to pay great attention to the sounds in their environment. For example, Arthur Rubinstein learned to recognize people by the tunes they sang to him, and to sing a well-known mazurka to obtain a 'mazurka' cake. This suggests that he was using music to communicate in the way that most children use speech, and musically talented children, for example Handel and Walton, do sometimes sing before they speak. This might suggest that the right hemisphere of their brains is prone to develop particularly readily. Though the conclusions to be drawn from bilaterality research remain uncertain, it seems possible that trained musicians are able to bring either or both hemispheres into use, according to the demands of a particular task. Musical children seem to show greater sensitivity to sounds (if not always musical ones), than ordinary children. Noy (1968) hypothesized that such over-sensitivity may be the basis of aptitude for music, since coping with sounds forces the infant to develop auditory discrimination. Specific interest in music might occur when the auditory channel was the especially potent mode of communication between mother and child.

The talented child does not just show attention to and delight in music; keen perception of music is also involved. Musical talent is perhaps most often recognized when the child of two or so sings accurately the tunes he hears around him. If the home provides access to a keyboard instrument, before long the child will begin to pick out tunes on it. Thus, both Charles and Samuel Wesley (nephews of John Wesley) began to play tunes on their mother's harpsichord before the age of three. Mozart would amuse himself picking out thirds and sixths which particularly pleased him. At two years three months, William Crotch played God Save the King on a small organ his father had built. A piano was bought for Rubinstein's elder sisters when he was two; Arthur became an avid listener, and would slap his sister's hands for playing a wrong note. He quickly taught himself to play any tune that caught his ear.

Musically gifted children like Rubinstein soon show the ability to add 'a just bass', and perfect pitch tends to appear in children who start learning an instrument at an early age (Sergeant, 1969). This may help to explain why so many gifted children develop the ability to sing and to name specific notes, on demand. Like ordinary children, very young musicians often display a marked attraction to the tone quality of certain instruments. Thus, Rubinstein rejected a fiddle that his father bought for him and Yehudi Menuhin broke a toy violin in disgust because it would not 'sing' with the beautiful tone of the violins at the concerts to which his parents took him. Among the many feats of memory recorded in the history of music is Mozart's in writing out Allegri's Miserere, after hearing it in the Sistine Chapel at the age of fourteen. The thirteen year-old pianist Dimitri Sgouros is reported to have thirty-five concertos in his repertoire already. Enesco, Toscanini, and Louis Kentner are but a few examples of musicians who could indelibly imprint upon their memories complete symphonies at a single reading.

Evidence of the talent of prodigies comes not only from their parents, but also from the eminent musicians who hear them play (and from their audiences, if they are performers). At three years six months, Rubinstein was required by Joachim to name the notes of some 'tricky' chords, to play back the second theme of Schubert's *Unfinished Symphony*, finding the right harmonies, and later to transpose it (Rubinstein, 1973). Barrington (1771) tested the young Mozart with sight-reading from a five-part score, with improvising a love song, and with playing one of his own compositions. He concluded that Mozart's genius was very similar to Handel's.

Attempts were made by early psychologists to study 'wonder children' objectively. Richet (1901) found that Pepito Areola could play twenty harmonized pieces from memory when he was three years six months; his improvisations showed some feeling for form, and Stumpf (1909) noted that at six, Pepito had perfect pitch.

The most notable of these studies was made by Revesz (1925), who observed and tested Erwin Nyiregyhazy for six years, from the age of seven. According to his father, a singer in the Royal Opera Chorus in Budapest, Erwin tried to imitate singing before he was one; in his second year, he could reproduce correctly tunes sung to him and, by the age of three, began to play everything he heard. Revesz found that at seven, the child could name any note or chord played to him, and could adjust a 'Sound Variator' to notes that deviated only slightly from international pitch. His success at analysing complicated chords exceeded that of a well-known cellist—a result confirmed by Stumpf when Erwin visited Berlin.

Revesz carried out an interesting series of experiments, which revealed the strengths and limitations of Erwin's musical memory. For example, at seven, he could reproduce faultlessly at the third attempt a thirteen-note tune that was played to him. However, only the treble part of a four-part theme was reproduced correctly; asked to read a four-part theme away from the piano, he succeeded in memorizing it after going through it eight or nine times, humming to himself, and moving his fingers as if playing. Two years later, Erwin was able to recall the themes correctly after repeating them only once. At this age, he learned from notation a three-bar theme from 'Electra' by Strauss in forty seconds, and retained it for (at least) a week. He could memorize Beethoven sonatas and Bach fugues after repeating them only three or four times. His piano playing impressed listeners not only because of his technique, but also by the musical quality of his interpretations.

Revesz was particularly impressed by Erwin's precocity at composition. As a means of assessing the development of his creativity, Revesz traced his progress in compositions produced between the ages of seven and twelve, noting especially the range of emotions portrayed. Such spontaneous productions may be stronger indications of creative talent than scores on 'Creativity' tests (see below).

Revesz (1953) rightly noted that genuinely creative powers of interpretation must be distinguished from clever technique. Musicality denotes 'the need and capacity to understand and to experience the autonomous effects of music'. Musicality is shown by ability to understand the structure of a work of art, to follow or even anticipate the composer's intentions, and to become so absorbed in the emotions expressed that the performer (and listener) feels as if he were creating it. Certainly, absorption in music characterizes great musicians, and indeed those with lesser talents. Of 103 first-year music students, most of whom were considered to be talented, 65 per cent endorsed the statement that they possessed 'a facility for becoming completely absorbed in making music', and 55 per cent that they had 'an acute sense of identification with and dedication to a particular musical instrument'. Only 29 per cent claimed to have 'an exceptionally keen ear for intonation and other minute differences between sounds', and 8 per cent to have an outstanding musical memory (Payne, 1980).

Of more importance than early successes are the ultimate achievements of composer or performer. From an examination of compositions frequently cited in source books, Lehman (1953) concluded that the years between ages thirty-five and thirty-nine were the most productive for grand operas, cantatas, and orchestral works of 'superior' quality. However, he also noted that, at least in the case of thirty-two composers of 'superior' grand operas, as compared with eighty-two composers of works of lesser merit, the more brilliant were early starters. While Revesz (1953) took the view that the real problem of creative activity was originality, Simonton (1980b) believed that originality is to be distinguished from creativity. Originality merely requires the objective calculation of probability, but creativity demands a consensus of subjective judgements regarding psycho-social merit. Simonton assessed merit by the fame of themes, and content-analysed by computer 15 618 themes by 479 composers; the data were extracted from two thematic dictionaries of the classical repertoire. Among his conclusions was that as a composer ages, the originality of his melodies tends at first to increase, and then to decline somewhat. The most famous melodies tend to be produced by the most productive composers, in those years when many themes are being composed by other composers. In the case of compositions by the ten composers who were responsible for 39 per cent of all music in the classical repertoire, the fame of a theme was linearly related to its originality (number of chromatic notes and unusual intervals). The more original melodies tended to be composed at times of stress in the composer's life (Simonton, 1980a).

Not all notable musicians have begun their careers with public displays of virtuosity. Michael Tippett had piano lessons as a child, but no other music training, and did not come from a musical family; however, after leaving grammar school, he decided to become a composer. Peter Maxwell Davies, from a working-class family, was enchanted by a performance of *The Gondoliers* when he was four, and began to make up tunes, considering in his head whether they should go up or down. A piano was moved from his grandmother's when he was eight; he began piano lessons and to write simple music, studying 'every damned score' from a Manchester Music Library. With no help from school, he passed A-level music, the examiner discovering that he could play on request not only 'set' pieces, but parts of Beethoven symphonies. He thus displayed 'self-initiated' learning, noted in the UK Council for Music Education and Training Guidelines for Teachers (1982) as a sign of potential giftedness. Conversely, many 'wonder children' fail to fulfil the promise of their youth. Leaving out of count those whose precocity is due merely to dexterity, facility for imitation, etc., we still have to explain why William Crotch and the Wesleys, who displayed at four as much talent as Mozart, should produce so much less. Obviously, many factors are involved in the development of the individual musician, and home background may well play a decisive role. Leopold Mozart apparently sacrificed the furtherance of his own career to take his children on tour; so did Menuhin's father. Such protection needs to be carried out with due regard to what is appropriate for the child's development. The Wesleys' father, in his fifties when they were born, regarded music with some ambivalence when it was not associated with religion. Even when Charles, the elder son, did receive lessons, the teacher seems to have been indolent, and left the boy to his own devices. Crotch did succeed in having a successful career as an academic musician, becoming the first principal of the Royal Academy of Music—no mean achievement, if not comparable to Mozart's. Erwin had the misfortune to lose his caring father when he was twelve; the family moved to Berlin, and Erwin developed a passion for the music of Liszt. After a sensational debut in America, his career declined, perhaps due to bad management and unfortunate marriages.

Crises are liable to occur when the adolescent musician has to come to terms with the demands of an adult career, and the professional guidance of friends who have distinguished careers themselves is valuable at this time. Menuhin had to undertake a period of 'retooling' his technique as a young adult; while Rubinstein at forty-six, when he became a father, withdrew to his studio to immerse himself in practice and by discipline, emerged renewed, as a consummate virtuoso. Music may be a uniquely demanding profession, but it is of course not the only demanding one. Certain personality traits may favour the musician's development (see below). What may most strike the observer, however, is what an 'ordinary' child the gifted youngster is, as soon as he is away from his instrument.

MUSICAL TALENT AND ITS RELATIONSHIP TO OTHER ABILITIES

Seashore (1938) contended that the 'basic' capacities assessed by his 'Measures of Musical Talents' were highly specific, while Wing (1968) believed that a strong general factor underlies ability to perform a wide variety of musical tests. Shuter-Dyson (1982) reviewed research based largely on testing and factor analytical studies. She concluded that: 'If a second-order factor (or factors) were to be extracted from the results of testing, it would account nicely for the existence of a number of musical abilities in varying degrees in individuals and also for the need for an overall, co-ordinated level of efficiency for success in music whether as listener, performer, or composer.' (Given that primary factors are themselves inter-correlated, further analysis can be carried out to produce second or even third-order factors of a more general nature, which are conceived as underlying the primaries.) Stankov and Horn (1980) reported evidence for a general auditory factor, Ga, at the second-order level, derived from primary factors of relevance to music. Stankov and Horn, however, regarded Ga as being predominantly perceptual—processing information for use by higher levels of general intelligence. Impressed by the evidence that specifically musical abilities often appear very early in life, sometimes in circumstances where high intelligence would find rather little material upon which to operate, Shuter-Dyson (1981) and Shuter-Dyson and Gabriel (1981) proposed a model of musical ability which would do justice to the high cognitive requirements involved in the processing of music.

This model followed the attempt of Horn and Donaldson (1980) to reconcile the findings of cognitive psychologists with those of psychologists

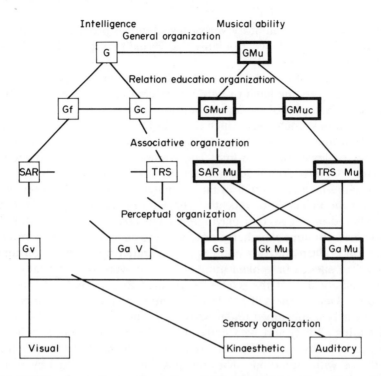

FIGURE 9.1 Diagrammatic representation of the highly talented musician. Double lines indicate an exceptional degree of ability. (Revised from Shuter-Dyson and Gabriel, 1981). G/GMu—General Intelligence/Music Ability. Gf/GMuf—General Intelligence Fluid/General Musical Ability fluid. Gc/GMuc—General Intelligence/Musical ability crystallised. SAR—Short-term Acquisition Retrieval. TSR—Tertiary Storage Retrieval. Gv—Visual perception. Ga V—Auditory perception, verbal. Gs—Perceptual Speed. GkMu—Kinaesthetic perception, music. GaMu—Auditory perception, music

interested in individual differences of intellectual functioning. Figure 9.1 shows how the model might apply to the individual with high musical talent. The connections are conceived as operating in both directions to represent, for example, the role of long-term memory in the processing of incoming musical stimuli, and various links with other intellectual abilities are also represented. Auditory acuity is part of sensory detection, although above a certain level, it does not seem to be especially related to musical talent. Indeed, cases of students making considerable headway in music in spite of being afflicted by deafness in middle childhood are not unknown (Cleall, 1983). Auditory sensory memory (pre-categorical acoustic store) has formed part of theories of speech perception (See Broadbent, 1983). Crowder, at Yale, is obtaining evidence of analogous findings with musical material, but this does not mean that efficiency at verbal processing tasks implies skill at processing music; auditory verbal tests tend to produce separate factors from musical ones. Hence, in Figure 9.1, verbal perception Ga (V) is shown as distinct from Ga (Mu).

No clear line of demarcation can be drawn between sensory and perceptual levels on the one hand or between perceptual and association levels on the other. Examples of perceptual music tasks are the Seashore, the Wing, and the Bentley pitch tests, which make only modest demands on memory. These typically ask the listener to judge whether the second of two tones is higher or lower than the first. The memory tests from the same batteries refer to short-term acquisition retrieval, though they often load highly on the same factors as pitch in factor analytical studies. All three tests are based on the principle of repeating short tunes and asking which tone has been altered on the second playing. In Deutsch's (1977) research task, the subject had to judge whether a note was the same or had been altered by a semitone, when the two notes were separated by interpolated tones, as opposed to silence or spoken numbers; errors were systematically affected by the relationship of the pitch of certain of the interpolated tones to the test tones. Deutsch herself speaks of retention of pitch information, so that this task is best subsumed under SAR. Short-term memory tasks were used by Dowling (1978) and by Cuddy et al. (1979), the subjects being asked to judge as 'same' or 'different', sequences which were transposed either exactly, or with alterations. The transpositions were affected by acculturation to the diatonic scale, implying a processing level where 'meaning' is important.

Attempts to assess long-term memory in music have usually involved the recognition of well-known tunes, often distorted in some way. Shuter-Dyson and Gabriel adopted the distinction, suggested by analogy with intelligence, between fluid and crystallized general musical ability. Fluid general intelligence is manifest in tasks that call for new solutions, is developed through incidental learning and, according to Cattell (1965), is measurable by 'culture-fair' tests. Crystallized intelligence results from the learning imparted at home, at school, and by other cultural agencies. The young child who, when picking out notes on a piano, discovers for himself the curious affinity of Middle C with lower and higher Cs, might be said to be displaying fluid musical ability. Crystallized musical ability would develop from informal and formal learning from parents and teachers.

Taking a broad definition of musical ability as a species-specific capacity to apprehend structure in sounds, we can agree with Suzuki that if a child can learn to speak his own language, he can learn music. In so far as fluid musical ability depends on incidental learning, it is a concept that could be applied to any milieu—Western, African, or Balinese. In a musical culture where tonality and harmony predominate, crystallized ability will reflect these aspects of music; in a culture where polyrhythms are important, ability will crystallize in that direction. What would constitute a measure of fluid musical ability? The Gordon Audiation Measures (see below) would seem to qualify; audiation can be described as 'inner hearing', and skill at it is a requirement for hearing syntax in music. The quality of formal achievement in either long-term or short-term music memory depends on how well one can derive immediate impressions and make intuitive responses (Gordon, 1979a, 1981). Karma (1979) is experimenting with a test based on the ability to structure acoustic material. For example, the subjects have to divide the first section of each item into three similar parts in their minds, and then decide whether the second section is similar. For his melody tests, Davies (1971) used tonal sequences based on statistical approximation to music in the equal-tempered scale, while envisaging the production of sequences based on a scale not common to any culture. Examples of tests of crystallized musical ability would be all those that claim to test achievement and 'appreciation', where the listener is required to judge which of a pair of excerpts is played as the composer intended. As in the case of intelligence, fluid and crystallized musical abilities are likely to be highly correlated and further analysis is required to produce a general factor of musical ability.

It is not clear how 'creativity' would fit into the above model, but attempts have been made to apply tests for it in music. For example, Tarratus (1964) used tests of fluency, flexibility, and originality based on those proposed by Guilford, along with an original test of humour, with 145 students at the Ohio State University. Scores on originality, the ratio of originality to fluency, humour, and the ratio of humour to fluency significantly differentiated the composers from other music students. Vaughan (1971) gave much thought to a theoretical model for creative ability in music. She developed a test scored for fluency, rhythmic security, ideation, and synthesis. Interjudge reliability indices ranged from 0.78 to 0.90 (Vaughan, 1977). Gorder (1980) produced a test requiring improvisation on short phrases, scored for fluency, flexibility, originality, and musical appeal. (See Richardson, 1983 for a useful review of creativity research in music education.) Such tests may not provide predictions of outstanding ability as a composer, but might rather be helpful for indicating the improvisation ability needed in many music careers. Improvisation is a complex skill in its own right, whether in jazz or sitar music, excellence requiring a large repertoire of procedures for accomplishing some end-result in a limited time (Sloboda, 1982).

Music depends primarily on what Drake (1939) called 'earmindedness', though the importance of kinaesthetic perception in music is well-documented. It is therefore shown on the diagram, as is visual perception, which is involved in such activities as the reading of notation and the visual cues utilized in instrumental performance. Horn (1973) found some common variance between comparable visual and auditory tests. Hidden

tunes (spotting whether or not a short melody is embedded in a more complicated one) seem the most promising test of such connections (Shuter-
Dyson and Gabriel, 1981). Barrett and Barker (1973) had some success
in finding statistically significant relationships between reproduction of single notes or melodic and rhythmic patterns, and tests of visual pattern
perception.

However, the most intriguing research from the point of view of talented children was reported by Hermelin and O'Connor (1980). They compared fourteen children with very high IQs (mean 151), fourteen musically
gifted children from the Yehudi Menuhin School (IQ range 102–130, mean
117), and a control group of fourteen children matched on IQ with the
musical group. Pairs of words and of pictures were presented on slides; the
words might be identical, or synonyms, or different in meaning. The children were required to press a 'Same' button for the identical or similar
words (or pictures) and a 'Different' button for those judged to be different. The musically gifted subjects gave significantly faster responses to
identical words than did the other two groups, but there was no significant
difference with synonyms; the musical were faster at making different judgements to unrelated words, and the controls significantly slower. In the case
of pictures, the musical children were fastest and the control group slowest.
To test whether the musically talented were fastest due to quicker reaction
times, because of their instrumental skills, a further experiment required
the children merely to press a button as soon as they saw the slide. The
control group was slower, but the other two groups did not differ significantly from each other. In a third experiment, perceptual speed at stimulus
identification was tested, words and pictures being presented by tachisto-
scope. The musical and highly intelligent groups required equal exposure
times for words and pictures, but the control children needed significantly
shorter times for pictures. Since identification of words was about equal for
all groups, the speed of the musically gifted in overall judgements could not
be accounted for by differences in reading speeds. Hermelin and O'Connor
speculated that this type of cognitive performance might be influenced by
factors of attention and motivation, but this would not explain why the
musically gifted should be more attentive to this non-musical task. Manturzewska (1979) found that the piano competitors were both better and
quicker at Raven's Matrices than were piano, musicology, or psychology
students.

It could be argued against Shuter-Dyson's emphasis on the specificity
of musical talent that success in music depends on fluid intelligence being applied to music from a very early age, in an infant possessing keen
auditory equipment and who has become 'imprinted' onto music. Thus,
Yehudi Menuhin would be viewed as an extremely bright boy with a good
ear for music, who had become enamoured with its sound in infancy. This

is indeed a possible theoretical position; he was certainly an extremely bright child, with a great interest in how things worked, and capable of considerable scientific inventiveness. On the way home from his first French lesson, he found he could remember all the words he had been set to learn. Schumann's early talents were as much literary as musical, Thomas Beecham memorized a whole act of Macbeth when he was eight, and Holst learned enough Sanskrit to be able to translate some poems he wished to set to music. How these musicians would have fared, had they taken up some different profession, it is of course impossible to say.

In general, the musical talent of outstanding musicians seems to exceed their general intellectual capacities, IQs at the Yehudi Menuhin School ranging from 93 to 166, with an average of about 130—a level which would be expected of undergraduates (Brackenbury, 1976). The young musician with the lowest IQ, who had had to have remedial teaching for reading and arithmetic, gained an award for advanced music study. Tested with an early form of the Simon-Binet scale, Erwin appeared to be at least two years in advance of his chronological age, but his intellect would hardly be on a par with his musical achievements; his conversation about music, though, suggested a more brilliant intellect. Cox (1926) estimated the intelligence of great men from biographical evidence of the activities of which they were capable at various ages. The IQs of the eleven composers included in her study ranged from 110 for Gluck and Palestrina to 150 for Mendelssohn, but as a group, the musicians were among the lowest in IQ of all the eminent persons she studied. White (1931) estimated the versatility of their abilities and interests and found them among the least versatile, perhaps through the demands of music on their time. Manturzewska (1978) reported that students at the Warsaw Academy of Music reached Percentile Rank 90 on Raven's Matrices and PR 60–70 on a Polish version of the Army General Classification Test. Cooley (1961) and Kemp (see below) both found that music students were superior in intelligence to other college students.

We can certainly agree with Seashore (1938) that in 'predicting success in musical education, we must always take intelligence into account'. However, Manturzewska (1979) suggested that there is an optimum range of intelligence (not too high, not too low) for music studies.

Personality characteristics

Kemp (1981a,b,c; 1982a,b) compared children from conservatoires, youth orchestras, and schools for the musically talented with children professing to have no musical or creative interests, using Cattell's High School Personality Questionnaire. Music students from conservatoires and universities filled in the Cattell 16PF questionnaire, and were contrasted with students with no musical interests, also, professional musicians were compared with

TABLE 9.1 Summary of results of group comparisons with the 16PF and HSPQ carried out to identify the personality profiles of secondary school, student and professional musicians, and of students and professional composers. (Adapted from A. E. Kemp 1981a and 1981b)

| | Criterion group numbers | | 16PF and HSPQ primary factors | | | | | | | | | | | | | | | | | |
| | | | Positive pole description | | | | | | | | | | | | | | | | | |
Group comparisons	m	f	A Outgoing	B More intelligent	C Emotionally stable	D Excitable	E Dominant	F Surgent	G Conscientious	H Adventurous	I Sensitive	J Individualistic	L Suspicious	M Imaginative	N Shrewd	O Apprehensive	Q1 Radical	Q2 Self-sufficient	Q3 Controlled	Q4 Tense
Secondary-school musicians vs non-musicians	259	237		*** B+			*** E−		*** G+		*** I+	*** J+						*** Q2+	*** Q3+	
Especially talented school musicians vs other school musicians	41	28	** A−			** D+				** H−		** J+				* O+				
Student musicians vs non-music students	329	359	*** A−	*** B+	*** C−			*** F−	** G+		*** I+			*** M+		** O+		*** Q2+		** Q4+

Comparison	Composers	Non-composers	Aloof	Less intelligent	Emotionally less stable	Undemonstrative	Submissive	Sober	Expedient	Shy	Tough-minded	Zestful	Trusting	Practical	Forthright	Self-assured	Conservative	Group-dependent	Undisciplined	Relaxed
Student performers *vs* other music students	118	105	A− **				E+ *		G−					M+ *			Q1+ **	Q2+ **		
Male professional musicians *vs* norms	121		A− ***	B+ ***	C− **						I+ ***		L+	M+ ****	N− ***	O+ ***	Q1+ *	Q2+ ***	Q3− **	
Female professional musicians *vs* norms	81		A− ***	B+ ***			E+ *				I+ ***			M+ ****	N− ***			Q2+ ***		Q4+ **
Male student composers *vs* non-composers	36	50	A− *				E+ **		G− **		I+ *			M+ ***	N− **		Q1+ **	Q2+ **	Q3−	
Male professional composers *vs* non-composers	28	41		B+ *			E+ *		G− **					M+ *						
Female professional composers *vs* non-composers	10	42					E+ *											Q2+ ***		

Negative pole description

***P < 0.001   **P < 0.01   *P < 0.05

norms for adults from higher socio-economic groups. Kemp (1982b) believed his results (Table 9.1) showed that all musicians possess a pattern of traits, which could be interpreted as facilitating the process of developing the motor, perceptive, and cognitive skills necessary for musical performance. Introversion, pathemia (second-order factors), and intelligence were stable traits from childhood through to professional life. The development of musicianship at certain stages appeared to be linked to additional traits that reflect temporary needs and demands.

Thus, it appeared that in childhood, superego strength and personal control (G and Q3) are required for the development of good practice habits. Among university students, superego continues to be important, but personal control is replaced by the seriousness indicated by desurgency (F−). At the adult level, where work habits are integrated into life-style, these traits become largely redundant. Anxiety appeared in the case of outstandingly gifted children (such as those from specialist music schools) in the form of excitability (D), sensitivity to threat (H−), and apprehensiveness (O). The two traits more associated with 'state' anxiety—emotional instability (C−), and ergic tension (Q4)—did not emerge until later. A comparison of males and females showed that the pattern of male anxiety (C−, L, O and Q3−) was quite different from the female one (Q4). The question of whether high levels of anxiety drive individuals to take refuge in creative activity, or whether living under a self-induced pressure gives rise to anxiety requires further research. Kemp (1981c) also noted differences in personality traits connected with instrumental performance. Singers tended to be extroverts, while instrumentalists tended more to be introverts, especially in the case of string and wood-wind players. For composers, the introversion and pathemia of the performer becomes linked with independence, subjectivity, and lower moral upbringing in the most distinctive profile of all groups of musicians. Kemp interpreted introversion in creative persons as indicating inner strength with richness and diversity of thought processes, and their independence and lower upbringing as reflecting personal autonomy and a need to break away from conventional modes of thinking. The link between the temperaments of performers and composers respectively reflects the fact that interpretation of music requires a creative temperament albeit at lower levels (Shuter, 1968). It is perhaps worth citing the words of Menuhin (1964): 'A musician above all others must be attuned to that inner voice which is audible in silence ... music demands of the musician that he listen as his work comes into being.'

Unlike the composer, the successful music teacher shows a modification of the 'musician profile' in the direction of general population norms, due to the need for down-to-earth attitudes in the classroom (Kemp, 1982c). Kemp (1982a) found sex differences in the traits related to musicianship, indicating that sex differences were eroded among musicians. Only those with a wider range of temperaments, which cut across sex-stereotyping, would seem suited to the music profession.

IDENTIFICATION OF TALENT

The correct identification of talent at the earliest possible age is put forward in the Gulbenkian report (1978) as a key issue. To stand a chance of becoming a professional violinist or pianist, the child should begin to play seriously by the age of seven or eight, while wind or brass players cannot normally afford to leave the beginning of training much later than about eleven. A high proportion of talented children come from families with some sort of musical background, so that their talent is probably nearly always spotted, but problems may arise if parents over-estimate their children's gifts. It is the talented children born into families with no particular musical or cultural background that often have to depend on class teachers, head teachers, or music advisers to seek them out. All musicians agree that the outstandingly gifted child is immediately recognizable, unmistakable, and very rare. We might indeed suppose that the talent of a Menuhin would make itself obvious, but we cannot be sure that there have been no mute inglorious Mozarts. Very possibly, it is the child with high, but not exceptional talent who is most likely to be missed.

The audition

This is the most common method of selection for musical training, and specialist music schools often employ extended audition and interview procedures. At Chetham's School of Music, Manchester, a method of selection has been developed which aims to reveal musical resourcefulness and creative responses, and to be flexible enough to suit the individual child. Brackenbury (1976), the former headmaster of the Yehudi Menuhin School, stated that what was sought there was the unequivocal musician, as revealed by a natural feeling for rhythm and pitch, and above all by evidence of an insatiable appetite for music (so that without it the child feels deprived), rather than early technical facility. However, even experienced musicians agree that it is much easier to assess attainment than potential. Even at that school, mistakes sometimes occurred and over-prepared candidates were admitted, their real inclinations coming to light only later. Payne (1980) concluded from the experience of setting up and running a junior music school in Lancashire that the judgements made by himself and his collaborators on musicality proved sound; if mistakes were made, they arose from the difficulty of assessing motivation to persist. Payne made every effort to conduct the auditions at a brisk pace, encouraging progressively more rapid and more individualized responses, although slowness of response was not regarded as necessarily indicative of slowness of perception. This type of audition tended to weed out candidates who were over-prepared.

The use of standardized tests

Auditions may be a satisfactory means of selecting potential musicians in situations where the selectors have clear ideas of what they are looking for, and the experience to recognize it. Moreover, the candidates are in some sense self-selected, in that they at least present themselves, or are induced by parents or teachers to do so. However, Ogilvie (1973) reported that a very large number of primary school teachers failed to respond to a request to record those characteristics which they thought most commonly formed the basic ability syndrome in musical activity, pointing out that 'they had neither the knowledge nor the experience of music to be able to recognize levels of ability, high or low'. Payne obtained completed questionnaires on provision for musically gifted children from local education authorities whose total school population (primary and secondary) amounted to about 3 900 000 children. While 69 per cent of the initial identification of giftedness was made by a combination of parents, teachers, and/or music advisers, 31 per cent depended on the teachers alone. The same proportion acknowledged using objective music tests, specifically the Bentley Measures.

Tests intended to be prognostic of musical aptitude have existed since 1919, when the Seashore Measures were first published. Used with an intelligence test and audition, they contributed to the entrance procedure at the Eastman School of Music, Rochester, NY. They also successfully formed part of a programme for selecting talented pupils for instrumental instruction and for helping to grade students into homogeneous groups. The Drake, the Wing, and the Bentley batteries have also proved effective at identifying children whose talents might otherwise have been overlooked. (For a detailed account of tests of musical aptitude and attainments, see George 1980, and Shuter-Dyson and Gabriel, 1981.)

All the above tests are intended for group testing, and hence for use with children old enough to cope with the answer sheets. However, Gordon (1979a,b) introduced the Primary Measures of Music Audiation (PMMA) to serve as a diagnostic aid for the strengths and weaknesses of children between five and eight; no knowledge of music, reading, or numbers is required to use the answer sheet. The child has to listen to a pair of short phrases and decide if they are the same or different. If they sound the same, he draws a circle around a picture of two same faces; if they sound different, he circles a pair of different faces. The patterns were selected on the basis of a taxonomy of tonal and rhythm patterns that had been extensively investigated for their perceptual difficulty and growth rate (Gordon, 1979a, pp. 8–9). The test is in two parts; tonal and rhythm, each requiring 15–20 minutes to administer.

Even with five-year-olds, reliability is good. Coefficients are: Tonal, 0.85–0.89 (split-halves), 0.68–0.73 (test-retest); Rhythm, 0.72–0.86 (split-halves), 0.60–0.73 (test-retest); and Composite, 0.90–0.92 (split-halves), 0.73–0.76 (test-retest). Each test item offers only two choices. However, in the norms, the guessing score (50 per cent correct) would earn only a very low percentile rank.

Gordon suggests that a percentile rank of 80 or higher on the Composite norms indicates that the child is gifted and could profit greatly from and contribute significantly to special music activities. Norton (1980) compared the PMMA and WISC scores of forty-one children with their performance of an auditory conservation task (identifying a tonal pattern when it has been rhythmically varied or a rhythm pattern when melodically varied). Nine out of the forty-one children, aged 6.6 years, were auditory conservers. Their mean IQ was 120 and percentile rank on the PMMA 89. The PMMA score, IQ and interaction of PMMA-IQ were significantly related to auditory conservation. Children of 6.6 years who are auditory conservers are likely to be musically gifted.

Then, in 1982, Gordon published the Intermediate Measures of Music Audiation (IMMA) for use with groups where a substantial number of the children have obtained exceptionally high scores on the PMMA. Unlike the PMMA, the Intermediate Measures include only patterns which were identified in research as difficult or 'not easy'. In both the tonal and the rhythm parts, six (out of forty) items are very difficult, but are placed among relatively easy questions; the answer sheets are similar to those for the PMMA. The IMMA is intended for use in grades 1–4 (ages six to nine). A 'Criterion' score, equal to a Percentile Rank of 95 or over, is to be considered indicative of exceptionally high musical aptitude. Gordon (1982) believes that instruction should be focused initially on the dimension (tonal or rhythm) on which the child has scored lower. When that is satisfactorily attended to, the dimension on which the child scored higher should be given emphasis. After some six months, Gordon recommends that the child should be retested, to see whether any adjustment in emphasis of instruction is needed. The split-halves reliability coefficients range from 0.72 to 0.78 for the tonal test, from 0.70 to 0.71 for the rhythm, and from 0.80 to 0.82 for the composite scores. Test-retest reliabilities were from 0.85 to 0.88 for the tonal, from 0.81 to 0.84 for the rhythm test, and from 0.90 to 0.91 for the composite test. A longitudinal study of individual children is being undertaken to try to establish predictive validity, but validity evidence so far available is highly promising.

Gordon emphasizes that the tests are intended to be used with discretion, as an aid to the parent and the teacher. The purpose is certainly not to exclude an interested child, even with very low scores, from participation in any type of musical activity.

However desirable it may be to recognize a child's talent early, it is also important not to stop seeking for gifted children who may be 'late bloomers' or just overlooked. Tatarunis (1981) urged music educators not to neglect cultural and ethnic minorities, where gifted children may be missed, and Karma (1982) drew attention to a type of child (with spatial ability) who is unlikely to be selected into musical instruction at an early age. A typical example is a boy who is interested in sports and/or engineering, but who has not achieved very well at school, because of lack of opportunities for using his spatial ability; he is not noticed in connection with music until his early teens, when he is found to have unexpected talent. However, one might hope that use of the PMMA would bring such children to light at an early age.

Some children who are identified as talented may show little interest in music, perhaps because their past encounters with it have been unrewarding, but the teacher may be able to discover an approach to music that is congenial to the individual. Then, success tends to foster interest. In the case of the music students questioned by Payne (1980), their first conscious interest in music occurred at around ten years six months, whereas the average age at which positive provision had been made was approximately 9.8 years. Thus, for nearly one-third of the students, interest was preceded by some form of positive provision.

ENVIRONMENTAL INFLUENCES ON TALENT

Home influences

The influence of a child's home (or substitute home in which he grows up) is literally incalculable. The child of outstanding talent is 'typically' born in a home where at least one of the parents is musical; the father may be a professional musician of no great distinction (Beethoven, Field, Holst), or the mother a gifted amateur (Chopin, Mendelssohn, Sgouros). Musicians like Schubert and Haydn grew up in families where music making at some level (Schubert would often have to point out his father's wrong notes!) was part of life. In the case of the virtuosi musicians studied by Scheinfeld (1956), 75 per cent of their fathers and 50 per cent of their mothers had some degree of musical talent, while the Juilliard students' fathers had talent in 50 per cent of cases and their mothers in 74 per cent; yet quite a few of the virtuosi reported no talent in either parent. Nor did the differences in family backgrounds or the talents of the parents seem to be related to the calibre of musicianship shown by the individual. Both the competitors and the piano students in Manturzewska's (1979) report came in 90 per cent of cases from homes with rich musical traditions, one-third of the competitors being the children of professional musicians. Payne

(1980) asked his sample of music students how much encouragement they had received at home; 89 per cent said their musical interest and activities had been encouraged at home, and only 3 per cent that they had been discouraged. The home environment was considered highly or moderately musical by 70 per cent, only 7 per cent regarded it as 'unmusical', and 29 per cent considered it 'not necessarily musical but artistically sympathetic'. On the whole, their homes appeared to be more encouraging than their schools. Shetler (1979) concluded from a survey of symphony orchestra musicians in the United States that music in the home and encouragement from parents and teachers were both of great importance. In general, the musicians had received more encouragement from their mothers than from their fathers, who tended to regard the choice of music as a career with some apprehension.

Suzuki would contend that the earlier the child can listen to music and learn to play, the better. Although his and other similar methods are undoubtedly successful in producing rapid command of instrumental performance, a correlation with a virtuoso career is not the rule (Abel-Struth, 1973). However, producing virtuosi was not Suzuki's prime aim; learning one's native language does not necessarily lead to becoming a great poet or dramatist.

Gordon (1979a) stresses the importance of the child being exposed to music so that he has the opportunity of absorbing it, adding that the most crucial time for unconscious listening is before the age of three. The child should be encouraged to sing and to engage in rhythmic activities as early as possible. The younger the child, the greater the possibility of increasing his musical powers by suitable education; by the age of nine, musical aptitude has become stabilized. During research for the development of his Musical Aptitude Profile, intended for ages nine to seventeen, Gordon (1965) found that the relative position of pupils remained the same as on an initial testing, in spite of concentrated music instruction. Wing (1968) and Bentley (1977) reported similar results. Gordon (1979b) tested two groups of children aged five to eight with the PMMA. One group, from privileged homes, attended a private school where excellent music instruction was available; the other group came from homes with limited cultural opportunities, but attended a community music school which offered individual music lessons. The scores of both groups were superior to the standardization sample norms, and the scores for the private school children were on the whole modestly superior to those made by the community music school children. Gordon suggested that the innate capacity of the private academy children was likely to be similar to that of the standardization group, so that their superior scores were due to home and school opportunities. Since attendance at the community music school was evidence of motivation to study music and possibly of higher innate capacities, this—along with good music instruction—

enabled the group to achieve superior scores in spite of their unfavourable backgrounds.

Freeman (1974) emphasized the importance of a home environment that is specifically musical. She matched twelve musically talented children of junior school age, and twelve artistically talented children with twenty-four children controlled for age, sex, social class, and intelligence. All the children were tested with the Wing Memory Test, an original test requiring the rearrangement of chime bars to produce a well-known tune (a very potent test), and a test of aesthetic discrimination. Equivalent tests of artistic abilities were also given to all the children, and the various tests confirmed the differing talents of the groups. Freeman visited the parents, and obtained replies to a detailed questionnaire. Artistic children appeared to be equally influenced by home and by school, but in the case of the musically talented children, she concluded that parental attitudes were of supreme importance, and that the influence of the home was greater than that of the school. Children in the control group who had been encouraged to try a musical instrument at school often gave up if the home was not sufficiently supportive. Manturzewska (1979) also noted a lack of music tradition in the home as a cause of dropout from music school. Excellent facilities for learning music were available in the area of Freeman's study, but the decision as to how far they were used seemed to rest with the headteacher, and some children in the control group were positively discouraged by their parents from aesthetic effort. Certain youngsters, in the tradition of Handel and Gluck, might find parental opposition a challenge. When Geoffrey Burgon's father showed no interest in his son, then in his teens, taking up the cornet, the son became all the more determined to do so.

Of the entrants to the Royal Northern College of Music, Manchester, 60 per cent came from superior socio-economic backgrounds. Zenatti (1981) also reported evidence that a rich musical environment, hence earlier acculturation to musical conventions, was associated with higher-social-class families, and considered that a battery of individual music tests for young children, which she had produced, might be a means of discovering talent among children from unfavourable backgrounds.

Provision in schools

Having identified what appears to be a musically talented child, the question arises of what should be done to educate him. 'The fundamental problem is to find a way of giving a thorough training in the art without loss to a child's general education' (Standing Conference for Amateur Music, 1966).

One of the conclusions reached in the Gulbenkian Report was that there was no automatically right answer on specialist music education. Essential requirements are opportunities for instrumental lessons, facilities for practice, opportunities for meeting and playing with other young musicians to help relieve the isolation of lone hours of practising, and ample encouragement from parents, teachers, and friends. If these needs can be met within the ordinary school system, it would have the advantage of enabling the child easily to reduce his commitment to music, if he should after all decide to pursue a different career. If he has outstanding talent, the specialist schools would seem to offer greater advantages, such as master classes by distinguished visiting musicians, and closer association with similarly gifted children who can provide stimulus and competition. However, concern about a 'hothouse atmosphere' or 'production of elites' is often expressed in relation to specialist schools. However, though such a system seems to be favoured in Eastern Europe, though there may be less pressure and publicity surrounding the launching of the young musicians' careers in those countries (Moshansky, 1978).

Ogilvie (1973) cited several case studies which confirm that the recognition and fostering of musical talent in ordinary schools are fraught with uncertainty. Very few of the music students encountered during the Gulbenkian enquiry attributed their development as performers to anything that happened to them in class music in primary school. Even if such interest and involvement has been aroused in a primary school with a good music tradition and enthusiastic teaching, the carry-over to secondary education may be disappointing (Wragg, 1974). The music students questioned by Payne (1980) were concerned by the lack of practice facilities in their schools, and especially about the status of music in the school curriculum.

A centre where children can attend on Saturdays is perhaps especially valuable in providing for children who are not wholly committed to a particular instrument and whose vocation in music is still uncertain. At such a centre, mastery of a traditional 'standard' repertoire need not be the primary aim, there being scope for jazz, avant-garde, and other forms of music. At his junior music school, for example, Payne adopted a curriculum core that stressed improvization and creative activities. A substantial number of its pupils did in fact go on to music colleges and university music departments.

Conservatoires do tend to stress the study of standard repertoires and academic traditions of composition, though this may not be the best preparation for many careers in music. Full-time practising performers make up only a small percentage of the actual numbers engaged in music-making as a career, while the only aspect of music that requires tertiary qualifications is class teaching. In the fields of popular music, in radio and TV and recording studios, it may be best to seek work as early as possible, in order to start building up a network of contacts. In these situations, it may be a considerable advantage to be a jack-of-all-trades.

To sum up, the many and complex factors involved in musical talent—
and hence in the question of why some children appear to be especially
gifted—have yet to be unravelled. Meanwhile, enough is known about the
development of musical talents to enable tests like the PMMA and the IMMA
to be used as aids in the decisions that have to be taken if such talents are
to be nurtured. The PMMA could be helpful in the musical education of
all children, and thereby eventually improve the social climate in which the
young musician must grow.

REFERENCES

Abel-Struth, S. (1973). Music in kindergarten and preschool years. *International Music Education*, ISME Yearbook I.

Barrett, H. C., and Barker, H. R. (1973). Cognitive pattern perception and musical performance. *Perceptual and Motor Skills*, **36**, 1187–1193.

Barrington, D. (1771). Account of a very remarkable musician. *Phil. Trans. R. Soc. Lond.* **60**, 54–64.

Bentley, A. (1977). International follow-up study of the Bentley 'Measures of Musical Abilities'. *Bull. Council Res. Mus. Ed.* No. 50, 6–10.

Brackenbury, A. (1976). Round the clock with gifted musicians. In *Gifted Children* (eds J. Gibson and P. Chennells), pp. 73–87, Latimer, London.

Broadbent, D. E. (Ed.). (1983) Functional aspects of human memory. *Phil. Trans. R. Soc. Lond.*, **B302**, 237–436.

Calouste Gulbenkian Foundation (1978). *Training Musicians*. London.

Cattell, R. B. (1965). *The Scientific Analysis of Personality*. Penguin, Harmondsworth.

Cleall, C. (1983). Notes on a young deaf musician. *Psychol. Music*, **11**, 101–102.

Cooley, J. (1961). A study of the relation between certain mental and personality traits and ratings of musical ability. *J. Res. Mus. Ed.* **9**, 108–17.

Cox, C. (1926). *Genetic Studies of Genius*, Vol. II, *The Early Mental Traits of Three Hundred Geniuses*. Stanford University Press, Stanford.

Cuddy, L. L., Cohen, A. J., and Miller. J. (1979). Melody recognition: The experimental application of musical scales. *Canad. J. Psychol.* **33**, 148–157.

Davies, J. B. (1971). New tests of musical aptitude. *Brit. J. Psychol.* 557–563.

Deutsch, D. (1977). Memory and attention in music. In *Music and the Brain* (eds Macdonald Critchley and R. A. Henson). Heinemann, London, pp. 95–130.

Dowling, W. J. (1978). Scale and contour: Two components of a theory of memory for melodies. *Psychol. Rev.* **85**, 341–354.

Drake, R. M. (1939). Factorial analysis of music tests by the Spearman tetrad-difference technique. *J. Musicol.* **1**, 1, 6–16.

Freeman, J. (1974). Musical and artistic talent in children. *Psychol. Music*, **2**, 1, 5–12.

George, W. E. (1980). Measurement and evaluation in musical behavior. In *Handbook of Music Psychology* (ed. D. A. Hodges). National Association for Music Therapy, Lawrence, Kansas.

Gorder, W. D. (1980). Divergent production abilities as constructs of musical creativity. *J. Res. Mus. Ed.* **28**, 34–42.

Gordon, E. (1965). *Musical Aptitude Profile Manual*. Houghton Mifflin, Boston.

Gordon, E. (1979a). *Primary Measures of Music Audiation Test Manual.* GIA, Chicago.

Gordon, E. (1979b). Developmental music aptitudes as measured by the Primary Measures of Music Audiation. *Psychol. Music,* **7**, 1, 42–49.

Gordon, E. (1981). *Tonal and Rhythm Pattern Audiation Cassettes Manual.* GIA, Chicago.

Gordon, E. (1982). *Intermediate Measures of Music Audiation.* GIA, Chicago.

Gulbenkian Report (1978). *The Arts in Schools.* Calouste Gulbenkian Foundation, London.

Hermelin, B., and O'Connor, N. (1980). Perceptual, motor, and decision speeds in specifically and generally gifted children. *Gifted Child Quarterly,* **24**, 180–5.

Horn, J. L. (1973). Theory of functions represented among auditory and visual test performances. In *Multivariate Analysis and Psychological Theory* (ed. J. R. Royce), Academic Press, London.

Horn, J. L., and Donaldson, G. (1980). Cognitive development II: Adulthood development of human abilities. In *Constancy and Change in Human Development* (eds O. G. Brim and J. Kagan). Harvard University Press, Cambridge, Mass.

Karma, K. (1979). Musical, spatial and verbal abilities. *Bull. Council Res. Mus. Ed.* No. 59, 50–53.

Karma, K. (1982). Musical, spatial and verbal abilities: A progress report. *Psychol. Music, Special Issue,* 69–71.

Kemp, A. E. (1981a). The personality structure of the musician I: Identifying a profile of traits for the performer. *Psychol. Music,* **9**, 1, 3–14.

Kemp, A. E. (1981b). The personality structure of the musician II: Identifying a profile of traits for the composer. *Psychol. Music,* **9**, 2, 67–75.

Kemp, A. E. (1981c). Personality differences between the players of string, woodwind, brass and keyboard instruments, and singers. *Bull. Council Res. Mus. Ed.* Nos. 66–67, 33–38.

Kemp, A. E. (1982a). The personality structure of the musician III: The significance of sex differences. *Psychol. Music,* **10**, 1, 48–58.

Kemp, A. E. (1982b). The personality structure of the musician IV: Incorporating group profiles into a comprehensive model. *Psychol. Music,* **10**, 2, 3–6.

Kemp, A. E. (1982c). Personality traits of successful music teachers. *Psychol. Music, Special Issue,* 72–75.

Lehman, H. C. (1953). *Age and Achievement.* Princeton University Press, Princeton, New Jersey.

Manturzewska, M. (1978). Psychology in the music schools. *Psychol. Music,* **6**, 2, 36–47.

Manturzewska, M. (1979). Results of psychological research on the progress of music practising and its effective shaping. *Bull. Council Res. Mus. Ed.* No. 59, 59–61.

Menuhin, Y. (1964). Bringing on the young musician. *The Sunday Telegraph,* 6 December, p. 13.

Moshansky, M. (1978). Practising the philosophy of constant renewal: Fou Ts'ong. *Classical Music,* 13 May, pp. 16–17.

Norton, D. (1980). Interrelationships among music aptitude, IQ, and auditory conservation. *J. Res. Mus. Ed.* **28**, 207–217.

Noy, P. (1968). The development of musical ability. *Psychoanal. Study of the Child,* **23**, 332–47.

Ogilvie, E. (1973). *Gifted Children in Primary Schools.* Macmillan Educational, London.

Payne, V. (1980). The special needs and problems of the musically gifted. M.Phil. Thesis, York University.

Revesz, G. (1925). *The Psychology of a Musical Prodigy*. Harcourt Brace, New York.

Revesz, G. (1953). *Introduction to the Psychology of Music*. Longman, Green, London.

Richardson, C. P. (1983). Creativity research in music education: A review. *Bull. Council Res. Mus. Ed.* No. 74, 1–21.

Richet, G. (1901). Note sur un cas remarquable de précocité musicale. *IV Congrès Internat. de Psychologie, Compterendu des Sciences*, 93–99, Paris.

Rubinstein, A. (1973). *My Young Years*. Jonathan Cape, London.

Scheinfeld, A. (1956). *New Heredity and You*. Chatto and Windus, London.

Seashore, C. E. (1938). *Psychology of Music*. McGraw-Hill, New York.

Sergeant, D. C. (1969). Experimental investigation of absolute pitch. *J. Res. Mus. Ed.* **21**, 3–19.

Shetler, D. J. (1979). A pilot study of the training and career experiences of symphony orchestra musicians. *International Music Education, ISME Yearbook VI*, 167–174.

Shuter, R. (1968). *The Psychology of Musical Ability*. Methuen, London.

Shuter-Dyson, R. (1981). Towards a Model of Musical Ability and its Relationship to other Abilities: Areas of Consensus and Areas of Controversy. Paper to 17th Meeting of the Society for Research in Psychology of Music and Music Education, University of Reading.

Shuter-Dyson, R. (1982). Musical ability. In *The Psychology of Music* (ed. D. Deutsch). Academic Press, New York.

Shuter-Dyson, R., and Gabriel, C. (1981). *The Psychology of Musical Ability*, 2nd edn. Methuen, London.

Simonton, D. K. (1980a). Thematic fame and melodic originality in classical music: A multivariate computer-content analysis. *J. Personal*, **39**, 206–219.

Simonton, D. K. (1980b). Thematic fame, melodic originality, and musical zeitgeist: A biographical and transhistorical content analysis. *J. Personal. and Soc. Psychol.* **38**, 972–983.

Sloboda, J. (1982). Music performance. In *The Psychology of Music* (ed. D. Deutsch). Academic Press, New York.

Standing Conference for Amateur Music (1966). *Music Centres and the Training of Specially Talented Children*. National Council of Social Service, London.

Stankov, L., and Horn, J. L. (1980). Human abilities revealed through auditory tests. *J. Educ. Psychol.* **72**, 19–43.

Stumpf, C. (1909). Akustische Versuche mit Pepito Areola. *Z. f. Angew. Psychol.* **21**, 1–11.

Tarratus, E. A. (1964). Creative processes in music and the identification of creative music students. Ph.D. Diss., Ohio State University.

Tatarunis, A. M. (1981). Exceptional programs for talented students. *Mus. Ed. J.* **68**, 3, 55–60.

UK Council for Music Education and Training (1982). *Musical Giftedness in the Primary School*. Pullen, Knebworth, Herts.

Vaughan, M. M. (1971). Music as model and metaphor in the cultivation and measurement of creative behavior in children. Ed. D. Diss., University of Georgia.

Vaughan, M. M. (1977). Musical creativity: Its cultivation and measurement. *Bull. Council Res. Mus. Ed.* No. 50, 72–77.

White, R. K. (1931). The versatility of genius. *J. Soc. Psychol.* **3**, 460–89.

Wing, H. D. (1936). Tests of musical ability in school children. Master's Diss., London University.
Wing, H. D. (1968). Tests of musical ability and appreciation. 2nd edn, *Brit. J. Psychol. Monogr. Suppl.*, No. 27.
Wragg, D. (1974). An investigation into some factors affecting the carry-over of music interest and involvement during the transition between primary and secondary education. *Psychol. Music*, **2**, 1, 13–23.
Zenatti, A. (1981). *L'Enfant et son Environnement Musical.* Issy-les-Moulineaux, EAP.

Theodore Lownik Library
Illinois Benedictine College
Lisle, Illinois 60532

The Psychology of Gifted Children
Edited by Joan Freeman
©1985, John Wiley & Sons, Ltd.

CHAPTER 10

Mathematical Gifts

D. T. E. MARJORAM AND R. D. NELSON

Mathematics is an area of intellectual activity in which children can display remarkable ability. There is a history of precocity in the childhood of many generally accepted mathematical geniuses, Pascal and Leibniz being famous examples (Lehman, 1953). The ten-year-old Gauss astonished the primary school teacher, who hoped to occupy his class in adding up the integers from 1 to 100, by quickly writing $50 \times 101 = 5050$ and saying 'There it lies.' Weirstrass, however, who began serious mathematics in his forties, is a notable exception. Though one can safely say that mathematical precocity is not a sufficient nor even a necessary condition for later achievement, these histories alone cause educators to feel a responsibility to identify and nourish early signs of talent by providing suitably qualified teachers and appropriate schemes of work (Cockcroft, 1982).

Systematic studies of gifted child mathematicians are a recent development, and the main purpose of this chapter is to describe research into the mathematical abilities, personal characteristics and aspirations of children identified as mathematically gifted. The other aim is to describe how educational systems are providing for these children.

PROFESSIONAL MATHEMATICIANS

There have been a number of important studies of professional mathematicians: by Poincaré (1952), Hadamard (1945), Aiken (1973) and Helson and Crutchfield (1970). Poincaré divided the creative process into stages— preparation, incubation, illumination, verification and explication. He also distinguished two types of mathematician—the logical (Weirstrass) and the intuitive (Riemann, Bertrand)—'The one preoccupied by logic—a Vauban besieging; a general of trench warfare ...', the other guided by intuition—'... a bold cavalryman'—who showed a marked preference for visual, geometric modes of thought. Hadamard investigated the cognitive style or primary mode of thought, of a number of eminent mathematicians: 'Practically all of them avoid not only the use of mental words, but also ... the mental use of algebraic or precise signs ... they use vague images.' Furthermore, '... the mental pictures of the mathematicians whose answers I have received are most frequently visual, but they may also be of another kind—for example, kinetic'.

The mathematical community gives pre-eminence to those whose discoveries change or develop the subject in important ways. A professional mathematician is judged, therefore, on the importance of his published work to his fellows. Though publication of original work by schoolchildren is not unknown, e.g. Youd (1970), this method of selection is hardly applicable to children at an early stage in their mathematical development. Methods of selection of the mathematically gifted include outstanding performance on conventional achievement tests, applying learned algorithms to routine problems, teacher nomination, or an outstanding score on tests of general intelligence or mathematical reasoning ability. But it is important to recognize that these measures are then identifying children as mathematically gifted by criteria which do not tap the ability to pose and solve new mathematical problems. Further research with children selected by these methods may then reflect a spectrum of abilities or characteristics related to the tests and criteria by which they were chosen in the first place.

STUDIES OF MATHEMATICAL GIFTEDNESS

The work of Krutetskii

Between 1955 and 1966, the Russian psychologist V. A. Krutetskii studied 192 children aged six to sixteen, of whom 34 were judged to be mathematically gifted. At the same time he surveyed over a hundred mathematics teachers, and collected information on a similar number of professional mathematicians and physicists. The children's cognitive processes were observed as they worked on a specially prepared series of problems, and they were also interviewed.

There were four groups of problems. The first three corresponded to Krutetskii's view of the stages in problem-solving: gathering the information to solve the problem, processing the information to obtain a solution, and retaining information about the solution. The fourth group involved specific types of ability, e.g. spatial. Though the problems involved very little taught mathematics beyond elementary arithmetic, they were non-standard, and varied in difficulty and type. Thus, some problems had multiple solutions, others involved fallacious proofs, and so on.

As a result of these studies, Krutetskii was able to describe the ways in which the mathematically gifted differed from less able children (in Bright, 1977). In summary, mathematically gifted children:

1. View the mathematical content of a problem both analytically and synthetically.
2. Are quick to generalize the content of a problem and its method of solution.
3. Exhibit curtailment when solving problems of similar type; i.e. after relatively short exposure, they come to regard certain steps in the solution as obvious and use abstracted abbreviated forms of reasoning, omitting intermediary steps.
4. Are flexible in their thinking and can change easily from one cognitive process to another even if it is qualitatively different.
5. Are not tied to techniques of solution that have been successful in the past, and can readjust when these fail (cf Luchins, 1942).
6. Look for simple, direct, elegant solutions.
7. Can easily reverse their train of thought.
8. Will investigate aspects of difficult problems before trying to solve them.
9. Tend to remember the generalized, curtailed structures of problems and their solutions.
10. Tire less when doing mathematics than in other classes.

Krutetskii noted the tendency of the gifted to prefer either visual/spatial modes of thought or a logical/analytic mode. He found three stages in the development of curtailed thinking: (a) generalization, (b) curtailed reasoning, (c) generalized, curtailed structures. Some of these characteristics can be found in the following solution to an unusual scholarship question by a gifted thirteen-year-old.

Q. Explain why the squares of odd numbers differ by a multiple of 4.
A. Odd square − odd square = (odd − odd)(odd + odd)

$$= (\text{even})(\text{even})$$

$$= \text{a multiple } 4$$

Krutetskii's findings suggest that his gifted pupils do not just have better memories and learn and work faster than their contemporaries; rather, they appear to think about mathematics in qualitatively different ways and already possess some of the problem-solving skills of adult mathematicians.

However, conventional, standardized, multiple-choice tests of mathematical achievement are unlikely to identify such characteristics, and organizers of educational provision for the gifted need to take these characteristics and their special development into account.

The Chelsea College studies

In the UK, a major enquiry into the understanding of mathematics in children aged eleven to sixteen, was carried out on a large sample ($n = 10\,000$) between 1974 and 1979 by a team at Chelsea College, University of London.

The research project (Concepts in Secondary Mathematics and Science) described hierarchies of understanding in ten topics commonly taught in the secondary school. The results were based on data from the children's written and oral solving of word problems. As they were all at school, and had therefore been taught some mathematics in ordinary classes, the highest achievers may have been demonstrating their ability to understand the teacher or text at an opportune moment, rather than any untutored innate giftedness. However, with this in mind, the type of question which the highest achievers could solve was considered to provide some insight into what makes a successful child mathematician (i.e. one successful at school mathematics).

The hierarchical results of the survey were divided into four stages of difficulty. The hardest items which formed stage four, had facilities of between 5 and 30 per cent (Hart, 1981). In order to solve a number of these, a child would need to be familiar with fractions and decimals to the extent that they are used and not avoided (Kerslake, 1983), as is the case with most children. The naive interpretations of the number operations, such as 'you can only divide smaller numbers into larger', which suffice for whole numbers, need to have been replaced by more mature concepts, so that the child can give a meaning to:

16/20 facility	12yr	13yr	14yr	15yr	
	7	11	25	36	%

For children whose only interpretation of division is that of sharing sweets between friends, the question above has no meaning and indeed 51 per cent of twelve-year-olds said that the question was 'impossible'.

The use of a letter in algebra to signify more than one numerical value distinguishes the child who is playing 'the mathematical game' from those who see a letter as an immediate (and often wasteful) replacement for a single number. The following CSMS algebra question illustrates this point.

Which is larger, $2n$ or $n + 2$? Explain.

Facility	13yr	14yr	15yr	
	4	6	10	%

(Küchemann in Hart, 1981)

Similarly, graphical questions which required the labelling with an algebraic equation of a given diagram had low facilities. In one example, the children were given the graphs of $y = 2x$, $y = 2$, $x = 2$ and $x + y = 2$. They were asked to indicate which was $y = 2x$ and to give equations for the other three:

			13yr	14yr	15yr
y	$=$	$2x$	18.8	18.2	26.9
y	$=$	2	16.7	10.3	14.3
x	$=$	2	15.2	9.8	14.0
$x + y$	$=$	2	5.9	3.9	5.1

(Kerslake in Hart, 1981)

Any question requiring the child to appreciate the infinite nature of numbers was found very difficult, e.g. 'How many different numbers could you write down which lie between 0.41 and 0.42?' All this evidence leads one to suspect that the successful child has an appreciation of the power of the mathematics within which he works and, perhaps of greater importance, luxuriates within that power rather than finding it intimidating.

Part of the work of the project 'Strategies and Errors in Secondary Mathematics' (also based at Chelsea College) was to interview some children thought by their teachers to be outstanding at mathematics. The comments of these were illuminating when they solved problems in 'proportion', as their flexibility and confidence in the use of fractions could be seen, even if their strategies were not teacher-taught.

Question: In a recipe for 8 people, half a pint of cream is needed. How much is needed for 6 people?

Facility	13yr	14yr	15yr	
	24	23	31	%

For example, one bright girl answering this question argued that one needed the fraction that came between a half and one-quarter, and managed to find it. This argument is used by many children, but the less successful opt for one-third for the answer, reasoning that the denominator between the 4 of one-quarter and the 2 of one-half is three. The girl was told 'Lots of children tell me the answer is one-third. What is wrong with that?' She replied, 'It's not right. What you need is the fraction that comes exactly in the middle between those two.'

Study of Mathematically Precocious Youth

This study (SMPY) is based at Johns Hopkins University and began officially in 1971. Its aims are to identify, study, and provide education for children who initially are in the first two years of junior high school, i.e. between 12 and 14 years of age. The instrument of selection is the mathematics section of the pre-college Scholastic Aptitude Test (SAT), which is designed to test the developed mathematical reasoning ability of older pupils (aged sixteen to eighteen), and has a top score of 800. Stanley and his co-workers used a score of 600 or more on SAT-M (maths) as their criterion of mathematical precocity. Thirteen year-olds achieving such scores are on a par with the top 11 per cent of high-school seniors, and are claimed to be in 'the upper half of one per cent of the distribution of developed mathematical talent in their age group' (Stanley et al., 1974). This is approximately the same percentage as the high IQ group who formed the basis for Terman's high IQ studies (1925–1959). For non-USA readers, it may be helpful here to say that roughly 5 per cent of English children attempt and pass the 18+ Advanced Mathematics Examination, and that about one in five (1 per cent) achieve the highest grade (A) in that examination.

Why did SMPY use SAT-M as its main criterion? 'We wanted to find youths who, at an early age (mostly 12 or 13), were already able to reason extremely well with simple mathematical facts ... we did not want scores to depend much on rote knowledge of mathematical knowledge or computational ability' (Stanley et al., 1977). Another reason was the belief that students with such accurate and swift reasoning powers would be capable of taking the intended educational provision—namely radical acceleration through the high-school curriculum.

The setting and rules of the talent searches have tended to attract able students who liked competition, and the entrants are regarded as being in the top 2 per cent of their age-group in mathematical reasoning ability.

Keating (in Stanley et al., 1974) reports studies of the 450 entrants for the 1972 talent search, 35 of whom were high scorers on SAT-M, and invited back for further testing. This group (all boys) will be referred to as the 'high group'. They also obtained high mean scores in tests of verbal ability, non-verbal reasoning, and spatial ability. Asked to rate their 'liking for school', the higher the boys' scores, the lower their reported level of 'liking for school'.

No statistically significant differences due to sibling position were found, though in the 'high group', those who were second-born had the highest mean for aptitude and achievement in mathematics. The relation between reported level of parents' education and children's test scores followed the standard pattern: the higher the level of education, the higher was the mean of the test scores of the children. However, there were noteworthy variations, with some of the 'high group' coming from homes which had low levels of formal education.

An attempt was made to assess the 'high group's' evaluative attitudes, using Spranger's classification of interests, into six types: theoretical, economic, aesthetic, social, political, and religious. One of the reasons for this was to see whether these gifted children had attitudes resembling Mackinnon's (1962) classic pattern of Theoretical-Aesthetic for eminent creative scientists. As would be expected, the theoretical value was usually the highest for members of this group. On the other hand, the aesthetic value was not particularly prominent in this group, and five of the thirty-five boys exhibited MacKinnon's 'classic' pattern. Interpretation of this result is difficult, however.

Another interesting study of the personality characteristics of 216 boys and girls who had been rated as highly gifted, able, or average in mathematical ability was by Solano (1983). She concludes that 'mathematically gifted and able boys are much alike in self-esteem and self-concept. Mathematically gifted and able girls are very much like equally able boys in self-esteem and self-concept'.

Benbow and Stanley (1980, 1983) have reported that large sex differences in mean scores on SAT-M were obtained by the gifted young children entering the Johns Hopkins Regional Talent searches since 1972. For their 1983 report, they used a group of 19 883 males and 19 937 females, drawn partly from the Middle Atlantic Region and partly via a national talent search open to any gifted pupil under the age of thirteen. The mean sex difference on SAT-M was 30 points—male mean = 416, female mean = 386, with respective standard deviations of 87 and 74; mean scores in verbal ability were almost equal. These results are consistent with their 1980 findings, and the authors drew particular attention to the ratio of males to females among the high scorers. For those scoring 600 or more in the regional search, the ratio was 4.1:1. In the national search, the ratio for those scoring 700 or more was 13:1.

Sex differences in mathematical performance vary with the type of mathematics being tested and with the age of testing. Thus, girls tend to be significantly better at computational tasks, whereas boys are more successful in application and problem-solving. Also a pattern of development in which a superiority of girls over boys in mathematical attainment in the primary years is transformed into superiority, increasing with age, of boys over girls in the secondary years is consistent with most studies (Maccoby and Jacklin, 1975; APU, 1980, 1982). Male superiority, increasing with age, in tests of spatial ability— the ability to perceive relations in space and visualize objects in three dimensions—is generally accepted (MacFarlane Smith, 1964; Maccoby and Jacklin, 1975), but the relationship between spatial ability and mathematics is not clear-cut (Blackwell, 1940). Explanations of sex differences in spatial ability are divided between the 'innate' (e.g. brain lateralization) and the 'environmental' (e.g. differential play experience). Another group of explanations of sex differences in mathematical performance centres on the social reinforcement of gender roles (Walden and Walkerdine, 1982).

The results of Benbow and Stanley with gifted students are of interest because they appear to cast doubt on 'socialization' as an explanation of sex differences for their students. 'It is not obvious how social conditioning could affect mathematical reasoning ability so adversely and significantly, yet have little detectable effect on stated interest in mathematics, the taking of maths courses during the high school years before SAT's are normally taken, and mathematics course grades.'

These studies can be criticized on the grounds that the search procedure may have been more successful in locating highly talented boys than girls. It should also be recalled that performances of twelve-year-olds are being compared on a single test, designed to measure developed mathematical reasoning ability of students aged sixteen and seventeen.

In a footnote to their 1983 paper, Benbow and Stanley report a high incidence of left-handedness and immune disorders among the high scorers in their study. Earlier work on left-handedness by Geschwind and Behan (1982) had found elevated frequencies of immune diseases in left-handed individuals and their relatives, and Geschwind has advanced the hypothesis that a major influence is asymmetrical development of the left and right cerebral hemispheres, caused by excess secretion of testosterone *in utero* . Testosterone not only retards neuronal development in the left hemisphere, but also affects immune development; the effect is more pronounced in males, since the foetal testes secrete large amounts of testosterone. Since right cerebral dominance is associated with greater spatial ability, this hypothesis is of considerable interest to those investigating 'innate' explanations of sex differences in mathematics.

MATHEMATICS AND MUSIC

Music is often strongly connected with exceptional ability in mathematics. However, it only seems to function in one direction, so that whereas mathematicians often relax with music, few musicians do mathematics for fun. Indeed, Revesz (1953) found that only 9 per cent of professional musicians had mathematical talents or interest in mathematics, though his survey of 500 Dutch and other mathematicians revealed significant musical bias among them. Shuter (1968) suggested that though their potential may well be equivalent, children's relatively poor uptake of music, when compared with mathematics, is due to practical reasons such as the time it takes in practice and the lack of opportunity.

Correlations between musical and mathematical tests are, however, modest, and Wing (1954) in his researches into musical ability, thought that even this could be attributed to common factors of memory, attention or general ability. However, the musical tests at their present stage of development, still have considerable room for improvement in both validity and reliablity, though of the maths tests, Whellams (1970) found that the algebra component was the most discriminatory measure of musical ability among the non-music tests. In Manturzewska's (1978) comparison of the 10 per cent most successful and the 10 per cent poorest students at an academy of music, the good students were especially distinguished by their high scores on the scientific and mechanical scales of the Kuder Preference record. It is possible, as Howes (1958) has suggested, that the connection is in the facility to think and feel in formal patterns of measurable units and relations, which could describe a sonata movement as well as mathematicizing, e.g. the clear harmony and counterpoint patterns which in the work of J. S. Bach, can all be recorded and analysed in mathematical form

IDENTIFYING MATHEMATICALLY GIFTED CHILDREN

Bright mathematical children sometimes show their early disposition in a liking for numbers and number games. They enjoy counting so much that they may count almost compulsively, remarking on the patterns in numbers of all kinds— on bus tickets, car registration plates, telephone numbers, etc. This delight in figures often takes on a personal meaning for the mathematical child, drawing him or her to prefer and enjoy certain numbers, while finding others unattractive. Very young children may show a fascination for shapes, jigsaws, spatial puzzles, patterns and designs, ever seeking arithmetical ideas, acquiring a precocious concept of the cardinality of numbers and a taste for rigorous thought.

The small but growing literature about mathematically gifted children already contains a variety of methods of identification. Straker (1983) has a checklist of behavioural characteristics of such pre-school or infant children:

—a liking for numbers, including use of them in stories and rhymes;
—an ability to argue, question and reason using logical connectives: if then, so, because, either, or ...;
—pattern-making revealing balance or symmetry;
—precision in positioning toys, e.g. cars set out in ordered rows, dolls arranged in order of size;
—use of sophisticated criteria for sorting and classification;
—pleasure in jig-saws and other constructional toys.

By contrast, to select bright children aged six to eight, Sawyer (1980) used

Passalong, a set of tests described by Alexander (1932). Each test is a geo-metrical puzzle, requiring determination and spatial skills for its solution.

The Johns Hopkins researchers used the standardised SAT-M test to iden-tify exceptional twelve-year-olds for study. In the UK, the annual National Mathematics Contest has been entered by some of the ablest young math-ematicians, aged fourteen to eighteen, in the country. The 90-minute test paper comprises around twenty items, restricted in content to elementary geometry, algebra and arithmetic, but requiring skill and ingenuity for their solution. High scorers in this contest are invited to compete in the British Mathematical Olympiad.

Problem-solving

A common feature of checklists of characteristics, and tests of mathematical giftedness is that they look for expertness in problem-solving, so that re-cent work on mathematical problem-solving appears relevant to the present discussion. The following account is highly simplified.

In general, a mathematical problem will need translation into strictly mathematical terms and then solution. The former process will require lin-guistic knowledge and general knowledge; the solution may require knowl-edge of problem types, implementation of algorithms and strategic knowl-edge, e.g. setting sub-goals, working backwards.

What distinguishes the expert from the novice? One answer appears to be that experts in a specific problem area have made routine for themselves many aspects which require creative problem-solving from novices. Though this has been informally observed of mathematicians, the best documented area is chess, where it is estimated that masters have stored something of the order of 50 000 configurations of chessmen, together with appropriate responses (de Groot, 1965; Chase and Simon, 1973; Simon and Gilmartin, 1973). In the same way, a mathematician has, for example, a repertoire of immediate responses when faced with a configuration, such as:

$$x^2 + 2x - 8 \qquad \text{viz. quadratic expression}$$
$$\text{sketch graph}$$
$$(x + 1)^2 - 9$$
$$(x + 4)(x - 2)$$
$$x(x + 2) - 8$$

Secondly, experts differ by planning their solutions. Thus, Larkin et al. (1980) found that when experts were presented with elementary problems in kinematics, (a) they tended to classify the type of problem being asked, and find a procedure for solving it before making calculations, and (b) liked to combine groups of procedures into single procedures when completing the solution. The latter might be termed 'instant curtailment'.

Thirdly, Polya (1968) and Schoenfield (1980) have described how experts call on a range of general problem-solving techniques in mathematics. Polya illustrated many of these general strategies or heuristics in terms of elementary mathematical problems.

The implications for the education of gifted young mathematicians are, firstly, that they need to acquire a large amount of mathematical knowledge—'there is no basis in current scientific knowledge for changing our present policy of intensive disciplined training for individuals who aspire to make creative changes in the domains in which they choose to work' (Greeno, 1980). Secondly, they need to develop general problem-solving strategies that can be applied to their mathematical knowledge.

There is a long history of attempts to teach general problem-solving skills (Mayer, 1983). While it is found that problem-solving programmes often improve performance on problems similar to those in the programme, there is only limited evidence of transfer to dissimilar problems. However, Schoenfield (1979, 1980) and Thornton (1978) have reported success in teaching heuristics that are directly related to mathematical problem-solving, and this seems a fruitful area for the development of the mathematics curriculum of able students.

Finally, a number of writers, such as Krutetskii (1976), Getzels (1981, 1982), and Sternberg (1982) have made a case for giving gifted mathematicians and scientists adequate training and opportunity to find and pose problems. Getzels points out that an important part of research is the framing of initial questions (see also Chapter 22).

PROVISION

While most non-selective schools have special curricula for their abler children, it is unusual to find special programmes for children in the top 1 per cent of mathematical ability. Even in a large school, there may be only one or two children of this ability in each year-group. Streaming by mathematical ability has long been advocated and used, but this goes only part of the way to giving the exceptional child challenging work. A recent survey in the UK found only 4 per cent of secondary schools making special provision in the first three years (DES, 1980).

At a time when many countries find it difficult to attract highly qualified mathematicians into school teaching, one of the most important findings of the British HMI report, *Gifted Children in Middle and Comprehensive Schools* (1977) was that the most effective teachers of the ablest children were those who were enthusiastic, still learning, and intellectually active themselves. The absence of such teachers is notable in this extract from Greitzer's (1975) report on the Sixteenth Mathematical Olympiad:

'During our training session, we asked the 24 students involved where and how they obtained their mathematical competence. Overwhelmingly they said they learned in spite of school. In some cases they learned by being in contact with other gifted students, in a mathematics team or club, or by having access to a college library. Guidance was minimal or absent. The training session was the first opportunity for many of the students to learn about some facets of mathematics and mathematical proof. In only one case did a participant mention an enthusiastic teacher, and in no case was an innovative curriculum mentioned.'

'Enrichment' of the curriculum is often advocated for exceptional pupils, and is termed 'in depth' or 'in breadth'. In the former case, the pupil is given more difficult problems on a topic than the rest of the class, and in the second case, the gifted pupil tackles topics outside the standard syllabus sequence. Teachers do not always find it easy to provide enrichment material of their own, nor is it a standard ingredient in published textbooks or individualized learning schemes. However, subject teaching journals often contain useful ideas. For example, in France, the regions of Poitiers, Limoges, Orleans, and Tours have for some years published a bulletin for their mathematics teachers (PLOT 1977, 1979). Each bulletin contains descriptions of some new school project, competition, or teaching idea recently tried in one of the region's schools. In Britain, the publications of the Spode Group (1982), though not specifically prepared for the exceptional pupil, are a valuable source of enrichment material; a comprehensive survey of sources of enrichment material available in the UK is given by Straker (1983).

Another approach is to 'accelerate' by either omitting a year, or by working through the normal syllabus at a faster rate. An account of the provision by Johns Hopkins University of 'radical acceleration' for selected pupils is given in Stanley (1977). The children attend fast-paced classes which work through the normal high school syllabus at speed; use is made of Saturday classes, summer schools and college courses. Some of these pupils have then graduated from university at seventeen and eighteen years. The emphasis of this approach is on working in a homogeneous class under a teacher, rather than on self-paced individualised learning.

Instances of published courses for children of exceptional ability are rare. An American scheme for children aged thirteen to eighteen, called 'Elements of Mathematics', was sponsored by the National Institute of Education. These texts are used with two projects for mathematically gifted children in the United States: The Gifted Maths Programme at the State University of New York, and Mathematics Education for Gifted Secondary School Students based at St Louis, Missouri. In both cases, children attend special courses away from their schools in place of normal mathematics classes; for detailed accounts of this work, see Krist and Rising (1981) and Kaufman, Fitzgerald and Harpel (1981).

In England, the school mathematics curriculum has allowed the gifted mathematician to accelerate and enrich at secondary level by taking courses in Additional Mathematics (which includes calculus) rather than Mathematics at sixteen, and Further Mathematics as well as Mathematics as Advanced-level subjects at eighteen. Both these accelerated courses contain more advanced material, but also require deeper study of the standard mathematics curriculum. In selective schools, these courses can be taught in special fast-paced sets, but in non-selective schools it is not always possible to find sufficient children to run accelerated courses of this kind. Further provision for the exceptional child at Advanced level is made in the form of 'special' papers in Mathematics and Further Mathematics. These contain harder questions on the normal syllabus and questions on more advanced topics.

Extra-curricular provision has generally been in the form of contests or lectures; the National Mathematics Contest (University of London), for example, has proved very popular since its introduction twenty years ago, and there have been parallel developments at local and regional level. Universities and polytechnics arrange lectures and events for sixth-formers, and also provide speakers for school maths clubs. The Royal Institution runs a series of mathematics master classes in London, and these have been followed by similar developments elsewhere. For activities in Scotland see Hunter (1980).

CONCLUSIONS

We began this chapter with creative mathematicians and it is appropriate to end by asking whether, amidst the evident concern for and activity on behalf of mathematically gifted children, we are doing enough in our classrooms, in our school prize-givings and regional contests to encourage and reward creative, independent work by these children. The energy and enthusiasm given to computer-program creation (Fletcher, 1983) and design and technology projects will perhaps encourage the mathematical community to reward and publish more 'original' work by schoolchildren than it does at present. As Sawyer (1983) has said: 'One of the main aims in educating the gifted ... is not to keep children dependent on information communicated by a teacher, but rather to teach them to read, to use libraries, to seek out sources of information for themselves.'

REFERENCES

Aiken, L. R. (1973). Ability and creativity in mathematics. *Review of Educational Research*, **43**, 4, 405–32.

Alexander, P. (1932). *British Journal of Psychology*, **23**, 52–63.

Assessment of Performance Unit: Department of Education and Science (1980,

1982). *Mathematical Development: Primary Survey Report No. 1. Mathematical Development: Secondary Survey Report No. 3*, HMSO, London.

Benbow, C. P., and Stanley, J. C. (1980). Sex differences in mathematics ability: fact or artifact?. *Science*, **210**, 1262–1264.

Benbow, C. P., and Stanley, J. C. (1983). Sex differences in mathematical reasoning ability: more facts. *Science*, **222**, 1029–1031.

Blackwell, A. M. (1940). A comparative investigation into the factors involved in the mathematical ability of boys and girls. *British Journal of Educational Psychology*, **10**, 4, 143–153 and 212–222.

Bright, G. S. (1977). Critique and Analysis of 'The psychology of mathematical abilities in school children'. *Investigations in Mathematics Education*, **10**, 2, 43–47.

Chase, W. G., and Simon, H. A. (1973). Perception in chess. *Cognitive Psychology*, **4**, 55–81.

Cockcroft, W. H. (1982). Report of the Committee of Inquiry into the teaching of mathematics in schools. *Mathematics Counts*. HMSO, London.

de Groot, A. D. (1965). *Thought and Choice in Chess*. Mouton, The Hague.

Department of Education and Science (1977). *Gifted Children in Middle and Comprehensive Schools*. HMSO, London.

Department of Education and Science (1980). *Aspects of Secondary Education in England: Supplementary Information on Mathematics*. HMSO, London.

Fletcher, T. J. (1983). Microcomputers and mathematics in schools. Department of Education and Science Discussion Paper, London.

Geschwind, N., and Behan, P. (1982). Left-handedness: Association with immune disease, migraine and developmental learning disorders. *Proc. Nat. Acad. Sci.* **79**, 5097–5100.

Getzels, J. W. (1981). Problem finding and the nature and nurture of giftedness. In *Gifted Children: Challenging their Potential* (ed. A. H. Kramer). Trillium Press, New York.

Getzels, J. W. (1982). The problem of the problem. In *New Directions for Methodology for Social and Behavioural Science: Question Framing and Response Consistency*, No. 11. Jossey-Bass, San Francisco.

Greeno, J. G. (1980). Trends in the theory of knowledge for problem solving. In *Problem Solving and Education: Issues in Teaching and Learning*. Erlbaum, Hillsdale, New Jersey.

Greitzer, S. L. (1975). The 16th International Olympiad and some implications. *Mathematics Teaching*, **5**, 68.

Hadamard, J. (1945). *The Psychology of Invention in the Mathematical Field*. Princeton University Press, Princeton.

Hart, K. M. (1981). *Childrens' Understanding of Mathematics, 11–16*. Murray, London.

Helson, R., and Crutchfield, R. S. (1970). Mathematicians: The creative researcher and the Ph.D. *Journal of Consulting and Clinical Psychology*, **34**, 2, 250–57.

Howes, F. (1958). *Music and its Meanings*. Three lectures given at the University of London, referenced in Shuter, R. (1968).

Hunter, J. (1980). Mathematically gifted children — the Scottish scene. *Bulletin IMA*, **16**, 45.

Kerslake, D. (1983). *Avoidance of Fractions*. Paper given at AERA, Montreal.

Kaufman, B., Fitzgerald, J., and Harpel, J. (1981). *MEGSS in Action*. Cemrel Inc., 3120 59th Street, St Louis, Missouri.

Krist, B. S., and Rising, G. R. (1981). The gifted maths program for secondary students at the State University of NY at Buffalo. Paper delivered at 4th World Conference on Gifted Children in Montreal.

Krutetskii, V. A. (1976). *The Psychology of Mathematical Abilities in School Children.* University of Chicago Press, Chicago.

Larkin, J. H., McDermott, J., Simon, D. P., and Simon, H. A. (1980). Expert and novice performance in solving physics problems. *Science*, **208**, 1335–1342.

Lehman, H. C. (1953). *Age and Achievement.* Princeton University Press, Princeton.

Luchins, A. S. (1942). Mechanisation in problem solving. *Psychological Monographs*, **54:6**Whole No. 248.

Maccoby, E. E., and Jacklin, C. N. (1975). *The Psychology of Sex Difference.* Stanford University Press.

MacFarlane Smith, I. (1964). *Spatial Ability.* University of London Press, London.

MacKinnon, D. W. (1962). The nature and nurture of creative talent. *American Psychologist*, **17**, 484–95.

Manturzewska, M. (1978) Psychology in the music school. *Psychology of Music*, **6**, 36–47.

Mayer, R. E. (1983). *Thinking, Problem Solving, Cognition.* W. H. Freeman, New York.

PLOT (1977; 1979). *Bulletin des Régionales APMEP de Poitiers, Limoges et Orléans et Tours.* Université de Orléans.

Poincaré, H. (1952). *Science and Method.* Dover, New York.

Polya, G. (1968). *Mathematical Discovery*, Vol. II, *On Understanding, Learning and Teaching Problem Solving.* Wiley, New York.

Revesz, G. (1953). *Introduction to the Psychology of Music.* London, Longmans.

Sawyer, W. W. (1980). Identifying very bright eight year-olds. *Bulletin IMA*, **16**, 51.

Sawyer, W. W. (1983). Some thoughts on education and mathematics. *Gifted Education International*, **1**, 65–69.

Schoenfield, A. H. (1979). Explicit heuristic training as a variable in problem solving performance. *Journal for Research in Mathematics Education*, **10**, 173–187.

Schoenfield, A. H. (1980). Teaching problem-solving skills. *American Mathematical Monthly*, **82**, 10.

Shuter, R. (1968). *The Psychology of Musical Ability.* Methuen, London.

Simon, H. A., and Gilmartin, K. A. (1973). A simulation of memory for chess positions. *Cognitive Psychology*, **5**, 29–46.

Solano, C. H. (1983). Self-concept in mathematically gifted adolescents. *Journal of General Psychology*, **108**, 33–42.

Stanley, J. C., Keating, D., and Fox, L. (1974). *Mathematical Talent: Discovery, description and development.* John Hopkins University Press, Baltimore.

Stanley, J. C., George, W. C., and Solano, C. H. (1977). *The Gifted and the Creative.* Johns Hopkins University Press, Baltimore.

Sternberg, R. J. (1982). Teaching scientific thinking to gifted children. *Roeper Review*, **4**, 4, 4–6.

Straker, A. (1983). *Mathematics for Gifted Pupils.* Schools Council Publication, London.

Terman, L. M. (1925). *Genetic Studies of Genius.* Stanford University Press, Stanford.

The Spode Group (1982). *Solving Real Problems with Mathematics.* Vol. 1. CIT Press, Bedford.

Thornton, C. A. (1978). Emphasising thinking strategies in basic fact instruction.

Journal for Research in Mathematics Education, **9**, 214–227.

Walden, R., and Walkerdine, V. (1982). *Girls and Mathematics: The Early Years.* University of London Institute of Education, London.

Whellams, F. S. (1970). The relative efficiency of aural-musical and non-musical tests as predictors of achievement in instrumental music. *Bulletin of the Council of Research and Education in Music.* **21**, 15–21.

Wing, H. D. (1954). Some applications of test results to education in music. *Brit. J. Educ. Psychol.* **24**, 161–170.

Youd, N. (1970). An original solution of a problem in calculus. *Mathematical Spectrum.* **3**, 17–21.

The Psychology of Gifted Children
Edited by Joan Freeman
©1985, John Wiley & Sons, Ltd.

CHAPTER 11

Social Giftedness and its Relationship with Intellectual Giftedness

KIPPY I. ABROMS

Psychological literature has flirted with the notion of social giftedness for almost a century. The earliest measure of intelligence, the Binet-Simon Scale produced in 1905, covered many areas of cognitive functioning, some of which may be viewed as rudimentary measures of social giftedness, and are still found in the 1972 Stanford-Binet Intelligence Scale. There are, for example, the components used to assess perception of people. At the age of five, children are presented with paired drawings of faces, and are asked, 'Which is the prettiest?', while children aged seven are asked to identify the missing parts of a human-figure drawing.

Freud used the term 'menschenkenner' for people who were notably good at perception of people, but was not specific about the make-up of this ability. Michael Argyle (1971), from his work on non-verbal communication, has suggested that social intelligence is similar in nature to skills in social interaction, though he too seems to be more concerned with its outcomes than its make-up.

A more direct approach to the phenomenon of social giftedness came in Hunt's (1928) George Washington University Social Intelligence Test, designed to tap 'the ability to deal with people' (in Strang, 1930). It had six sub-tests—Judgement in Social Situations; Memory for Names and Faces; Recognition of Mental States from Facial Expression; Observation of Human Behaviour, with elicited knowledge of motives prompting behaviour; Social Information, with knowledge of things such as magazines, movies, cars, and sports; and Recognition of the Mental States Behind Words. Hunt found that 'those who are most adept at the recognition of emotional states from the face are adept at recognizing them also from the word'. More recently, Davitz (1964) found that facial expression was more informative about another's emotional state than verbal description.

Hunt's data suggested that social intelligence is developmental until about the age of seventeen or eighteen. Both social and abstract intelligence scores were found to be equally good predictors of academic success among college entrants, especially where both scores were high, but not when abstract intellectual ability was poor. However, Hunt doubted whether paper and pencil tests could ever be reliable indicators of the functional, real-life aspects of social intelligence.

Since then, the term 'social intelligence' has been largely supplanted by 'psychosocial intelligence' or 'social giftedness'. In this chapter, the construct of social giftedness is examined in terms of social cognition, prosocial behaviour, moral reasoning and leadership. Social development in these areas is compared between intellectually and non-intellectually gifted children.

SOCIAL COGNITION

Social cognition is the way an individual perceives other people and comes to understand their thoughts, emotions, intentions, and viewpoints (Shantz, 1975). This social role-taking, an ability to 'stand in another's shoes', can be considered the converse of Piaget's conception of egocentrism (Piaget and Inhelder, 1969).

Visual perspective taking

This is a facet of social cognition which involves inferring another's visual experience. In its most basic form, it can be observed by the age of three (Masangkey et al., 1974; Fishbein et al., 1972; Lewis and Fishbein, 1969; Walker and Gollin, 1977; Zahn et al., 1977; Flavell et al., 1968).

Tasks involving visual perspective were given to twenty three-year-olds, with a mean IQ of 134 (Abroms and Gollin, 1980). Each child was shown a picture on a card and asked—'See this picture ... is it a picture of a man or a lady? Now, put it so that the man is looking at me.' Using another card, the child was asked—'Do you see the clown with the smiling face or the clown with a frowning face?' When the child had answered correctly, the experimenter switched the sides of the stimulus card and asked, 'Do you see the smiling face or the frowning face?' and 'Do I see the smiling face or the frowning face?' Though the brightest children had scored well on this test when they entered nursery school, eight months later, there was an even closer relationship between their perceptual and intellectual levels. The brightest three-year-olds had improved their visual perception scores, were more self-assured in their awareness, and better able to express themselves.

However, a similar study by Kennedy (1979) with nineteen four- and five-year-olds found that, whatever their intellects, older children were better at visual role-taking skills, and she suggested that this ability was identifiable in developmental stages.

Conceptual perspective taking

This is an aspect of social cognition—being aware of another person's wants, needs, ideas, thoughts, knowledge, and preferences. Flavell *et al.* (1968) created a 'birthday task' to explore this area. Children aged three to six years old were asked to predict what someone else would like as a birthday present, rather than what the subject might choose for himself. Each child was presented with an array of objects and asked to select a birthday present for each of his or her parents, siblings, and teachers. Choices were judged as role-appropriate on the basis of age and gender. Three-year-olds disregarded both the age and gender of the intended recipient, four- and five-year-olds' choices represented a type of transitional level, and all the six-year-olds made appropriate role responses. Among the intellectually gifted three-year-olds in the Abroms and Gollin (1980) study, conceptual and visual perspective taking scores were strongly related to each other ($r = 0.9197$), i.e., these bright little ones made correct choices in most cases.

Conceptual perspective taking also implies the development of an understanding of gender. In a study of gifted three- and four-year-olds, Miller *et al.* (1978) found a strong positive relationship between the development of gender concept and cognitive development. When matched for age, children with IQs of 130 or above were correct significantly more often than those with IQs of less than 130 on the answers to gender constancy items.

Employing Piaget's ideas of conservation, Jordan (1980) examined the understanding of kinship among five- to seven-year-old intellectually gifted children, with the following procedures:

1. Conservation of Single-Kinship Roles consisted of posing questions involving time, e.g. 'When two boys grow up, are they still brothers? Here is Susan, who is seventeen years old: is she still a daughter on her birthday ten years from now, when she is twenty-seven years-old?'
2. Conservation of Multiple-Kinship Roles used six logical (inclusive) and six illogical (exclusive) kinship pairs. Examples of the former include mother–daughter, brother–son, sister–mother, while exclusive kinship pairs included daughter–father, sister–son, mother–brother. Responses were elicited by asking questions about dolls which had been given kinship roles, e.g. 'These dolls are mothers and these are daughters. This mother also wants to be a daughter. Can a mother be a daughter at the same time?' (Jordan, 1980).

3. Conservation of Kinship-Social Roles contained three conventional and
   three unconventional kinship social pairs, e.g. father–doctor vs father–
   nurse. Cardboard stick figures, ambiguous as to sex, were again used
   as role models in questioning the children.

By the age of five, the children had reached their highest level on exclusive kinship roles, probably because they were sensitive to the fact that it
was logically impossible for both roles to occur at once, e.g. 'brother–sister'.
However, regardless of sex, by the age of five, the children were aware of
their membership in child and sibling roles over time-spans, and conservation of inclusive pairs was still improving at the age of seven. A significant
age effect, both mental and chronological, was found among all the tasks except exclusive kinship roles. According to Jordan's review of the literature,
this sample demonstrated precocious kinship conservation, with the unexpected finding that higher levels of role-taking were found among gifted
girls than gifted boys. Both this study of Jordan's and Abroms' (1982a) observations of gifted preschoolers engaged in kinship role play, offer further
indications that young gifted children go through similar stages of mental
processing as other children—but much more quickly.

Affective perspective taking

This is understanding how the other is feeling, which involves inferring
another person's emotional state. Much of the data on affective perspective taking comes from measures similar to Borke's (1971) Interpersonal
Perception Test, which consists of twenty-three situational stories (half accompanied by a descriptive picture), in which a youngster may be perceived
as happy, sad, angry, or afraid. Four cards with faces which depict each of
these emotions are presented to the child, who is asked to point to the one
which shows best how the child in the story might feel. Borke found that
by the age of three, American children were able to differentiate between
happy and unhappy responses, and that the perception of anger and fear
increased between the ages of three and five.

In 1973, Borke published the results of a cross-cultural study, using her
test with American and Chinese three-year-olds, and found that happy situations were easily recognized by both groups. In the identification of fearful situations, middle-class Chinese children proved to be not only more
accurate than lower-class Chinese children, but were more advanced than
middle- and lower-class American chidren. Chinese children aged three and
four were also more accurate than American children of the same age in
identifying sad situations. The recognition of fear and sadness appeared to
be not only a function of age, but also of socialization. Among the upper-
middle-class sample of Caucasian preschoolers in the Abroms and Gollins

study (1980), females performed better than males on the Borke test; also, children of parents rated low in strictness tended to perform better on this test.

Piaget and Inhelder (1969) have described how egocentrism is so pervasive among young children that it showed itself in a number of 'contents', i.e. spatial representation, moral judgment, communication skills, concepts of relational words, etc. However, the studies of young gifted children presented here challenge this notion and suggest that gifted youngsters 'decentre', in Piaget's terms, i.e. take a broader perspective, earlier than the non-gifted on experimental tasks of social cognition.

Unfortunately, the few studies available (summarized above) have used gifted children only from middle-class families and in unnatural experimental situations rather than home environments. To improve veracity, we need broader-based and longitudinal research comparing social cognition among gifted and non-gifted children. It has been suggested (Mussen and Eisenber-Berg, 1977; Shantz, 1975; Bryan, 1975; Hoffman, 1973; Baumrind, 1971; Hoffman and Saltzstein, 1967) that more open and democratic ('inductive') child-rearing practices are more prevalent in middle-class than in lower-class families. In the latter, a relatively authoritarian, punishment-orientated mode is more likely to prevail. Shantz (1975) has commented that inductive practices 'include giving the child reasons for requiring a change in his behavior and pointing out the consequences (material and psychological) of his behavior for other people and himself', which may be an important variable in the development of superior role-taking skills.

Rubin (1973) and Van Lieshout *et al.* (1973) found that social cognitive skills were highly intercorrelated. However, the low to moderate relationship between measures of social cognition and IQ in children who are not identified as gifted suggests that social cognition may exist as a factor somewhat detached from IQ. Social giftedness, in terms of superior social cognition, may exist among non-intellectually gifted children, as suggested by Guilford's (1959) behavioural content area. At present, we can only say that intellectually gifted young children appear to reach stages of social cognition earlier than other young children. By learning more about the ways in which intellectually gifted youngsters are aware of others, we may hope to be able to see how it affects their social behaviour.

PROSOCIAL BEHAVIOURS

Prosocial behaviour consists of a variety of voluntary acts such as helping, sharing, donating, reacting to distress, and expressing physical affection for the benefit of another, without the anticipation of external rewards (Bar-Tal, 1976; Mussen and Eisenberg-Berg, 1977).

Variables which have an effect on pro-social behaviour can be:

1. Situational, which includes observation of a model, mood of the individual, presence of others, compliance with previous requests, degree of dependency of the person in need, familiarity with the person in need, prior help received, amount of freedom the helping person has in deciding whether to attempt to help or not, and emergency or non-emergency situations.
2. Personal, which includes race, sex, age, social class, family size, ordinal position, socialization experiences within the family, and some personal characteristics such as aggression, activity level, expressiveness, and social and emotional adjustment (Bar-Tal, 1976; Mussen and Eisenberg-Berg, 1977).

Most studies of prosocial behaviour in young children have been designed on the theory that social cognition—the understanding of another's perspective (feelings, thoughts, and intentions)—should be reflected in social behaviour. These have mostly been laboratory investigations, which have attempted to manipulate prosocial behaviour by means of modelling and social reinforcement, employing a single age-group, or which have a cross-sectional design to investigate age differences (Bryan, 1975; Staub, 1975; Yarrow and Zahn-Waxler, 1976). They ask whether young gifted children, who seem to be able take the perspective of another at an earlier age than the non-gifted, are actually more responsive to another's needs, and whether they more often act in ways which benefit others.

Rheingold (1982) studied the prosocial behaviours of children eighteen, twenty-four, and thirty months of age, in a laboratory setting which simulated a home. Although she did not measure the parents directly for intelligence or social cognition, their educational levels suggested that they had an advanced level of cognitive functioning (Abroms, 1982b; Jordan, 1981). Parents, other adults, and the children were asked to do domestic-style tasks such as sweeping up a litter of paper bits, folding laundry, and placing crumpled papers in a waste basket. They were told to perform the tasks slowly and to talk about what they were doing. 'All the children, even at 18 months of age, not only participated in their parents' performance of the tasks but did so to a considerable extent. Specifically, 13 of the 20 eighteen month-old children helped on half or more of the tasks their parents performed' (Rheingold, 1982).

The frequency of prosocial behaviours was found to increase with age, as did the nature of participation. Only one child of eighteen months folded a laundry item, for example, though eight children of thirty months folded laundry items in a precise manner. These acts were accompanied by increasingly sophisticated language. For example, eighteen-month-old children said

'Fold clothes', and 30 month-old children said 'I'm going to pick up these books …' Furthermore, some children in the older groups were already spontaneously incorporating the word 'help' in their statements (Rheingold, 1982). The manner in which the tasks were completed and the talk which accompanied them led Rheingold (1982) to conclude that 'to assist another is a positive social behaviour not to be denied the very young'.

Abroms and Gollin (1980) investigated the relationship of scores on measures of both social cognition and the prosocial behaviours of sharing, helping, reaction to distress, and physical affection among gifted three-year-olds during free play time. They tried to discern whether there was a consistent relationship between the children's scores on tasks of visual, conceptual, and affective role-taking, and the measurements of their prosocial behaviours. On ten different days, at the beginning and at the end of nursery school, the researchers observed each child for ten four-minute periods.

In this sample of upper-middle-class, gifted three-year-olds, the relationship between IQ (as measured by the Slosson Intelligence Test) and perceptual and conceptual role-taking skills was found to increase during the school year. Initially, IQ, rather than social cognitive skills, was the more significant predictor of prosocial behaviours, but eight months later, neither IQ nor scores on role-taking tasks were efficient predictors. This sample of gifted children showed trends in prosocial behaviours which were similar to those expressed by non-gifted preschoolers in a naturalistic setting (Jersild and Markey, 1935). They showed only a slight increase in the frequency of their prosocial behaviours, and there was more verbal aggression ('I'm not gonna have you to my party') as the year progressed.

Despite their precocious mental skills, many gifted three- and four-year-olds 'tend to hit and kick other children when frustrated, have trouble communicating needs and feelings to other children, lack the skill to inititate cooperative play or to join a group, have not learned to share and take turns and so on. In short, these children appear to be socially similar to three- and four-year-olds of average intelligence, but at the same time, they think and reason like much older children' (Roedell et al., 1980). The bottom line in the Abroms and Gollin (1980) study was: 'Let's share. I'll go first.'

In middle-class homes, sharing and helping are often taught and rewarded in young children. Thus, when bright three-year-olds enter nursery school, they are relatively adept at meeting expectations for prosocial behaviours. Given free play situations on an extended basis and a child-care setting which emphasizes a philosophy of gradual, self-initiated social development with teachers as guides, rather than dictators of social skills, clever children can experiment and assess the benefits to themselves of prosocial behaviour. Basically, they are asking, 'Where is the payoff?'

SOME WORK WITH OLDER CHILDREN

In a study of altruistic behaviour, Berkowitz (1966) found that middle-class American and English boys were only helpful to boys from whom they had previously received help. Other research in the United States (Muir and Weinstein, 1962) and in Israel (Dreman and Greenbaum, 1973) has indicated that middle-class individuals are more likely to exchange help and favours, rather than give them altruistically (Webb *et al.*, 1977).

Rothenberg (1970) conducted a cross-sectional study of the relationships between age, intellectual ability, social cognition, and measures of social competence (which subsumed prosocial behaviour), as measured by teacher ratings and peer nominations among ten- to fifteen-year-old children. She presented them with four tape-recorded stories, involving adult males and females, in dialogues depicting changes of feelings (happiness, anger, sadness, and distress or anxiety). Social sensitivity was found to be higher in the older children and, for the total sample of 108, there was also a significant relationship between social cognition and intelligence scores, as measured by the Peabody Picture Vocabulary Test and the Block Design sub-test of the Wechsler Intelligence Scale for Children (WISC). Rothenberg concluded that 'social sensitivity increases as intelligence increases', and suggested that there is a positive relationship between social cognition, measures of intelligence, and prosocial behaviour among young adolescents.

Obviously, relationships between social cognition, intelligence and prosocial behaviours are complex. The paucity of studies to date, for the most part, suggest that an understanding of others, whether intellectual or emotional, does not seem to be indicative of a child's actual behaviour towards them.

MORAL REASONING

Much of the current research on moral reasoning comes from the cognitive-developmental paradigm advanced by Lawrence Kohlberg (1967), who has attempted to discern the various orientations that older children use in making moral judgments. He focused upon the form rather than the content of his subjects' responses and subsequently suggested three levels of moral functioning—'Preconventional', 'Conventional', and 'Autonomous'. His Moral Judgment Scale (MJS) of nine hypothetical dilemmas has been used primarily with adolescents and young adults (Haan *et al.*, 1968; Kohlberg, 1968; Rest *et al.*, 1969; Schwartz *et al.*, 1969; Rest, 1973). Kohlberg (1971) refers to the work of Turiel (1966) and of Rest (1968) to validate his contention that the his stages of moral development are hierarchical, each higher stage subsuming the lower ones. Kurtines and Grief (1974), however, contend that the stages are coarse measures at best, and only 'moderately effective in discriminating between unsophisticated and sophisticated reasoning'.

Kohlberg (1971) and others (Selman, 1971a; Eisenberg-Berg and Hand, 1979; Walker, 1980; Blasi, 1980) have described social cognition—advanced role taking—as the common core of each of the successive stages of moral judgment, the order of which is universally invariant (Kohlberg, 1968, 1969, 1971). This assumption is based upon Kohlberg's (1968) somewhat sketchy reporting of research among ten-, thirteen-, and sixteen-year-old males in the United States, Taiwan, Mexico, and Turkey, initially presented in *Psychology Today*, though given a degree of legitimacy by inclusion in Goslin's *Handbook of Socialization Theory and Research* (1969).

Reports of the relationship between intelligence scores and those obtained from Kohlberg's MJS are enigmatic. With the support of one reference, Kohlberg (1969) concluded that there was no relationship between moral judgment and high IQ scores: 'Children above average in IQ are equally likely to be low or high in moral maturity.'

Other researchers, though, have concluded that moral reasoning is positively related to cognitive maturity (Selman, 1971b; Kuhn, Langer and (in a later study) Kohlberg, 1971). Selman suggested that children with a mental age of about ten years are beginning to exercise their newly developed reciprocal role-taking skills in making Kohlberg's stage 2 and 3 judgments, while children 'who are at a higher mental age probably developed this skill at an earlier chronological age'. He suggested that the time period for examining the co-development of these two processes appears to be critical. Abroms and Gollin's results (1980) suggested that a confluence between role-taking and IQ occurs as early as age three among gifted pre-school children. Further studies of children combining measures of role-taking, IQ, and moral reasoning are undoubtedly needed.

Again intellectually gifted children appear to reach a relatively high stage of moral reasoning earlier than their chronological peers (Karnes and Brown, 1981; Tan-Willman and Gutteridge, 1981). Some may even be able to use principled reasoning during their mid-teens, though it is most typically reached in adulthood, if by only a small segment of the population. There is some evidence that gifted children differ from their peers at an early age by their extreme social sensitivity to attitudes, values, and morals (Gowan and Bruch, 1971; Drews, 1971; Tannenbaum, 1975). There is little doubt that the gifted show precocity within Piagetian stages, and reach concrete and formal operations earlier than their peers (Webb, 1974; Rader, 1975; Shigaki and Wolf, 1980).

Both Kohlberg (1971) and Piaget (1948) have suggested a parallelism between cognition and moral reasoning, though the level of one does not assure the equivalent level of the other. Neither, however, appears to give any credit to the effects of socialization on moral reasoning. Indeed, Kohlberg (1968) contends that a number of internalized moral judgments 'do not come in any direct and obvious way from parents, teachers or even peers'. Yet, according to other sources, inductive child-rearing practices often appear as a common thread in the nurturance of social cognition, prosocial behaviours, and moral reasoning (Uguerel-Semin, 1952; Hoffman and Saltzstein, 1967; Haan *et al.*, 1968; Hoffman, 1970; Mussen *et al.*, 1970; Bryan, 1975; Hoffman, 1975; Mussen and Eisenberg-Berg, 1977; Parikh, 1980).

It seems, however, that children are not passive and may influence the structure of the child-rearing practices which they experience. A cognitively advanced child, because of her own better ability to reason, is more likely to elicit inductive reasoning than a child less able to comprehend and to interact with the dominating verbal content of such an approach (Hoffman, 1975). Modelling can also be an aspect of inductive reasoning which is closely associated with moral reasoning. Mussen and Eisenberg-Berg (1977) argue that if 'parents reason with their children, pointing out the "rights" and "wrongs" of their actions, they inevitably model consideration for others, and, at the same time, stress the social implications of one's own behaviour'. Although they have suggested a link between levels of moral judgment and prosocial behaviours, their correlations are neither sufficiently robust nor consistent to provide empirical predictions of prosocial behaviour.

We are therefore left with a highly imperfect understanding of the relationship between moral cognition and moral action. The paucity of research on moral cognition and moral action applies to both gifted and non-gifted children, and precludes a reliable interpretation of social giftedness as developing from socialization.

LEADERSHIP

Outstanding leadership capabilities are regarded in the United States (if not in Europe) as a legitimate form of giftedness, often being considered synonymous with 'social giftedness' (Zettel, 1979; Alvino *et al.*, 1981). The literature contains a plethora of material describing various aspects of leadership, but it is impossible to define leadership ability let alone gifted leadership, from them. 'There are almost as many different definitions of leadership as there are persons who have attempted to define the concept' (Stogdill, 1974). For working purposes, though, leadership can be viewed as a process which focuses on change through the influence on and the control of people.

Gifted leadership in North America implies superior role-taking skills (social cognition), elevated moral reasoning, and an interplay with prosocial behaviours. It is recognized that Machiavellianism lies at the other end of the spectrum, so that notorious leaders, such as Hitler and Jim Jones who have dramatically influenced, controlled, and led large masses of people toward unprincipled goals, are excluded from consideration in this discussion.

Though there is a lack of empirical data on leadership among young children, Karnes and Shwedel (1981) have made a significant attempt to operationalize the complex construct of leadership at the pre-school level, using teacher and parent ratings. They began by using a global screening instrument in which children were rated on a scale of 1–4 by a teacher or parent as follows:

- a. Shows an awareness of the needs of others.
- b. Seems to enjoy being around other people: is sociable, and prefers not to be alone.
- c. Tends to influence others when they are around: generally directs the activity in which s/he is involved.
- d. Assumes responsibility beyond what is expected for his/her age.

If a child received an overall rating of 8 or above from the teacher, or 10 from the parent, he or she was then observed during a specific activity. For example, the youngster was taught to make paint by mixing water and dry paint, then asked to choose two other children, a girl and a boy, to teach them how to mix paints. The following types of leadership behaviours were scored on a quantitative basis:

1. Was the child willing to choose partners? If not, why?
2. How did the child go about enlisting others? (a) Did s/he invite or ask others to participate in a positive manner on order or command in a negative manner? (b) Did the child make the task seem exciting to others?
3. How did the child go about teaching the task? (a) Did s/he verbally describe the sequence of steps? (b) Did s/he demonstrate the sequence of steps? (c) Did s/he monitor the work of the others?
4. Did at least one of the children succeed at the new task?

When a child received a comparatively high score on tasks such as the above, a more in-depth assessment, based upon curricular areas, was made by the teacher's observation. Dramatic play provides a useful example; it was measured on the Karnes and Shwedel's (1981) Talent Checklist, which has been effective in identifying gifted leadership among handicapped, non-handicapped, and intellectually gifted preschool children, viz:

1. Is the child sought out by others to become involved?
2. Is the child joined by others, once they see his/her involvement?

3. Does the child initiate dramatic play without prompting?
4. Does the child bring materials from home for dramatic play?
5. Does the child assign roles to other participants?
6. Is the child's behaviour copied by peers?
7. Does the child require little direction to sustain or elaborate dramatic play?
8. Does the child allow others to take major roles?
9. Does the child allow turn-taking?

This study suggests that gifted leadership, a comparative phenomenon as defined by these instruments, can be observed and documented among pre-school children of varying intellectual potential; i.e. gifted leadership is not a phenomenon exclusive to the intellectually gifted preschooler. Although advanced verbal skills are a prominent characteristic of gifted preschool children, most youngsters between the ages of three and four appear to modify the form and content of their speech according to what they presume their listener will understand (Maratsos, 1973; Garvey and Hogan, 1973; Menig-Peterson, 1975). Given precocious levels of social cognition on laboratory tasks among young gifted children, it would appear that the gifted might effectively combine them with verbal skills in the service of outstanding leadership communication. But this is not necessarily so in practice; advanced knowledge, verbal skills, and lower levels of *in situ* role-taking skills may literally 'turn off' other children (Abroms, 1982a).

Gifted leadership is not dependent on a gifted level of intelligence, since personality characteristics and situational variables play a major role. A few studies do provide insight into personality dimensions among identified intellectually gifted pupils who exhibit leadership potential. Jarecky (1959), for example, found that gifted thirteen to fifteen year-olds who received high ratings on sociograms, descriptive statements of 'good' characteristics from teacher ratings, the Vineland Social Maturity Scale, and on a composition entitled 'The Sort of Person I Am', correlated well with the following leadership characteristics:

1. The children were accepted for their leadership qualities by the majority of the people who knew them—peers and adults alike.
2. They were often involved in a social venture in which they made constructive contributions.
3. They were frequently regarded as arbitrators or policy-makers in peer groups.
4. They made lasting relationships with both peers and adults.
5. They stimulated positive productive behaviour in their peers.
6. They appeared to exercise a protean approach to social complexities, coping with a mixture of humour, intelligence, and insight.

Other studies of gifted pupils report similar findings (Payne and Halpin, 1974; Hynes *et al*, 1978–79; Gordon, 1952). Jarecky (1959) suggested that though leadership abilities and intelligence were interrelated, intelligence alone did not account for social giftedness. Though Gordon (1952) found a low but positive relationship between leadership and intelligence among university students, Chauvin (1982) did not find a significant independent relationship between the IQ scores of 181 gifted adolescents and a leadership profile, as measured by the High School Personality Questionnaire (Cattell and Cattell, 1975).

Both Lindsay (1978) and Renzulli and Hartman (1971) caution that because the extraordinarily bright child may not view a group's problems in the same way as less-able children, he or she may not be interested or concerned in actually offering help to the group. Alternatively, the gifted may offer their advice in an insensitive, domineering manner.

The difficulties in describing leadership *per se* have resulted in a modest body of studies on gifted leadership and its relationship with intellectual giftedness. It would seem, however, that the cornerstone of leadership, from preschool age to adolescence, is probably social cognition, rather than intellectual giftedness. This seems logical, since in order to effect change, one must understand the perspective of others. Personality characteristics which are commonly associated with the leadership profile include enthusiasm, easy communication skills, problem-solving skills, humour, self-control, conscientiousness, and a degree of intelligence (Stodgill, 1974)—all of which point to the situational nature of leadership.

CONCLUSIONS

Comparative profiles and studies of the development of both normal and gifted children have been presented above with respect to the constructs of social cognition, prosocial behaviours, moral reasoning, and leadership. The intellectually gifted appear to reach measurable levels of social cognition as young as the age of three, with some confluence between their scores of intelligence and social cognition. However, no significant relationship has been consistently demonstrated between social cognition and pro-social behaviours among differently able children. Indeed, at the pre-school level, however advanced their social cognition, gifted children still 'tend to hit and kick other children when frustrated' (Roedell and Robinson, 1977).

Kohlberg has suggested that social cognition is a necessary component of moral reasoning and that although intelligence is also a factor, high levels of intelligence do not ensure high levels of moral reasoning. The relationship between moral judgment and moral action remains murky.

Social cognition appears to be an aspect of leadership, assuming that the leader's understanding of social perspectives within a group is a crucial element for change. A truly gifted leader, as defined here, must exercise higher levels of moral reasoning, and prosocial behaviour. Intellectually gifted adolescents appear to score significantly higher than their non-gifted peers on paper-and-pencil tasks of moral reasoning, and also appear to possess a greater number of leadership characteristics, as indicated by self-report profiles and nominations. But any relationship between practical leadership and intellectual giftedness remains, at best, inconclusive.

Social giftedness can be said to exist when the link between mind and behaviour is expressed on a consistently remarkable basis. So far, research does not support the notion that intellectual giftedness is tantamount to social giftedness. In a theoretical profile of the socially gifted individual, superlative social cognition, readily recognizing the thoughts and feelings of others, would probably be the cornerstone of mental processes and behaviours. Thus, the socially gifted individual should be able to reason at a highly principled level and also to show behaviours at the individual and group level which induce change of a universally acceptable nature, without anticipation of reward. Clearly, the challenge of modern education is to develop these behaviours among all pupils, not merely those who possess a high IQ.

ACKNOWLEDGEMENTS

This chapter is dedicated to Bess J. Seligman. Her thoughts and actions truly epitomize social giftedness. Much appreciation is expressed to Andrea L. Wert for her enthusiastic and competant assistance.

REFERENCES

Abroms, K. (1982a). Classroom interactions of gifted preschoolers. *Teaching Exceptional Children.* **14**, 223–225.

Abroms, K. (1982b). The gifted infant: tantalizing behaviors and provocative correlates. *Journal of the Division of Early Childhood,* **5**, 3–18.

Abroms, K., and Gollin, J. (1980). Developmental study of gifted preschool children and measures of psychosocial giftedness. *Exceptional Children,* **46**, 334–341.

Alvino, J., McDonnel, R., and Richert, S. (1981). National survey of identification practices in gifted and talented education. *Exceptional Children,* **48**, 124–132.

Argyle, M. (1971). *The Psychology of Interpersonal Behaviour.* Penguin, Harmondsworth.

Bar-Tal, D. (1976). *Prosocial Behavior.* Hemisphere Publishing Corporation, Washington.

Baumrind, D. (1971). Current patterns of parental authority. *Developmental Psychology Monograph,* **4**, 1–105.

Berkowitz, L. (1966). A laboratory investigation of social class and national differences in helping behavior. *International Journal of Psychology,* **1**, pp. 231–242.

Blasi, A. (1980). Bridging cognition and moral action: a critical review of the literature. *Psychological Bulletin*, **88**, 1–45.

Borke, H. (1971). Interpersonal perception of young children: Egocentrism or empathy? *Developmental Psychology*, **5**, 263–269.

Borke, H. (1973). The development of empathy in Chinese and American children between three and six years of age: a cross-cultural study. *Developmental Psychology*, **9**, 102–108.

Bryan, J. (1975). Children's cooperation and helping behaviors. In *Review of Child Development Research*, Vol. 5 (ed. C. M. Hetherington). University of Chicago Press, Chicago.

Cattell, R., and Cattell, M. (1975). *Handbook for Junior-Senior High School Personality Questionnaire*. IPAT, Champaign, Illinois.

Chauvin, J. (1982). A study of leadership potential in a selected group of gifted students. Unpublished doctoral dissertation, University of Southern Mississippi.

Davitz, J. R. (1964). *The Communication of Motional Meaning*. McGraw Hill, New York.

Dreman, S., and Greenbaum, C. (1973). Altruism or reciprocity: Sharing behavior in Israeli kindergarten children. *Child Development*, **44**, pp. 61–68.

Drews, E. (1971). Beyond curriculum. In *Educating the Ablest* (eds J. Gowan and E. P. Torrance), F. E. Peacock, HO-D, Itasca, Illinois, pp. 110–126.

Eisenberg-Berg, N., and Hand, M. (1979). The relationship of preschoolers' reasoning about prosocial moral conflicts to prosocial behavior. *Child Development*, **50**, 356–363.

Fishbein, H., Lewis, S., and Kieffer, K. (1972). Children's understanding of spatial relations: coordination of perspectives. *Developmental Psychology*, **7**, 21–32.

Flavell, J., Botkin, P., Fry, C., Wright, J., and Jarvis, P. (1968). *The Development of Role-taking and Communication Skills in Young Children*. Wiley, New York.

Garvey, C., and Hogan, R. (1973). Social speech and social interaction: Egocentrism revisited. *Child Development*, **44**, 562–568.

Gordon, L. (1952). Personal factors in leadership. *Journal of Social Psychology*, **36**, 249–254.

Goslin, D. (Ed.). *Handbook of Socialization Theory and Research*. Rand McNally, 1969, Chicago.

Gowan, J., and Bruch, C. (1971). *The Academically Talented Student and Guidance*. Houghton-Mifflin, Boston.

Guilford, J. (1959). Three faces of intellect. *American Psychologist*, **14**, 469–477.

Haan, N., Smith, M., and Block, J. (1968). Moral reasoning of young adults: political-social behavior, family background, and personality correlates. *Journal of Personality and Social Psychology*, **10**, 3, 183–201.

Hoffman, M. (1970). Moral development. In *Carmichael's Manual of Child Psychology*, Vol. II (ed. P. Mussen), Wiley, New York, 261-359.

Hoffman, M. (1973). Altruistic behavior and the parent–child relationship. Report No. 36, Developmental Program, Department of Psychology, University of Michigan, Ann Arbor, Michigan.

Hoffman, M. (1975). Moral internalization, parental power, and the nature of parent–child interaction. *Developmental Psychology*, **11**, pp. 228–239.

Hoffman, M., and Saltzstein, H. (1967). Parent discipline and the child's moral development. *Journal of Personality and Social Psychology*, **5**, 45–47.

Hunt, T. (1928). The measurement of social intelligence. *Journal of Applied Psychology*, 317–334.

Hynes, K., Richardson, W., and Asher, W. (1978-79). Project talent revisited: Cross-validating self-report measures of leadership. *Journal of Experimental Education*, 54–70.

Jarecky, R. (1959). Identification of the socially gifted. *Exceptional Children*, **25**, 415–419.

Jersild, A., and Markey, F. (1935). Conflicts between preschool children. *Child Development Monographs*, No. 21.

Jordan, T. (1981). St. Louis baby study. Technical report No. 43: Prospective longitudinal study of bright children: Cognitive development from one to seven years, University of Missouri, St. Louis.

Jordan V. (1980). Conserving kinship concepts: a developmental study in social cognition. *Child Development*, **51**, 146–155.

Karnes, M. B., and Shwedel, A. (1981). *RAPYHT Project: Activities for Talent Identification*. Mimeograph, Institute for Child Behavior, University of Illinois, Urbana, Illinois.

Karnes, F., and Brown, K.E. (1981). Moral development and the gifted: an initial investigation. *Roeper Review*, **3**, 8–10.

Kennedy, M. (1979). Unpublished manuscript, Tulane University.

Kohlberg, L. (1967). Moral and religious education and the public schools: A developmental view. In *Religion and Public Education* (ed. T. Sizer), Houghton-Mifflin, Boston.

Kohlberg, L. (1968). The child as a moral philosopher. *Psychology Today*, **2**, 25–30.

Kohlberg, L. (1969). Stage and sequence: the cognitive developmental approach to socialization. In *Handbook of Socialization Theory and Research* (ed. D. Goslin), Rand-McNally, Chicago.

Kohlberg, L. (1971). From is to ought: How to commit the naturalistic fallacy and get away with it in the study of moral development. In *Cognitive Development and Epistemology* (ed. T. Mischel), Academic Press, New York.

Kohlberg, L., and De Vries, R. (1969). Relations between Piaget and psychometric assessments of intelligence. Paper presented at the Conference on the Natural Curriculum, Urbana, Illinois.

Kuhn, D., Langer, J., and Kohlberg, L. (1971). Relations between logical and moral development. In *Recent Research in Moral Development* (eds. L. Kohlberg and E. Turiel), Holt, New York.

Kurtines, W., and Greif, E. (1974). The development of moral thought: review and evaluation of Kohlberg's approach. *Psychological Bulletin*, **81**, 453–470.

Lewis, S., and Fishbein, H. (1969). Space perception in children: a disconfirmation of Piaget's developmental hypothesis. Paper presented at the meeting of the Psychonomic Society, St Louis, Missouri.

Lindsay, B. (1978). Leadership giftedness: Developing a profile. *Journal for the Education of the Gifted*, **1**, 63–69.

Maratsos, M. (1973). Nonegocentric communication abilities in preschool children. *Child Development*, **44**, 697–700.

Masangkay, K., McCluskey, K., McIntyre, C., Sims-Knight, J., Vaughn, R., and Flavell, J. (1974). The early development of inferences about the visual percepts of others. *Child Development*, **45**, 357–366.

Menig-Peterson, C. (1975). The modification of communicative behavior in preschool-aged children as a function of the listeners' perspective. *Child Development*, **46**, 1015–1018.

Miller, J., Roedell, W., Slaby, R. and Robinson, H. (1978). Sex-role development in intellectually precocious preschool children. Paper presented at the meeting of the Western Psychological Association, San Francisco.

Muir, D. and Weinstein, E. (1962). The social debt: An investigation of lower class and middle-class norms of social obligation. *American Sociological Review*, 27, 532–539.

Mussen, P., and Eisenberg Berg, N. (1977). *Roots of Caring, Sharing, and Helping* W. H. Freeman, San Francisco.

Mussen, P., Rutherford, E., Harris, S., and Keasey, C. (1970). Honesty and altruism among preadolescents. *Developmental Psychology*, 3, 2, 169–194.

Parikh, B. (1980). Development of moral judgment and its relation to family environmental factors in Indian and American families. *Child Development*, 51, 1030–1039.

Payne, D., and Halpin, W. (1974). Use of a factored biographical inventory to identify differentially gifted adolescents. *Psychological Reports*, 35, 1195–1204.

Piaget, J. (1948). *Moral Judgment of the Child.* The Free Press, Glencoe, Illinois.

Piaget, J. and Inhelder, B. (1969). *The Psychology of the Child.* Basic Books, New York.

Rader, J. (1975). Piagetian assessment of conservation skills in the gifted first grader. *The Gifted Child Quarterly*, 19, 226–229.

Renzulli, J. and Hartman, R. (1971) Scale for rating behavioral characteristics of superior students. *Exceptional Children*, 38, 243–247.

Rest, J. (1968). Developmental hierarchy in preference and comprehension of moral judgment. Unpublished doctoral dissertation, University of Chicago.

Rest, J. (1973). The hierarchical nature of moral judgment: A study of patterns of comprehension and preference of moral stages. *Journal of Personality*, 41, 86–109.

Rest, J., Turiel, E., and Kohlberg, L. (1969). Level of moral development as a determinant of preference and comprehension of moral judgments made by others. *Journal of Personality*, 37, 225–252.

Rheingold, H. (1982). Little children's participation in the work of adults, a nascent prosocial behavior. *Child Development*, 53, 114–125.

Roedell, W. C., and Robinson, H. B. (1977). *Programming for Intellectually Advanced Children: A Program Development Guide.* Child Development Research Group, University of Washington, Seattle (ERIC ED 151 094).

Roedell, W., Jackson, N., and Robinson, H. (1980). *Gifted Young Children.* Teachers College, Columbia University, New York.

Rothenberg, B. (1970). Social sensitivity and the relationship to interpersonal competence, intrapersonal comfort, and intellectual level. *Developmental Psychology*, 2, 335–350.

Rubin, K. (1973). Egocentrism in childhood: a unitary construct? *Child Development*, 44, 102–110.

Schwartz, S. H., Feldman, K. A., Brown, M. E., and Heingartner, A. (1969). Some personality correlates of conduct in two situations of moral conflict. *Journal of Personality*, 37, 41–57.

Selman, R. (1971a). The importance of reciprocal role-taking for the development of conventional moral thought. In *Recent Research in Moral Development* (eds L. Kohlberg and E. Turiel). Holt, New York.

Selman, R. (1971b). The relation of role taking to the development of moral judgment in children. *Child Development*, 42, 79–91.

Shantz, C. M. (1975). The development of social cognition. In *Review of Child Development Research*, Vol. 5 (ed. E. M. Hetherington), University of Chicago Press, Chicago.

Shigaki, I., and Wolf, W. (1980). 'Hierarchies of formal syllogistic reasoning of young gifted children. *Child Study Journal*, **10**, 87–106.

Staub, E. (1975). *The Development of Prosocial Behavior in Children*. General Learning, Morristown, New Jersey.

Stogdill, R. (1974). *Handbook of Leadership*. Free Press, New York.

Strang, R. (1930). Measures of social intelligence. *American Journal of Sociology*, **36**, 263–269.

Tannenbaum, G. (1975). A backward and forward glance at the gifted. In *Psychology and Education of the Gifted* (eds W. Barbe and J. Renzulli), Irvington Publishers, New York, pp. 21–31.

Tan-Willman, C., and Gutteridge, D. (1981). Creative thinking and moral reasoning of academically gifted secondary school adolescents. *Gifted Child Quarterly*, **25**, 149–153.

Turiel, E. (1966). An experimental test of the sequentiality of developmental stages in the child's moral judgments. *Journal of Personality and Social Psychology*, **3**, 611–618.

Ugurel-Semin, R. (1952). Moral behavior and moral judgment of children. *Journal of Abnormal and Social Psychology*, **47**, 463–474.

Van Lieshout, C., Leckie, G., and Smits Van Sonsbeek, B. (1973). The effect of a social perspective-taking training on empathy and role-taking ability of preschool children. Paper presented at the meeting of the International Society for the Study of Behavioral Development, Ann Arbor, Michigan.

Walker, L. (1980). Cognitive and perspective-taking prerequisites for moral development. *Child Development*, **51**, 131–139.

Walker, L., and Gollin, E. (1977). Perspective role-taking in young children. *Journal of Experimental Child Psychiatry*, **24**, 343–357.

Webb, R. (1974). Concrete and formal operations in very bright 6- to 11-year olds. *Human Development*, **17**, 292–300.

Webb, R., Oliverie, M., and Harnick, F. (1977). The socialization of intelligence: implications for educational intervention. In *Social Development in Childhood* (ed. R. A. Webb). Johns Hopkins University Press, Baltimore.

White, C. (1975). Moral development in Bahamian school children: A cross cultural examination of Kohlberg's stages of moral reasoning. *Developmental Psychology*, **11**, 535–536.

Yarrow, M., and Zahn-Waxler, C. (1976). Dimensions and correlates of prosocial behavior in young children. *Child Development*, **47**, 118–125.

Zahn-Waxler, C., Radke-Yarrow, M., and Brady-Smith, J. (1977) Perspective taking and prosocial behavior. *Developmental Psychology*, **13**, 87–88.

Zettel, J. (1979). Gifted and talented education over a half decade of change. *Journal for the Education of the Gifted*, **3**, 14–37.

The Psychology of Gifted Children
Edited by Joan Freeman
©1985, John Wiley & Sons, Ltd.

CHAPTER 12

Gifted Women

Lynn H. Fox and Wendy Z. Zimmerman

Most descriptions of the gifted and talented refer to potential in children and to manifest achievement in adults; when children are selected for special education by measures of potential (as on tests of intelligence or creativity) boys and girls participate in roughly equal proportions. But since in adult life men far outnumber women in positions of eminence and leadership in the sciences, social sciences, arts, and humanities, as well as in politics, business, and industry, it is obvious that the disparity between potential and achievement is considerably less for men than it is for women. This is dramatically illustrated by the following statistics from the United States.

Although women now make up 42 per cent of the labour force, nearly 80 per cent of them are employed in low-level sales, clerical, plant, and factory jobs (Stencel, 1981). Results of the 1980 Census revealed that of 441 described jobs, only 60 had enough women in them to be classified as female-dominated, all the others being predominantly male (NACWEP, 1981). In 1971 and 1972, the percentages of women earning first degrees in the professions of dentistry, medicine, and law were 1, 9, and 7 per cent respectively, and though there was an improved balance between 1979 and 1980, with increases to 13, 23, and 31 per cent (Grant and Eiden, 1982), the proportion of women is still small. In truth, most of the 16 per cent of women classified as professionals are in the traditionally female fields of education, nursing, health technology, and library science (Stencel, 1981), and although the majority of all teachers are women, they are still unlikely to reach the top school posts. For example in 1978, women represented only 14 per cent of school principals, and in 1980 less than 1 per cent of school superintendents were women (Title IX, 1981).

These facts are not surprising in the light of present societal expectations and sex-roles, though they have begun to change over the past decade or so, and in the United States, for example, it is predicted that most women will soon be spending a sizable number of years in the labour force (Title IX, 1981). Thus, any discussion of gifted females must deal with the issue of changing views of women's roles, including potential improvements in opportunities to compete for leadership, yet not ignore the possible effects of biological factors. The selective review of the literature on gender-based differences given below, provides some tentative answers to questions concerning male and female potentials and achievements.

GENDER-BASED DIFFERENCES IN APTITUDE AND ACHIEVEMENT

Although global measures of intellectual aptitude are specifically designed to give equivalent mean scores for both sexes, there are slightly more males than females at either end of the normal distribution (Maccoby, 1963; Maccoby and Jacklin, 1974). Terman (1925), for example, found more males scoring above 140 on the Stanford-Binet Intelligence Test, and suggested that it was due to the instability of the male XY chromosome pair (Terman and Oden, 1947). Nevertheless, the differences in the numbers of boys and girls at or above IQ 140 on intelligence tests is really too small to explain the differences in their adult attainments. When achievement is measured by grades in school, girls tend to do better than boys, though Hall (1980) found that among a group of gifted high-school pupils, grade-point average was not correlated with intelligence for girls, though it was for boys.

Age differences associated with gender emerge when achievement is measured by tests; studies of early admission to kindergarten or first grade reported that there were more girls than boys, by as much as two to one (Birch, 1954; Hobson, 1963). Young girls are better than young boys at verbal skills, usually implying early school readiness (Maccoby and Jacklin, 1974), and conversely, more young boys than girls are identified as having reading problems or learning disabilities. But by the time children reach early adolescence, girl's verbal advantages seem to disappear. The Study of Verbally Gifted Youth at The Johns Hopkins University did not find sex differences on the Scholastic Aptitude Test, Verbal (SAT-V), for gifted twelve and thirteen year-olds, nor was there a sex difference among either the college-bound or general high-school populations on this test at ages sixteen and seventeen (results of the OTID Talent Search, 1982). Either the boys caught up with the girls due to the heavy verbal emphasis of most school education, or the tests for older populations failed to measure any continued female verbal advantage (Tittle et al., 1974).

The most dramatic cognitive difference between males and females is in the area of mathematical aptitude, when at about the age of twelve, boys perform better than girls on difficult mathematical reasoning tests (Fox/break and Cohn, 1980), while in later adolescence, boys excel on measures of spatial and mechanical reasoning also (Maccoby and Jacklin, 1974). A recent National Assessment of Educational Progress report noted that seventeen year-old boys out-scored girls in several areas of achievement such as science and mathematics, but girls out-performed boys in only one measure—writing. Whether or not males are inherently more mathematically able, they do seem to have a greater interest in the subject than girls at the high-school and college levels. Gifted boys are also more likely than gifted girls to accelerate their study of mathematics, and even girls who are clearly very gifted sometimes elect not to study calculus at high school (Brody and Fox, 1980).

Although sex differences in science abilities have not been thoroughly investigated, they do appear to be related to both mathematical and verbal interests and abilities. The physical sciences, for example, demand more mathematical competence than the biological sciences, which in some areas emphasize the more verbal activities of nomenclature. Among college-bound, high-school senior pupils in the United States in 1978, 26.1 per cent of the males but only 6.3 per cent of the females planned to specialize in the physical sciences and related areas, whereas, 19.2 per cent of the males and 27.9 per cent of the females planned to study the biological and related sciences (CEEB, 1978). In 1976–77, women received 20 per cent of the doctoral degrees in the biological sciences, but only 13 per cent and 8.9 per cent in mathematics and the physical sciences respectively (Grant and Lind, 1979).

Talent in the visual and performing arts is more difficult to assess than in academic areas, yet it is clear that there are some gender differences in such interests in adolescence. More girls than boys are likely to nominate themselves for gifted programmes in the visual and performing arts. For example, in a 1975 summer programme for the gifted in Maryland, no boy elected for dance, and girls outnumbered boys by two to one in art and drama, though boys did outnumber girls in the jazz band (Fox, 1976a). Among adult artists, writers, and composers there are more men than women, but this may have resulted from their differential pursuit of careers rather than differences in innate abilities.

Attempts to explain the causes of sex differences in achievement are confounded in three ways.

1. The exact nature and extent of the relationship of abilities with achievement is not certain; test results may be merely artifacts of test construction, rather than indicators of true underlying abilities (Tittle et al., 1974). In large samples, for instance, statistically significant

differences on tests of mathematics may have very little practical significance, and be less than one item difference in mean scores for the
two sexes (Fennema, 1977).

2. Although there may be differences in mean scores for boys and girls,
   not all boys score higher than all girls, and vice versa. For example,
   while more boys than girls appear to be mathematically gifted, there is
   still a sizable number of gifted girls who score better than the majority
   of boys their age.

3. Aptitude tests for advanced mathematics and science do not necessarily
   predict the successful pursuit of careers in those fields; the differences
   in the numbers of males and females studying these subjects at university or having careers in them is actually much greater than the tests
   would predict. For example, approximately twice as many gifted boys
   as girls scored 500 on the SAT-M at age twelve or thirteen, and of
   those, the proportion of boys who went on to study calculus at high
   school or college was much greater (Fox, et al., 1979), while males are
   not two, but ten times more likely to get PhD degrees in mathematics,
   engineering, or computer science.

Research on relationships between cognitive information processing and
brain functioning with hormonal or other biological correlates is not sophisticated enough to answer questions about the relative importance of
gender to any specific form of giftedness. Even research studies which hypothesize a sex-linked inherited factor for spatial or mathematical ability,
or a differential lateral specialization of the brain for men and women, are
very tenuous (Sherman, 1977; Wittig and Peterson, 1979). Nor is there much
evidence to support or refute hypotheses about the impact of gender *per se*
upon the pattern or level of talent in any area except athletics, and even
there some old assumptions are being challenged.

On the other hand, there is a considerable body of research to support
the hypothesis that males and females are subjected to very different socialization experiences, though exactly how important these differences are for
the development of specific abilities is not known. The most reasonable social explanatory model of gender differences in attitudes and achievements
seems to be of socializing pressures from parents, teachers, peers, and the
media helping to shape the developing child's view about interests and behaviours, which are appropriate to sex-role, and which in turn influence
expectations and achievements.

GENDER DIFFERENCES IN PERSONALITY VARIABLES

Psycho-educational profiles collected on 1593 gifted high school pupils (789
females, 804 males) showed that their self-concept scores were higher than

those of the general population for academic ability, and equivalent for self-esteem (Tidwell, 1980). On measures of locus of control, they viewed themselves as largely in control of their own life-events, and expected high-level careers; unfortunately, sex differences were not investigated. Profiles of gifted eighth-grade boys and girls on the California Psychological Inventory (CPI) were compared by Lessinger and Martinson (1961), who found few sex differences. However, a similar study of eighth-grade mathematically gifted girls by Haier and Denham (1976) found few sex differences, when compared with a random sample of eighth-grade pupils, though the mathematical girls were decidedly non-conforming.

Research on gifted adults in professions such as psychology, biology, chemistry, art, writing, politics, and mathematics has reported strong similarities in the personality characteristics of males and females within each occupational category (Bachtold and Werner, 1970, 1972, 1973; Blaubergs, 1978; Helson, 1971). In a review of the literature on personality and background characteristics of women in male-dominated occupations, without reference to ability levels, Lemkau (1979) found them to be high on competency traits such as independence, assertiveness, and rationality—features normally identified as the masculine stereotype. Yet, although they were slightly more orientated towards ideas than people, the women had retained the warmth and expressiveness of the traditional feminine stereotype. Carney and Morgan (1981) found that women college students in non-traditional areas had higher American College Test (ACT) scores and higher grades in high-school mathematics, suggesting that many women presently in male-dominated occupations were likely to have been gifted adolescents.

SEX-ROLE ORIENTATION

It can be seen in the recent literature on sex roles that the traditional concept of masculinity and femininity as a single bipolar dimension or trait has been replaced by the independent yet complementary concepts of psychological masculinity and femininity (Bem, 1974; Block, 1973; Constantinople, 1973; Spence, et al., 1975), and these changing perspectives have stimulated new ways of measurement and research.

Psychological masculinity is viewed in terms of instrumental or agentic characteristics. For example, Parson and Bales (1955) have described the instrumental role responsibilities assigned to men in most societies as boss-manager, leader, final judge, and executor of discipline and control with regard to the children of the family, and Bakan (1966) found a masculine sense of agency in characteristics such as self-assertiveness, self-protectiveness, and self-aggrandisement. Psychological femininity is seen in terms of expressive or communal characteristics, as in Parsons and Bales's feminine domestic role responsibilities of mediator, 'comforter' of the family provider, and general emotional support. Communal feminine characteristics were described by Bakan as selflessness and a desire to be at one with others.

This new perspective of sex-role orientation lends significance to the idea of psychological androgyny—defined as having a balance of a high degree of both masculine and feminine traits—as distinct from the undifferentiated state in which there is a low degree of both. Undifferentiated individuals have been found to possess lower self-esteem than androgynous ones (Bem, 1977; Spence et al., 1975).

Comparisons have revealed that proportionally more high-school girls than college women were classified as androgynous, but that the boys were proportionally less androgynous than college men (Spence and Helmreich, 1978). In a study of gifted high-school pupils, over half the girls endorsed androgynous or cross sex-typing orientation, but boys were more likely to fall into the undifferentiated category (Spence and Helmreich, 1978; Mills, 1981; Wells, et al., 1982). Fox and Cohn (1980) found that in a sample of seventh- and eighth-grade pupils who were gifted in mathematics, significantly more girls than boys were cross-sex identified.

It seems possible that the conflict between masculine and feminine traits is less easily resolved for gifted females than males and leads to lower levels of self-confidence for girls than it does for gifted boys (Bem, 1975; Bem and Lenney, 1976; Spence, et al., 1975). The sparsity of the evidence, however, points to the need for further research in this area for the gifted. Efforts are currently underway at The Johns Hopkins University, Baltimore, to investigate the stability of gifted adolescents' sex-role development as well as the predictive validity of sex-role orientation measures with regard to behaviours and expectations related to achievement, in both sexes.

ACHIEVEMENT MOTIVATION

Although the motive to achieve is sometimes treated as a personality characteristic (Callahan, 1979), it is less likely to be an innate than a learned response or attitude. Based on studies of college students, Horner (1968, 1972) has postulated a female 'fear of success', which explains why females may be ambiguous towards success in areas which have a societal label of 'masculine'. Although work by Maccoby and Jacklin (1974) with school-age children, designed to arouse their motives in competitive situations, did not find any consistent sex differences, Fox (1977) and Fox et al., (1979) did identify sex differences in self-confidence among the gifted in the area of mathematics. However, in a review of literature concerning the 'fear of success' construct, Spence and Helmreich (1978) considered the findings inconsistent, and noted failures to replicate Horner's original results.

Perhaps it is sex-role orientation and not gender per se which affects achievement needs. Investigating a high-school population with the Work and Family Orientation Questionnaire (WOFO), consisting of six achieve-ment scales (Work Orientation, Mastery, Competitiveness, Effort, Job Con-cern, Spouse–Career Aspirations), Spence and Helmreich (1978) found ma-jor effects for sex-role orientation on each achievement scale, except Spouse–Career Aspirations. Overall, androgynous pupils showed the highest achieve-ment motivation, followed by masculine, then feminine, then undifferenti-ated individuals. In women, the only exception in that descending order was for competitiveness; masculine-typed women scored as most competi-tive and most likely to have high educational aspirations, followed by those typed as androgynous, feminine, and finally the undifferentiated. These re-sults suggest that gifted females with an androgynous orientation, or perhaps stronger masculine traits (cross sex-typed), will strive to fulfill their intellec-tual abilities both personally and professionally (Mills, 1980; Orlofsky and Stake, 1981). Though the relative effects of biological and environmental factors are unclear, efforts to provide a well-balanced socialization expe-rience for gifted females seem to be vital in assisting them to grow and develop fully.

GENDER DIFFERENCES IN VALUES, CAREER INTERESTS AND ORIENTATION

From high school, through college and adulthood, the sexes appear to have different value systems, as measured by the Allport-Vernon Lindzey Study of Values (AVL)—males scoring higher on the Theoretical, Economic, and Political scales, and females on the Social, Aesthetic, and Religious scales (Allport, *et al.*, 1970). Fox and Denham (1974) found significant differences on the Theoretical, Social, and Artistic scales, between gifted seventh-grade boys and girls, matched on measures of ability and socio-economic back-ground. The gifted boys had similar values to their normative controls, but the gifted girls ranked the Theoretical value higher and the Religious value lower than these controls. Thus, the gifted girls differed from both their male and female peers on measures of values.

Values appear to be related to behaviours, interests, and perhaps intellec-tual ability. In a sample of mathematically gifted youth, Mills (1980) found that a feminine value orientation (high Social, Religious, and Artistic val-ues) was often positively related to verbal scores, and negatively to maths scores, on the Scholastic Aptitude Test (SAT). In reverse, a high mascu-line value orientation (high Theoretical, Economic, and Political values) was negatively related to verbal scores and positively to mathematics scores, The-oretical values also being positively related to science interests (Allport, *et al.*,1970). Boys who have both mathematical ability and theoretical interests are clearly eager to accelerate their progress in school (Fox and Denham, 1974). It seems likely that different value orientations of gifted boys and girls account for some of the sex differences in the study of mathematics and science and in related career orientations.

There are surprisingly few studies of career orientation among the gifted, although that of mathematically precocious youth at The Johns Hopkins University is providing some data about gifted adolescents. Of seventh- and eighth-grade children who competed in a 1972 mathematics contest (Fox and Denham, 1974), the majority of boys had a higher score for investigative occupations, while the girls showed preferences for investigative, social, and artistic occupations on an abbreviated form of the Vocational Preference Inventory (VPI) (Hollan, 1965). However, continued research with this population has revealed an increasing interest in investigative careers among the girls. The analysis for the 1979 group suggests that many gifted girls may be selecting careers in medicine as a way to integrate their social and scientific talents and values (Fox *et al.*, 1982).

Although gifted boys and girls do differ with respect to career interests and orientations, it is important to note that gifted adolescent girls also differ from those of average ability in their greater preference for professional and scientific careers. When Fox *et al.* (1976) compared gifted seventh- grade boys and girls with a normative sample of ninth-grade children on the fourteen basic interest scales of the Strong-Campbell Interest Inventory, they found the gifted pupils scoring significantly higher on the scales of Writing, Mathematics, Science, Public Speaking, and Medical Science, and having more interest in intellectual pursuits. Gifted girls also scored higher than the normative girls on the scales of Law and Political and Mechanical Activity, and although the latter reversed their position on scales of Domestic Arts and Office Practice, those differences were not statistically significant. Thus, gifted girls may not be less interested in the traditional female careers, but simply more interested than girls in general, in areas traditionally viewed as masculine, such as science, mathematics, and mechanical activities.

Gifted girls may experience more conflict than boys in making career choices because, unlike the boys, they expect to have their careers interrupted while they raise children. In a study of gifted seventh-grade children who participated in a talent search in 1978 at The Johns Hopkins University, only 46 per cent of the girls but 98 per cent of the boys expected always to have a full-time career (Fox, *et al.*, 1979); 30 per cent of the girls expected to have a part-time career or a career interruption, and 25 per cent did not expect to work outside the home after they had had children. The view that careers are still only an option for gifted girls was demonstrated when 51 per cent of the boys and only 27 per cent of the girls gave financial necessity as the primary reason for working. Nearly half the gifted girls (46 per cent) thought that the most important reason for working was an obligation to themselves to use their talents, and another 20 per cent saw it as an escape from boredom—a feature considered by only 7 per cent of the boys.

Educational aspirations and behaviours of gifted girls, such as willingness to be accelerated, are related to long-term thinking about the future. Among girls who expected to have a full-time career always, 80 per cent were aiming for a higher degree, which was close to the 79 per cent of all boys, though only 36 per cent of girls with limited career goals expected to get that far. Also, the majority of girls who had agreed to acceleration in school mathematics were the ones planning a full-time career, the others having more limited career plans.

Entwistle and Greenberger (1972) concluded that peers, especially male peers, exert considerable pressure against adolescent girls' occupational aspirations. Only 18 per cent of the boys in the Johns Hopkins study expected their wives to have full-time careers, and 57 per cent did not expect them to work outside the home after they had had children. When asked why fewer women than men pursue careers in mathematics, science, and engineering, over 75 per cent of both the gifted boys and girls thought family responsibilities were a problem. In a similar sample (Fox, *et al.*, 1982), 70 per cent of gifted girls, but none of the gifted boys, expected to work part-time or interrupt their career in order to raise their children. It is interesting that so many males perceive a conflict between family and career responsibilities for gifted girls, but not for themselves.

Parents too shape girls' expectations in their different expectations for girls and boys. In the above study, parents of the poorly motivated, mathematically gifted girls (those choosing not to accelerate, or expressing greater interest in the humanities) were unlikely to have encouraged them in mathematical and scientific careers, and had lower educational aspirations for them. But not all the parents stereotyped mathematics as a more masculine than feminine activity; parents of the well-motivated girls, and all the boys, were happy with a mathematical or scientific career for their child.

Many people believe that women who work outside the home will have less time and therefore less satisfaction with their families, yet the married, mostly professional, men in the Terman longitudinal study said that their greatest life satisfaction came primarily from their families, and then their careers (Oden, 1968; Sears, 1976). A follow-up study of the gifted women in the Terman sample found that the small percentage of women who had careers, rather than just a job, had derived satisfaction from these, whether or not they had families (Sears, 1976; Holahan, 1981), and many women without careers said that if they could plan their life over again, they would pursue one. In a study of younger gifted women who were combining a career with family life, their career, family, and personal relationships all provided high satisfaction, though work satisfaction was less for the comparison group of gifted women who were full-time housewives (Rodenstein and Glickhauf-Hughes, 1979).

Astin (1974a) hypothesized that if a woman anticipates a conflict between the home-making role and a career, she is likely to forego the career, but more recent studies suggest that though today's gifted women may be prepared to interrupt their career to have a family, they will not give it up altogether. Of very gifted eighth-grade girls in 1980, 94 per cent wanted a career, even if it were not financially necessary, though over 70 per cent of them anticipated working only part-time or not at all when their children were young (Fox, et al., 1982). The vast majority of 3000 college students of both sexes in the United States (Leland, 1980) felt that mothers should either not work or work only part-time until their children were five years-old. In spite of the fact that the women respondents were preparing for careers and planned to take higher degrees, they still perceived a conflict between their career goals and hopes for marriage and children. They wanted maternity leaves of several years so that their careers would not have to be sacrificed: yet in the future, long career interuptions may greatly deter career progress due to rapidly advancing technology.

A longitudinal study of gifted women aged twenty-four to thirty-five (Rodenstein and Glickhauf-Hughes, 1979) classified them into three groups. First, the career group who were unmarried, childless, and had a full-time career; secondly, the housewives with children, who had listed this as their occupation; and thirdly, the integrators who were married with children and had a full-time career. Examination of these women's career choices as high-school senior pupils revealed that the career and integrator women had found investigative occupations much more appealing than the housewives, who had been more attracted to social occupations. The latter group also reported that their career choices had been more influenced by their parents than women in the other two groups.

Gifted girls could be expected to be influenced by women they see, and Astin et al. (1976) speculated that while many young women may be attracted to a career, they refocus on the familiar roles of wife and mother due to the lack of 'career' female role models. When gifted eighth-grade children were asked whether or not they knew a man or woman or both in a particular career to whom they could talk about that profession (Fox, et al., 1982), same-sex models were found to be much more available to boys than to girls, particularly in mathematical or scientific careers, such as computer-systems analyst, mathematician, accountant, and chemist. The most extreme example was that of engineer, where only two girls knew a woman, while twenty-five boys knew a man.

Although careers in law and medicine were attractive to the gifted girls of this sample, the boys still knew twice as many male role models as the girls knew female ones. Careers for which access to same-sex models were equal were banker, psychiatrist, and writer-journalist. The careers for which girls knew more women than boys knew men were in fields reflecting social and artistic interests, such as social work and fine arts. The girls were asked whether or not lack of role models led to fewer women in science, mathematics, and engineering; 40 per cent thought it was a serious problem, 44 per cent thought it was a minor problem, and only 17 per cent did not perceive it as a problem at all.

CREATIVITY

Perhaps it is because more men than women pursue full-time careers that they achieve greater public recognition for their creative acts, and consequently studies of creative adults have usually focused on men (MacKinnon, 1960, 1962). Torrance (1972, 1977) suggested that creative women find outlets for their creative energies in the home and community, in ways which are important but do not lead to wider recognition. However, as the number of women making careers increases, presumably more will emerge among the recognized creative contributors to society.

Creative men are reported to possess both masculine and feminine interests and an openness to self (MacKinnon, 1960, 1962). Androgynous women were found by Harrington and Andersen (1981) and by Morse and Bruch (1978) to have stronger creative self-concepts, relative to feminine and undifferentiated subjects, due almost exclusively to their greater masculine advantage, while Weinstein and Bobko (1980) found a positive correlation between androgyny and creativity (unrelated to intelligence), indicating that flexibility in sex-role perceptions is of benefit to the development of the creative person (MacKinnon, 1960, 1962; Getzels and Jackson, 1975). They suggest that women striving to be creative in Western society may experience considerable conflict between the masculine components of their creative self-concepts and pressures toward 'sex-appropriate' characteristics and behaviours; in such a situation, energies which could be expended in creative endeavours are diverted to resolving conflicts.

Although scores on tests of creative potential are equally distributed among males and females (Maccoby and Jacklin, 1974), the expression of creative ideas may involve risks; in one study more gifted boys than girls took part in controversial classroom discussions (Gallagher, 1967), while another found gifted boys to be eight times as likely as gifted girls to challenge the ideas of teachers and peers (Gallagher, et al., 1967); indeed, some teachers encourage and reward independent behaviours more for boys than girls (Dwech and Bush, 1976). On the other hand, when either teachers or parents reinforce sex-role stereotypes they effectively hinder the development of giftedness and creativity.

An alternative approach by Bruch and Morse (Morse, 1978) suggests that creative productivity in women should be studied and explained in terms of dimensions of dependence, femininity, aggression, and aestheticism. Although more research is needed to validate the Bruch-Morse model, it does provide an interesting basis for studying and counselling gifted girls, including an instrument for self-assessment in terms of the model (Morse, 1978). Morse suggests that women can be helped to transform over-dependent behaviour or excessively hostile and aggressive acts to the more ideal state of productive independence by balancing a masculine–feminine trait approach.

IMPLICATIONS OF THE EVIDENCE

Though parents have the first and most important impact on the developing child's self-perceptions of her creative and intellectual abilities, socialization experiences both in the home and in the educational environment are also influential. For the gifted female, those perceptions of stereotyped and non-stereotyped views of women's roles may lead to conflict between who or what she wants to be, as opposed to who or what she is supposed to be, which can become internalized as anxiety and guilt. The following sections will discuss the implications of research findings for parents, educationalists, and counsellors in their guidance of gifted females towards full personal development.

PARENTING

Either parent may become a prime behavioural model for a child, early identification with an intellectual and analytical father being correlated with problem-solving, quantitative interests, and ability for both boys and girls (Milton, 1957), while in reverse, a father's absence in the early years results in children's relatively higher verbal ability (Carlsmith, 1964). Studies of productive and creative female mathematicians found that they tended to be eldest daughters without brothers, but with dominant professional fathers with whom most identified (Helson, 1971). Though their femininity scores were not low, this identification had perhaps enabled them to develop a more typically 'masculine' analytical cognitive style. But even if a gifted girl does not model herself on her father, she may still elicit cues from him to help shape her views of sex-role appropriate behaviour. For example, if her father rewards her solely for her beauty and social behaviour, rather than her curiosity and intellect, she may form the impression that she will not be valued by men if she appears to be 'smart'.

Hoffman (1972) has described several studies showing that the more a girl identified with her mother and the more feminine she was, the less her likelihood of becoming a high achiever. However, Hoffman has pointed out that the mother's actual characteristics had been ignored by these investigators, and the significant factor may not have been one of identification with the mother *per se*, but rather with a theoretical stereotyped passive and dependent woman. Referring to the belief that highly achieving females had hostile mothers, she redefined 'maternal hostility' as the replacement of 'smother love' with the encouragement of independence and autonomy.

Early interest in mathematics is more likely to be noticed and supported by parents of boys than of girls. Gifted girls who took high-school advanced placement courses in science and mathematics reported their early frustrations in trying to get chemistry or construction sets as toys (Casserly, 1980); their parents seemed to fear that they would hurt themselves with a chemistry set, though not in the kitchen. Fox *et al.* (1982) found that mathematically well-motivated girls had experienced strong support for acceleration and high educational expectations from both parents, particularly their mothers, in mathematics or the sciences. Girls seem to need sufficient parental support to enable them to carry out 'atypical' risk-taking behaviour such as accelerating in mathematics, though parental attitudes appear to make little difference to boys' behaviour in this respect.

EDUCATIONAL PLANNING

Once children have been identified as gifted, they may be offered special educational opportunities, such as some form of grade-skipping, or at least subject matter acceleration by one or two years, which is generally successful (Marland, 1972). To be most effective, however, it should be timed to avoid adjustment problems, which are compounded by the variation in the developmental stages of boys and girls.

Since girls are often developmentally ahead of boys, early admission to kindergarten or first grade should be even more effective for them than for boys. But in the secondary school years, the balance is likely to change. A sample of gifted seventh- and eighth-grade boys and girls who entered a mathematics contest at The Johns Hopkins University were canvassed as to their attitudes toward acceleration. Girls were significantly less in favour of acceleration for themselves than boys, only 54 per cent of the girls approving of this, compared with 73 per cent of the boys (Fox, 1976a). The girls were also more fearful than the boys both of possible rejection by peers for academic acceleration, and of trying something different because they might not succeed. Girls who had high self-esteem, as measured by expectations for success in the contest, were more likely to favour acceleration than girls who predicted they would score average or poorly, relative to the other girls in the contest; but the most-able girls were not necessarily high on self-esteem or on eagerness to accelerate. Perhaps gifted girls are more willing than boys to suffer intellectual boredom, if it will ensure their social standing in a peer group.

Sex differences in acceleration and course-taking are reflected through participation in the Advanced Placement Program (APP) in the United

States. These are courses specifically designed for the academically talented, which allow pupils to earn advancement in college for work done in high school. Gifted girls take fewer of these courses than boys—particularly in mathematics and science. For example, in 1974, girls made up only between 7 and 17 per cent of the APP candidates in different levels of chemistry and physics, and 28 per cent in mathematics (Casserly, 1975). In 1975, 50 384 exams were taken by boys and 34 402 were taken by girls. Of the nineteen different exams given, girls outnumbered the boys in only six: Art history, Studio art, English, French language, French literature, and Spanish. Boys outnumber girls in American history, European history, the Classics, German, and all the science and mathematics courses including Biology (CEEB, 1978).

The Study of Mathematically Precocious Youth has encouraged gifted students to enter college one or more years early, via college work taken while still in high school, but far more boys than girls who were counselled have done so. Only a few girls have been willing to take college courses while still in junior or senior high school (Solano and George, 1976), and the number of girls among considerably accelerated pupils is miniscule (Stanley, 1977). The boys' agreement to swift acceleration may be due to their greater willingness to take risks and to their career interests and values. Rapid acceleration is also more feasible in the sciences and mathematics than the humanities and social sciences at the present time, and as noted before, more gifted boys than girls are interested in these areas.

If some degree of acceleration in the rate of learning is necessary for gifted pupils, it is suggested here that it must be provided for girls in a way which reduces social conflicts and pressures for them. At the elementary- and junior- high-school levels, across-age-grouping and more individualized approaches to teaching may be more appealing to gifted girls than grade-skipping or half-day arrangements, where the pupil is assigned to different grade levels and classes for specific subjects. Accelerated classes in mathematics in mixed-sex junior high schools have worked well for boys, but may not work as well for girls, unless there is a sizable number of girls in the class (Fox, 1977). Hall (1982) has reported how university credit courses, held directly in high schools, were clearly effective in attracting girls, this success being attributed to their integration into the regular school day.

There is little research on the relative effects of enrichment education for boys versus girls. However, it could be expected that, though there may be little difference at the elementary school level, enrichment classes in literature, writing, and art would have greater appeal to girls, and mathematics or science to boys at the secondary school. But it may be that the style, conduct, and ratio of the sexes in the enrichment class may have more important influences on pupils' reception of the material than the actual subject matter.

Enrichment classes which focus on the development of psychological risk-taking and independence of thought may be particularly beneficial for girls, as would enrichment which focused on career exploration, providing role models and work involvement to broaden their horizons and reduce sex-role stereotyped thinking. Because the intellectually gifted female has fewer female role models with whom she can identify (Fox *et al.*, 1982), her fears related to being a 'pioneer' are intensified. Opportunities should be provided to allow girls to get to know professional women, to help their career awareness and exploration experiences, such as that developed by the Intellectually Gifted Child Study Group at The Johns Hopkins University (Fox and Tobin, 1978). However, the removal of adolescent girls from their peers for special attention may make them as resistant to enrichment as they are to acceleration. Activities could be provided on Saturdays, after school, during the summer, or interwoven into the regular classroom so that the nature of this 'gifted' experience (as opposed to accelerative practices) would cause fewer conflicts.

Grouping by sex can be valuable for some school subjects at certain ages, but over the past decade, grouping of children by either ability or sex has become rare in the United States. This is an unfortunate situation for some gifted girls, who need supportive networks of girlfriends with similar interests, as well as opportunities to develop their intellectual aggressiveness. In mixed-sex classes, some adolescent girls are reluctant to participate actively in competition with male peers, either from fear that they may be wrong and appear stupid, or that they will be correct and appear too smart—notably in lessons on subjects traditionally considered to be male-orientated (Gallagher, 1967; Gallagher, *et al.*, 1967; Walber, 1969). Sometimes if the element of choice is removed, it leads to more girls taking those subjects; for example, Farley (1969) has shown that girls who were required to take advanced mathematics achieved as well as those who had elected to do so, and the 'required' girls proved to be the more self-confident.

An all-girl accelerated algebra class was more effective in recruiting girls than were several mixed-sex classes (Fox, 1976b; Fox and Cohn, 1980). Girls in all-female physical-science classes viewed the subject matter as less masculine than girls in co-educational classes (Vockell and Lobanc, 1981). It is suggested that in such classes, girls are not a deviant minority, and therefore they are able to develop their subject preferences without inhibition. Findings from the Brown Project, 'Men and women learning together' (Leland, 1980) have shown that a higher than average proportion of women felt they had gained confidence at single-sex colleges, as well as having been prepared for further studies. Tidball (1980) also found that highly selective women's colleges produced more than twice as many achievers as highly selective co-educational institutions. If it is not possible to group by sex, efforts should at least be made to involve enough girls in a class to create a supportive atmosphere for them.

The use of more diagnostic-prescriptive teaching techniques would allow gifted girls to proceed at whatever pace their abilities dictate, without being labelled as 'special'. In fact, the ultimate solution for the gifted girl, as in the case of the slow learner, may be the abolishment of age-grade segregation.

COUNSELLING AND GUIDANCE

Counselling and guidance strategies should focus on the whole individual, thus providing both academic guidance, as it relates to achievement, career development, and decision-making, as well as counselling for the social-emotional issues of growth and development. Strategies for the gifted girl should be focused on her unconditional acceptance of her exceptional abilities, along with an exploration of the often contradictory and emotionally disturbing socialization messages which can result in underachievement.

While some of these messages are loud and clear, others can be so subtle! For example, Colangelo and Zaffran (1979) provided a framework for differential guidance and counselling within gifted populations of both 'enriched-gifted' and 'accelerated-gifted' personalities. The 'enriched-gifted' pupils were described as having an interest and ability to establish a relationship with a problem, enabling them to delve into the investigation with extraordinary depth. On the other hand, accelerated-gifted pupils were described as primarily interested in the mastery and integration of new material. Colangelo and Zaffran must have realized the inherent danger of sex-role stereotyping with regard to their framework—their example of the enriched pupil is male and the accelerated one is female, which is quite contrary to research findings on sex differences with regard to attitudes towards acceleration (Fox, 1976a). The significant point is that if counsellors and teachers view gifted females as stereotyped 'enriched' personalities, without supportively exploring and challenging why they appear to be so (in an attempt to heighten the pupil's level of awareness, as well as their own), the social-emotional component of counselling and guidance services will have been lost, and under-achievement will continue.

Support from teachers and counsellors is vital for gifted girls to facilitate the development of their giftedness, competence, independence, and self-confidence. Female mathematicians often credit the encouragement of a teacher as a major factor in their pursuit of the study of mathematics (Luchins and Luchins, 1980; Chapter 10). Casserly (1980) found that teachers in American high schools which had over twice the national percentage of girls enrolled in their APP (Advanced Placement Program) courses in mathematics and science, showed few signs of sex-role stereotyping in either their thinking or classroom behaviour; they expected and demanded high-level performances from the girls as well as the boys. Additionally, many of the pupils interviewed by Casserly reported that they had been 'tracked' as early as the fourth grade into gifted education, so that for them, taking APP courses was just a natural progression.

However, interviews with high-school counsellors in the Casserly investigation (1980) revealed that they often discouraged gifted girls from taking APP courses. Casserly hypothesized that women counsellors tended to project their own dislike or fear of science and mathematics in their counselling of girls. Their stated reasons for advising the girls out of APP courses included the loss of time needed for social activities, and the fear that the girls might obtain low grades in these courses, thereby harming their otherwise excellent academic records. Yet, those who took the APP courses actually earned high grades in them. The men counsellors' argument for counselling girls out of APP courses was different. They explained that it would be 'unfair to the girls' to encourage them to take the courses because the physical sciences job market was so tight and, of course, the jobs should go to the men. This study clearly illuminates the barriers which still exist for gifted girls.

While there are some counsellors who do seek to discourage gifted girls openly, the subtle transmissions which take place in counsellors' offices are perhaps even more dangerous, because they are more difficult to identify, and therefore even harder to change. The results of Buczek's study (1981) failed to support her hypothesis that counsellors would ignore the vocational concerns of female clients, but she did find that male counsellors asked girls more questions about family relationships and their social functioning. Buczek suggested that male counsellors expected these issues to be more relevant to the girls, even though the issues presented by the male and female clients in the study were the same. The implication seems to be that though most counsellors do not directly discourage female clients from taking up non-traditional vocational concerns, they may be indirectly discouraging them by focusing on potential social conflicts. Without encouragement and sound support from networks, most girls are likely to opt for the 'no go' path of least resistance, pursuing traditional career options.

Whether a gifted girl is taking an APP course, accelerating her high-school academic studies, or choosing a male-dominated career path, she may, in addition to her internal conflicts, at times find peer pressures acute, so that she either fears or experiences being rejected for pursuing 'masculine' interests. How many gifted girls counsel themselves out of enjoying extra provision because they fear becoming either 'social misfits' or 'academic brainheads', which would place their social relationships in jeopardy—particularly with the opposite sex?

Girls' perceptions of the possible negative consequences of appearing too bright or creative are all too often accurate. Both teachers and adolescent pupils hold a more negative stereotype of mathematically gifted girls than of boys (Solano, 1977). Of children who scored high on measures of creativity, the 'deviant' boys were found to be popular, but the girls were not (Torrance, 1959). However, Tidwell (1980) found that while gifted male and female pupils considered themselves 'happy', they also saw themselves—in apparent contradiction—as 'unpopular' with their peers. She offered the explanation that feelings of happiness for this population were not contingent upon the approval of others. Interestingly, Ross and Parker (1980) also found that gifted pupils possess significantly lower expectations of success in social, as opposed to academic pursuits, which they thought was possibly because gifted students focus their attention on accelerating academic skills, at the expense of interpersonal development. It seems from the two previous studies that gifted adolescent girls feel they have to make some sort of choice, either in improving their social obligations and interpersonal development, or by participating in gifted education.

Sometimes a change in the curriculum can be quicker and more effective for gifted girls than counselling, as Safter and Bruch (1981) have pointed out. However, curriculum changes are not usually made by counsellors, but administrators, whose approval at the very least, must be secured before any measures can be adopted—however long it takes!

But the real key initial stimulus for rapid and far-reaching change is awareness. An extended network of change agents could be brought about by the provision of in-service programmes for administrators and school personnel, designed to alert these professionals to the special needs of this population. It should, of course, also include the girls themselves, as well as their parents and significant others who could be reached through awareness activities. However, responsibility for effecting change is not a one-way burden, for investment and involvement in the gifted female's future leads to all-round growth, progress, and prosperity.

CONCLUSIONS

To pretend that gifted women and girls are not different from gifted men and boys is to diminish respect for the qualities of both sexes. Although early brain research results indicate different cognitive styles for males and females, personality differences appear to be more the result of sex-specific expectations, which are reinforced at home and in school. It is feasible, however, that some of the presently recognized sex differences may decrease as attitudes and values change, most particularly with the diligent and continued efforts to reduce sex-stereotyped thinking and behaviour on the part of parents, educators, and the young people themselves. The 'seeds' of achievement/career/marriage/family conflicts are planted early.

Women in the United States, notably those in the labour force, are experiencing feelings of ambiguity over their gender roles, as are the men with whom they are involved. These evolutionary changes are seen in the provision of on-site child-care facilities at places of employment, requests for paternity leave, and dual-career couples' attempts to build flexibility into their work in order to share their parenting responsibilities. While the changes themselves are significant, the actual numbers of people participating in them are not. It is probably due as much to economic responsibilities as to conscious gender-role changes that the dual career couple phenomenon has arisen; but whatever the reasons, combining a career and a family still presents more problems for women than for men. Thus, gifted girls will most likely continue to need more counselling and support in planning their career and life goals, than boys. However, with early identification, they can enjoy and benefit from improved support and encouragement, as they move through the developmental stages of childhood and adolescence to become gifted women.

It is important to ask the following questions when planning and evaluating educational provision for the gifted.

1. Are approximately equal number of boys and girls being identified? If not, why not? Are the selection procedures biased or the provision more attractive to one sex than the other?
2. Do girls and boys who participate in educational provision for the gifted achieve equally well? If not, why not?
3. Are efforts made to use non-sexist instructional materials and language laid down in the programme? If not, why not?
4. Are girls and boys encouraged to participate in intellectual risk-taking activities to the same degree? If not, why not?
5. Are the expectations, aspirations, and confidence levels of boys and girls in the classes about the same? If not, why not?

There is need for more research on how gifted females should be treated, as distinct from gifted males. Efforts should be made to investigate the effects of personality variables and of socialization experiences at different developmental stages, on achievement, behaviours, and expectations of both sexes. But it is important to stress that the finding of differences should not be interpreted as superior versus inferior, better or worse—just different. Our goal as educators is to facilitate optimal human growth and development, which includes helping gifted girls to achieve both good peer relationships and a challenging educational experience. We should not aim to educate women to be more like men, but instead design and adapt educational and career situations to accommodate and produce competent and productive adults of both sexes.

REFERENCES

Allport, G. W., Vernon, P. E., and Lindzey, G. (1970). *Manual for the Study of Values: A Scale for Measuring the Dominant Interests in Personality.* Houghton Mifflin, Boston.

Astin, H. S. (1974a). Overview of the findings. In *Women: A Bibliography on Their Education and Careers* (eds H. Astin, H. Suniewick and S. Dweck). Behavioral Publications Incorporated, New York, 1–10.

Astin H. S. (1974b). Sex differences in mathematical and scientific precocity. In *Mathematical Talent: Discovery, Description and Development* (eds J. C. Stanley, D. P. Keating and L. H. Fox), The Johns Hopkins University Press, Baltimore.

Astin H. S., Harway, M., and McNamara, P. (1976). *Sex Discrimination in Education: Access to Post Secondary Education.* National Center for Education Statistics, Education Division, Department of Health, Education and Welfare, February, p. 284.

Bachtold, L. M., and Werner, E. G. (1970). Personality profiles of gifted women: psychologists. *American Psychologist,* 25, 234–243.

Bachtold, L. M., and Werner, E. E. (1972). Personality characteristics of women scientists. *Psychological Reports,* 31, 2, 391–396.

Bachtold, L. M., and Werner, E. (1973). Personality characteristics of creative women. *Perceptual and Motor Skills.* 36, 1, 311–319.

Bakan, D. (1966). *The Duality of Human Existence.* Rand McNally, Chicago. Bem, S. (1974). The measurement of psychological androgyny. *Journal of Consulting and Clinical Psychology,* 42, 2, 155–162.

Bem, S. (1975). Sex role adaptability: One consequence of psychological androgyny. *Journal of Personality and Social Psychology,* 31, 4, 634–643.

Bem, S. (1977). On the utility of alternative procedures for assessing psychological androgyny. *Journal of Consulting and Clinical Psychology,* 45, 2, 196–205.

Bem, S., Martyna, W., and Watson, C. (1975). Sex typing and androgyny: Further explorations of the expressive domain. *Journal of Personality and Social Psychology,* 34, 5, 1016–1023.

Bem, S., and Lenney, E. (1976). Sex typing and the avoidance of cross sex behaviour. *Journal of Personality and Social Psychology,* 33, 1, 48–54.

Birch, J. W. (1954). Early school admission for mentally advanced children. *Exceptional Children,* 21, 3, 84–87.

Blaubergs, M. S. (1978). Personality studies of gifted females: An overview and commentary. *The Gifted Child Quarterly,* 22, 4, 539–547.

Block, J. H. (1973). Conception of sex role: Some cross-cultural and longitudinal perceptives. *American Psychologist,* 28, 6, 512–526.

Brody, L., and Fox, L. H. (1980). An accelerative intervention program for mathematically gifted girls. In *Women and the Mathematical Mystique* (eds L. H. Fox, L. Brody and D. Tobin). The Johns Hopkins University Press, Baltimore, 164–178.

Buczek, T. A. (1981). Sex biases in counseling: Counselor retention of the concerns of a female and male client. *Journal of Counseling Psychology,* 28, 1, 13–21.

Callahan, C. M. (1979). The gifted and talented women. In *Education of the Gifted and Talented* (ed. A. H. Passow). The Seventy-eighth Yearbook of the National Society for the Study of Education, University of Chicago Press, Chicago.

Carlsmith, L. (1964). Effect of early father absence on scholastic aptitude. *Harvard Educational Review,* 34, 3–21.

Carney, M., and Morgan, C. S. (1981). Female college persisters: Non-traditional career fields. *Journal of College Student Personnel,* 22, 5, 418–423.

Casserly, P. L. (1975). An assessment of factors affecting female participation in advanced placement programs in mathematics, chemistry and physics. Unpublished report of National Science Foundation, Grant No. GY-11325.

Casserly P. L. (1980). Factors affecting female participation in advanced placement programs in mathematics, chemistry and physics. In *Women and the Mathematical Mystique* (eds L. H. Fox, L. Brody and D. Tobin). The Johns Hopkins University Press, Baltimore.

Colangelo, N., and Zaffran, R. T. (1979). Special issues in counseling the gifted. *Counseling and Human Development,* 11, 5, 1–12.

(CEEB) College Entrance Examination Board (1978). *National Report on College Bound Seniors,* Box 886, New York, NY 10101, USA.

Constantinople, A. (1973). Masculinity-femininity: An exception to a famous dictum? *Psychological Bulletin,* 80, 5, 389–407.

Dweck, D. S., and Bush, E. S. (1976). Sex differences in learned helplessness: I. Differential debilitation with peer and adult evaluators. *Developmental Psychology,* 12, 2, 147–156.

Entwisle, D. R., and Greenberger, E. (1972). Adolescents' views of women's work role. *American Journal of Orthopsychiatry,* 42, 4, 648–656.

Farley, M. C. (1969). A study of the mathematical interests, attitudes and achievement of tenth and eleventh grade students. Doctoral dissertation, University of Michigan, 1968, *Dissertation Abstracts International,* 29, 3039A. (University Microfilms No. 69-2312.)

Fennema, E. (1977). Influences of selected cognitive, affective, and educational variables on sex-related differences in mathematics learning and studying. *Women and Mathematics: Research Perspectives for Change,* (NIE Papers in Education and Work: No. 8) Education and Work Group, The National Institute of Education, US Department of Health, Education and Welfare, Washington, DC.

Fox, L. H. (1976a). Second annual report to the Spencer Foundation on its three-year grant to the Evening College and Summer Session of The Johns Hopkins University, covering the second year of the grant, September 1, 1975 through August 31, 1976. Intellectually Gifted Child Study Group (IGCSG), The Johns Hopkins University. Baltimore.

Fox, L. H. (1976b). Sex differences in mathematical talent: Bridging the gap. In *Intellectual Talent: Research and Development* (ed. D. P. Keating), The Johns Hopkins University Press, Baltimore, chapter 9, pp. 183–214.

Fox, L. H. (1977). The effects of sex role socialization on mathematics participation and achievement. In *Women and Mathematics: Research Perspectives for Change* (ed. Shoemaker). (NIE Papers in Education and Work: No. 8), Education and Work Group, The National Institute of Education, US Department of Health, Education and Welfare, Washington, DC.

Fox, L. H., and Denham, S. A. (1974). Values and career interests of mathematically and scientifically precocious youth. In *Mathematical Talent: Discovery, Description, and Development* (eds J. C. Stanley, D. P. Keating and L. H. Fox), The Johns Hopkins University Press, Baltimore, pp. 140–175.

Fox, L. H., Pasternak, S. R., and Peiser, N. L. (1976). Career related interests of adolescent boys and girls. In *Intellectual Talent: Research and Development* (ed. D. P. Keating), The Johns Hopkins University Press, Baltimore.

Fox, L. H., and Tobin, D. (1978). Broadening career horizons of gifted girls. G/C/T, September/October, 45, 18–22.

Fox, L. H., Brody, L., and Tobin, D. (1979). *Women and Mathematics: The Impact of Early Intervention upon Course-Taking and Attitudes in High School.* Final Report to the National Institute of Education on its Grant No. NIE-G-77-0062, The Johns Hopkins University Press, Baltimore.

Fox, L. H., and Cohn, S. J. (1980). Sex differences in the development of precocious mathematical talent. In *Women and the Mathematical Mystique* (eds L. H. Fox, L. Brody and D. Tobin), The Johns Hopkins University Press, Baltimore, pp. 94–112.

Fox, L. H., Brody, L., and Robin, D. (1982). The study of social processes that inhibit or enhance the development of competence and interest in mathematics among highly able young women. Report to the National Institute of Education on its two year grant, No. NIE-G-79-0113, Intellectually Gifted Child Study Group, The Johns Hopkins University, Baltimore.

Gallagher, J. J. (1967). Teachers variation in concept presentation in Biological Science Curriculum Study curriculum program. *Biological Science Curriculum Newsletter*, **30**, 8–19.

Gallagher, J. J., Aschner, M., and Jenne, W. (1967). *Productive Thinking of Gifted Children in Classroom Interaction.* Council for Exceptional Children Research Monograph Series B5, Council for Exceptional Children, Arlington, Virginia.

Getzels, J. W., and Jackson, P. W. (1975). The study of giftedness: A multidimensional approach. In *Psychology and Education of the Gifted*, 2nd edn. (eds W. B. Barbe and J. S. Renzulli), Irvington Publishers, New York.

Grant, W. V., and Lind, C. G. (1979). *Digest of Education Statistics*, 17th edn, National Center for Education Statistics, US Government Printing Office, Washington, DC.

Grant, W. V., and Eiden, L. J. (1982). *Digest of Education Statistics—1982.* National Center for Education Statistics, US Government Printing Office, Washington, DC.

Haier, R., and Denham, S. A. (1976). A summary profile of the non-intellectual correlates of mathematical precocity in boys and girls. In *Intellectual Talent: Research and Development* (ed. D. P. Keating). The Johns Hopkins University Press, Baltimore.

Hall, E. G. (1980). Sex differences in IQ development for intellectually gifted students. *Roeper Review*, **2**, 3, 25–28.

Hall, E. G. (1982). Accelerating gifted girls. *G/C/T*, **25**, 48–50.

Harrington, D. M., and Anderson, S.M. (1981). Creativity, masculinity, and three models of psychological androgyny. *Journal of Personality and Social Psychology*, **41**, 4, 744–757.

Helson, R. (1971). Women mathematicians and the creative personality. *Journal of Counseling and Clinical Psychology*, **36**, 2, 210–220.

Hobson, J. R. (1963). High school performance of underage pupils initially admitted to kindergarten on the basis of physical and psychological examinations. *Educational and Psychological Measurement*, **23**, 1, 159–170.

Hoffman, L. W. (1972). Early childhood experiences and women's achievement motives. *Journal of Social Issues*, **28**, 2, 129–155.

Holahan, C. K. (1981). Lifetime achievement patterns, retirement and life satisfaction of gifted aged women. *Journal of Gerontology*, **36**, 6, 741–749.

Hollan, J. L. (1965). *Manual for the Vocational Preference Inventory.* Consulting Psychologists Press, Palo Alto, Calif.

Horner, M. (1968). Sex differences in achievement motivation and performance in competitive and non-competitive situations. Unpublished Doctoral dissertation, University of Michigan.

Horner, M. (1972). Toward an understanding of achievement-related conflicts in women. *Journal of Social Issues*, **28**, 2, 157–173.

Leland, C. (1980). Men and women learning together: A study of college students in the late 70s. Unpublished manuscript, Brown University.

Lemkau, J. P. (1979). Personality and background characteristics of women in male-dominated occupations: A review. *Psychology of Women Quarterly*, **4**, 2, 221–240.

Lessinger, L. M., and Martinson, R. A. (1961). The use of the CPI with gifted pupils. Personnel and Guidance Journal, **39**, 572–575.

Luchins, E. H., and Luchins, A. S. (1980). Female mathematicians: A contemporary appraisal. In *Women and the Mathematical Mystique* (eds L. H. Fox, L. Brody and D. Tobin). The Johns Hopkins University Press, Baltimore.

Maccoby, E. E. (1963). Women's intellect. In *The Potential of Woman* (eds S. M. Farber and R. H. L. Wilson). McGraw-Hill, New York.

Maccoby, E. E., and Jacklin, C. N. (1974). *The Psychology of Sex Differences*, Stanford University Press, Stanford, Calif.

MacKinnon, D. W. (1960). The highly effective individual. *Teachers College Record*, **61**, 367–378.

MacKinnon, D. W. (1962). The nature and nurture of creative talent. *American Psychologist*, **17**, 7, 484–495.

Marland, S. P., Jnr. (1972). *Education of the Gifted and Talented*. Report to the Congress of the United States by the US Commissioner of Education, Department of Health, Education and Welfare, Washington, DC.

Mills, C. (1980). Sex-role-related personality correlates of intellectual abilities in adolescents. *Roeper Review*, **2**, 3, 29–31.

Mills, C. J. (1981). Sex roles, personality, and intellectual abilities in adolescents. Journal of Youth and Adolescence, **10**, 2, 85–112.

Milton, G. A. (1957). The effects of sex role identification on problem-solving skill. *Journal of Abnormal and Social Psychology*, **55**, 208–212.

Morse, J. A. (1978). Freeing women's creative potential. *The Gifted Child Quarterly*, **22**, 4, 459–467.

Morse, J. A., and Bruch, C. B. (1978). A comparison of sex roles of creative-productive versus non-productive women. *The Gifted Child Quarterly*, **22**, 4, 520–525.

Oden, M. H. (1968). The fulfillment of promise: 4O-year follow-up of the Terman gifted group. *Genetic Psychology Monographs*, **77**, 3–93.

Orlofsky, J. L., and Stake, J. E. (1981). Psychological masculinity and femininity: Relationship to striving and self-concept in achievement and inter-personal domains. *Psychology of Women Quarterly*, **6**, 2, 218–233.

Parsons, T., and Bales, R. F. (1955). *Family, Socialization and Interaction Process*. Free Press, Glencoe, Illinois.

Results of the OTID (1982). *Talent Search and Possible Educational Strategies*. Office of Talent Identification and Development (OTID) publication.

Rodenstein, J. M., and Glickhauf-Hughes, C. (1979). Career and lifestyle determinants of gifted women. In *New Voices in Counseling the Gifted* (eds N. Colangelo and R. T. Zaffran). Kendall/Hunt Publishing Company, Dubuque, Iowa.

Ross, A., and Parker, M. (1980). Academic and social self concepts of the academically gifted. *Exceptional Children*, **47**, 2, 6–10.

Safter, H. T., and Bruch, C. B. (1981). Use of the DGG model for differential guidance for the gifted. *The Gifted Child Quarterly*, **25**, 4, 167–174.

Sears, R. R. (1976). Sources of life satisfaction in the Terman gifted men. Paper presented at the 1976 meeting of the American Psychological Association, September, Washington, DC.

Sherman, J. (1977). The effects of biological factors on sex-related differences in mathematics achievement. *Women and Mathematics Research Perspectives for Change* (NIE papers in Education and Work: No. 8), Educational and Work Group, The National Institute for Education, US Department of Education and Welfare, Washington, DC.

Solano, C. H. (1977). Teacher and pupil stereotypes of gifted boys and girls. *Talents and Gifts*, **19**, 4, 4.

Solano, C. H., and George, W. C. (1976). College courses for the gifted. *Gifted Child Quarterly*, **20**, 3, 274–285.

Spence, J. T., and Helmreich, R. L. (1978). *Masculinity and Femininity: Their Psychological Dimensions, Correlates and Antecedents*. University of Texas Press, Austin.

Spence, J. L., Helmreich, R., and Stapp, J. (1975). Ratings of self and peers on sex role attributes and their relation to self esteem and conceptions of masculinity and femininity. *Journal of Personality and Social Psychology*, **32**, 1, 29–39.

Stanley, J. C. (1977). Rationale of the study of mathematically precocious youth (SMPY) during its first five years of promoting educational acceleration. In *The Gifted and the Creative: A Fifty-year Perspective* (eds J. C. Stanley, W. C. George and C. H. Solano). The Johns Hopkins University Press, Baltimore, pp. 75–112.

Stencel, S. (1981). Equal pay fight. In *Editorial Research Reports*, **1**, 209–228.

Terman, L. M. (ed.) (1925). Mental and physical traits of a thousand gifted children. *Genetic Studies of Genius*, Vol. 1, Stanford University Press, Stanford.

Terman, L. M., and Oden, M. H. (eds) (1947). *Genetic Studies of Genius*, Vol IV, *The Gifted Child Grows Up*. Stanford University Press, Stanford.

Tidball, M. E. (1980). Women's colleges and women achievers revisited. *SIGNS— Journal of Women in Culture and Society*, **5**, 3, 504–517.

Tidwell, R. (1980). A psycho-educational profile of 1,593 gifted high school students. *The Gifted Child Quarterly*, **24**, 2, 63–68.

Title IX: (1981). The half full, half empty glass. National Advisory Council on Women's Educational Programs, US Government Printing Office, Washington, DC.

Tittle, C. K., McCarthy, K., and Steckler, J. F. (1974). *Women and Educational Testing*. Educational Testing Service, Princeton, New Jersey.

Torrance, E. P. (1959). Explorations in creative thinking in the early school years. Highly intelligent and highly creative in a laboratory school. Research Memorandum, Bureau of Educational Research, College of Education, University of Minnesota, Minneapolis, (BER 59-7).

Torrance, E. P. (1972). Creative young women in today's world. *Exceptional Children*, **39**, 597–603.

Torrance, E. P. (1977). Creativity gifted and disadvantaged gifted students. In *The Gifted and Creative: A Fifty-year Perspective* (eds J. C. Stanley, W. C. George and C. H. Solano). The Johns Hopkins University Press, Baltimore.

Vockell, E. L., and Lobonc, S. (1981). Sex-role stereotyping by high school females in science. *Journal of Research in Science Teaching*, **18**, 3, 209–219.

Walberg, H. (1969). Physics, femininity and creativity. *Developmental Psychology*, **1**, 47–54.

Weinstein, J. B., and Bobko, P. (1980). The relationship between creativity and androgyny when moderated by an intelligence threshold. *The Gifted Child Quarterly*, **24**, 4, 162–166.

Wells, M. A., Peltier, S., and Glickhauf-Hughes, C. (1982). The analysis of the sex role orientation of gifted male and female adolescents. *Roeper Review*, **4**, 4, 46–48.

Wittig, M. A., and Peterson, A. C. (eds.) (1979). *Determinants of Sex-related Differences in Cognitive Functioning.* Academic Press, New York.

Being Gifted

The Psychology of Gifted Children
Edited by Joan Freeman
©1985, John Wiley & Sons, Ltd.

CHAPTER 13

Emotional Aspects of Giftedness

JOAN FREEMAN

It must be said at the outset that most gifted children can be expected to be as well balanced and happy as other children; the primary difference between gifted and other children is one of ability. Giftedness, however, is a relative quality, its meaning varying over cultures and centuries, so that it cannot be described as excellence *per se*, but is always to some extent a matter of subjective judgement. Recognition may not only be in terms of ability, but influenced by personal and socially bound behavioural expectations, so that it is important to know how children come to be selected as gifted, especially when general conclusions may be drawn from such investigations. For these reasons, it is unlikely that any group of children identified as gifted can be typical of all gifted children.

STEREOTYPES OF THE GIFTED

The effect of identifying, and labelling a child as gifted is not only likely to alter relationships between the child and others, it may also alter her physical circumstances—by placing her in some form of special education. The powerful effects of the label can be seen in the controversies about very high ability (whether it exists and if so, what to do about it), and for the individual child, of creating emotional pressure by prejudicing his own and others' perceptions and expectations about him.

Popular stereotypes of the gifted child seem to be somewhat opposed on either side of the Atlantic. The American image is largely positive, based on Terman's (1925) findings, corroborated by many others, that his Californian sample (who had a high proportion of children from the upper socio-economic levels) were above average in most things, including intelligence, physique, and creativity. In his Michigan study of the effects of labelling children 'gifted', Cornell (1983) found that those who were identified by the school, on either teacher recommendations or tests, were given an idealized role of all-round superiority to fulfil. This is a dangerous feature, also pointed out by Whitmore (1980, and Chapter 3), who calls for a repudiation of the 'Terman Myth' and a more realistic appraisal of the gifted. Even when they did not agree with the school verdict, the parents of Cornell's sample were seen to have a special relationship of pride and closeness with these children, as Renzulli (1979) also found. The effects of this positive stereotyping of the gifted can be, (a) to raise expectations (Marland, 1972), risking neglect of the children's special needs, as they are expected to do well on their own, (b) the build-up of others' resentment of their 'unearned', passively accepted gifts, especially in a society which functions on the principle of rewards for effort (Mead, 1954), and (c) increased pressure on the child to be superb at everything all the time, though he may only be gifted in specific ways.

The evidence for the greater stability of the gifted is, however, far greater than that for their instability, since the research is either specific to certain groups or inconclusive in this respect. For example, Knepper et al. (1983) found in their sample of matched gifted and average eleven year-olds, that the superior cognitive ability of the former was significantly related to improved interpersonal and intrapersonal skills, because they had better coping abilities. The researchers suggested that if these skills were to be thought of as cognitive schemata, then their growth could be stimulated in all children. In adolescence also, Khoury and Appel (1977) concluded from a review of the evidence, that the gifted were not only emotionally more stable, but were more independent, socially active, and imaginative than their average counterparts.

In Britain, though, the stereotype is mainly negative, associating giftedness with 'difficulty', so that parents and teachers of outstanding children expect — and thus often find — emotional problems. This has often been described to the author by the parents of 'difficult' gifted children as the result of such children having to live in a mediocre world or, as Hopkinson (1978) put it, gifted children: 'are prone to sudden bursts of rage resulting from frustration'. This view is illustrated by the father of an English unrecognized gifted child of IQ 166: 'We don't think he's outstanding; not bright enough to be a problem'; another parent of an unrecognized gifted child of IQ 162 said: 'He's not outstanding; he's very happy' (Freeman, 1979). For some children, it can seem to be a licence for anti-social behaviour. This association of gifts with emotional instability is possibly a dilution of the 'genius is akin to madness' outlook, which is strongly held in literature and in the popular imagination in many parts of the world.

The negative stereotype was seen in action in the Gulbenkian Project on Gifted Children in England (Freeman, 1979), where seventy children whose parents had identified them as gifted by joining the National Association for Gifted Children—which did not require objective testing—were studied over a four-year period. Each was compared with two matched control children from the same school class (one having the same non-verbal intellectual ability and the other taken at random for ability), while the 210 homes, the children's schools, parents, teachers, and children were all visited and investigated. When the children who had been identified as gifted by their parents were compared with their controls in terms of emotional behaviour, they were found to be significantly (1 per cent) more disturbed, as described by both parents and teachers. Their equally able classmates, whose parents had not joined the association and did not identify them as gifted, showed a rate of emotional deviance which was no different from that in the general population. All the children with IQs of over 140 were then examined in terms of their emotional ratings, but no relationship could be found between this objective measure and emotional behaviour. The negative stereotype of the gifted child as odd and likely to have emotional problems was found to be rife among parents and teachers, both of whom had sometimes judged the child's giftedness as an aspect of his social behaviour. This procedure would serve to reinforce the image—since only emotionally troubled children would be chosen as gifted— while detracting from the identification as gifted of children who are well balanced, particularly if they are underachieving.

SPECIAL VULNERABILITIES OF THE GIFTED

In spite of the undoubted benefits of being more able than one's fellows, such gifts cannot be treated separately from children's emotional, physical, and educational development. By whatever means giftedness is assessed—by achievement, talent, or potential—these factors act upon each other, often challenging the social structure of many cultures at different levels of intimacy. Because of their exceptionality, gifted children have particular vulnerabilities, which can cause conflict and disruption in their lives, and some of these are outlined below.

Family life

When parents raise a family, they usually expect their children to have abilities and outlooks rather like their own, and their expectations of the children's behaviour will be based on both their own experiences and information about the 'normal' stages of child development. Problems can arise when this is not so, for instance, where one or more of the children is highly able. It is particularly difficult for parents to cope with the relative differences between a child's precocious ability and his chronological age (Khatena, 1982). Not only are different types of behaviour associated with each of them, but as in all child development, though across a wider spectrum, the gifted will slip confusingly into either precocity or childishness without warning.

Questions of negative and positive stereotypes often arise, so that parents may fear both that their child will be 'odd', and that he may outshine them. Most parents, in fact, do not want a gifted child, preferring normal children. Bridges (1973) has suggested that parents of gifted children can be concerned with feelings of their own inadequacy, either in supplying the emotional support that a 'different' child may need, and/or being able to provide a sufficiently stimulating educational environment. However, he found that some parents saw social promotion in being the parents of a gifted child, and were not displeased to live vicariously through him—a dangerous emotional state, when parents can forget that their child is still a child, in their urge to register more and more success.

It would not be unreasonable to expect discord in families to be related to the relative difference between the parents' and children's abilities, though this is perhaps not so much of a problem as that of co-ordination between the gifted child and his less-able siblings, who may feel dominated by the gifted 'know all'. There is some indication that sibling relationships are disrupted when just one of them is gifted (Cornell, 1983). An example of this was described to the author by the mother of an older girl with an IQ of 170, who had a younger brother of average ability—when they went into the garden and she asked the children the names of the flowers, the daughter always knew. If she told her to be quiet and let the boy speak, she felt that she was stifling her and depriving her of her rightful praise, but if she let the girl get it right every time, the boy's morale was constantly being diminished. In the end, the problem was partly solved by sending the boy to boarding school.

It is now well recognized that 'life events', such as divorce, bereavement, or even moving house, can bring about both psychological and physical stress reactions in adults, and also in children (Rutter, 1981). Behaviour problems in highly intelligent children (Pringle, 1970; Freeman, 1979) were clearly related to styles of upbringing and family circumstances. Parents who come for counselling to the National Association for Gifted Children (UK) (Sieghart, 1981) complain mainly about the poor sleep and constant rain of demanding questions from their children, though the Association does recognize that the sample which comes for help is unlikely to be typical of all families with gifted children, and that neither sleep nor questioning habits are free of the effects of parental expectations. The presence of one exceptionally able child in a family can also alter the parents' perceptions of the other children, so that they appear less bright than they really are. Alternatively, the gifted one may adapt to the level of the rest of the family, and under-achieve.

Heightened sensitivity

Some researchers, e.g. Gesell *et al.* (1965), have described gifted children as being particularly alert at birth, though there is no systematically gathered evidence on this matter. Attentiveness, though, has been found to be related to social-class more than IQ. A follow up study of thirty-five ten-year-old boys and thirty-three girls, who had been assessed for attentiveness (among other things) starting at four months old (Kagan *et al.*, 1979), found that though it did predict IQ and reading ability, these outcomes were more closely associated with those of parental characteristics, especially social-class, rather than infant attributes.

Others, such as Cruickshank (1963), have argued that it is the child's supersensitivity itself which creates intellectual giftedness by allowing him to assimilate extraordinary amounts of sensory input, a theory recently underlined by Scarr and McCartney (1983) from genetic evidence. Certainly, children in the Gulbenkian sample who scored in the top 1 per cent of the Ravens' Matrices non-verbal test of intellectual functioning described themselves as very sensitive, able to empathize, and able to attend simultaneously to more than one source of input. However, those with even mild emotional problems were less so, their disturbance appearing to blunt the very fine edge of their perceptual processing.

It is possible that the intellectually gifted child is better able to pick up communication signals, though acute perception on the basis of little experience can also result in some misinterpretation of signals. For example, gifted children can be overly responsive to criticism, some appearing to take it more to heart than average children. In addition, perhaps due to their perfectionism, the resulting poor self-image produces stress, and some degree of social isolation, which in turn, can hamper normal reconfirming communication. A high intelligence can construct a great variety of complex and effective defensive outer shields against such painful emotion, the level of which depends to some extent on the support they receive for their 'differentness' from others, as well as on their own ability to cope. In younger gifted children, it may give them the appearance of compliance and achievement, but leave them overly controlled emotionally, possibly erupting in adolescence into either rejection of adult values or withdrawal. Defensive self-isolation from close contact with age-peers, with whom they are out of step, can also bring about anxiety and depression (see Chapter 15), though it has been claimed that such specific problems of interpersonal dynamics can respond well to psychotherapeutic intervention (Osborne and Taylor, 1980).

Unrealistic expectations

McClelland (1955) has pointed out how children who expect too much of themselves perforce begin to develop a sense of failure, to the extent that they may give up trying. Some intellectually gifted children, well balanced in other respects, may set themselves unattainable goals, being aware of what could be accomplished, without making allowance for their own child-level skills. Failure to achieve the aimed-for standard may then be seen as a personal fault, rather than as the result of the child's age and experience. Adults can also make unreasonable demands on such children, perhaps being unaware of the emotional support which they need in their efforts. They may also generalize, unjustifiably, from a child's high ability in one area of development, such as advanced verbal ability, to assume high ability and emotional maturity in others. Children have been found to be more influenced by their parents' estimates about their own abilities than by their own past achievements (Parsons et al., 1982). A possible result of these unreal expectations is a fear in the child of disappointing others, which interferes with her psychological freedom to explore. These expectations, whether coming from home or school, are largely social in origin and one likely outcome, where they are too much for the child to cope with, is for him to take refuge in poor performance to escape the constant pressure.

Gifted children can be a source of vicarious success for some parents and teachers, and the temptation for them to 'stretch' the child in the name of educational justice can be punishing to the recipient. The burden of constantly living up to high expectations handicaps a child from accepting himself as a whole person with imperfections, especially where love may seem to be dependent on success, yet failure to reach every set goal is inevitable. Pressure by parents on children to achieve was almost palpable in a few of the homes visited in the author's research (Freeman, 1979). Some parents did not allow their children to 'waste' their time reading comics or watching television, so that they tended to comply by collecting more and more information. They were less able to mix equally with others, were sometimes more 'childish' for their age, and were found to have generally less well integrated intellectual and emotional lives. It would be understandable if the roots of later guilt and dissatisfaction were to be found there.

Emotional causes of under-achievement

Achievement is normally defined in terms of expectations of performance, based on assessements of ability, whether these are subjective, or by scores on tests, such as IQ, verbal reasoning, or school assessments. The measurement of giftedness, however, by an IQ score of 130 or more has been found to be progressively affected as IQ rises by children's environments

(Freeman, 1981; and Chapter 1), and also by other factors such as emotional disturbance and being in a minority culture (see Chapter 3). Though Hildreth's (1966) proposal that intellectual giftedness be assessed using both clinical and long-term approaches would doubtless improve the accuracy of identification, it would be helpful to consider achievement in broader, 'whole child' terms. A high IQ could be recognized as a measure of what a child has learned informally from the environment, and school achievement tests as the child's uptake from systematic teaching. The question would then change from simply asking why a child is under-achieving to why he has learned so well in one environment and not in the other. Such a child might show his giftedness in his knowledgeablity about 'non-school' subjects, be 'street wise', orally bright in class though poor at presenting written work, and perhaps show an adult maturity in social circumstances. The gifted child who is not achieving well at school often has the unattractive traits of a bored appearance, cynical talk, low self-esteem, emotional instability, obviously poor motivation, and often comes from a culturally poor home. Investigation and counselling, however, can bring to light the reasons why a child is functioning well outside school, and provide clues as to how the school can help him to do better within its confines.

Because of their exceptionally high ability to absorb information, particularly of an abstract nature, intellectually gifted children would be expected to be affected more than others by symbolic learning such as modelling. If any small child observed her mother's fear of mathematics, and heard her say 'I'm no good at arithemetic', it could be supposed that the child would restructure her cognitive processes and subsequently her learning behaviour when in a situation where arithmetic was presented to be learned. Even being told that 'science is hard' is a form of psychological setting which is likely to be conjured up, along with some anxiety, when the key word 'science' is heard. The set of self-expectations which a person can have about himself has been termed 'self-efficacy' by Bandura (1979). His thesis is different from a conditioning one, in that for low expectations due to modelling, the situation is not that people receive poor reinforcement, or that traumatic events from the environment deter their behaviour; they fail even before they start, because they do not expect their efforts to produce results.

Fear of the achievement is brought about by events which the individual does not feel herself competant to deal with, though her actual ability is irrelevant (such children are most often girls). It is the 'low efficacy' which is responsible, and Bandura believes this is caused by observational learning. A behavioural procedure to overcoming this barrier to achievement would be to try to supplant the unacceptable learned response with a better one, but results have not been successful. According to Marks (1978), neither relaxation training nor carefully graded hierarchies of responses are effective in changing this learned behaviour. Bandura argues that social learning theory provides the explanation, and describes studies which show that it is the opportunity for 'enactive mastery' ie. exposure to the desired behaviour or role model, which produces the desired change. The essential fulcrum of change is the child's ability to be aware and take learning from the exposure—something a gifted child would be expected to do well.

Stress

For all individuals, the difference in their emotional behaviour is largely dependent on their perception of the environment. What one child may see as stressful, may be challenging to another; where one sees school as threatening, to another it is fun; each individual reacts according to his appraisal of the situation. Stress is most often the result of an imbalance between what the child sees as being demanded of him and what he can do (Cox, 1978). Resulting discord can then lead to personal distress, such as anxiety and depression, and to all the behaviour problems which are likely to follow, such as a poorer performance in both the acquisition and recall phases of the academic learning process. It could mean, for example, that when a gifted child takes the avoidance way out of an understimulating classroom situation by conforming to the group norm, the self-perpetuating aspect of this discord takes effect. Once this style of life has been accepted and commitments have been made, the virtues of the chosen way become overestimated, and those of the discarded way diminished. This behaviour was described by Festinger (1951) as the result of the human desire to reduce what he called 'cognitive dissonance', i.e. the inbalance between perceptions of ideas and emotions, circumstances, etc. Gifted children, with their powerful reasoning ability, would be likely to reinforce the decision to under-achieve, making it particularly difficult for them to change, as the years of practice accumulate.

Stress can be brought about both by situations in which the individual feels he cannot cope and by situations in which he feels understimulated. For the gifted child, the former may be the result of mixing with intellectual ability-peers who are chronologically much older than him, so that he is exposed early to adult problems which call for greater maturity than he possesses. Another difficult situation for the gifted to cope with is when they attempt to do things in their own non-conforming way or to express thoughts in a divergent manner, and find that people and circumstances serve to prevent the expected outcome. The alternative stress of understimulation or boredom may result when gifted children find themselves in an environment, either in or out of school, where the demands on them are slight, and do not match up to what they know they are capable of; the effects may be as severe as in cases of excessive demand (Steptoe, 1983). Children in either of these stress situations may perceive themselves as having little influence over their own actions, and as the locus of control begins to slip outwards, those of very high ability have been found to develop lower self-concepts than their average counterparts (Stipek and Weisz, 1981). Again, as in the effects of role modelling, the clue to the highly intelligent individual's behaviour is usually in his cognitive appraisal of the situation.

Moderate anxiety, however, is recognized as improving performance, and Wade (1981) suggested that it may be particularly relevant for the attainment of higher-ability children. She found that of 956 English pupils of ten and eleven years old, high-ability boys (but not girls) who used an approach style of coping with their anxiety, achieved much better results than those who used an avoidance style, especially in formal classrooms. The girls' strong link between anxiety and attainment, at all levels of ability, included the component of motivation, which Wade considered to be due to their female conformity with adult expectations.

Gender

Although this is not specific to the gifted, high intelligence does appear to enhance the 'normal' sex-role problems of development. For example, boys are more likely to be selected as gifted—2:1 in the Gulbenkian sample (Freeman, 1979), and in the teacher nominations of 1330 gifted children in Essex (Wallace 1983)—while no less than 90 per cent of the children referred as 'under-achieving gifted' in California were boys (Whitmore, 1980). Studies of gifted delinquents have also normally been carried out with boys (Pringle, 1970; Chapter 16). However, nice little girls who sit quietly in class, never demand, and produce excellent tidy work but no more, may be covertly gifted, remaining quietly under-achieving, though not necessarily distressed and anti-social in their reactions. There is evidence that cultural pressure on girls to achieve at school (and in general) is very much less than for boys; consequently, they under-value their school-work, and their self-esteem is not lowered by poor school results as it is for boys (see Chapter 12). King (1983) found amongst gifted adolescents, whether measured by IQ or achievement, that boys who are given good emotional support are nevertheless low in self-concept; she suggests this is because they do not compare themselves with their own age-group, but instead make excessive demands on themselves by aiming for what they perceive as their high potential for achievement. To make full use of their intellectual abilities, gifted girls needed to perceive more independence and boys more structure in their environment, and both needed to perceive considerable support from their parents to do their best.

Osborne and Taylor (1980) have pointed out that even today, some gifted girls have difficulty in reconciling high achievement, particularly involving intellectual striving (or aggression), with femininity, so that it often seems simpler to drop one of these qualities deliberately. Highly intelligent and achieving girls tend to be bossy and domineering, but collapse easily when criticized due to the deep conflicts in their lives which sap their self-confidence; they can also be hypercritical of their mothers, especially if these women are not high achievers. As part of their striving for more perfect outcomes, gifted boys (more than girls) may try to dominate their peers, for example in the application of the rules in playground games. The poor welcome this usually receives can be taken by them as yet further rejection.

Emotional concerns in school

There is some evidence that gifted children are generally happy and functioning well, within the variety of British educational institutions, but two surveys by the Department of Education and Science (DES, 1967 and 1977), describe how gifted children were not always recognized or catered for, especially in primary schools. Using measured IQ as the criterion of giftedness, Painter (1980) concluded that almost all the gifted children in the secondary comprehensive schools she studied in England were not only underestimated by their teachers, but were also under-achieving and emotionally frustrated at school. Hitchfield (1973), as part of a national study of children in Britain, took the opposite view—'other than in a few extreme cases'—though there are doubts that the level of ability in her sample was sufficiently high to be termed gifted. Many American states have made considerable efforts to withdraw gifted children from the supposedly 'lock-step' tuition of the public-school system into special education; the Assisted Place Scheme recently introduced in the UK represents a similar approach.

In France, Terrassier (Chapter 14) has described how present school provision there is inadequately responsive to gifted children's individual needs, causing them emotional problems, especially when different aspects of their development proceed in uneven and unexpected ways. Such children are most likely to be in a relatively isolated situation, as they will be developing well outside the normal range of their contemporaries, and so do not have the benefit of the mutual understanding and sympathy of friends. Their often swift progress though the developmental stages is also emotionally distressing to them. Where giftedness is in a relatively narrow field, it may only be the parent or classroom teacher in regular contact with the child who would be able to identify this ability and help it along.

Since special provision for the education of the gifted is at best minimal in most parts of the world, it is more than likely that a child of very high ability will find himself in an educational situation which is not appropriate to his needs. Thus, there are three potential problem areas which a gifted child may encounter in a normal classroom.

The first is the curriculum (Tempest, 1974; Wallace, 1983; and see

Chapter 6), which has not been designed for children who are advanced— both intellectually and in terms of their acquired knowledge. This can wear gifted children down, through repetitive teaching and the drudgery of basic skills learning, which the rest of the class need. The literature on the effects of emotion on learning is surveyed by Boyle (1983); he found with 135 student teachers in Australia that only when the material to be learned was intellectually challenging did the combined influences of the non-ability variables of personality, motivation and mood states have a positive significant effect on their learning. The lesson seems to be that even if these personal states are positive for intellectually gifted children, they will not be moved to learn as well as they could if the learning is set at too low a level.

Secondly, the style of teaching may be inappropriate, since the needs of gifted children are more bound up with 'permission' for intellectual exploration than are those of other children. In one study, the higher the IQ scores of children the less likely they felt themselves to be in need of spoon-feeding from their teachers, and the more they wanted to take part in planning their own education (Freeman, 1979).

Thirdly, the learning climate of the classroom can be negatively influenced by the insensitive mores of classmates, which can be emotionally disturbing to a child who enjoys academic study. Even in highly selective academic schools, there is sometimes an atmosphere of anti-intellectualism, where 'swots' are assigned a distanced social position (Hargreaves et al., 1975; Hartup, 1978).

The gifted child's sometimes conflicting, and therefore potentially disturbing, needs for both intellectual exercise and social acceptance in school are greater than those of other children, and can result in a variety of defensive behaviours, from conformity (usually girls) to hostility (usually boys), most probably accompanied by tension, if not anxiety. The degree of this distress is likely to be tied to the child's relative deviance from the peer group norm, and to that extent, may interfere with his school achievement (Kohn, 1977; and Chapter 15). These emotional blocks can become lifetime habits, though early recognition and intervention can break the cycle of reconfirmed negative self-concepts by reinstating feelings of competence. Group counselling, i.e. intense social support, has been found to be effective, since the children involved benefit from recognition that others have the same problems (Zilli, 1971). On the other hand, less specifically psychological intervention, such as altering a child's schooling, may provide a deeper and longer-lasting solution (Whitmore, 1980; and Chapter 6).

Education specifically designed for the gifted

This has to be considered in terms of the development of both affect and the ways in which the child is gifted; a brief outline of some of the concerns to be taken into account is given here.

Separate education

The greatest experiment on the effects of selection was launched in Britain in 1944 with the formulation of the selective sytem of secondary education, taken at eleven-plus years. But its long-term emotional effects on children who 'passed' or 'failed' have never been properly investigated from the emotional point of view of the children. It was not, of course, meant to be an experiment, but rather the provision of appropriate education for all secondary-school children in the country. Though the idea that some are born hewers of wood and drawers of water is not exactly new, this was the first nationally concerted attempt to adjust education and consequent opportunities according to children's measured ability. At the end of the first decade of its operation, however, a British Psychological Society report (Vernon, 1957) pointed out the possible effects on life of these tests, which sent approximately 10 per cent of children into the 'wrong' form of education, and also the effects of the pre-examination stress in the junior schools, especially in districts which had low provision of secondary academic grammar school places (it varied between 10 and 40 per cent). This system has now largely been replaced by 'mixed-ability' comprehensive schools.

The negative effects of rigid selection by ability for separate education by the occasional inclusion of non-ability factors such as appearance and behaviour, other errors in the process, and the distressing effects they bring with them, are now generally recognized. Though there is a case for special schools for ballet and music (Povey, 1980), most writers on giftedness in children do not consider a separate education to be good for them; the extra intellectual stimulation they receive seems to be outweighed by the strong possibility of unbalanced emotional development (see DES, 1977).

Acceleration

By allowing a highly achieving pupil to jump some of the formal school curriculum, moving in with an older class, it is hoped that she will be less bored or intellectually frustrated than when she is kept back below the level of her ability, and will be more stimulated to enjoy her school learning. It is also the easiest administrative way of solving the problem of the highly achieving child in school. The most obvious emotional problem of acceleration is that it removes the pupil from the orbit of her emotionally compatible class-mates—a situation which can lead to difficulties in the development of her ability to make good social relationships and to consequent long-term personal unhappiness. This risk is considerably modified, however, when acceleration is modifed to part-time attendance in a higher class for specific subjects. There is some evidence (Vernon *et al.*, 1977) that adverse effects can be minimalized when the following provisos are carefully judged for each individual.

1. Mastery must be seen to be in depth, rather than as merely a superficial collection of top grades.
2. Adequate psychological preparation is given to the child for the move.
3. The child is seen to be sufficiently physically and emotionally mature.
4. The jump is of not more than one year.
5. The teaching in the new class recognizes what has happened and is appropriately sensitive.

Enrichment

This is the least controversial of the possible educational extras for the gifted, and is usually welcomed by pupils, teachers and parents. It is the provision of learning opportunities, outside the normal school curriculum, which are designed to challenge the gifted mind. These may be offered in school time, at weekends, or in the holidays, and are provided by the education authorities or by voluntary groups of parents. The purpose is not to offer more of the same, which would be study in depth, but to broaden the child's horizons, introducing such areas of study as astrology or world affairs. It is important, though, for the normal classroom teacher to be involved, and to be able to co-ordinate his teaching with what is being offered to just a few of his pupils, since his disapproval can undermine the possible benefit. Gifted children who receive extra stimulation in this way do not seem to have difficulties in fitting in with normal class learning. Enrichment activities for the gifted can be seen as improving teachers' awareness of alternative teaching strategies, and thus as raising the motivational and cognitive level of the other children—a beneficial 'spin-off' from concern for the gifted. A practical example is the use of teaching materials, developed by the School's Council Curriculum Enrichment Project for Gifted Children in Primary Schools (Ogilvie, 1980), which are now being promoted for the enrichment of all children who are able to study alone.

Meeting peers

Gifted children have a need to meet others, of approximately their own age and ability level, though not necessarily in the same area of expertise. Dishart (1983) has explained how child–child relationships transcend those of adult–child, being more congruent and a better psychological fit. Using the the same verbal and body language, not only can the gifted work together towards quality, excellence, and extending their ranges, but they can play together and confide in each other without fear of being considered foolish or peculiar in their fantasies and ideas. This meeting with same-age peers is particularly important for the gifted for their reality verification, self-image, and context.

Reality verification

A child needs appropriate feedback to reaffirm the reality of his perceptions, thoughts, reasoning, and creativity. If the gifted child receives response and feedback to only a proportion of her realities, as she will from non-gifted age-mates, the other parts are effectively denied, and she can sometimes find it difficult to know what is reality and what is fantasy. After a while, she may only respond to that portion of her own realities which the others recognize, maybe hiding and suppressing her exceptionality as unreal. If she also suffers stigma and ridicule for her 'deviance', she may repress her gifted capacities, to the extent that they may be functionally lost.

Self-image

All children find emotional support in experiencing others like themselves. In an equable relationship, a gifted child can feel accepted as an individual, rather than a stereotype, and being accepted can increase the ability to accept others. Being with peers relieves the gifted of the frequent conflict between their feeling of freedom to express their percieved truth where it may be unwelcome, and their need for approval.

Context

Learning about possible relationships and applications of their capacities, as well as what they know, helps the gifted to avoid the stifling of creativity which comes with conformity to the accepted norms of thought. This inter-action is particularly important when the child is very much brighter than the rest of the class, when it is almost impossible for the teacher to give him enough time for reflection and working through new ideas. Fellow gifted children are also more concerned with the trial and error of experimenting with new information than the teacher, who is usually keener to assist the child simply to more knowledge.

SUMMARY OF THE GIFTED CHILD'S PSYCHOLOGICAL NEEDS

By whatever means it is assessed, there is no reliable evidence that gift-edness is of itself directly related to emotional adjustment; the causes of adverse emotional effects on the gifted are usually the same life circumstances which can bring about poor adjustment in most children. In fact, it is generally accepted that the gifted are psychologically more sturdy than other children. However, there are secondary aspects of being gifted which can cause emotional problems for some, bringing them conflict and anxiety, and producing consequent unwelcome behaviour. Typical problems may ensue, for example, from the interaction between other people's responses to exceptionally high ability and many gifted children's hypersensitivity and perfectionism. Nor do gifted children appear to benefit by the imposition of the label 'gifted', which often trails distorting mythologies and stereotypes with it.

Though the gifted have the same emotional needs as other children, their reactions to certain circumstances concerned with their exceptional abilities are often particularly intense. As with other children, if their psychological needs are not met, then the efficiency of their functioning, such as capacity for selective attention, is likely to be disrupted so that they do not give of their best. But the gifted are more likely than other children to find themselves in frustrating situations, and the thwarting of their intense needs often brings about a stronger reaction than in the average child. This, together with a higher ability to direct their actions, enables gifted children to be more effective in choosing their reactions, whether these are bringing their frustration to attention or conforming to the average.

The gifted have the same educational needs of expression and exploration as other children. But because of their extraordinary abilities, they are likely to be more distressed by highly directive, inflexible school systems which practice, for example, rote-learning and repetitive exercises, and by too low teacher expectations. For the same reason, they are capable relatively more than other children, of thriving in a positive educational environment. They do, however, have some specific educational requirements.

1. Possibly more than other children, the gifted can appreciate and use honest feedback—offered with respect.
2. Open communication with learning groups—particularly to acquire social skills.
3. An intellectually challenging, meaningful, and flexible curriculum.
4. Exposure to like minds—especially of their own age.
5. Suitable material to work with.
6. The opportunity to pursue personal interests.

Whether at home or at school, gifted children are unlikely to satisfy their considerable potential for development on an average and for them, inadequate educational diet. Teachers, parents, and other care-givers should be more aware, in recognizing the ability of these children and the special situations this produces, to adjust to their individual requirements, and to provide as appropriately as they can for the children's needs.

ACKNOWLEDGEMENT

This chapter is a much expanded version of the invited Annotation, 'Emotional problems of the gifted child', *J. Child Psycho. Psychiat.***24**, 481–485.

REFERENCES

Bandura, A. (1979). Reflections on self-efficacy. In *Ann. Rev. Behav. Ther. Theory Pract.* Vol.7 (eds C. M. Franks and C. T. Wilson) Brunner/Mazel, New York.

Boyle, G. J. (1983). Effects on academic learning of manipulating emotional states and motivational dynamics. *Br. J. Educ. Psychol.* **53**, 347–357.

Bridges, S. (1973). *IQ—150.* Priory Press, London.

Cornell, D. G. (1983). Gifted children: the impact of positive labelling on the family system. *Amer. J. Orthopsychiat.* **53**, 322–335.

Cox, T. (1978). *Stress.* Macmillan, London.

Cruickshank, W. (1963). *Psychology of Exceptional Children and Youth.* Prentice-Hall, Englewood Cliffs, New Jersey.

DES (1967). *Children and Their Primary Schools. The Plowden Report.* HMSO, London.

DES (1977). *Gifted Children in Middle and Comprehensive Schools.* HMSO, London.

Dishart, M. (1983). Psychosocial facilitators, enhancers, and inhibitors of gifted children. In *Face to Face with Giftedness* (eds B. M. Shore, F. Gagné, S. Larivée, R. H. Tali and R. E. Tremblay). Trillium Press, New York.

Festinger, (1951). *A Theory of Cognitive Dissonance.* Tavistock, London.

Freeman, J. (1979). *Gifted Children: Their Identification and Development in a Social Context.* MTP Press, Lancaster; University Park Press, Baltimore.

Freeman, J. (1981). The intellectually gifted. In *Genetics and Exceptional Children,* No. 7, *New Directions for Exceptional Children* (eds K. Abroms and J. J. Bennett), Jossey-Bass, San Francisco, California, pp. 75–66.

Freeman, J. (1982). Some emotional aspects of giftedness. In *The Gifted Child at School* (ed. D. Grubb), Oxford Society for Applied Studies in Education, Oxford, 53-65.

Gesell, A., Ilg, F. L., and Ames, L. B. (1965). *The Child from Five to Ten.* Hamish Hamilton, London.

Hargreaves, D. H., Hestor, S. K., and Mellor, F. J. (1975). *Deviance in Classrooms.* Routledge and Kegan Paul, London.

Hartup, W. W., (1978). Children and their friends. In *Issues in Childhood Social Development* (ed H. McGurk), Methuen, London, pp. 130-170.

Hildreth, G. (1966). *Introduction to the Gifted.* McGraw-Hill, New York.

Hitchfield, E. M. (1973). *In Search of Promise.* Longman, London.

Hopkinson, (1978). *The Education of Gifted Children.* The Woburn Press, London.

Kagan, J., Lapidus, D. R., and Moore, M. (1979). Infant antecedents of cognitive functioning: a longitudinal study. In *Annual Progress in Child Psychiatry and Child Development* (eds S. Chess and A. Thomas). Brunner/Mazel, New York.

Khatena, J. (1982). *Educational Psychology of the Gifted.* Wiley, New York.

Khoury, T. J., and Appel, M. A. (1977). Gifted children: current trends and issues. *J. Clin. Child Psychol.* 6, 49–55.

King, M. L. (1983). Environmental availability, giftedness, and delinquency proneness. In *Face to Face with Giftedness* (eds B. M. Shore, F. Gagné, S. Larivée, R. H. Tali and R. E. Tremblay), Trillium Press, New York.

Knepper, W., Obrzut, J. E., and Copeland, E. P. (1983). Emotional and social problem solving thinking in gifted and average elementary school children. *The Journal of Genetic Psychology*, **142**, 25–30.

Kohn, M. (1977). *Social Competence, Symptoms and Underachievement in Childhood: a Longitudinal Perspective.* V. H. Winston and Sons, Washington.

Marland, S. P. (1972). *Education of the Gifted and Talented*, Vol. 1, US Printing Office, Washington DC.

Mead, M. (1954). The gifted child in the American culture of today. *J. Teacher Ed.* **5**, 211–214.

Marks, I. M. (1978). Behavioural psychotherapy of adult neurosis. In *Handbook of Psychotherapy and Behaviour Change*, 2nd edn, (eds S. L. Garfield and A. E. Bergin). Wiley, New York.

McClelland, D. C. (1955). Measuring motivation in fantasy. In *Studies in Motivation* (ed. D. C. McClelland), Appleton Press, New York.

Ogilvie, E. (1980). The Schools Council Curriculum Enrichment Project. In *Educating the Gifted Child* (ed. R. Povey), Harper and Row, London.

Osborne, E., and Taylor, D. (1980). Address given at Leonardo Trust Conference on Gifted Children, London. (Reference: Tavistock Clinic, London).

Painter, F. (1980). Gifted children at home and school. In *Educating the Gifted Child* (ed R. Povey). Harper and Row, London.

Parsons, J. E., Adler, T. F., and Kaczala, C. (1982). Socialization of achievement attitudes and beliefs: parental influences. *Child Development*, **53**, 310–321.

Povey, R. (1980). Educating the gifted child: an overview. In *Educating the Gifted Child* (ed. R. Povey), Harper and Row, London.

Pringle, M. K. (1970). *Able Misfits.* Longman, London.

Renzulli, J. (1979). The attitudes of gifted students towards participation in special programs, *GATE*, **1**, 127–133.

Rutter, M. (1981). *Maternal Deprivation Reassessed*, 2nd edn. Penguin, Harmondsworth.

Scarr, S., and McCartney, K., (1983). How people make their own environments: a theory of genotype → environment effects. *Child Development*, **54**, 424–435.

Seighart, F. (1981). The voluntary counselling service of the NAGC. In *Gifted Children: Challenging Their Potential* (ed A. Kramer). Trillium Press, New York.

Steptoe, (1983). Emotion and stress. In *The Scientific Basis of Psychiatry* (ed. M. Weller), Baillièr Tindall, London.

Stipek, J. J., and Weisz, J. R. (1981). Perceived personal control and academic achievement. *Review of Educational Research*, **51**, 101–137.

Tempest, N. R. (1974). *Teaching Clever Children*, Routledge and Kegan Paul, London.

Terman, L. M. (ed.) (1925–1959). *Genetic Studies of Genius*, Vols. I–V. Stanford University Press, Stanford.

Vernon, P. E. (ed.) (1957). *Secondary School Selection.* Methuen, London.

Vernon, P. E., Adamson, A., and Vernon, D. F. (1977). *The Psychology and Education of Gifted Children.* Methuen, London.

Wade, B. E. (1981). Highly anxious pupils in formal and informal primary classrooms; the relationship between inferred coping strategies and: cognitive attainment. *Br. J. Educ. Psychol.* **51**, 39–49.

Wallace, B. (1983). *Teaching the very able child.* Ward Lock, London.

Whitmore, J. R. (1980). *Giftedness, Conflict and Underachievement.* Allyn and Bacon, Boston.
Zilli, M. J. (1971). Reasons why the gifted adolescent underachieves and some of the implications of guidance and counselling to this problem. *Gifted Child Quart.* **15**, 279–292.

The Psychology of Gifted Children
Edited by Joan Freeman
©1985, John Wiley & Sons, Ltd.

CHAPTER 14

Dyssynchrony—Uneven Development

JEAN-CHARLES TERRASSIER

In my practice as an educational psychologist in France, I have examined, over the years, at least 500 gifted children. It has become clear to me that they very often experience modes of psychological and social development which are specific to them and which can bring them problems. The most obvious ones appear to come about because of the considerable discrepancy between their very high intellectual functioning and their equally common difficulties over more practical matters.

Gifted children often suffer from a lack of synchronicity in the rates of development of their intellectual, affective and motor progress, which has its effect in a number of aspects of their lives, and its results in turn produce further psychological problems. This developmental imbalance appeared to be sufficiently prevalent among gifted children to merit classification in terms of a pattern or syndrome, which I have termed dyssynchrony.

THE ORIGINS OF THE TERM DYSSYNCHRONY

The idea that children's rates of development could vary and produce problems was first suggested by Zazzo (1969) in the notion of heterochrony, though it was a description which he reserved for the mentally retarded, who 'compared with the normal child, develops at different speeds in the various sectors of his psychological development'. However, the connotations of this term as it stood would obviously be inappropriate, and indeed merely confusing, were it to be applied to gifted children.

A similar word, 'dysharmony', was also rejected, as it implies a serious damage to the child's personality, and refers to a pre psychotic structure. 'Dischrony', coined by Gibello (1976), is concerned with time sequencing, again implying some mental disturbance, so that dyschronic children appear as hyperkinetic, impulsive, disorganized in time, and consequently unadapted to school. This was not a term which could usefully be applied to the gifted.

However, the term which I have chosen—dyssynchrony—can be conceived as having two aspects: internal, where it concerns the particular heterogeneous rates of development of gifted children; and social, where it expresses the children's resultant relationships with their environmental circumstances. Dyssynchrony is the overall syndrome, including both internal and external unevenness in development and their consequences.

The suggested merit of this concept lies not so much in the presentation of new observations, but in providing a clear structure in which to place child behaviours which have already been recognized and recorded. It is hoped that this structure will assist educationalists to understand better the development of gifted children, and to take the most appropriate consequent action in terms of teaching or psychological help.

INTERNAL DYSSYNCHRONY

It would be pertinent here to look at some examples of the difficulties which can come about due to the uneven development of gifted children's abilities.

Intellectual—psychomotor dyssynchrony

Gifted children are often found to have an advantage over children of average ability in early walking and speech. A study by Donald Kincaid (1971) of 561 children with Stanford-Binet IQ scores of over 150 in Los Angeles, confirmed this, especially for girls, who were advanced by one-and-a-half months in speech. However, it is not so much the speeded-up developmental progress which causes problems, but its frequent imbalance; this is the particular cause of difficulties in school, notably in relation to reading and writing.

Auzias et al. (1977) have shown how precocity is much more frequently found in reading than in writing. In France, gifted children can often read 'illegally' before they go to school at the age of six; indeed, some can manage it by the time they are four, through watching the television game for adults ('Numbers and Letters'). Of course, parents often help their children along by making suggestions and answering questions, all of which gifted children readily absorb. Half Kincaid's Californian sample could read by the time they were four years old, and in England, Joan Freeman (1979), investigating a group of sixty-three gifted children (IQ 140+), found that two-thirds had been able to read before the age of five, but that a highly significant proportion had problems with handwriting. In France, Leroy-Boussion (1971) offered 179 five-year-olds the option of learning to read with half the usual amount of tuition—one hour per day, instead of two. Only the children of IQ 130 or more were sufficiently mature to be able to do it in that way, and they were directly admitted the following year into the second grade at school.

The concomitant problem with children who read so easily is their exceptional difficulty in learning to write. Their early attempts produce awkward hand movements, and they find it hard to co-ordinate writing with their natural, fast mental rhythm. The gifted child often seems to try by sheer willpower to master this anxiety-wrought situation, so that the resulting tension and effort may well produce muscle rigidity, which in turn causes an exaggerated, trembling, irregular tracing of letters. Alternatively, the child may become almost obsessionally careful; although this improves his graphic presentation, it will still prevent him from following his own mental rhythm, and the result is yet again failure.

A child may try these procedures for a while, but they consume energy, and are tiresome and unfulfilling, so that it is often easier to avoid the situation altogether. This negative attitude then affects not only the skill of writing, but also the level of spelling and written expression. Like others, I have found this problem to be more common among boys than girls.

Language—reasoning dyssynchrony

Whether measured verbally or non-verbally, reasoning ability is always in advance of a gifted child's language ability. For example, among the verbal sub-tests of the Weschler Intelligence Scale for Children (WISC) (Weschler, 1949), where mental age rather than IQ is the meaningful measurement, 'information' 'vocabulary' and 'arithmetic' are often the least well performed. On these, six-year-old gifted children rarely have scores which are more than two or three years above their age-norms. However, in the sub-test 'analogies', in which a child must discover relationships between two elements, it is not unusual to see the same child obtain an increment of four to six years above his age-norm. This sub-test taps intelligent thinking abilities more than knowledge.

On non-verbal tests of intellectual development such as the WISC 'performance' sub-test, the Raven's Progressive Matrices (Raven, 1965), or Cattell's Culture-Free tests (Cattell, 1950), children who have been recorded as having a verbally-based IQ of 130–140 can reach a score of 160–170. These great differences between children's levels of capacity for different mental functions are neither recognized nor catered for educationally—an omission which can only diminish the fulfilment of children's potentials, and add to their internal dyssynchrony.

In mathematics lessons also, the gifted child's rapid comprehension causes him to believe he knows the lesson, just because he understands it. However, on being asked to explain it, he may do less well than a less-gifted child, whose greater efforts of attention and memory will repay him with better marks and the teacher's approval. Gifted children seem somewhat reluctant to make use of their memories, and to make the necessary effort to retain their school learning.

Intellectual—affective dyssynchrony

Too often, intelligence and affect do not develop in parallel ways in the gifted. Children may use their brilliance to disguise their emotional immaturity, though this may emerge at key moments, such as bedtimes. The night often holds anxieties and fears for the gifted child, which he cannot dissipate or alleviate, even with his great reasoning power, and the failure causes him yet more distress. For their part, parents often find it difficult to come to terms with this dyssynchronous behaviour.

The child is again in a difficult situation when his sharp intelligence provides him with anxiety-provoking information, which he is unable to process appropriately. His lively mind elaborates associations with the great reservoir of information he has accumulated, and which becomes a source of both intellectual riches and neurotic behaviour.

One method of defensive processing might be in the form of sublimation, but the preferred defence is usually that of intellectualization. This was described by Anna Freud (1937) as a method by which the ego of the child or adolescent is able to defend her drives by taking refuge in a coldly intellectual, but much more reassuring, mode. Nevertheless, if the feeling is still too over-powering to be contained by the unconscious censor, the child will explain his resultant behaviour quite rationally. Alternatively, intelligence can have a calming effect on immature emotions, by bringing reason and possibly mastery to bear on potentially anxious situations, thus removing their sting. This particular form of intellectual defence, however, if taken to an extreme, does put the child at risk of being identified as neurotic. In this connection, Guillemaut (1978), a psychoanalyst, stated that 'this child must be allowed to express his impulses and pleasures, his loathings, shames and angers. He also must be left with some difficulties to overcome, so he can have to risk, to protest, to lack. If he cannot either wish, or lack he will sink into boredom, and boredom is a form of depression with this child'. My own experience confirms this view.

DYSSYNCHRONY AND THE SCHOOL

The most obvious form of dyssynchrony for the gifted child is the discrepancy between the speed of his mental development and that of the rest of the class in standard school progression. In France the educational approach at present is overly and inflexibly concerned with chronological age, producing a system which neglects a child's own self and originality. This situation could be though of as equivalent, in some respects, to placing a normally able child in a class for the mentally retarded, with not surprisingly resultant problems in the development of relationships and in identification with his schoolfellows.

Current educational policies in many countries, including France, appear to treat each child as identical to all the others, and as a result, fail in the education of a large proportion of them. It is an unfair system. In France, at a typical, totally standardized primary school, the required age of entry to the Preparatory Course is between five years, nine months and six years, eight months; that is when the child begins to learn to read, write, and count. Three groups of children are affected differently by this system.

First, by the end of the first school year, nearly a third of the pupils are observed by their teachers to have failed to reach the required level. Some of these children will have fallen behind because of specific learning difficulties, but most of them simply have an IQ of below 100, and could never cope with what had been set for them. However, for children who are intellectually far behind, special 'improvement' classes have been functioning in France for seventy years. An effort is made in them to offer the retarded child a more concrete and individualized form of teaching, which is more adapted to his potentialities.

In order to prevent both these cracks in the present school system from showing, and to shield the children concerned from feelings of incapacity, those children who fail are not kept down in the first grade for a second year. This policy also has the effect of reassuring the parents, whose postponed disappointment is then sometimes all the more painful. However, to disguise the intellectual diversity of children even more, there has been a definite proposal recently to reduce the level of the required standard in this first year.

In contrast, the second group of children, whose IQs range from 100 to 130, is very clearly priviledged by the present system, which appears to be made for them. The education they are offered is correctly geared to their developmental progress, and they integrate easily. They account for about 45 per cent of the total number in schools.

Gifted children, whose IQs range from 125 to 200, form the third and most neglected group; they are a minority of 2–5 per cent of the school population. Sometimes an infant-school teacher may spot a child's precocity and ask for him to be tested; if the child is found to be gifted, and if the next headteacher is not biased against it, he can enter the Preparatory Course a few months earlier. However, for an eight-year-old gifted child with a mental age which is between three and seven years ahead of the average, there is no way out of this lock-step education, and no consideration is given to her personality and special needs.

The abilities of such advanced children will deteriorate over the years, if they are not exercised. The French school system asks the gifted child to be content with minimum knowledge until he reaches the end of the fourth form, at about the age of fifteen. This offers him disappointment in return for his curiosity, and teaches him that school work does not deserve his efforts. The school is thus contributing to the formation of intellectual inhibitions.

But then, having been intellectually so underfed for nine school years, the child enters the fifth secondary year to a suddenly increased and inconsistent change of rhythm, especially if he goes into the scientific section. However, the setting up in 1981 of an undifferentiated fifth form cannot be considered an improvement. Recent reform does include a few safe-guarding measures for these bright children, but these are too often not respected in practice, and teachers are not infrequently discouraging to parents who ask for the age-limit for their child's advance to be waived. Although it was a part of the reform that gifted children in the first and second secondary forms should receive educational enrichment by attending special courses for a few hours a week, this also is far from being entirely honoured in practice.

There are some who argue that it is dangerous to 'push' children; but who are these 'pushed' children? In fact, they are the less bright ones, who have difficulty in following the class course, while their more able classmates are slowed down. Under-stimulated gifted children may then work at between three and five years below their potential, which is describable in terms of a School quotient: the relation of school age to mental age.

$$\text{School quotient} = \frac{\text{School age}}{\text{Mental age}}$$

When these two ages are evenly balanced, the quotient equals one, or close to it, which indicates that the child is progressing well. The school age is determined by the child's school grade, with its implied level of education. For instance, in France, Elementary Course 2 will have a school age of eight years, though one might also take the time of the school year into account. If a second grade child shows a mental age of twelve, then his school quotient will be:

$$\text{School quotient} = \frac{\text{School age}}{\text{Mental age}} = \frac{8}{12} = 0.67$$

This means that such a gifted child is functioning at two-thirds of his potential—an unwarranted situation, comparable to delaying the entry of normal children into school by several years. It implies great difficulties, even for a teacher of considerable goodwill, to do his best by the child. In these terms, gifted children constitute the most 'retarded' group in French schools, while the standard of education continues to be adapted to those of still lower ability. For example, a child entering secondary school a few years ago who had five mistakes in his dictation received a score of 0. Now, even with the length and difficulty of the dictation reduced, he can score an average mark with the same number of mistakes. Hence, fewer children get 0, but is this really an educational victory?

RELATIONSHIPS

With parents

Both parents and other children often expect the gifted child to behave according to his age. Although parents are often the ones who spot their child's giftedness (especially if they have other children), it does not imply their willingness to promote it, for parents also experience the problems caused by the dyssynchrony between their gifted child's intellectual and affective development.

In my experience, gifted children are concerned at a very early age about what can be called 'the problem of limits'—limits of life such as birth, death, God, and of the universe. When expressed as early as three or four years-old these concerns only contribute to the parents' perplexity. This tendency to precocious philosophy causes particular difficulties for children in families of a low cultural level. It stresses their already problematic situation, where parents do not understand the child, and it brings her added distress when she realizes that others do understand her also. She is then placed with two cruel alternatives—either to be loyal to the family and renounce her brilliance, or go for intellectual development, with its inevitably associated guilt. To retain its harmony, in this situation the family may well need professional guidance.

Children from poor social environments are well recognized as enjoying fewer educational opportunities, and this shows through the generations. The family milieu may be deficient in language, thinking, and identifying support, but in addition the school, which could act to palliate these negative forces, is not at present taking adequate intellectual care of the child. Consequently, the standardized educational system is acting to perpetuate this injustice and inequality of opportunities.

With other children

In line with the theory of dyssynchrony, gifted children tend to have characteristic choices of friends, who may be of the same intellectual ability but older and taller, or intellectually inferior. Most of the time, they will choose either older and more interesting children or adults for indoor games and conversation. For outside games, they usually choose their age-peers. If, however, a child can find one or more friends of his own ability, as Gowan and Torrance (1971) report, he becomes happier—an unlikely outcome with the present structure of education. In a study of American primary schools,

Gallagher and Crowder (1957) observed a rise in the level of school interest by gifted children when others like themselves are present; they estimated that only 29 per cent of gifted children are correctly placed in schools.

There are other standardizing elements in the environment. Television, for example, delivers information which unfolds at a determined speed, which some passive gifted children will watch indiscriminately. Others, who are more dynamic, take their personal rhythms to books, which can take a child's interests further, and are generally more conducive to deep, organized thought.

SOME CONCLUSIONS ABOUT DYSSYNCHRONY

It must be stressed that the dyssynchrony described here is not a pathological condition, beyond the bounds of what can be considered normal. It is a description of the actual conditions in which many gifted children develop; in most cases, their problems are the result of maladaptation between society and education. This situation calls for considerable effort from the gifted child, who must solve not only normal childhood concerns, but also those peculiar to the gifted.

PYGMALION EFFECTS

Positive Pygmalion Effect

There are two types of children who become advanced above their age-groups in school. The first are the gifted, who profit by their experience, while the second find themselves there by mistake, and to their discomfort. No less than 19.3 per cent of all the children who proceeded into the second year of junior school had an IQ of less than 100; two years later, there were still 6.4 per cent remaining in this position. These children suffer from a sense of failure, and from feeling a lack of being appreciated. If the effect of teacher expectation—the Pygmalion Effect (Rosenthal and Jacobson, 1971)—were to be seen, it would surely be there. But these children could not live up to their teacher's expectations of them.

Though there may have been some improvement in these children's performances, it cannot be compared with the Pygmalion Effect as originally described. That first research was carried out on only ten pupils in each class, and described IQ gains of up to 40 points, when teachers had been led to believe that certain of their pupils were brilliant, the youngest children making the greatest gains. However, the statistical tables show that the class scored an average of only 55 points on the reasoning test. A year later, seven pupils from the experimental group were again said to have gained on average nearly 50 IQ points, and forty-eight pupils from the control group more than 40 IQ points. That explosive inflation of IQs makes the validity of this particular study hardly credible, though the Positive Pygmalion phenomenon may yet be proved to exist by other researchers. In fact, when a teacher is informed of her pupil's actual potentials, she is in a far better position to help realize them. For those pupils who are truly gifted, the consequences are the most positively of a Pygmalion type.

Negative Pygmalion Effect

In both France and many other countries, the majority of gifted children remain unrecognized. For them, the situation is the reverse of the above, and can be called the Negative Pygmalion Effect. Where a teacher is ignorant of a child's intellectual precocity, she will expect her pupil to be within the normal range of ability, and will help him to stay in that position by virtue of these expectations. Some American studies have shown that only 10–20 per cent of gifted children are identified by their teachers in primary schools, though identification will occasionally rise to 50 per cent. The Negative Pygmalion Effect thus applies to about two-thirds of gifted children in a standardized educational system.

In school, it provokes inattention in these children, who may daydream in order to ward off the boredom they feel in a poorly stimulating atmosphere. Where an interest is taken in school activities, it will be concentrated on those which the pupil finds difficult and interesting. Hence he may be seen to be successful at complex problems, but remain superficial, and make mistakes in simple tasks. Slavin (1980) found that positive feedback could act to counter the Negative Pygmalion effect with 389 6th, 7th and 8th grade pupils. However, Stipek and Hoffman (1980) concluded that the beneficial effects of positive feedback on children's expectation of future achievements was modified by their perceptions of the reasons for their past performances.

Families may also under-expect from their gifted children. Though the negative effect is less important than that of the school, where the families are of good socio-cultural level, it becomes significant in families where concern with the child's development is minimal. Under-expectation from other children adds to the social pressure for the gifted child to conform.

As with dyssynchrony, the Negative Pygmalion Effect is both external and internal. Internally, it affects the child's self-image, which he assumes as a reflection of society's view of his potential. It makes it difficult for him to discover and accept his precocity. He attempts to accommodate to the given social norm, sometimes compulsively, inhibiting his natural potential so that his intelligence may well become a source of socially induced guilt.

This Negative Pygmalion Effect varies amongst different children, both in strength and incidence, according to the characteristics of the children and of the social contexts. Some children remain at its mercy for a long time, resulting in their under-achievement, which reinforces the effect in a downward spiral. But in a favourable background, where the gifted child is accepted as such by others and for himself, there will be no negative effect. However, in spite of adverse conditions, some gifted children still have the courage to know their precocity, to such an extent that they can convince others to see them differently. Do not let gifted children fall into this trap.

ACKNOWLEDGEMENT

This is a translation of material from Les Enfants Surdoues, by Jean-Charles Terrassier, published by Les Editions ESF, Paris.

REFERENCES

Auzias, M., Casati, I., Cellier, C., Delaye, R., and Verleure F. (1977). *Ecrire a 5 ans?* FUF.

Cattell, R. B. (1950). *The Culture Free Intelligence Test.* IPAT, Illinois.

Freeman, J. (1979). *Gifted Children: Their Identification and Development in a Social Context.* MTP Press, Lancaster.

Freud, A. (1937). *The Ego and the Mechanisms of Defence.* Hogarth Press. London.

Gallagher, J. J., and Crowder, T. (1957). The adjustment of gifted children in regular classroom. *Exceptional Children,* **23**, 306–312; 317–319.

Gallagher, J. J. (ed.) (1979). *Gifted Children: Reaching Their Potential,* (Actes du 2éme Congres Mondial pour les Enfants Surdoues). Koller and Son, Jerusalem, Israel.

Gibello, B. (1976). Dysharmonie cognitive. *La Revue de Neuropsychiatric Infantile,* **9**, 539–542.

Gowan, J. C., and Torrance, P. (eds) (1971). In *Educating the Ablest: a book of readings on the education of gifted children.* F. E. Peacock, Ithaca, Illinois.

Guillemaut, J. (1978). L'enfant surdoue et les autres: une recontre de quel type? *Actes du Congrés de Nice.*

Kincaid, D. (1971). A story of highly gifted pupils. In *Educating the Ablest: a book of readings on the education of gifted children.* (eds Gowan, J. C., and Torance, P.) F. E. Peacock, Ithaca, Illinois.

Kincaid, D. (1975). For parents of academically talented children. *The Gifted Child Quarterly,* **XIX**, 3, 246–249.

Leroy-Boussion, I. (1971). Maturite mentale et apprentissage de la lecture. *Enfance,* **3**.

Raven, J. C. (1965). *Guide to Using the Coloured Progressive Matrices.* H. K. Lewis, London.

Rosenthal, R. A., and Jacobson, L. (1971). *Pygmalion a l'ecole.* Casterman.

Slavin, R.E. (1980). Effects of individual learning expectations on student achievement. *J. of Educ. Psychol.,* **4**, 520–524.

Stipek, D. J., and Hoffman, J. M. (1980). Children's achievement related expectancies as a function of academic performance histories and sex. *J. of Educ. Psychol.,* **6**, 861–865.

Weschler, D. (1949). *Weschler Intelligence Scale for Children.* Psychological Corporation, New York.

Zazzo, René. (1969). *Les Debilites Mentales,* Collection V, Armand Colin.

The Psychology of Gifted Children
Edited by Joan Freeman
©1985, John Wiley & Sons, Ltd.

CHAPTER 15

Gifted Adolescents: A Developmental Perspective

FRANZ J. MÖNKS AND HERMAN W. VAN BOXTEL

Adolescence is considered in this chapter as part of a developmental, life-long process, which is affected by a network of biological, social, historical, and cultural situations, so that change in one aspect of development effects changes in the others. This approach does not merely describe such developmental changes, but is also concerned with explanation, because understanding the circumstances and variables which influence behaviour, provides a guide to optimizing them for individuals. Though this essentially preventive approach is important for all children, it is particularly so for those, such as the gifted, who are seen as 'divergent' from the average.

This discussion of the gifted adolescent focuses on Renzulli's (1978) 'Three-ring' conception of giftedness—an interlocking combination of three clusters of traits; above-average abilities, task commitment and creativity—which the present writers suggest is reset in a developmental dimension to include the specific social settings of school, peers and family, to be called the Triadic Model. The gifted person is not, however, seen merely as a product of the relationships between social dimensions and personal characteristics, but has a strong influence on them during the transformations which take place between puberty and adulthood, i.e. adolescence. An outline of adolescent development is first described and then those aspects of it which are particular to the gifted are identified.

ADOLESCENCE IN A LIFE-SPAN PERSPECTIVE

Adolescence is a time of specific transitions with specific outcomes (Ausubel, 1965), when novel and often strong behaviour patterns can emerge. There is also a differentiation of cognitive abilities, when youngsters become capable of reflecting on their thoughts, and of engaging in meta-cognitive activities, i.e. thinking about the structure, function, and content of the cognitive processes. At the end of this period, most young people have a better idea of their social and moral values, and a deeper insight into their personal abilities and social requirements.

All adolescents experience changes in their life situations, such as position in the family, peer group, and society, as well as biological and cognitive changes, which bring about changes in behaviour. This means that much adolescent development can be better understood when considered in terms of the continuities which bind it to the childhood that went before (Hill and Mönks, 1977). Figure 15.1 represents a generally accepted theoretical framework of adolescent development in a life-span view (see also Mönks and Ferguson, 1983).

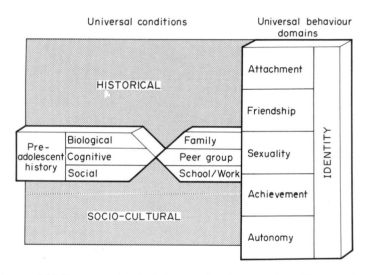

FIGURE 15.1 Frame-work of adolescent development in a life-span view

PSYCHO-SOCIAL CHANGES

Individual differences within the dynamic network of socializing systems and political necessities result in a great variety of behavioural changes during adolescence; especially in the six psychosocial areas described below.

1. Attachment is a fundamental life experience, which determines human bondings from early life. Though emotional ties with the family undergo modifications in middle childhood, detachment is increased during adolescence, so that friends and others outside the family become

more significant; often a dramatic and conflict-loaded change (Hartup, 1978). The increasing numbers of friendships as well as conformity to peer influence in early adolescence, can appear to be at the expense of the quality of the parent–child relationships (Hill, 1980); an influence sometimes seen by the parents as a negation of their values and norms though empirical findings do not seem to confirm this (Andersson, 1979; Berndt, 1979; Hill, 1980; La Gaipa, 1979). However, it is important for the adolescent to initiate and stabilize new attachments, in order to achieve a personal equilibrium (Rutter, 1980).

2. Friendships have a specific meaning when defined as peer relationships, a peer being someone who is an equal in developmental terms, but different from an age-mate. This distinction is extremely important for gifted adolescents, since the development of their social and intellectual abilities is often ahead of that of their age-mates. Whatever their relationship, though, these friendships do have a significant influence on the regulation and integration of developing behaviours such as social competence, aggression, and sexuality (Hartup, 1978).

3. Sexuality begins at puberty with new sensations and experiences, and the reorganization of sex-role identity, which will have a fundamental influence on future life. Though it is the peer and age-groups which provide a learning environment for coping with these new behavioural possibilities (McCandless, 1970), sexual behaviour and identity will also be affected by socio-cultural influences.

4. Achievement is strongly related to careers in Western societies, with the motivation, especially for the gifted, to reach high standards of excellence. Though young children often have unrealistic and fantastic ideas about careers (Ginzberg et al., 1951; Ginzberg, 1972), they become more realistic and knowledgeable from about the age of eleven, this trend accelerating during adolescence due to growing awareness of skills, aptitudes, and interests. This is also the time when abilities become manifest in a significant way, due to their differentiation and specialization (Lerner and Spanier, 1980; Stanley, 1977), enabling young people to make realistic compromises; balancing wishes and ambitions against the constraints and opportunities of society, which are important matters for the appropriate education of gifted adolescents.

5. Independence, or more positively the increase of autonomy, is another prominent characteristic of adolescent development. It is the capacity 'to cope independently and in a self-assertive manner with one's own desires and abilities in relation to society's requirements and possibilities' (Mönks and Ferguson, 1983), which Havighurst (1951) called a developmental task. Emotional autonomy is related to the loosening of attachment with parents; behavioural autonomy (independence of

decision-making) is more dependent on an interplay between changing responsiveness to peers and parents (Hill and Mönks, 1977); the development of moral and value autonomy during late adolescence, though related to previous experiences, is still largely dependent on personal choices and preferences. These ongoing processes of adaptation and integration of values towards autonomy are heavily dependent on cognitive capacities. The ways in which precocious gifted adolescents cope with these developmental tasks, and what support they can expect from parents and peers are important to the understanding of how they attain individual identities.

6. Identity is an umbrella characteristic, related to the above five transformations, representing the person's feelings of self-esteem and self-confidence (Mönks and Ferguson, 1983). Taking a more descriptive and idealized view, Erikson (1968) sees identity at its best as a form of psycho-social well-being—'Its most obvious concomitants are a feeling of being at home in one's body, a sense of "knowing where one is going", and an inner assuredness of anticipated recognition from those who count.'

Though these six psychosocial transformations are developmentally embedded in the total life-span, they manifest themselves and are significantly shaped during adolescence. The prominence in them of cognitive abilities, creativity, and task commitment has implications for the social interaction of the gifted, and therefore affects their identity formation.

THE RENZULLI THREE-RING CONCEPTION OF GIFTEDNESS

Early definitions of giftedness, such as Terman's (1925) use of the top 1 per cent on an intelligence scale, were often one-sided. However, as early as 1916, William Stern (1967) had argued that ability is only a necessary condition; the production of outstanding performances depends on other properties, especially interest and will, which Terman recognized in his later work (1954) (see also Mönks, 1983).

Based on extensive empirical research, Renzulli (1978) and his co-workers has evolved a 'Three-ring' conception of giftedness which involves cognitive and other factors. They describe giftedness as consisting of

> an interaction among three basic clusters of human traits—these clusters being above average general abilities, high levels of task commitment and high levels of creativity. Gifted and talented children are those possessing or capable of developing this composite set of traits and applying them to any potentially valuable area of human performance (Renzulli *et al.*, 1981, p. 27)

They also explain (p. 18) that: 'It is important to point out that no single cluster "makes giftedness"... each cluster contributes equally—task commitment and creativity are not simply extras; they are equally important ingredients in the make-up of a gifted person.' The three clusters are represented in the form of three interlocking rings, shown in Figure 15.2 and described below.

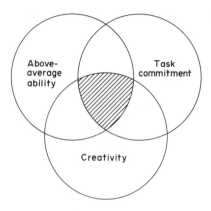

FIGURE 15.2 Three-ring conception of giftedness (RENZULLI, 1978)

Above-average ability

Like the other two clusters, above-average ability is a psychological construct, which, in order to be measured, has to be operationalized. This is usually done with tests of general intelligence or achievement, though tests of special abilities (e.g. for critical thinking, mechanical aptitude, or non-verbal reasoning) can also be added. Renzulli does not define the concept of 'general abilities', but uses instead the implicit operational definitions of the measures. However, he warns against too heavy a reliance on these traditional indications of ability, in view of their questionable reliability—especially in the upper ranges—and their tendency to favour good test-takers and lesson-learners (Wassermann, 1982). For the same reason, the use of high cut-off points is avoided, so that about 15–20 per cent of the total population can be included. As an alternative or in addition to these test scores, Renzulli recommends using performance scores such as school grades and grade point averages, or anecdotal reports and examples of the pupils' work. He also advocates the use of teacher, parent, peer and self ratings.

Creativity

The precise meaning of the concept of creativity is not yet agreed among educators, possibly because it can refer to either, (a) a disposition—

flexibility combined with well-developed intelligence, (b) a process— exploratory behaviour, with the ability to make combinations, or (c) a product —which elicits admiration for the originality and ingenuity of its creator (Baacke, 1979; and see Chapters 5 and 23). Though he does not provide a definition, it is implicit in Renzulli's argument that creativity is a function of characteristics such as originality of thinking, freshness of approach, the ability to set aside established conventions and procedures (with reference to MacKinnon, 1964), and 'the originality, novelty, or uniqueness of a person's contribution' (Renzulli *et al.*, 1981, p. 22). Probably for the same reasons that it is hard to give such a definition, the validity and reliability of creativity measures are very low. Because of these measurement problems, Renzulli does not advocate creativity tests, but suggests that a better impression of a person's creativity can be formed by rating procedures which evaluate his past or present performances and products.

Task commitment

Renzulli defines task commitment as a refined or focused form of motivation: 'Whereas motivation is usually defined in terms of a general energizing process that triggers responses in organisms, task commitment represents energy brought to bear on a particular problem (task) of specific performance area' (Renzulli *et al.*, 1981). In reviewing studies on this subject, he mentions factors which have been associated with task commitment, such as persistence in the accomplishment of ends, intrinsic motivation, and a driving absorption in work, independence, self-reliance, and self-initiative. Some writers see task commitment as strongly grounded in identity formation, but this cluster of factors is hard to operationalize and not easily or objectively measured; Renzulli again proposes their identification without measurement, relying even more heavily on ratings of performance than with the other two clusters.

AN EXTENSION OF THE THREE-RING CONCEPT: PLACING GIFTEDNESS IN A DEVELOPMENTAL AND SOCIAL CONTEXT

Developmental aspects

Although Renzulli's Three-ring concept of giftedness does constitute an important extension and correction of existing definitions, his model suggests that the described personal characteristics have a static nature, emphasized by constant reference to 'traits'. But as adolescence is a developmental period of complex transformational processes in social settings, when experiences and socialization processes are often of crucial importance for their development, that context is where Renzulli's three essential ingredients of giftedness should be placed.

Piaget, and others who have built on his stage-theory of cognitive development, recognize that general cognitive and intellectual abilities are still developing in adolescence. The adolescent transition from the concrete to the formal operational stage increases the capacity for abstract thought, so that thinking becomes more orderly and systematic, conclusions can then be based on hypothetical possibilities, and operations performed on mentally created ideas (Arlin, 1975; Flavell, 1977; Dacey, 1982). Baacke (1979) too is clear that adolescent intelligence cannot be represented as a global ability, since it is undergoing a differentiation into several components, and he stresses the importance of this period for intellectual development. He also suggests that both the quality and expression of youngsters' learning abilities are very dependent on social factors, though affected less by the basic environmental influences of primary socialization than by the incentives and directing of interests mediated by secondary socialization.

Adolescence can be regarded as the critical period in life, in which the young person is particularly open to changes in creative thinking. For example, Dacey (1982) states that 'since creativity is so much a matter of one's self-concept and motivation, and since adolescence is a period in which self-concept is being defined, creativity may be fostered during this period' (p. 135). However some writers, particularly the psychoanalytical, believe that it cannot be influenced after the decisive experiences and subconscious processes of early childhood.

The personality characteristic of task commitment is not new to adolescence, but can be seen as a form of achievement motivation. Oerter (1967) even argues that from twelve years on, no observable changes in achievement motivation take place, though McClelland (1961) and Heckhausen (1980) state that substantial transformations may occur in adolescence. It is during adolescence that it becomes possible to make some commitments, with growing awareness of abilities and interests, and as the outcome of a developmental process. Perry (1981) points out in his theory of intellectual/ethical development that the last three of the nine stages, which are distinguished in it, refer to the ability to choose and to explore commitments. Reaching these stages should be strongly associated with the formation and refinement of one's personal identity, which is the meta-transformational process pervading all the psycho-social dynamics of adolescent development.

Social Aspects

The social settings in which the developmental processes described above take place are extremely important. Gifted adolescents do not exist in a vacuum, but perform (or fail to perform) in a constant, dynamic inter-action with significant others. A promising approach to the topic is the social ecology of adolescence; analogous in a sense to biological ecology (the science of the relations between organism and surrounding environment), this studies the interaction between the social environment and the social behaviour of mankind. Baacke (1979) distinguishes the different ecological zones in the world of adolescents, and envisages them as concentric circles; family, school, and peer-group being clearly recognized as the most important social settings.

The importance of the family has recently been emphasized by Hill (1980), who explains how transformations in family relationships come about in early adolescence due to changes in the social circumstances of both children and parents, though research and consequent knowledge about this intersection of parental and early adolescent influences is poor. One of the few studies dealing with the family environment of gifted adolescents is that of Tabackman (1976), who sought to identify family factors which might be associated with giftedness, and to determine the validity of family environment measures for predicting academic achievement of gifted pupils. It was found that the families of gifted children were significantly higher than the norm on a factor of 'adult orientation'; these families saw themselves as more independent, permissive, intellectual, unstructured, and harmonious than the average in their interactions. Tabackman's study stressed both the importance of the family for the functioning and development of gifted children, and the need for more research in this direction.

The relevance of social settings such as the school and the peer-group for the developing adolescent has been well documented (Mönks and Ferguson, 1983), but strategies for the education of gifted and talented young people which take these facts fully into account are rare. In a discussion of the selection of children for 'one-sided' acceleration projects such as the Study of Mathematically Precocious Youth (Stanley, 1980), Rüppell (1981) made the following criticisms.

1. Giftedness is statistically defined as efficient teachability in the given school conditions.
2. Gifted children are identified only on the basis of aptitude tests, without reference to parent and/or teacher judgements; so that potentially gifted pupils may not be recognized, and no attention is given to individual weak and strong points.
3. The individual gifted child is isolated and is wrenched from his peer-group; he is placed in a strange and different learning environment.
4. Content-specific acceleration leads to the increasingly faster processing of learning-contents, without explicit attention to the development of general thinking abilities.

As an alternative, Rüppell proposed an ecologically acceptable stimulation model, which makes it possible for potentially gifted children to acquire complex thinking strategies, under various stimulating environmental conditions, within the context of their own peer-group. Optimal development of individual cognitive and other talents is made possible by the allocation of specific roles and activities, again within the same context of the peer-group, and with respect to the child's social and emotional development.

Models for research and educational practice which take the special importance of the social setting into account (as in this and similar projects) do justice to gifted children as social and emotional human beings, and therefore are most promising. Although Renzulli's team did gather some 'developmental' and 'sociometric' information, for his identification model for gifted children, further theoretical elaboration of these aspects seems to be required. An extended and modified conceptualization of Renzulli's Three-ring conception, which includes the social settings, is visualized in a new Triadic Model (Figure 15.3).

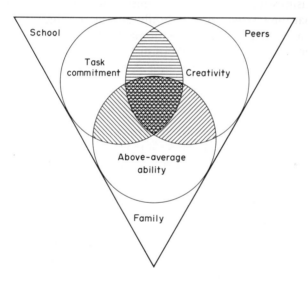

FIGURE 15.3 Triadic model of giftedness

SOME ILLUSTRATIONS OF OUR APPROACH

The social-emotional development and functioning of gifted adolescents are much more complicated, and need much more differentiation, than most studies in the literature have recognized. In the above sections we have tried to identify them within a general framework of adolescent development, but the following sections will be more specific, with more detailed description of the variables which are potentially relevant to the gifted and their interactions within the framework. Though many studies have been limited in their measurements of few variables, simple operationalization and their results often over-generalized and contradictory, nevertheless, aspects of the framework have to be discussed in the light of the existing literature, and are also illustrated by examples of gifted adolescents from a pilot study being carried out at present at the University of Nijmegen, Holland.

In the study giftedness is seen as characterizing youngsters by giving them very special social positions, and in coping with these, the gifted children and adolescents can be expected to develop varying strategies which allow them to feel as comfortable as possible (Lazarus, 1966). These coping strategies have different consequences both for their personal development and for their position amongst peers or age-mates. We are trying to identify the most important of the variables which determine the emergence of coping strategies, and which in turn become part of adolescents' behavioural repertoire, eventually to be described in terms of the Triadic Model.

So far, in the Nijmegen project, ten gifted adolescents (eight boys and two girls) have been interviewed with a pre-structured in-depth interview, with particular regard to the following areas, (a) pre-adolescent history, (b) peer relationships, (c) relationships at home, and (d) the socio-cultural context.

Pre-adolescent history

In pre-adolescent history, all three clusters in our Triadic Model of giftedness undergo developmental changes—a person at the onset of adolescence is not a tabula rasa. The development of task commitment, for example, is influenced by social settings, particularly the school. Boensch (1977) presents an impressive argument describing the way school systems in many countries fail to meet the needs of children who deviate from the mean. In his view, learning abilities can only be fully utilized when motivation (the will of an individual to aim his sensory, cognitive and motor functions at the attainment of an objective in the future) is also being developed. To encourage this, all children, not only the gifted, should be offered open and interest-arousing educational opportunities.

However, the gifted do have the problem that in most school systems, education is orientated toward the middle area of the normal distribution of ability, so that young gifted children can find the work too easy and may become lazy. For them the organization of the curriculum has to be flexible, exciting and differentiated for individuals to evoke their potentialities. Where the school climate is inadequate, the effects of its early deficiencies are still likely to carry over to adolescence. This is not to say that all children who lack a certain degree of challenge will end up the same way—much can be compensated for by a stimulating home environment—but these special situations should be recognized. We had a clear example of this effect in our Nijmegen sample. A decidedly under-achieving fifteen-year old boy, who was a member of Mensa (an organization which demands a very high intelligence for entry), had had to repeat his second year of secondary education because of his poor grades. He said of his elementary school years: 'I was too hard-working in the first and second year, but after that, I became extremely lazy. I was equally good in all subjects anyhow; my marks stayed the same, but I no longer did a thing, or not much.'

Peer relationships

For all adolescents, the importance of the peer group (inside as well as outside school) increases sharply, becoming more frequent and intensive, with increasing detachment from the family (Hartup, 1978; Mönks and Ferguson, 1983). This is a particularly important psychological time for the highly able because of the possible distinction for them between age mates and ability peers. Freeman (1979) found that though children with very high IQs had normal peer relationships in everyday activities at school with age mates, they generally preferred ability peers (defined in terms of behavioural complexity), who were older than themselves for out of school activities, and did not have as many friends as other children at home. They did seem to have more problems than the average in making friends, at least with their age mates.

Though there are always exceptions, the harmonious friendship of gifted adolescents with their age mates is not normally hampered by their differences in behavioural complexity and developmental levels. There are many other variables, of at least as great an importance, which form bonds between them. In fact, the exceptional circumstances of the gifted can enhance their potential friendships; for example, when gifted young people make a greater effort to develop engaging personal characteristics, such as friendliness, or show willingness to make their extra intellectual and creative abilities available to their age mates (see Chapter 11). Indications of this outgoing spirit, combined with conscious social adaptation were found in a number of our interviews, e.g. with a thirteen-year-old boy:

> The advantages and disadvantages of being good outweigh each other; you can help a lot more people. If I wasn't so good in school, I would probably be rather less popular. I try to act as normally as possible, and not show that I'm proud of my results; that's something you shouldn't do. I try to help wherever I can, and whenever I'm asked. That is also important for my popularity; if I didn't help, I think it would make a big difference.

Some variables such as physical performance, are relatively important at this age, so that if the gifted have reached an acceptable (to age peers) minimum on these, differences in development and degree of complexity on other variables become less important. A thirteen-year-old girl, for instance, said that being very bad at athletics would make you much less appreciated, or even a social outcast.

The ways in which gifted adolescents (wittingly or unwittingly) develop their own ways of handling their exceptional position, will depend on the interaction of personality characteristics and features of the social environment. Where there are many variables potentially relevant to the social position of gifted adolescents in their class or peer group, the value of each should be considered in the formation of coping strategies. Research should focus on possible patterns in the formation of strategies which are relevant to gifted adolescents, and use the consequences of any discovered patterns to help in the young people's personal development.

Much of the existing research literature generalizes widely about gifted adolescents, often suggesting that they are less socially accepted than others. But research which takes the differences amongst gifted adolescents themselves into account, particularly with regard to social skills, is more relevant and promising. For instance, Hogan and Weiss (1974) made a distinction between pupils with high academic achievement and those with an 'intellectual orientation' (i.e. high scores on an intellectual efficiency scale but rather lower actual performance). The second group had higher scores than either the first or the control group on 'interpersonal effectiveness' and 'self-assurance'. The first group, on the other hand, was more 'responsible' and 'interpersonally mature', liked to work within the limits of conventional constraints, and was characterized by 'unusual conscientiousness', 'industry' and 'dependability', rather than by tolerance or empathy. These pupils seemed to have the essential personality characteristics to make them able to perform at the highest level, but (at least in some cases) seemed to lack certain social skills.

Results compatible with these were reported by Elshout et al. (1983), who isolated a group of adolescents with high scientific performance, representing less than 5 per cent of the population, and characterized by habits of self-study, high task commitment, and academic interest, shown by a rather reserved and distant attitude towards people. A residual group whose performance was lower, though within the 25 per cent of highest achievers, were found, on the other hand, to be characterized by social activities, interests, and skills, and by extraversion and social dominance. Other research which seems to be in agreement is that of Viernstein and Hogan (1974); they made a distinction between high- and low-aspiring talented adolescents (based on occupational choices), and analysed differences between these groups in terms of Holland's theory of six personality types and codes. They found that 'high and low aspirers of both sexes are distinctly different: the dominant code of high aspirers is Investigative, while the dominant code of low aspirers is Social' (p. 186).

All these findings seem to suggest, on the one hand, an academically orientated group of highly performing, science-interested, industrious, and rather socially withdrawn gifted adolescents, and on the other a group of somewhat less achieving but still gifted adolescents, who are more socially interested. However, it would be a mistake to over-generalize, for the way in which the two groups were formulated makes them easy to caricature, and many other factors are also relevant to the topic. Furthermore, no data were gathered on the actual social position of the subjects in any of these research projects, in terms of acceptance or rejection by peers, or class-mates and of other sociometric data. In addition, the use of different definitions of giftedness makes the results of these studies hard to interpret; none use a definition as in the Triadic Model (see Figure 15.3). Yet these studies make it possible to say something about the particular roles of the different elements in our definition.

In this respect it is regrettable that the concept of creativity was not involved in these studies, possibly because it is somewhat more associated with the less highly achieving and more socially accomplished group of gifted adolescents, a conclusion which is suggested by Walberg's (1971) research. Though he found only a weak relationship between gifted adolescents' involvement in school activities and their level of creativity, they were seen to be well integrated into the social hierarchy of the school. Schaefer (1980) found the same for a group of ten gifted adolescent girls, who often took charge in group activities and were relatively active in activities outside school, but it is possible that in this respect, sex-role differences play a part. Thus, Kurtzman (1980) determined that highly creative boys were more sociable and received greater peer acceptance than less-creative boys; though highly creative girls were less accepted by their classmates.

A subject closely related to the functioning of gifted adolescents amongst peers is the self-concept, involving such concepts as self-confidence and self-acceptance, all as aspects of the metatransformational process of identity formation, discussed earlier. For gifted adolescents, there seems to be a positive association between intelligence, self-confidence, positive self-image, and self-acceptance. The same can be said, but with much weaker evidence, of the association between achievement, self-confidence, and self-acceptance (Mönks and Ferguson, 1983), though some results are contradictory. What is needed here is the same degree of differentiation that was suggested above in relation to social functioning. The self-concept has to be thought of as a complex psychological construct, not only in its features, (Shavelson et al. (1976) distinguish seven different aspects), but also in its contents.

If the self-concept is regarded as a result of the growing awareness of one's own talents and qualities, it can be conceived of as consisting of different 'compartments', associated with different behavioural domains; this chapter will consider only those of social relations and intellectual or academic achievement. Winne *et al.* (1982) used the Coopersmith Self-Esteem Inventory, which consists of four sub-scales (general, self–peer relations, home and academic) and the Sears Self-Concept Scale (nine sub-scales: physical ability, physical appearance, social relations, social virtues, happy qualities, convergent mental abilities, divergent mental abilities, school subjects and work habits). They found that gifted pupils scored more highly on academic self-esteem, but could not determine any reliable differences in the social and physical domain. Ross and Parker (1980) hypothesize a discrepancy between the academic and the social self-image of the 'academically gifted', the first proving to be significantly more positive. They offer two possible explanations, which are seen as complementary: on the one hand, these pupils might be developing their academic skills in too one-sided a way, at the cost of the development of their social skills; on the other hand, they might experience a certain uneasiness and insecurity in finding a place in the peer group. In the light of the selection procedure that the authors used (they selected high-level performers in a strictly academic and intellectual sense) this might well be the case. In this respect, research in which under-achieving and not under-achieving gifted pupils are compared (see for example Ziv *et al.*, 1977 and Kirk and Gallagher, 1979) is interesting. Unfortunately again, no information was gathered in these studies on the actual social skills of the subjects, nor was any sociometric data or reports of their actual social behaviour.

It was remarkable how uniform all the subjects in our pilot study were, in terms of such personality characteristics as autonomy and independence: this, in spite of the adolescent's still developing self-concepts, which varied with their different performances on socially and non-socially relevant variables. For example, most subjects did not need to be encouraged to begin their homework, and the ways in which they structured their studies and organized their lives gave evidence of high levels of self-determination. In addition, insight into their own behaviour and into the quality of their relationships with others was often astonishing. A sixteen-year-old boy, speaking about being popular, said:

> You have to make a distinction between people that I myself appreciate very much and people who are very popular in class. The people I like have to be the same person in front of anybody; they must stand up for the things they say, and be who they are. Children who are popular in class like to be very tough or infantile. In recent years, it seems to be more and more possible to join in with the others by being yourself. Sometimes you are rejected, but I don't like to fool myself ... My popularity got less

until I came into the fourth grade. Things are stable now; you know a few people with whom you can get along very well in a more permanent way. The number of people with whom you can't get along at all is certainly higher; at first, there weren't such people, but now there are those that really reject you.

Relationships at home

Another important social setting which is relevant to the development and functioning of gifted adolescents is the home environment; a review of the relevant literature by Colangelo and Deltman (1983) mentions a number of important family characteristics. For example, families of gifted children tend to show strong family-ties and warm relationships between their members; parents are found to give their children more freedom and to be more involved with their gifted child. However, under-achievers more often experience rejection and hostility from their parents than achievers, whilst reasonably high expectations, combined with involvement, seem to represent the optimal family backgrounds for highly achieving gifted children.

For one boy in our sample, under-achievement was not so much due to rejection, but rather to indifferent parental behaviour. This gifted boy also trained his parents so that they no longer raised questions about school matters: 'By not answering their questions, I discouraged their interest in my school career.'

Another study which attempts to isolate such family background factors is that of Tabackman (1976). Families with gifted adolescents saw themselves as more independent, permissive, intellectual, unstructured, and harmonious in their interactions. Walberg (1971, 1980) reports that the creative adolescents in his study generally came from stimulating home environments.

Most of the characteristics mentioned above seem more likely to be found in families of higher socio-economic status. In our own study, practically all the adolescents we have interviewed come from families in which one or both of the parents had a high professional status. These families were characterized by a positive intellectual climate, relationships of mutual trust between parents and children, a positive attitude by the parents towards their children's study, without becoming too exigent; in fact, in the existing climate, little encouragement or reward were necessary to motivate the children.

The following example illustrates such supportive home atmospheres:

I can get along with my parents; they are interested in many things in which I am also interested. I always tell everything at home; I show them everything. Sometimes they ask something too, but most often they don't have to: I tell them everything. When I come home, I have to get rid of my story. I always enjoy everything I'm doing, and my parents always show a keen interest in me ... It stimulates you; they help to extend your interests. On holidays, we go to the museum and that sort of thing; it's the sort of thing they were educated with themselves. In this respect, my parents are more important than school. But everything is connected with everything, school, home and my own interests.

The possibility that giftedness and being born in families with a high socio-economic status are closely related variables is confirmed by a number of research studies. For example Schmidt (1981) found that the vast majority of his research group of gifted pupils originated from higher social class families, and the same is suggested by the work of Ketcham and Snyder (1977). However, there is evidence that in lower-class families, outstanding performances are often regarded as non-conformist behaviour, so that such behaviour is not so much positively reinforced. This might lead to the conclusion that socio-economic class as such is not a determining factor for the optimal development of giftedness, but rather the adverse reactions to expressions of outstanding (intellectual) performances that are brought about in some socio-economic classes.

The socio-cultural context

Figure 15.1 showed how the universal conditions for children's development are influenced by socio-cultural and historical factors, which manifest themselves in social settings; illustrated here by sex-role expectations, and the way in which these expectations influence the developmental processes of gifted adolescents. Hill (1980) has put it as follows:

And there is information that girls in early adolescence differentiate skills on a gender-role basis more than in childhood and begin to opt out and to do less well in 'male subjects' in school. They even may begin to underachieve in relation to their ability, apparently in response to the paired norms that 'good children get good grades' but 'not too good'. Indeed the aversive consequences for girls for expending efforts, persisting in the face of obstacles, competing and actually succeeding may lead to an internalised avoidance of and withdrawal from achievement situations, the so-called 'fear of success'. (p. 50)

Freeman (1983) also supposes that high intelligence might enhance the normal developmental sex-role problems, and cites Osborne and Taylor (1980), who report from their clinical practice that 'some gifted girls have difficulty in reconciling high achievement with femininity, even today, so that it often seems simpler to drop one of the qualities deliberately' (p. 483). Schaefer (1980), in his study of ten highly creative adolescent girls, suggests that their need for autonomy and achievement was in conflict with their needs for parental and peer-group acceptance, which required being feminine and socially acceptable. This is consistent with the results of Kurzman (1980); highly creative boys were proved to receive greater acceptance from their classmates, whereas highly creative girls were less accepted.

Kirk and Gallagher (1979) assume that gifted girls especially meet problems when they are confronted with the sex-role stereotypes of their parents and educators. It is suggested that these stereotypes also exist in the peer-culture, where creativity, the need for achievement, and the taking of intellectual risks are discouraged. Viernstein and Hogan (1974), found in an empirical study that gifted girls with very high levels of aspiration had feelings of insecurity; it is possible that these girls felt badly socialized and in conflict with norms of their parents and social groups.

Finally, Tomlinson-Keasy and Smith-Winberry (1983), in a research project comparing gifted and average pupils, found that with gifted girls, one could speak of a superior social adjustment as contrasted with the less good adjustments of the gifted boys. These differences were explained by hypothesizing that boys met higher expectations and experienced more competitive pressure (they also attended more prestigious universities). But a follow-up study of the Maryland Talent Searches by Solano (1983), found that there were no significant differences in the self-esteem or self-concepts of boys and girls gifted in mathematics (a traditional male subject), though the gifted girls did think rather better of themselves than average-ability girls. The conclusion seems to be that traditional sex-role expectations for girls can interfere with their actual performances, but not necessarily with their sense of self. But since these expectations and behaviours are socioculturally and historically determined, it makes it hard to generalize results of studies to other situations.

CONCLUSIONS

In this chapter, we have stressed the importance of using definitions of giftedness which cover more than cognitive-intellectual factors, particularly the concepts of creativity and task commitment. Even though this might mean that one is forced to use relatively subjective identification procedures (e.g. rating scales) in addition to standardized psychometric measurements, it is the price to be paid for more valid criteria of identification.

Secondly, we have attempted to give some indications of the specific behaviours and developments of the gifted adolescent within the outlined framework of normal adolescent development. We have tried to make clear that giftedness is not something which exists in a vacuum: like other adolescents, the gifted act in social settings and experience complex developmental processes, which have to be studied in the same conceptual framework. But as a consequence of their exceptional position with regard to a number of factors, most noteably ability, they may act and develop in different ways.

Finally, we wish to state that research in this field seems to show little consistency and many apparent contradictions. The most important cause of this inconsistency is due to the use of many different definitions of giftedness, so that many unrelated variables are operationalized, making it hard to interpret and integrate the results of the research. What research on aspects of the social functioning of gifted adolescents has most missed, especially in relation to the peer group, is an integral approach in which all relevant aspects are operationalized, and in which quantitative as well as qualitative data are gathered. Such research would make it possible to give answers to problems that so far remain unresolved.

More refinement and differentiation in theorizing and operationalizing are clearly needed, and the Triadic Model is suggested as being of value in this respect. It is hoped that future research projects in which many relevant variables, suggested by the elaborated life-span developmental perspective, are measured together, would be most valuable. In theory, at least, it would make it possible to study relationships that have so far remained undiscovered, and to explain research findings which point, for the moment, in different directions.

REFERENCES

Andersson, B. W. (1979). Developmental trends in reaction to social pressure from adults versus peers. *International Journal of Behavioral Development*, **2**, 269–286.

Arlin, P. K. (1975). 'Cognitive development in adulthood: a fifth stage? *Developmental Psychology*, **11**, 5, 602–605.

Ausubel, D. P. (1965). *Theories and Problems of Adolescent Development.* Grune & Stratton, New York.

Baacke, D. (1979). *Die Dreizehn—bis Achtzehnjährige: Einführung in Probleme des Jugendalters.* Urban & Schwarzenberg, München, Wien, Baltimore.

Berndt, T. J. (1979). Developmental changes in conformity to peers and parents. *Developmental Psychology*, **15**, 608–616.

Boensch, M. (1977). Zum gegenwärtigen Stand der Begabungsforschung und seiner Berücksichtigung in der Unterrichtspraxis. *Unterrichtswissenschaft*, 1, 66–76.

Colangelo, N., and Deltman, D. F. (1983). A review of research on parents and families of gifted children. *Exc. Children*, **50**, 20–27.

Dacey, J. S. (1982). *Adolescents Today*, Scott, Foresman, Glenview, Illinois.

Elshout, J. J., Kouwenhoven, K., and Tromp, D. (1983). De identificatie van hoogbegaafde jonge mensen. *Paedagogische Studien*, **60**, 209–219.

Erikson, E. H. (1968). *Identity, Youth and Crisis.* Norton, New York.

Flavell, J. (1977). *Cognitive Development.* Prentice-Hall, Englewood Cliffs, New Jersey.

Freeman, J. (1979). *Gifted Children*. MTP Press, Lancaster.
Freeman J. (1983). Emotional problems of the gifted child. *J. Child Psychol. Psychiat.* **24**, 481–485.
Ginzberg, E. (1972). Toward a theory of occupational choice: A restatement. *Vocational Guidance Quarterly*, **20**, 169–176.
Ginzberg, E., Ginsberg, S. W., Axelrad, S., and Herman, J. L. (1951). *Occupational Choice: An Approach to a General Theory*. Columbia University Press, New York.
Hartup, W. W. (1978). Children and their friends. In *Issues in Childhood Social Development* (ed. H. McGurk). Methuen, London.
Havighurst, R. J. (1951). *Developmental Tasks and Education*. Longman, New York.
Heckhausen, H. (1980). *Motivation und Handeln*. Springer, Berlin.
Hill, J. P. (1980). The family. In *Toward Adolescence: The Middle School Years. Seventy-ninth Yearbook of the Study of Education* (ed. M. Johnson). University of Chicago Press, Chicago.
Hill, J. P., and Mönks, F. J. (Eds.) (1977). *Adolescence and Youth in Prospect*. IPC Science and Technology Press, Guildford.
Hogan, R., and Weiss, D. (1974). Personality correlates of superior academic achievement. *Journal of Counselling Psychol.*, **21**, 144–149.
Ketcham, B., and Snyder, R. T. (1977). Self attitudes of the intellectually and socially advantaged student: normative study of the Piers Harris children's self-concept-scale. *Psychological Reports*, **40**, 111–116.
Kirk, S. A., and Gallagher, J. J. (1979). *Educating Exceptional Children*. Houghton Mifflin, Boston.
Kurtzman, K. A. (1980). A study of school attitudes, peer acceptance, and personality of creative adolescents. In *Gifted and Talented Education in Perspective* (eds. J. S. Renzulli and E. P. Stoddard). The Council for Exceptional Children, Reston, Virginia.
La Gaipa, J. J. (1979). A developmental study of the meaning of friendship in adolescence. *Journal of Adolescence*, **2**, 201–213.
Lazarus, R. S. (1966). *Psychological Stress and the Coping Process*. McGraw-Hill, New York.
Lerner, R. M., and Spanier, G. B. (1980). *Adolescent Development*. McGraw-Hill, New York.
MacKinnon, D. W. (1964). The creativity of architects. In *Widening Horizon in Creativity* (ed. C. W. Taylor). Wiley, New York.
McCandless, B. R. (1970). *Adolescents*. Dryden Pres, Hinsdale, Illinois.
McClelland, D. C. (1961). *The Achieving Society*. Free Press, New York.
Mönks, F. J. (1983). Hoogbegaafde kinderen: een benadeelde groep? *Pedagogische Studien*, **60**, 195–208.
Mönks, F. J., and Ferguson, T. J. (1983). Gifted adolescents: An analysis of their psychosocial development. *Journal of Youth and Adolescence*, **12**, 1–18.
Oerter, R. (1967). *Moderne Entwicklungspsychologie*. Verlag Ludwig Auer, Donauwoerth.
Osborne, E., and Taylor D. (1980). Address given at Leonardo Trust Conference on Gifted Children, London.
Perry, W. (1981). Cognitive and ethical growth. In *The Modern American College* (ed. A. Chickering). Jossey-Bass, San Francisco.
Renzulli, J. S. (1978). What makes giftedness? Re-examining a definition. *Phi Delta Kappan*, **60**, 180–184 and 261.

Renzulli, J. S., Reis, S. M., and Smith, L. H. (1981). *The Revolving Door Identification Model.* Creative Learning Press, Mansfield Center, Connecticut.

Ross, A., and Parker, M. (1980). Academic social self concepts of the academically gifted. *Exc. Children,* **47,** 6–10.

Rüppell, H. (1981). Ein ökologisches Förderungsmodell für Hochbegabte. Eine Modifikation des Bonner-Lehr-Lern-Systems. In *Das Hochbegabte Kind* (eds W. Wieczerkowsky and H. Wagner). Pädagogischer Verlag Schwann, Düsseldorf.

Rutter, M. (ed.) (1980). Attachment and the development of social relationships. In *Scientific Foundation of Developmental Psychiatry.* William Heineman, London.

Schaefer, C. E. (1980). A psychological study of 10 exceptionally creative adolescent girls. In *Gifted and Talented Education in Perspective* (eds J. S. Renzulli and E. P. Stoddard). The Council for Exceptional Children, Reston, Virginia.

Schmidt, M. H. (1981). Psychiatrische Aspekte der Hochbegabung. In *Das Hochbegabte Kind* (eds W. Wieczerkowsky and H. Wagner). Pädagogischer Verlag Schwann, Düsseldorf.

Shavelson, R. J., Hubner, J. J., and Stanton, J. C. (1976). Self concept: validation of construct interpretations. *Review of Educational Research,* **46,** 407–441.

Solano, C. H. (1983). Self concept in mathematically gifted adolescents. *The Journal of General Psychology,* **108,** 33–42.

Stanley, J. C. (1977). Rationale of the study of mathematically precocious youth (SMPY) during its first five years of promoting educational acceleration. In *The Gifted and the Creative: A Fifty-Year Perspective* (eds J. C. Stanley, W. C. George and C. H. Solano). Johns Hopkins University, Baltimore, Md.

Stanley, J. C. (1980). On educating the gifted. *Educational Researcher,* **9,** 8–12.

Stern, W. (1967). Psychologische Begabungsforschung und Begabungsdiagnose. In *Begabungsförderung und Schule* (eds Th. Ballauf and H. Hettwer). Wissenschaftliche Buchgesellschaft, Darmstadt.

Tabackman, M. J. (1976). *A Study of Family Psycho-social Environment and its Relationship to Academic Achievement in Gifted Adolescents.* University of Illinois, Urbana-Champaign.

Terman, L. M. (1954). The discovery and encouragement of exceptional talent. *American Psychologist,* **9,** 221–230.

Terman, L. M. (ed.) (1925). *Genetic Studies of Genius: Mental and Physical Traits of a Thousand Gifted Children.* Stanford University Press, Stanford.

Tomlinson-Keasy, C., and Smith-Winberry, C. (1983). Educational strategies and personality outcomes of gifted and non-gifted college students. *Gifted Child Quarterly,* **27,** 35–41.

Viernstein, M. C., and Hogan, R. (1974). Parental personality factors and achievement motivation in talented adolescents. *Journal of Youth and Adolescence,* **4,** 2, 183–190.

Walberg, H. (1971). Varieties of adolescent creativity and the high school environment. *Exc. Children,* **38,** 111–116.

Walberg, H. J. (1980). Varieties of adolescent creativity and the High school environment. In *Gifted and Talented Education in Perspective* (eds J. S. Renzulli and E. P. Stoddard). The Council for Exceptional Children, Reston, Virginia.

Wasserman, S. (1962). The gifted can't weigh that giraffe. *Phi Delta Kappan,* **53,** 621–625.

Winne, P. H., Woodlands, M. J., and Wong, B. Y. C. (1982). Comparability of self-concepts among learning disabled, normal and gifted students. *Journal of Learning Disabilities*, **15**, 470–475.

Ziv, A., Rimon, J., and Dori, M. (1977). Parental perception and self-concept of gifted and average underachievers. *Perceptual and Motor Skills*, **44**, 563–568.

The Psychology of Gifted Children
Edited by Joan Freeman
©1985, John Wiley & Sons, Ltd.

CHAPTER 16

Delinquency Among Gifted Children

ROBERT BROOKS

Although frequently used to describe the 'very naughty' child, the term 'delinquent' is properly reserved for children over the age at which they are presumed to have the ability to form intent, who engage in behaviour contrary to the law of the society in which they live. Most delinquent acts, when committed by adults, are punishable as crimes, but there are some which are specific to juveniles, including such behaviours as truancy, under-age drinking, the purchase or possession of certain substances, and proscribed sexual activity.

Delinquency is a specific term, whereas maladjustment is a psycho-social concept, which, though it may overlap, is not synonymous with delinquency. But because delinquency is often associated with other behaviours which are maladaptive, it has been suggested that all delinquents are maladjusted, though not all maladjusted children are delinquent. Though this is a reasonable working hypothesis, instances may occur when a juvenile presents a pattern of 'pure' delinquency as learned responses to the perceptions held of the self and society. In a few cases of gifted children, it might appear that their behaviour deviations are exclusively confined to delinquent acts, revealing a sort of rationality in their conduct not so readily observable in less-able misfits. However, whilst some gifted delinquents may graduate to become significant figures in the adult criminal world, many of the offences they commit are ill-planned, stupidly executed, and have scant regard to the outcome (Brooks, 1980).

Delinquency is no new phenomenon, but since the 1940s, the number of young people reported for or detected engaging in it has increased dramatically, and part of this increase can be attributed to greater numbers of children and young people in the total population. Although this pattern is presently being reversed, the actual rate of delinquency seems likely to rise in most Western countries to a level where it is estimated that some 12 per cent of all young people (up to the age of eighteen years) and 22 per cent of all boys up to the same age will be likely to have records of it.

Virtually all children engage in delinquent acts at some time during their development, but for most, these episodes will be transitory and will not merit formal intervention. The official identification of a child as delinquent rests on quantitative rather than qualitative considerations; it is only when the behaviour becomes so persistent or grave as to be socially intolerable that formal psycho-social intervention appears necessary. For the most part, children grow out of the delinquent acts which seem to form part of the normal process of maturation, so that those who justify being formally labelled as delinquent represent a threat to and a burden on society.

Because delinquency is a legal rather than a psychological concept— although it may have considerable psychological significance—what is considered at one time or in one society as unlawful may be perfectly lawful at another time or place. Since delinquency relates to the infraction of rules established by societies, variations in the rules forming the legal framework must result in changes in the patterns of delinquency. However, delinquency is not necessarily a moral issue. The legal statutes of a society are not always based on moral considerations; they may stem from social or economic factors, so that delinquent 'guilt' cannot be invariably equated with moral turpitude. On the other hand, delinquents alienate themselves from a legitimate value system established by a society, and are attracted to an illegitimate value system. This process of alienation and attraction stems from their perceptions of themselves, of others, and of the structures of society; such perceptions may be false or irrational, but are not necessarily immoral.

What are gifted delinquents like? In addition to the general intellectual and reasoning abilities measured by IQ tests, giftedness may include superior innate abilities and skills in particular academic areas, in visual and performing arts, in creative thinking, in psycho-motor activities, or in social leadership. Whilst young people of high intellectual potential usually possess some special talents, it is quite wrong to suppose that high levels of measured intelligence are indicative of outstanding ability across the whole spectrum of human endeavour. For many highly intelligent children, their giftedness may be a burden rather than a delight—often as a result of inappropriate expectations imposed upon them by parents, teachers, and significant others. These expectations may be conditioned by educational conventions, social attitudes, economic criteria, sex-role stereotyping, and other factors. Gifted children ought not to be regarded as 'better' purely on the grounds of special innate talents, nor should they be considered specially blameworthy when circumstances have thwarted the full development of their various potentials.

The average juvenile delinquent scores somewhat below average on tests of intelligence, when compared with the general population, and there is a slightly greater incidence of educational retardation among delinquents than in the school population at large. Gath, Tennant and Pidduck (1970a) found that delinquent boys with an IQ of 115 and above comprised 7.8 per cent of those tested, whereas they would have expected to have found 16.5 per cent on the basis of a normal distribution of intelligence. The Cambridge Study of Delinquency Development (West and Farrington, 1973) indicated that delinquents were significantly under-represented among youths of IQ 115 plus. On the other hand, surveys of boys admitted to approved schools between 1956 and 1961 showed that some 12 per cent had IQs of over 110, a finding supported by studies conducted in the United States by Caplan and Siebert (1964), Merrill (1947), and Conger and Miller (1966).

Identifying the actual number of gifted delinquents is difficult because a child who presents behaviour problems which include delinquent acts along with other maladaptive symptoms may not be formally identified as delinquent, but be the subject of intervention on the wider grounds of maladjustment. The group formally identified as delinquent will be likely to comprise those children who are the most seriously disaffected and who appear to constitute the gravest social threat. In any event, it would appear from the rather limited evidence available that low intelligence cannot, as it once was, be considered the major causal factor of delinquency. This has implications for therapeutic strategies, and tends to support the view that educational provision can only be regarded as a part of much wider social and emotional therapy, and that academic progress should only be regarded as offering a partial indication of developing stability.

For those juvenile delinquents who were assessed as needing residential care, the provision used to be primarily custodial. The regimes adopted in the approved schools generally were typified by close supervision, strict routines and compliance with detailed sets of rules. The educational provision was remedial in character, with the older children receiving some training in practical skills. Such units failed to meet the needs of the more able children and when, in the post-war period, a significant number of gifted delinquents had to be catered for, it became clear that some special units would have to be created. Although some work had been carried out in the private sector by people such as Lyward, Lennhoff and Shaw, the decision was taken in 1948 to establish state provision for gifted delinquent boys. This offered unique opportunities for assessing the special needs of this group and to evolve appropriate therapeutic strategies. Contrary to the expectations of some, it soon became apparent that effective therapy would not be achieved through the medium of purely intellectual activities nor in an environment the ethos of which would be perceived as primarily custodial. The first and most difficult task which emerged was the creation of a sense of community and it was only when that had been achieved that the group developed a sense of stability.

In due course, it was possible to undertake a longitudinal study of gifted delinquents, using as a sample 135 boys aged thirteen to fifteen years on admission to the Unit. The sample constituted consecutive admissions and the IQ range was from 120+ measured on the Weschler Intelligence Scale for Children. Detailed analyses were made of the boys' behavioural responses to their social, educational and emotional experiences. The survey was extended to cover a period of ten years following release from the unit in order to evaluate the outcome of therapy. The study was made possible as there were detailed records available from Classifying Units (which incorporated school and other reports) and the Home Office made available copies of subsequent criminal records of those boys who formed the sample. This research has been reported (Brooks 1972).

It was noted that there was significant regression during the two-year period following return to the community of society which was evidenced by poor employment records and the commission of further offences. These regressive patterns are similar to those noted by Tremblay (1983) and the evidence supports the view that the effectiveness of residential therapy for gifted children is conditioned by the quality of 'after-care' which should be an integral and on-going aspect of treatment. 'After-care' ought not to be a new provision tacked on to the end of a period of residential therapy but should be initiated during the time of residence so that the transition back into society becomes nothing more than a further step in the total therapeutic process. It was found that those leaving the therapeutic atmosphere were at greatest risk of regression during the first year back in society. Any evaluation of the success rates of a residential therapeutic unit has to be made after a reasonable period has elapsed after the 'clients' have left and the quality of the after-care cannot therefore be divorced from the work of the unit itself.

All the case studies of the sample were analysed in order to establish any traits which might have been common to practically all those forming the group. It was found that their behaviour was typified by a rejection of the ethic of hard work, a low threshold of frustration tolerance, and a very thinly disguised contempt for the common values of society (Brooks, 1972). They resisted anything perceived as coercion, and were suspicious of any influences which emanated from their parents or teachers. This suspicion was displayed to the staff of the treatment units, until confidence and trust was won through slow and painful patience. What appeared to be a deep-seated delinquent culture was usually the outcome of the failure of homes and schools to provide the boys with reinforcements for the identities which they had vainly tried to establish for themselves. Indeed, a great deal of their behaviour was not so much a direct confrontation with society, but rather a dismissal of the demands felt to come from parents and teachers, which were perceived as irrelevant to their needs and self-actualization. The boys seemed to be shut up within themselves and their aggression was a sort of defence of what they perceived as their own integrity.

It seemed that the boys felt a need to rid themselves of false identities which had been imposed on them, or to be reaching out for a quality of caring concern through which they could be enabled to satisfy their inner competence drives. The attitudes of their parents and teachers ranged from a form of selfish pride in the boys' giftedness through to a denial of their potential, which was seen by some adults as posing a sort of threat to their own status. The boys felt that the social models of the institutions of which they were nominally members had scant relevance for them; many found the models to which they were expected to conform to be profoundly constricting. Their experience appeared to have either eroded their social and cognitive development, or had never included positive recognition of their special needs. Only rarely did they see their parents and teachers as demanding anything other than unquestioning compliance with what they perceived as being infantile, empty, and artificial rituals.

Those boys who formed my 'gifted' sample appeared to have sought to bolster up their sense of worth and individuality through a delinquent subculture, but most of them were more certain of what they were not than what they were. They tended to lack hindsight and foresight, placing store by immediate sensation and gratification. In a study of Shakespeare's Lear, one boy wrote: 'At the end of the play Lear is capable of being humble; of loving others as well as himself and begging forgiveness for his foolishness. This sort of thing does not very often happen here but people, when they have been here some time, are not afraid to be humble or look foolish unlike some new boys who will do anything rather than lose their brash and brittle facades'. The boys seemed to be shut up within themselves, and their aggression was a sort of defence of what they perceived as their own integrity.

The development of identities which are confirmed by intellectual endeavour or the use of motor skills held little attraction for them, and they pitied their peers who conformed to the social ethics and expectations of society. Nearly all the boys studied possessed an irresistable urge to hold the centre of the stage in any conversation or activity, and this made them appear very egocentric, even though this stance was more likely to be the outcome of their own uncertainty rather than of any real authority. Although they all gave ample evidence of having failed to have learned how to cope with being gifted, they did perceive themselves in some way as being 'special'. Their IQ scores were very important to them, but they were quite unable to accept them as mere indicators of potential. One boy commented in interview that: 'Because we are more intelligent, there is more in us to get twisted up'.

Psychiatric evidence suggested that the level of emotional disturbance was higher in those delinquents in the gifted group than amongst those of average intellectual potential, but matched for age and social class. The physical health of the gifted group was notably good.

Their relationships with their peers were marked by the lack of insight they displayed. Whilst giving an impression of forming close friendships, any depth of commitment within a relationship was usually lacking, so much so that if one of two boys who appeared to be inseparable was removed from or left the therapeutic group, the other showed scant remorse. An emotional outburst seemed all that was likely to mark the ending of the relationship. Their relationships within the therapeutic unit seemed to reflect those which existed within their homes—there was a lack of real binding between the members of the family groups, and the boys had never learned to appreciate the real meaning and significance of personal relationships.

Much of the work undertaken with gifted delinquents tends to have been limited to isolated reports on individual and 'experimental' units. Only now is a body of fragmentary information being brought together in ways which might eventually lead to a recognition of the therapeutic needs common to the majority of this group. There is, for example, a striking similarity between the characteristics of the group of 135 gifted delinquent boys forming the basis for this particular study and those detailed by Margaret Parker (1983). She identifies a number of factors which were almost uniformly typical of the gifted law breakers she investigated. These included children who were effectively non-parented, achieved only low levels of success in schools, experienced enhanced learning difficulties, adopted strong ego-centric attitudes, were deeply deprived of caring experience, and had low levels of frustration tolerance and expressed rebellious attitudes through withdrawal or aggressive patterns of behaviour.

Pringle (1970) undertook a study of the educational and behaviour difficulties of 103 very intelligent children (IQs 120–200 with an average of 130). She found evidence of a wide range of problems associated with this group, including behavioural difficulties ranging from slight to severely neurotic. She also identified symptoms of aggression associated frequently with withdrawal, noted that the group had undistinguished educational records and commented that the social competence was much lower than might have been expected of such an intelligent group.

Klein and Cantor (1976) found that gifted children were more than normally sensitive to their environment and Lowenstein (1981) identifies some of the problems associated with relatively less-able or intellectually limited parents and teachers charged with the care of more able children.

This coincidence of views by even a limited number of scholars makes it reasonable to hypothesize that the treatment response to gifted children who lapse into delinquency should not be restricted to the traditional concept of security-oriented convenience but be aimed towards capitalizing on their inherent strengths of which their very delinquency is evidence.

A COMPARATIVE STUDY

A further study was conducted to compare gifted delinquent boys with their peers of average intelligence. A control group was established by taking 135 boys of average intelligence (WISC 90–105), who were made the subjects of court orders during a similar period to that of the index group (WISC IQ range 120+) and who were matched for age and social grouping.

The mean age at the first court appearance in which a finding of 'guilt' was recorded varied between the two groups; that for the control group was 132.6 months, whereas the mean age for the index group was 150.1 months. It might appear from this that the gifted group were treated more leniently by those in authority. The court records reveal that more gifted boys received formal cautions regarding their first offences than those who formed the control group. However, this variation may be accounted for by various factors, including:

1. The possibility that the gifted boys and their families might have displayed a superior level of articulation.
2. Those in authority might have felt that a court appearance could be more detrimental to the gifted boy than to his less-able peers.
3. A number of gifted potential delinquents might have been ascertained as maladjusted earlier in their careers and have been placed in special schools, thereby avoiding the stigma of being delinquent.
4. There are a number of private units catering for or offering places to gifted but maladaptive children.

In fact, the records indicated that although the gifted group tended to make fewer appearances before juvenile courts, they committed a larger number of admitted offences than the control group.

An analysis was undertaken of the numbers of subjects who had experienced significant disruption of parental relationships. This analysis indicates that paternal deprivation represents a very significant factor for the gifted group of boys, and that the degree of significance of paternal deprivation for the gifted group exceeds that of maternal deprivation for the control group. Although maternal deprivation is notable for both groups, it appears that the paternal role has particular significance for the gifted group.

TABLE 16.1 Comparison of the numbers of subjects who had experienced disruption of parental relationships with those not so affected

	Index group N = 135	Control group N = 135
Number where mother absent or relationship interrupted	47	73
Mother present	88	62
Number where father absent or relationship interrupted	92	57
Father present	43	78

The levels of educational attainment and reactions to school experience, as reflected by test results and teacher evaluations, were also reviewed. It appears that the under-achieving factor is more pronounced for the gifted group than for the group of average intelligence. This may be accounted for—in part at least—by teacher expectations, which may be more stringent for the gifted group than for less-talented children.

TABLE 16.2 Levels of educational attainment and reactions to school experience as reflected by test results and teacher evaluation

	Index group N = 135	Control group N = 135
Attainment commensurate with potential	21	59
Under-achievers	77	35
Hostile (including persistent truancy)	37	41

CLASSIFICATION OF OFFENCES

An analysis of the offences committed by the gifted group and the control group respectively revealed no significant differences. However, the classification yields little of empirical value, because theft or other property offences form a disproportionately large number of the crimes with which young offenders are charged. This may be partly because certainty of obtaining a finding of guilt influences the police in selecting the charges which they prosecute; for example, what in actual fact might be a case of assault with sexual overtones may be prosecuted as a case of simple assault.

Differences in the patterns of delinquency of highly intelligent boys have been proposed by various authors; Merrill (1947) suggested that they might favour a particular type of offence, and Simmons (1962) that they displayed a surprising degree of ineptitude—a view supported by Gath et al. (1971). It must be recognized, though, that any offence tends to be conditioned by chance factors. Very few young offenders display the professionalism of the confirmed adult criminal, and even in the apparently planned offences committed by juveniles, the principal consideration appears to centre around escaping detection rather than ensuring a good haul. The details of offences committed by the gifted group indicated that some catalyst or trigger mechanism sparked off the behaviour, such as the car key left in, or the shop with a very tempting display. The rewards from their offences appear to have been perceived more in terms of excitement—'for a lark'—such as the joy-ride in a stolen car, than in terms of calculated gain. Even where material gain was achieved, a great deal of stolen property was discarded.

When the offences committed by the index group were compared with those committed by the control group, there was some evidence that the gifted group committed rather more with psychological implications. This supports the view of Simmons (1956, 1962) and of Gath et al. (1970b) that gifted delinquents reveal a greater degree of psychiatric disturbance than their less-able peers.

TOWARDS A PROFILE OF THE GIFTED DELINQUENT

Attempts to clarify all the differences between the less-able child and his gifted peers are frustrated because no accepted system operates to identify gifted children, such as exists to ascertain the intellectually handicapped. However, comparison of the index with the control group in this study seems to reveal certain tendencies amongst the gifted group which, under certain circumstances, particularly predispose them to some degree of emotional or developmental disturbance, resulting in delinquent behaviour. These can be summarized as follows.

1. A heightened sensitivity to experience, including that of personal relationships. This is not to suggest that gifted children have superior capacities to love and to be loved, but they do appear to be able to articulate and to interpret their experiences. They appear to see more in their experiences than the less able.
2. A potentially heightened level of intellectual curiosity which, unless satisfied, may lead to feelings of frustration, anxiety, or even rejection.

Those who formed the gifted sample appear to have suffered from a lack of cultural stimuli, suggesting that failure to provide a stimulating home and social background impedes the optimum social, emotional, and intellectual development of the gifted child.

3. More pronounced potential levels of creativity and perception, although in practical terms, their perceptions may be quite unrealistic.

4. Deeper critical faculties, which can result in a refusal to accept social models unless they can be convinced intellectually and emotionally of the validity of social dogmas as these apply to them.

5. Stronger levels of self-regard (which may be founded on illusion), often associated with an awareness that they are intelligent. This tendency often revealed itself as a sort of insufferable arrogance, which alienated them from other people.

6. A need for strong levels of perceived security. Changes in environment seemed to have had a much more profound impact on the index than on the control group, the members of which seemed, on the whole, to accept changes in environment with a greater degree of passivity.

7. Possibly associated with 5 above, a potential ability to lead others in a dominative way. The index group appear to have lower frustration tolerance thresholds than the controls, and this seems to have led a number of index subjects to exercise an apparently more potent influence on others. In reviewing the careers of the gifted group, it was notable that many frequently 'used' less-able children to do their bidding, with scant regard for the cost or consequences.

In addition to these tendencies, which appear to predispose the gifted children to delinquent behaviour, certain other features emerged from the study. Isolation from peers seemed to be a significant feature, though less amenable to identification than the more overt forms of anti-social conduct. The potentially gifted but shy and sensitive child is often overlooked, yet can be at greater risk than is generally appreciated. In interviews, a number of the gifted subjects revealed that they felt their very giftedness was resented by some adults, who regarded them as precocious, and by many of their peers, who appeared to resent their skills and insights.

It was clear from this study that the gifted child adjusts more successfully when given a stable home background, associated with consistent and normal child-rearing practices. Over-permissive or over-strict regimes within the home or school appeared to enhance the degree of risk, but the most significant risk-factor emerged as erratic and inconsistent handling. Linked to the need for a consistent home environment was that for each gifted child's special talents to be recognized and gently fostered. The frustration of potential clearly enhanced the risk element towards poor social and emotional adjustment. It was also notable that undue pressure to achieve high levels of intellectual competence was damaging to the total development of the child. Many parents and teachers of those gifted children who became delinquent appear to have been over-concerned with intellectual achievement without being sufficiently concerned for their emotional and social maturation. Children in the index group were often subjected to cognitive expectations with which they were unable to cope emotionally. These pressures may be reflected in the level of hostility to school experience which was a significant factor in the aetiology of the gifted delinquent.

In reviewing the environment of the gifted delinquent, the very high level of statistical correlation between interrupted paternal relationships and delinquent behaviour serves to endorse the view that for gifted delinquent boys, paternal deprivation had a much more positive reaction than maternal deprivation. The findings drawn from the study of the group of 135 subjects confirms those of R. G. Andry (1960) who found that 'delinquents strongly tend to recognise their fathers as head of their families'. Environmental and psychological communication between the father and the gifted delinquent is of a significance which has often been ignored in past studies of gifted children.

The gifted manifest a diversity of potential and needs, including the need to be encouraged and enabled to develop that delicate balance between social interaction and the right to enjoy a healthy degree of privacy. They must be given a freedom for their particular talents and interests to flourish, and not be subjected to rigid patterns of expectations which often stem from parents wishing to fulfil themselves vicariously. Finally, whilst the gifted must learn to relate to the less able, the latter should be encouraged to accord to the gifted that measure of psychological isolation as is vital for their full self-actualization. This suggestion may raise a fear of elitism in the minds of some but the fact remains that there are and always have been some people who can do some things better than others. The phenomenon of individual differences has to be accepted. In our society it appears that the most competent are admired. This is fairly obvious in the area of physical endeavour where achievement is tangible and observable. Gifted children, however, often reveal their talents in less overt ways which can tend to result in their being ignored, scorned or even feared. The gifted have a claim to proper recognition of their potential.

REFERENCES

Andry, R. G. (1960). *Delinquency and Parental Pathology.* Methuen, London.
Brooks, R. (1972). *Bright Delinquents: The Story of a Unique School.* NFER, Windsor.
Brooks, R. (1980). *Bright Delinquents.* Brighton Polytechnic, Brighton.

Caplan, N. S., and Siebert, L. A. (1964). A distribution of juvenile deliquent intelligence test scores over a 34 year period (N = 51,808). *Journal of Clinical Psychology*, **20**, 242–247.

Conger, J. J., and Miller, W. C. (1966). *Personality, Social Class and Delinquency.* Wiley, New York.

Gath, D., Tennent, G., and Pidduck, R. (1970a). Educational characteristics of bright delinquents. *Journal of Educational Psychology*, **40**, 2.

Gath, D., Tennent, G., and Pidduck, R. (1970b). Psychiatric and social characteristics of bright delinquents. *British Journal of Psychology*, **116**, 531, 515–516.

Gath, D., Tennent, G., and Pidduck, R. (1971). Criminological characteristics of bright delinquents. *British Journal of Criminology*, **11**, 3, 275–279.

Klein, P. S., and Cantor, L. (1976). Gifted children and their self-concept. *Creative child and adult quarterly*, **1**, 98–101.

Lowenstein, L. F. (1981). *The Psychological Problems of Gifted-Children.* Pullen Publications, Knebworth.

Merrill, M. A. (1947). *Problems of Juvenile Delinquency.* Harrap, London.

Parker, M. (1983). Trouble with the law. In *Face to Face with Giftedness* (eds B. M. Shore, F. Gagne, S. Larivee, R. H. Tali, and R. E. Tremblay). Trillium Press, New York.

Pringle, M. L. K. (1970). *Able Misfits.* Longman, London.

Simmons, M. M. (1956). Intelligent delinquents. *Times Ed. Supp.*, 2 March.

Simmons, M. M. (1962). Contribution to a symposium on highly intelligent children. *Times Ed. Supp.*, 26 January.

Tremblay, R. E. (1983). Bright juvenile delinquents in residential treatment: are they different?. In *Face to Face with Giftedness* (eds B. M. Shore, F. Gagne, S. Larivee, R. H. Tali, and R. E. Tremblay). Trillium Press, New York.

West, D. J., and Farrington, D. P. (1973). *Who Becomes Delinquent?* Heinemann, London.

West, D. J., and Farrington, D. P. (1977). *The Delinquent Way of Life.* Crane Russak, New York.

The Psychology of Gifted Children
Edited by Joan Freeman
©1985, John Wiley & Sons, Ltd.

CHAPTER 17

Gifted Children in Three Israeli Cultures

NAVA BUTLER-POR

Much recent research into the development and manifestation of giftedness in children has been concerned with the serious problem of abilities which remain undetected and unfulfilled. Prevailing Western educational ideology is attempting to look beyond performance to potential with the aim of optimal development of all children, thereby enhancing their contributions to society.

In many countries, the recognition of this need has stimulated the provision of special education for the gifted. However, the pupil participants in such endeavours are predominately the children of middle-class Western parents; a description which certainly applies to the composition of classes for the gifted in Israel (Butler, 1976; Butler-Por and Lancer, 1979). The reasons for this, as Getzels (1969) has summarized, are that

> Explicitly or implicitly the school requires an achievement ethic with consequent high valuation of the future, deferred gratification and symbolic commitment to success. Not only are these the values of the school, but they are the values of the environment in which most middle-class children are brought up. In seeking to spread appropriate educational provision to all those who need it, probably the major problem is how to discover the untapped talents of children who have been socialised in a subculture whose values and cognitive experiences are different from those of the dominant culture.

Unfortunately, the traditional intelligence test has not been entirely successful as an all-round measure of giftedness. Indeed, Vernon (1975) in his comprehensive survey of intelligence across cultures, even suggests that: 'It is probable that Terman and Burt's IQ and the statistician's factors have to some extent held up progress by their inflexiblity and their tendency to obscure cultural differences.' Some researchers have attempted instead to measure intellectual giftedness with tests of creativity, but the results have been disappointing (Getzels and Jackson, 1962; Torrance, 1973; Butler-Por and Lancer, 1981).

There is, however, a particularly difficult problem in the identification of differently cultured children whose orientations, aptitudes and abilities may vary from those of the majority. Their situation calls for the extension of research on the identification of talent to encompass these cultural influences (Reissman, 1962; Torrance, 1980). In the light of such considerations it is essential to investigate those features of a culture which may obscure a child's ability—features which may be of paramount importance if he or she is to reap the full educational benefits provided by the school. The work of Rokeach (1973) and of Feather (1975) on the nature of values, particularly in education, suggests that investigation of the effects of the dominant values in cultural groups is likely to contribute towards a better understanding of the development of children's abilities.

The study of values in countries such as Israel is of particular educational relevance to the problem of cultural interactions and influences, because of the variety of cultural groups which make up the national population, whose children participate in the Western middle-class school milieu. The investigation presented here has studied such interactions, with particular concern for the different perceptions of giftedness across cultures.

THE INVESTIGATION

The research populations was made up of 138 children and their parents. The children were selected from the fourth grade (aged nine to ten) and eighth grade (aged thirteen to fourteen) lists of schools in Haifa and the Northern region of Israel as follows.

Group 1: Gifted middle-class children and their parents

Children in this group attended a special class for the gifted in Haifa ($n=34$). They had been selected as being within the top 2 per cent of the school population, measured on a battery of ability and aptitude tests.Their parents were of European origin, defined as 'middle-class' in terms of their socio-economic status.

Group 2: Middle-class children of normal ability and their parents

These children went to regular classes in the same schools in which the gifted classes were held ($n = 32$). Their parents were of middle-class, European descent.

Group 3: Differently cultured disadvantaged children and their parents

These were children who attended either a primary school for the educationally disadvantaged, as defined by the Israeli Ministry of Education and Culture, using the criteria of father's education, income, persons per room, and ethnic origin, or a mixed-ability middle school, ($n=24$). Their parents were mostly first or second generation immigrants from Arab countries.

Group 4: Kibbutz children and their parents

This group of children were pupils in local and regional kibbutz schools, drawing their populations from five kibbutzim ($n=24$). Their parents were mostly of European origin and constituted a representative sample of the population of the older kibbutzim.

Group 5: Arab children and their parents

The children in this group were the more able of those who attended village schools near Nazareth ($n=24$). Their parents provided a representative sample of this population.

Interviews were given individually to ascertain the significance of educational values to the subject, both at home and in school. This technique was chosen for its flexibility in exploring how people behaved with regard to both their specifically educational and overall value systems. The interview schedule proceeded in a funnel style, starting with a broad question, and then narrowing down to more detailed points (Cannel and Kahn, 1953). All the interviews took place in the children's homes. The child and each of the parents were interviewed separately, care being taken to explain objectives at the start of each interview and to maintain an open and informal climate throughout.

Responses were coded and tabulated separately for each subject on the basis of a content analysis of each interview. Values which received the highest number of responses were ranked highly and the remaining values in decreasing order.

The following comparisons were coded:

1. Fathers of boys
   vs
2. Fathers of girls

3. Mothers of boys
   vs
4. Mothers of girls

5. Boys
   vs
6. Girls

RESULTS

The results are shown separately here for each group. Those of the nine- to ten-year-old, fourth-grade children and their parents are given first, followed by a description and comparison of the differences in the responses of the adolescent thirteen- to fourteen-year-old children of eighth grade and their parents.

Analysis of the interviews indicated that ten values were common to most of the groups, wheareas additional values only appeared in one or two specific groups.

Group 1: Gifted middle-class children and their parents (Table 17.1)

TABLE 17.1 Group 1: Percentage of responses of highly gifted middle-class children and their parents

No.	Values	Responses (%)
1	School achievement	88
2	Social success	77
3	Individuality	77
4	Independence	67
5	Tidiness and cleanliness	57
6	Material success	53
7	Happiness	43
8	Initiative	40
9	Good citizenship	21
10	Loyalty	6

This was the most representative group in terms of the ten values selected for investigation, in which two influences could be detected. First, the middle-class composition of the group, which placed high emphasis on achievement, and secondly the participation of the children in the class for the gifted, which would have raised their expectations, in spite of the variety of developmental objectives built into the educational programme for the gifted. However, although every parent had put school achievement at the top of their list, only three-quarters of the children had done the same.

Within-group differences showed that although social success was ranked very highly, it was considered to be more important for girls than boys, for whom parents had other expectations. Tidiness and cleanliness was often described by parents as a training which would affect school practices, and indeed the group's class teacher had made a great educational issue of it.

Material success was seen by parents as being related to academic achievement, especially for boys, in terms of high-status academic professions. Interestingly, though 50 per cent of the fathers thought it important for their daughters, none of the mothers did, and the same pattern was repeated in the children's responses; none of the girls attributed importance to material success.

Parents and children differed in their valuation of happiness and initiative. None of the children mentioned either one, but parents gave both a higher rating for boys. More importance was placed on good citizenship for girls than boys—a finding which suggests that even for these middle-class Israeli children, it is part of the traditional role in the education of girls.

Adolescent values for gifted middle-class children and their parents

Achievement-orientated values still received the highest rank, with school achievement in top place. Again, mothers of daughters and the girls themselves ranked it lower than the males. The ranking for independence dropped from 77 per cent to 22 per cent in eighth grade, possibly reflecting a move away from individual toward future orientated values.

Group 2: Middle-class children of normal ability and their parents (Table 17.2)

Socio-economic influences similar to the previous group also appeared to be active in this one. Achievement came high, but only 50 per cent of the children responded to the concept of independence. However, good citizenship was rated higher by this average ability group than by the gifted group, 50 per cent of the children responding, compared with none of the gifted group who rated material success more highly. Individuality came low and happiness was again ranked as more important for boys.

Adolescent values for middle-class children of normal ability and their parents

This average-ability group was characterized by a shift towards non-academic achievement-orientated values, as well as a high correlation between children and parents with respect to sex differentiation. Thus the highest ranking was awarded to the value of material success, wheareas school achievement had been coded in top place for fourth grade. Again, values in eighth grade did appear to be more directed towards future images and roles, as indicated perhaps by the lower response of 8 per cent given to independence, compared with the 40 per cent of responses in fourth grade.

TABLE 17.2　Group 2:　Percentage of responses of middle-class children of normal ability and their parents

No.	Values	Responses (%)
1	School achievement	81
2	Independence	70
3	Social success	66
4	Good citizenship	49
5	Tidiness and cleanliness	42
6	Material success	42
7	Individuality	40
8	Happiness	25
9	Initiative	25
10	Loyalty	19

Group 3: Differently cultured disadvantaged children and their parents (Table 17.3)

All the respondents in this group attributed the greatest importance to social success, which may be due to the emphasis the community school puts on social awareness and to the participation of its pupils in the social life of the school and of the outside world.

Every parent valued school achievement for boys, but only 25 per cent for girls, wheareas the children disagreed, in that 75 per cent of the girls responded to this value, and seemed to identify more with school than home values here. This was also true for independence; only 30 per cent of the mothers responded positively for girls, but 70 per cent of the girls responded for themselves in respect of this quality.

In contrast to the previous two groups, 50 per cent both of the mothers and girls responded to the idea of material success; this may be understood in the light of the lower income in these families, which makes material success for women appear necessary. Tidiness, cleanliness, and individuality were largely seen as within the mother's housework domain, though some felt that 'If children would clean their rooms, it would be easier.'

TABLE 17.3 Group 3:   Percentage of responses of differently cultured disadvantaged children and their parents

No.	Values	Responses (%)
1	Social success	91
2	School achievement	71
3	Material success	69
4	Independence	66
5	Tidiness and cleanliness	34
6	Individuality	34

Adolescent values for differently cultured disadvantaged children and their parents

The most striking change for this group was in the lowest rank given to the value of school achievement. Whereas this value had been placed second in the fourth grade value system at 71 per cent, it received the lowest proportion of responses in eighth grade at 17 per cent. This supports previous research results showing that cultural and societal expectations for this group are low, and thus have a negative effect on achievements in school (Passow, 1980).

Material success achieved the highest rank, which may indicate that this success value is believed to be an obtainable goal—a factor Torrance and Reynolds (1978) found to be significant in constructing future roles. However, it was pertinent that though both the parents of boys and the sons coded nearly 100 per cent responses to this value, mothers of girls and the daughters did not respond to this value at all! It is sad to note that though girls had identified with school values in fourth grade, with the onset of adolescence they seem to adopt the traditional role for women, which does not perceive academic success or success in male roles as possible (Horner, 1968; Butler and Nisan, 1975).

Group 4: Kibbutz children and their parents (Table 17.4)

Analyses of the interviews in this group revealed a striking picture of a society in a state of transformation. Conflicts which had arisen as a result of a situation in which outside influences impinged on long-accepted and established values became evident in the ranking of the values and their contents.

It was not surprising that in a closely knit society, such as that of a kibbutz, social success received overall top place, though mothers ranked it higher than fathers and boys more than girls. The social structure of the kibbutz emphasizes peer-group cohesiveness and children spend most of their time with their peer group. However, in three out of the five kibbutzim in this sample, the children no longer slept in the children's home—originally an important ingredient of kibbutz ideology—but went to their parent's homes at night. The discrepancy found between values held by the two parents may have been due to the situation that while mothers were anxious to adopt 'home sleeping', they may also have been concerned about the possible negative effects this might have on their children's social education.

TABLE 17.4   Group 4:   Percentage of responses of kibbutz children and their parents

No.	Values	Responses (%)
1	Social success	74
2	School achievement	49
3	Individuality	46
4	Independence	34
5	Membership in the kibbutz	34
6	Loyalty	31
7	Good citizenship	26
8	Academic profession	26
9	Happiness	3

Fathers valued school achievement more than social success within this group, though only one mother mentioned it. The children, of both sexes, rated it nearly as high as social success. Perhaps they were not yet as concerned as their parents with ideological issues of society, or they had identified more with their peer and school groups than the home.

As individuality was coded at a level close to that of social success, it seemed that there was some variance between the values of the kibbutz subculture for conformity to the group, and the personal needs of its members. Possibly this awakening awareness of a need for individuality had come about in this second-generation kibbutz population, which had been reared in the traditional way, by exposure to alternative ways of living such as Army service. Similarly, the values of independence, loyalty and good citizenship failed to register a consistent pattern other than that of children's loyalty to their friends.

Membership in the kibbutz and aquisition of an academic profession were values specific to this group, though the responses were only coded by the parents, these young children being perhaps not so future orientated. Of the mothers, 90 per cent responded to the value of membership in the kibbutz in relation to boys, which may be seen as an aspect of their anxiety that their sons would leave the kibbutz on marriage. Though only one mother had responded to the value of school achievement, 30 per cent valued an academic profession for their children.

Only the mothers responded to the value of happiness and in the same way as that of the culturally disadvantaged group—with a low rating. This is at odds with the generally high emphasis on good interpersonal relationships which was expressed in the interviews.

Adolescent values for kibbutz children and their parents

When the contents of the interviews were analysed a high correlation was found between these older children and their parents in the importance they gave to the values unique to kibbutz life. However, analysis of the value systems showed that such values as work, help to others and kibbutz membership were coded by a higher proportion of parents than children.

Though the children attributed greater value to school achievement than their parents, the tendency for sex differentiation found in fourth grade was maintained. For example, school achievement coded 100 per cent responses by boys, but only 50 per cent by girls. In comparison, the value of social success was ranked in top place by 83 per cent of the teenage girls, but by just one boy. This was a value which had been placed at the top of the system for the fourth grade children. It seemed that once again, the values for this age group were more future orientated than for the younger children. The different roles that the young people would be expected to fulfill—agriculture, industrial and political management for the men, child care, education and service for the women—were now influential in their value systems.

Group 5: Arab children and their parents

This group differed from the others in two ways, (a) the number of values mentioned was much larger at 25, (b) there was hardly any within group variance. As some of the values were similar, they were grouped as shown in Table 17.5. All respondents without exception attributed the highest importance to school achievement, which was remarkable, considering that

Arab education for girls is a fairly new concept. However, the interviews did disclose some ambivalence. Several fathers, for example, mentioned that they attached great importance to the intellectual development of boys and to artistic development in girls.

TABLE 17.5   Group 5:   Percentage of responses of Arab children and their parents

No.	Values	Responses (%)
1	School achievement	100
2	Tidiness and cleanliness	97
3	Competitiveness	94
4	Material success	92
5	Freedom	92
6	Sense of humour	92
7	Discipline	89
8	Positive attitude to games	83
9	Social success	83
10	Independence	78
11	Artistic creativity	78
12	Respect for teachers	75
13	Leadership	67

Nearly all (eleven of twelve) fathers responded to the value of independence for both boys and girls; mothers coded responses for girls, but only 50 per cent of them for boys. This is possibly due to the traditional role of women in this culture, which is the running of the home, and may have been seen by the respondents as independence. The children responded in a similar pattern.

Social success was seen to be more valuable for boys than girls by the parents, and though all the boys responded to this value only about 75 per cent of the girls did. Again, this may be due to cultural norms which place social restrictions on girls, though 75 per cent of them did respond to this value, possibly anticipating some future problems.

It was only in this group that the value of respect for teachers was coded—a value rated highly in Arab culture. However, the girls were surprisingly lax at only 50 per cent response, possibly due to the high proportion of male teachers in Arab schools compared with the preponderance of female teachers in Jewish schools. Obedience would be expected towards a male and the girls may have been expressing their objections to their cultural role perceptions of women.

The value of leadership rated surprisingly low. It was considered important for boys by 75 per cent and for girls by 50 per cent of the fathers. Mothers, daughters and sons, however, accorded more importance (75 per cent) to this value for girls. As leadership among the Arab Israeli population is an important issue, it may be that these results reflect dissatisfaction with the present situation, but it is also possible that because of the cultural tradition of family privacy, the results are not truly representative.

Adolescent values for Arab children and their parents

The picture for this older group was very similar to that for the younger children with the same wide spread of values and small group variance. This group gave the greatest importance of all to identification with the school ethos. The 100 per cent responses to school achievement in fourth grade was broadened for these older children to include social success and respect for the teacher. Rutter *et al.* (1979) found this outlook to be positive in its influence on school achievement. Tidiness and cleanliness, which coded 97 per cent of the responses on fourth grade, now coded only 39 per cent of the responses. Values for this group appeared to have changed with the increased age such that socialization practices were now regarded as less important and success in school had become the more 'important business'. This can be understood in terms of the high motivation to succeed in achievement-orientated areas within a society in which this group is in a minority.

There were still sex differences in personal values such as for independence, but the parents of girls coded a smaller proportion of responses to this value than the girls themselves. Possibly the girls in this culture were becoming less accepting of their traditional role.

Across all the groups the proportion of responses coded at eighth grade was lower than for fourth grade. This may have reflected some of the uncertainty and diffusion of values in these adolescents who, in developmental terms, were seeking self-identity—a process which involves some rejection of the values and norms which the younger children had accepted.

DISCUSSION

Contrary to our expectations, the similarities in the value systems of the five research groups were greater than their differences, particularly in the area of achievement orientation. School achievement, for example, was placed at the top of the value scale by three out of the five fourth-grade groups. However, by eighth grade, the non-academic values of social and material success had gained in prominence across the groups. Social success, which is so highly regarded in Israel as to constitute an educational objective, received high ratings at both grade levels of children.

This apparent shift away from more personal values towards societal norms of success supports Getzels *et al.* (1968) proposal that role expectations must be seen both in relation to each other and to prevailing cultural values. Hence the kibbutz group, which gave the highest importance to membership in the kibbutz, was probably expressing the greater need for survival of its society, thus additionally emphasizing the effects of future orientation and image on behaviour (Torrance, 1977; Torrance and Reynolds, 1978).

The relative agreement on achievement values among these varied groups is somewhat at odds with much of the research evidence of the last two decades, which emphasizes the effects of the gap between home and school cultures (Passow, 1972, 1980)—a gap which appeared to increase in this study at the secondary-school level. However, the effects of this gap may operate in Israel at more 'pervasive than visible' levels for the following reasons.

1. Although Israeli society is generally recognized as highly achievement orientated, the middle-class groups could have been expected to predominate in their valuation of school achievement. That they did not is possibly due to the tradition of respect for religious scholarship which characterizes both Moslem and Jewish cultures—a factor which may explain the great importance attributed to this value in all the groups.
2. Interactions between the greatly varied cultures in Israel is increased by conscription at eighteen; the three years of heterogeneous experience provide a process of acculturization, which alters the effects of the socialization and values with which the young people grew up.
3. There is a high rate of mobility within the groups which threatens their traditional values and ideologies. Many Arab fathers, for example, commute from their villages to work in neighbouring towns; members of developing new towns, often of oriental origin, are employed in the kibbutzim; and members of the kibbutzim may work in town or serve in the army and only return home for weekends.

Without exception, all the groups coded achievement-orientated values much more highly for boys than for girls. The two middle-class groups had higher occupational expectations for boys than for girls, and moreover considered that the personal values of happiness and initiative were also more important for boys.

These traditional role perceptions were revealed in both the expressed and the more hidden values noted during the interviews. For example, when parents complained that the school was failing to develop the intellectual abilities of their children, greater concern was expressed for the boys. As one father said, 'I don't think that the school really stretches my daughter. If she were a boy I would have sent her to the science enrichment course at the Technion.' Such attitudes were also prevalent in the kibbutz group revealing the discrepancy between the official kibbutz ideology of equality between the sexes and actual value-related behaviour. These findings add to understanding of the ambivalence felt by women and girls towards success, even in an ostensibly egalitarian society (Horner, 1968; Butler and Nisan, 1975; Hyde, 1981).

Sex-related attitudes towards achievement are important factors in the study of giftedness. Recent research by Nevo *et al.* (1982) has indicated that they are probably more extreme in Israel than in the West, and this is a significant matter with regard to the participation of girls in education for the gifted in Israel, where they are heavily outnumbered by boys. It is evident that the search for 'untapped' talent should include not only the differently cultured, but also the female child population. But perhaps this would have to be coupled with some significant social behavioural changes towards achievement by women.

Some incongruity was found between traditional values and ideologies in the Arab and Kibbutz groups, when compared with those of the society at large. Rokeach (1973) explains them as aspects of the relationships between needs and values; values are transformations of needs, through the influence of societal demands. In the Arab groups, for example, the value of obedience to parents and adults was coded equally with those of independence and personal freedom for the child. In the kibbutz group the traditional values of contribution to the community, working in a kibbutz enterprise, and serving other members of the kibbutz were held in equal esteem with such conflicting values as individuality and the aquisition of academic professional qualifications.

There were also discrepancies between the values parents described themselves as holding and their actual behaviour with the children. In the gifted groups, for instance, individuality was ranked in third place for fourth grade, yet it was not reinforced at home. The interviews revealed that children were generally required to conform to the accepted middle-class norms of social success, tidiness, obedience, and learning useful things for school. Similarly, in the differently culturally disadvantaged groups, social success was coded highly, but the children were often prevented from following outside school activites, and were kept at home to help with domestic chores.

CONCLUSION

Although this investigation was too limited to permit wide generalizations, it does indicate that the cross-cultural approach to the study of giftedness could prove fruitful in a larger context, enhancing understanding of the effects of cultural factors on children's development. it has also high-lighted the need for further research into the incongruities which exist between described and actually practised values in different cultures. This form of incongruity seems to be more evident in multi-cultural societies which are in a state of transition, and probably constitutes a major factor in the identification and development of the child's talents there.

ACKNOWLEDGEMENT

Thanks are due to Professor Getzels for his advice on the methodology of the study, and to Ms Ruth Barzili for her great help in the collection and organization of the data.

REFERENCES

Butler, N. 1976. Israel's first experiment in special classes for gifted children within regular schools. In *Gifted Children: Looking to their Future.* (eds J. Gibson and P. Chennells). Latimer, London.

Butler, R., and Nisan, M. (1975). Who is afraid of success and why. *Journal of Youth and Adolescence,* **4**, 259–270.

Butler, N., and Butler, R. (1979). Parents and children's perception of special classes for highly gifted children. In *Gifted Children Reaching their Potential* (ed. J. J. Gallager). Kollek, Jerusalem, pp. 223–245.

Butler-Por, N., and Lancer, I. (1981). Gifted middle-class and disadvantaged children in Israel. In *Gifted Children: Challenging their Potential.* (ed A. Kramer). Trillium, New York.

Cannel, C., and Kahn, R. (1953). The collection of data by interviewing. In *Research Methods* (eds L. Festinger and D. Katz). Holt, Rinehart and Winston, New York.

Erikson, E. H. (1963). *Childhood and Society.* 2nd edn. Norton, New York.

Feather, N. T. (1975). *Values in Education and Society.* Free Press, New York.

Getzels, J. W. (1969). A social psychology of education. In *The Handbook of Social Psychology,* Vol. 5 (eds G. Lindzey and E. Aronson), Addison-Wesley.

Getzels, J. W., and Jackson, P. W. (1962). *Creativity and Intelligence.* Wiley, New York.

Horner, M. S. (1968). Sex differences in achievement motivation and performance in competitive and non-competitive situations. Unpublished doctoral dissertation, University of Michigan.

Hyde, J. S. (1981). How large are cognitive gender differences? *American Psychologist,* **36**, 892–901.

Nevo, B., Safir M., and Ramraz, R. (1982). Gender differences in cognitive functioning among university applicants in Israel. A paper delivered at the International Interdisciplinary Congress on Women, December, University of Haifa.

Passow, A. H. (1972). The gifted and the disadvantaged. *The National Elementary Principal,* **11**, 24–31.

Passow, A. H. (1980). There is gold in them thou hills. *Teachers College, Columbia University,* New York.

Reissman, F. (1962). *The Culturally Deprived Child.* Harper and Row, New York.
Rokeach, M. (1973). *The Nature of Human Values.* Free Press, New York.
Rutter, M., Maughan, N., Mortimore, P., and Ouston, J. (1979). *Fifteen Thousand Hours.* Open Books, Somerset.
Torrance, E. P. (1973). Non-test indicators of creative talent among disadvantaged children. *Gifted Child Quarterly,* **17**, 3–9.
Torrance, E. P. (1977). Today's students' images of the future. In *Creative Thinking* (eds S. L. Carmen and B. L. Grover), Western Washington University, Bellingham, Washington.
Torrance, E. P. (1980). Educating the gifted in the 1980's: removing the limits on learning. *Journal for the Education of the Gifted,* **4**, 43–48.
Torrance, E. P., and Reynolds, C.R. (1978). Images of the future of gifted adolescents:
effects of alienation and specialized cerebral functioning. *Gifted Child Quarterly,* **22**, 40–54.
Vernon, P. E. (1975). Intelligence across cultures. In *Race and Education Across Cultures* (eds G. K. Verma and C. Bagley). Heineman, London.

The Psychology of Gifted Children
Edited by Joan Freeman
©1985, John Wiley & Sons, Ltd.

CHAPTER 18

The Psychological Development of Supernormal Children

ZHA ZI-XIU (Writer)

In 1978, in accordance with the four modernization programmes of the People's Republic of China—agriculture, industry, national defence, and science and technology—research was begun on supernormal children. It had four objectives. The first was that of identity, to overcome the problem of distinguishing children of supernormal intelligence from others, providing the basis for the second, the formulation of a plan for the research procedure. Thirdly, an investigation was to be made of the ways in which such children might be given an education, both appropriate to their needs and as early as possible, in order to enhance the proper flowering of their full potential. Lastly, it was anticipated that this research might add to our present knowledge of child psychology and provide a foundation for the future collection and development of data in China.

As a result of these research findings, it has also been possible to suggest improvements in the education of ordinary children, which would enable more children and young people to develop their special talents to work towards the realization of the country's objectives.

This chapter describes the year's research and its results, focusing on the five emergent characteristics of the supernormal, and ending with suggestions for further co-operative research.

THE RESEARCH

The sample was composed of twenty-nine supernormal children—eighteen boys and eleven girls—seen by fourteen units of the Co-operative Research Team in different parts of the country. Their ages ranged from four to fifteen years-old.

Most units adopted a battery of integrated procedures which included observations, psychological tests, analysis of the children's school work, interviews with parents, etc. Some units, which were concerned with both the research and the supernormal children's education, also worked with teachers and parents in groups. Each supernormal child was investigated in respect of the following points.

General information

This included the history of the child's development, state of health, family and educational conditions etc., and was chiefly obtained from enquiries made during family visits.

Education and academic results

These were obtained both from tests of the different school subjects and from other analyses of the children's schoolwork. The supernormal children who had not yet started school were tested with questions based on the textbooks (or test questions) which were used by specific school grades, so as to assess the scholastic level of their linguistic, mathematical knowledge, etc.

Process, characteristics, and level of intellectual development

Some units used the co-operative research group's intelligence testing system to test supernormal children's perception (power of observation), memory, and way of thought. Other units selected two control groups of normal children; one was of the same age but of a lower school grade, the other was of children of the same grade but older by two or three years. To provide comparison with the level of intellectual development of supernormal children, and using the collected work of the Co-operative Research Team, other units focused on comparative levels and characteristics of memory, ways of thinking, etc., in different age-groups of normal children. Records were kept, both of the details of the experimental procedures and the results.

Personality features (e.g. curiosity, determination)

This was based on ordinary observation by the researchers in the course of their investigations, as well as that of teachers and parents.

RESULTS AND ANALYSIS

After a year's research and experimentation, it could be seen that the scholastic performances of these supernormal children were unusual, with distinct individual characteristics. Some of the children showed great mathematical ability, some read voraciously at an early age, some were accomplished at foreign languages, some were talented at drawing, some could write poems, etc. Their personalities differed also; some were lively and keen on games, some quiet and thoughtful, some enjoyed science, some liked arts subjects, etc. However, they all had certain qualities in common, which are given below in terms of the five primary characteristics to emerge from this study.

Strong, cognitive interests and intellectual curiosity

The supernormal children were intensely curious, loved to question from an early age, and were especially keen to learn. They regarded learning as a game, and were very relaxed about it. Their cognitive interests were strong and wide.

As early as the age of two or three, some children when playing 'Maths Chess', instead of playing with the chess pieces, would get the numerals together, and ask their parents to teach them the figures for calculating. At the same age, many were not satisfied with looking at picture books and listening to stories from a children's book, and asked their parents to read and show them the text word for word. In this way they read, listened and learned new words. When some children were themselves looking at 'word from picture' texts, they would not be satisfied with just looking at the pictures, but would learn words based upon them. Then when these children were able to read, their thirst for reading went so far as to make them continue while they were eating; when one four-year-old went to the zoo, instead of just seeing what the animals were like, he read all the details about each one.

A four-year-old 'scientist', having learned about seeds in his first year at primary school, spontaneously put three in a flower-pot and observed their germination. After he had learned 'What am I?', he got a cup of water and boiled it, observing the process of vaporization. When he had learned about 'care of teeth' and the effects of acid foods, he asked his parents to put eggs into vinegar, and attempted to observe and investigate the way they changed through experiments.

Concentrated attention and good memory

The supernormal children often had outstandingly high levels of concentration, especially over issues of particular interest to them. Some young children could be attentive for several hours, and were not easily distracted by other happenings—even television.

In general, both their long- and short-term memories were above average for normal children of the same age; they could grasp material quickly and retain it for a long time. By relying on his short-term memory, a five-year-old, second-grade primary school child was able to recite a twelve-digit number better than six top pupils in the same grade, who were three or four years older than him. With this five-year-old, after the teacher had finished reading aloud a chapter of *The Beautiful Cock*, he could recite more than half the chapter accurately when he was tested immediately afterwards. His parents only had to tell him once that a complex Chinese character 霸 was made of three radicals, 雨 and 革 and 月 and he still remembered it six months later. He could recite multiplication tables in normal and reverse order. Another five-year-old could recite a thirteen-digit figure (5138427960358) exactly after reading it three times, and then after one more reading, reverse the figure. He had continued to remember the figures when he was tested up to six months later.

Keen perception and power of observation

In the perception tests, these children were again found to be superior to children of the same age. Both in reaction time and method of approach, some scored more highly than children who were two or three years older. These three- and four-year-olds could not only correctly differentiate big and small, long and short, up and down, but even left and right. For example, two three- year-old twins, besides being able to answer correctly which their right hand was, could correctly point out another's right hand. When the researcher asked why his and the child's right hand were not the same, the child immediately turned around to face the researcher's direction, and raising his right hand, said: 'This makes them the same now.'

The level of development of visual and auditory ability was outstanding in these children, shown in their precise identification of the minute differences in sounds and shapes of Chinese characters. A child of one could imitate the sounds of animals. Some children were very quick to identify the syllables, four tones, and alphabet of the easily confused Chinese 'pin-yin'. A four year-old child scored 98 marks when taking the city 'pin-yin' assessment, and was also very quick in mastering the radicals and structural build-up of Chinese characters, as well as making few mistakes in dictation. Some children, besides being able to identify the side radicals of characters and their structural build-up, could discover minute mistakes of certain characters in publications. Others could distinguish characters which look very alike, involving more than twenty characters, and could identify the difference in written shape and meaning of similar sounding words, e.g. 蓝 'lan'—basket, for basket ball, 篮 'lan'—blue, for blue cloth, and 南 'nan'—south, for direction south. The children were generally very observant, being able to recognize certain herbs from the meadows on the basis of illustrations in a Chinese herbal book.

Quick thinking, good comprehension and creativity

In several tests of their thinking ability, these children showed that the development of their deductive and inductive abilities was far superior to the level of other children of the same age, and even of that of children two or three years older in the same grade. This difference was most obvious when the class was set particularly difficult problems to solve. For example, in geometrical awareness inductive tests, the correct response rates of all the four supernormal middle- and top-class pre-school children, were higher by one standard deviation than those of the middle- and top-class control children. On two especially difficult questions, the supernormal children gave absolutely correct answers. The correct response rate of the top-class supernormal children was 62.1 per cent and 51.3 per cent, and that of the middle-class supernormal children 46.6 per cent and 20 per cent, for the two mathematical inductive tests. Three of the four supernormal children exceeded the mean correct response of children two or three years older; one even exceeded the mean by more than one standard deviation. The mean rate of the youngest was close to that for the normal children who were three or four years older, minus one standard deviation.

In several groups of very difficult problems in the mathematical inductive tests, the supernormal children performed very obviously more successfully than children of the control class, being particularly quick at mental arithmetic. For example, one child, from the time he was small, followed his mother around in recording the commune's achievement points, and so learned to calculate. At the age of five, he could calculate them accurately using an abacus, and could also calculate the four operations of numbers, with two or three digits, rapidly and accurately in his head. Another child, aged five-and-a-half, could find the multiples of a six-digit number multiplied by a six-digit number in ten minutes (e.g. $365427 \times 243682 = 89047982214$); he could also answer problems involving chickens and rabbits placed in the same cage correctly in three to six minutes, e.g. calculate the respective number of chickens and rabbits in a cage, if there were altogether 100 heads and 280 legs. Yet another child, at the age of seven, could give the answers to mathematical problems such as abcd $\times$ 9 = dcba in ten minutes. At the age of nine, he had solved the following mathematical problem in less than fifteen minutes—the sum of four numbers is 100; if four is added to the first numbers, deducted from the second, multiplied by the third, and divided by the fourth, the result would still be the same; what are the numbers?

Moreover, the supernormal children had very good comprehension and creative powers, such as the two-year-old child who played with wooden blocks and produced a new pattern each time. At five-and-a-half, he took this creative ability into language when he did not merely follow the structure shown by the teacher in sentence making, but produced his own; similarly, in doing arithmetic, he was not satisfied with the way the teacher solved questions, and tried to find his own solutions. Like the five-and-a-half-year-old child who was able to do multiplications of six-digit numbers by six-digit numbers, he had a unique combination of mental and pen-and-paper calculative ability.

The thinking processes of the supernormal children also showed unusual characteristics. Some showed advanced development mainly in logical thinking (e.g. early mathematical ability), whilst others were mainly outstanding in imaginative thinking (e.g. young singers and artists).

Confidence, competitiveness and persistence

These supernormal children were generally, more confident and more highly achieving than the average. They took great pleasure in competition, not only with children of the same age, but some even wanted to compete with adults in solving problems, playing chess, etc. They had their own ideas about things, and were not easily guided. There was, for example, the child who had entered the primary-school first grade when he was not yet four years old. When his parents taught him how to construct sentences and pointed out some new words, he did not use them but made sentences with words of his own.

When they wanted to learn or do anything, these supernormal children were so enthusiastic that they would not allow any alteration of their objective. The child, mentioned previously, who would read each description of the animals at the zoo, had also been to the museum five times. On the last occasion, his parents told him they would go after his nap. But when he woke up it was late, and the museum would have been closed even if they had gone there quickly. Though his parents tried to persuade him not to go, they failed—he insisted on going. When they arrived at the closed museum, this insistence so moved the guards that they let the family in, and he returned home justifiably satisfied.

The supernormal children were noteably very persistent about doing specific things which intrigued them. For example, a three-and-a-half-year-old child started to follow the English broadcasts; and whenever he heard it start, no matter what he was playing with, he immediately sat down in front of the radio to listen to the lessons. He persisted in this for two years from the elementary to the intermediate level.

Above all, these children were able to avoid distractions and to persevere to the completion of a task. Some could stand the temptation of television programmes or films, the irritation of noise made by younger siblings in the same room, the summer heat and insect bites, to concentrate on learning and on finishing school exercises. Whilst wiping away their tears, when faced with difficult problems which they could not do, they would carry on until they finally succeeded. Some would even insist on going to school while ill with 'flu or fevers, thus showing their strong determination and purposeful nature.

Before they were four years old, some of these supernormal children knew 2000 Chinese characters, as well as the addition and subtraction of numbers between 10 and 20. Some entered primary school early, at the age of four or five, some joined second grade at the age of five or six, others entered lower-secondary school through examination at eight or nine, and at fourteen or fifteen, some became young university students.

They did have certain problems though. For example, their physical development and stamina were not always good, and after skipping a grade, they were often not as good as their classmates at writing and physical education. There were also supernormal children who, after skipping a grade, could only perform at average or below-average level for a while in some subjects. But generally speaking, the development of their mental ability was obviously superior to that of children of the same age.

SOME THOUGHTS ON FURTHER CO-OPERATIVE RESEARCH

More than a year's research on supernormal children has highlighted both the lack of developmental data on the supernormal in our country and its potential importance for future theory and practice. Individually, the children were found to be very different, which means that very large numbers would have to be studied to find reliable indicators of supernormality. Future researchers would have to be flexible in their approach too, and adopt a variety of techniques, which should include observation, experiments, and close contact with teachers and parents, etc.

As the intelligence of supernormal children is unlikely to be linear in its development, it is difficult to measure with conventional tests, even if more than one is used. Specially designed intelligence tests for them would provide a valuable differentiating tool. In this and previous investigations, supernormal children have been found to score more highly than same or older-aged children on measures involving thought, notably the most difficult problems; therefore the development of such measures should take priority in further research. In perceptual abilities too, supernormal children are often distinguished as superior to normal ones, especially in their perceptions which are allied to a particular talent.

Future researchers should be careful to avoid merely recording their observations of the children's responses, and should take note of the whole process of the response. The duration of each stage of an investigation on supernormal children should be determined by the children's ages—one to three months for the little ones and six months for older children—with participation, observation, and recording by parents and teachers. Research units should conduct follow-up studies, which would include educational experiments, both to analyse and to further the children's abilities. Investigations should be modified by repeated trials, according to each child's circumstances, and guided by a Marxist-Leninist philosophy.

Some of the experiments used in this research were found to be valuable with normal children, and would surely be improved upon with more information. It is hoped that more of this kind of research will take place during the next five years, involving large numbers of children, to enable a foundation of knowledge of the psychological development of gifted children to be built up.

POST SCRIPT 1982

This chapter presents the report of our first year's research on the development of supernormal children. Since then, the work has been continued for a further four years; about a hundred children have been surveyed, and nearly fifty of them followed-up.

Within these years, most of the supernormal children have continued to show an accelerated pattern of mental development, some having jumped a whole educational age-stage. They have all retained their mental advancement and are growing up healthily.

It seems to the researchers that there is a variety of types of supernormal children, and though there are similarities between them, no two such children are identical. We consider that inherent endowment provides only the potential for development; it is the good appropriate, educational and home environments which transform this possibility into actual supernormality. The children's personality characteristics, such as interests, initiative, and perseverance are important factors also, and it is through them that the environmental variables can play their parts.

ACKNOWLEDGEMENT

This chapter is a translation of the report of The Co-operative Research Group of SC, in *Acta Psychologica Sinica*, **13**, 35–41.

Education of the Gifted

The Psychology of Gifted Children
Edited by Joan Freeman
©1985, John Wiley & Sons, Ltd.

CHAPTER 19

The Evolution of Education for the Gifted in Differing Cultures

JAMES J. GALLAGHER

Over the past two decades, increasing interest in gifted and talented children throughout the world, has resulted in an international variety of educational provision for them. This appears to stem from the growing recognition of the formidable nature of many of the world's problems. Whether at a local, national, or international level, major issues such as the availability of sufficient food, increasing pollution, diminishing energy resources, and the continuing threat of global conflict are matters of universal concern, which call for the application of the best of mankind's abilities. Each culture has evolved its own systems of providing special education for the gifted, and this chapter will try to identify and discuss common patterns and needs, and to suggest potential strategies for meeting them. The establishment of the World Council for Gifted and Talented Children in 1975, bringing together representatives from over forty countries throughout the world, is but one indication of the mutual concern to share ideas and effective practices for the gifted across cultures (Gallagher, 1979; Kramer, 1981; Passow, 1983).

Investigation for this chapter has depended upon the analysis of available written papers (substantially helped by a computerized ERIC search), with the particular question in mind as to whether issues of gifted education, about which people feel strongly in the United States, are of similar import in other countries. Six of these issues, chosen as representative of the present major concerns in the United States, are described and discussed below in terms of the international picture.

COMMON CONCERNS

Countries which have more than one literary reference to their educational provision for the gifted are represented in Table 19.1. The number inserted in the blocks for each country for each of the six issues represents a reference, which is given in the bibliography at the end of this chapter. Japan, Israel and Taiwan, for example, do not appear to be concerned about the problems of educational acceleration, Britain is very concerned about grouping by ability, and the United States about productive thinking.

TABLE 19.1   Common concern in gifted education

Country	Grouping by instruction	Acceleration	Productive thinking	Teacher training	Minority gifted	Talent search
Australia	36	50				
Bulgaria			2,56			1,56
Canada	38	8,37	7,42	7		
France	61,62					
Great Britain	9,14,15,60,65		9,26,52	66	26	
India		54	47,53			54
Israel	5,11,34		12,46,47	12,57	39,57,58	
Japan	13		23,42,63			
Peoples Republic of China						3
Republic of China (Taiwan)	32			67		
US	49	20,21,59	6,25,30 41,42,64	21,43	20	59
USSR	4,8					28,35
Venezuela		51	42			

Grouping by ability for special instruction

One of the most frequently aired issues in the education of gifted children in the United States is the manner and type of their grouping. It is centred on two questions: Will such grouping cause unfavourable attitudinal changes or social consequences? Will it create a less valuable overall educational milieu, by removing the gifted from contact with the average pupil? The spread of pupil ability and performance in secondary schools in the United States has been increased by the government policy to keep virtually all pupils in a comprehensive or heterogeneous educational environment until the age of seventeen (Passow, 1979).

Internationally, there has probably been more written on this issue of grouping than any other. The move to separate the gifted from other children, in order to provide them with a more suitable education, runs into some form of difficulty in almost every culture because of its potential for favouritism and encouraging class distinctions.

In Great Britain, there has been a long tradition of separating talented pupils, who have shown their high capabilities in academic achievement and test performance (Bridges, 1975; Vernon, 1977; Flack and Flack, 1979). Particularly relevant is the selective sixth-form system, which gives one to three years of specialized study at school, prior to higher education. Nevertheless, concerns over egalitarian issues are identifiable there as well. The influential Plowden Report noted the existence of an egalitarian suspicion of giftedness among teachers, and decided against separate schools for the gifted, except in music and ballet. It did, however, support the development of enrichment programmes within the framework of the regular education system (DES, 1967). The implications of the spread of comprehensive secondary schools serving children of many ability levels in Great Britain, and the elimination of the eleven-plus examinations were discussed by Stevens (1980). She was concerned with the problems of maintaining high academic standards in the face of a much greater heterogeneity of pupil populations and with the possible losses suffered by the gifted as the price that Great Britain may be paying in order to improve the chances of the less talented. Other writers (Hopkinson, 1978) have made the same point.

An enthusiastic acceptance of the principle of grouping has been noted in several Israeli publications (Bitan, 1976; Butler, 1976; Landau, 1979); a variety of special classes and special schools have been designed to enhance gifted children in that society.

The ebb and flow of interest in grouping by ability at the secondary level is illustrated by a report from Australia, where the practice has been abandoned in one of their states (Lett, 1976), parallelling a similar early pattern in the United States. Whenever interest in a society becomes keen on the issue of equity there appears to be a strong trend to abandon visible educational practices (i.e. grouping), which provide separate learning opportunities for the gifted, in favour of enrichment in a heterogeneous class. A similar ambivalence is reported from France, West Germany, and Canada where education and political philosophy have become intertwined to the apparent detriment of the gifted (MacLean, 1976; Terrassier, 1981; Urban, 1982; Chapters 14 and 20). These different governments, not wishing to be charged with elitism, have shifted to heterogeneous classes. However, the separation of gifted children in the creative arts does not seem to engender quite the same degree of worry about negative effects in some educators as similar grouping in academic fields.

The Scandinavian nations have provided outstanding examples of cultures deliberately avoiding special attention to gifted and talented youngsters. Although economically and educationally advanced, they have adopted a policy which avoids giving these children special attention. One of the most influential spokesmen for that point of view has been Husén (1974), who sees a fundamental dilemma between meritocracy and democracy. He is convinced that 'redemptive equality' can only come about by playing down the rewards, status, and authority connected with superior competence. However, other nations with similar concern for equal rights and opportunities have interpreted equality to mean the provision for each child of those opportunities for which they are uniquely qualified.

Concern about elitism or about the possible perversion of special educational privileges for gifted children is not restricted to Western Europe; there has also been substantial policy fluctuation on this issue in Eastern Europe. Prior to the October Revolution, the Russian educational system provided education for the academically talented of the upper classes which gave them access to the professions, but even after the Revolution, there was a period where pedology (child study) continued to show an interest in the identification and education of the gifted. In 1936, however, pedology was denounced as anti-Marxist, and a policy of heterogeneous grouping was adopted.

Analysis of Soviet press reports and scientific journals reveals a continuing debate in which proponents of the special schools and provision point to the national interest, while those opposed point to favouritism, elitism, and the development of wrong attitudes in children. At the present time, Dunstan (1983) finds that the majority of the comments in the press and journals are favourable to special provisions, but that the opposition is strong enough to keep the development of such special schools at a modest level. Despite this dilemma, however, a variety of special schools have been set up for mathematics and science, and through the device of the Olympiad, a major talent search has been conducted in mathematics, physics, and literature, with additional contests in the fields of biology, geography, and philology (Berezina and Foteyeva 1972; Dunstan, 1978). However, as in Western countries, the Soviet Union has found it much easier to provide direct support for the artistically talented. The well-known ballet school of the Bolshoi Theatre provides a special nine-year course of study through adolescence, and other opportunities are available in music at the Moscow Conservatory or the Leningrad Orphanage for Musically Talented Children. In his review of the history of special provisions for the gifted in the USSR, Dunstan (1983) noted how the initial 1960s provision of special boarding schools for physics and mathematics later became extended to encompass language and general intellectual abilities.

In many respects, provision for the talented child in the Peoples Republic of China has paralleled that of the Soviet Union (Butler, 1983). Until 1966, there had been a two-track system of education, with the gifted being channeled to 'key-point schools', which received more resources and better staffing—essentially feeder schools for the universities—while most children went to schools which prepared them for entry into the work force (not totally unlike the old Euorpean system). After the ten years of the Cultural Revolution, the country abandoned the two-track system, closed many schools, and decided attendance at university on the basis of political acceptability rather than academic performance; however, after the death of Mao Tse Tung in 1976, the two-track system was brought back. With the new policy of the four modernizations (agriculture, industry, national defence, science and technology) came a strong need to re-establish the key-point schools, streaming of classes, and competitive enrolment examinations for higher education. Additional opportunities for gifted children to learn in special groups is now provided through the extra-curricular activity of Pioneer Houses and Camps. Through these devices, the regular school curriculum can be enriched by special instruction in fields such as technology, astronomy, and history (Brickman, 1979) (see Chapter 21).

Extra-curricular activities are presented in a unique project in France, which was begun by parents (Rossillon and Castillion du Perron, 1983). Operating outside regular school hours, two days a week, the Jeunes Vocations Artistiques, Litteraires et Scientifiques in Paris provides a wide range of experiences for eligible children, selected by IQ tests. Defining their provision as Twentieth Century Humanism, the volunteer teachers provide experiences for children aged five to fifteen, in topics as diverse as computers, astronomy, drawing, writing, mime, and physical chemistry.

There have been specific attempts to group gifted children in the Far East. The Republic of China (Taiwan) has established an extensive number of special classes and resources for the education of gifted children, placing them in the category of exceptional, as in many States of the United States. It also offers both initial and in-service training to teachers, as well as summer training programmes for work with gifted children. Kuo (1981) concluded that investigations to test the consequences of placing gifted children in special class settings do not demonstrate any negative effects. Pupils did not show elevated levels of anxiety, nor were there negative effects on their self-concepts, so that the results were presented to support the continuation of special class programmes.

Chiba (1981) reported an early grouping-by-ability programme in Japan, which began at the age of two and focused on teaching materials designed around the Guilford Structure of Intellect model. Major gains in measured intellectual ability were reported in an investigation with 102 children, between the ages of two and nine, showing an average IQ gain of 15.9 points over a year. Most of the gains were in the semantic and symbolic dimensions stressed in the tuition.

ACCELERATION

The increasing availability of rapidly expanding bodies of knowledge has resulted in a longer and longer educational experience, until it is easily possible that some gifted children will spend a quarter of a century or more of their lives in an educational setting, prior to beginning an artistic, professional, business, or scientific career. In the United States, one strategy for coping with these extended academic demands has been to move the youngster through the educational programme at a more rapid rate, if this can be done without causing other adjustment problems. A moderate form of acceleration, reducing the total time in education by one or two years, is usually well accepted (Gallagher, 1975), though recently a more radical form of acceleration, placing highly selected pre-adolescents in universities to study specific subjects (particularly mathematics), has been proposed by Stanley (1979).

The movement of children through the educational sequence at a faster than average pace undoubtedly occurs in individual instances in every society. However, the institutionalization of such a policy, such as in the United States, where the Advanced Placement Program yields college credit for pupils who take advanced courses while still at high school, is relatively rare (Gallagher *et al.*, 1983).

MacKinnon (1973) has reported an early admission provision in Saskatchewan, Canada as one means of providing the child with a speedier exit from school, but many educationalists agree with Marjoram (1979) in Britain, who felt that moving the intellectually superior child ahead, without regard to his physical and social development, could lead to unhappiness and a failure to adjust in a class of older children. This conclusion was also reached in Venezuela (Plaza, 1979), where the disadvantages of placing a child in classes with much older children were considered too great. As in Britain, Plaza preferred the alternative path of enrichment, which seemed to suit Venezuela's situation best.

The pros and cons of acceleration have been weighed in Australia (Pirozzo, 1981) and in India (Saxena, 1976), for instance. Trying to provide a balanced education for individual children, who are different in intellectual and social development, appears to be difficult for educators in educational systems which were not designed to cope with such disparities. If gifted children are placed with their intellectual peers, then they may be out of step socially; placed socially, they are far out of line intellectually. Most educators faced with this decision have either rejected it entirely, or tried to split the difference by moving the children ahead one or two years in the direction of their intellectual peers, without placing them under damaging social pressure.

Productive thinking

For the past twenty years, growing attention has been paid in the United States to children who have enhanced skills in productive thinking, due to the increased premium being placed on their potential ability to generate new ideas to meet changing circumstances. The educational goal for them is to find better ways in which they could think more fluently, originally, and creatively, and use their outstanding talents more efficiently. Progress in that direction has been helped by the emergence of two complex models of intellectual performance—one by Guilford (1972) and the other by Bloom (1956). Using these models as a base, a variety of new measuring instruments, and even larger numbers of suggestions for teachers, have been developed so that it has become the single most important recent educational innovation in the US (Meeker, 1969; Torrance, 1979; and others). The implications of such additional developments are that, unlike acceleration (which merely moves the child from one place to another), the area of productive thinking requires changes in the teacher training and styles, and demands substantial modifications of existing educational procedures. However, it is a complex area, and the fact that it is less actively pursued than the much easier route of initiating talent searches is not surprising.

Few nations active in gifted education have been unaffected by similar efforts to measure and enhance creativity (Khatena, 1977). Comprehensive descriptions of activities in Great Britain (Bridges, 1975; Povey, 1980), Canada (Borthwick et al., 1980), and India (Mitra et al., 1968; Raina, 1979) all include an interest in creative and productive thinking. Meeker (1983) reported interest in the teaching of creative intelligence in Japan, the United States, Canada, and Venezuela. The concepts from the Guilford and Bloom models have also been utilized in extensive work in Israel by Butler (1976) and by Milgram and Milgram (1976a). The latter compared the intellectual and creative performances of members of a high-school senior class in Israel, and found that creativity was highly related to test dimensions of ideational fluency and originality, as had been noted in the United States. They concluded that a distinction should be made between intelligence and creativity, and that sufficient quantity of ideas is a necessary condition for the emergence of unusual responses. A similar distinction between creativity and intelligence was noted in a longitudinal study in Great Britain, conducted as part of the survey of all babies born in England, Scotland, and Wales during a one-week period in 1958 (Hitchfield, 1978). In a similar study, Milgram and Milgram

(1976b), working with groups of Israeli children of superior intelligence in the fourth to eighth grades, found that differences in creativity seem to be linked more closely to personal and social adjustment than are differences in intelligence. In this fashion, they have confirmed that creative performance has a sizable personality component, as well as a cognitive dimension—a fact noted in studies in a variety of cultures. Similarly, a review of Indian research by Raina (1979) described a link between a lack of conformity and high creativity which has also been noted in other societies.

A number of observers have commented upon the outstanding productive thinking performances of many pupils in Japan called by one observer (Torrance, 1980) 'a nation of 115 million over-achievers'. The cultural characteristics identified as being linked with that over-achievement are substantial rewards for creative achievement, the importance placed on intuitive ways of knowing, training in persistence and hard work, an ideal of self-directed learning, and emphasis on group learning and problem-solving. The important element in the circumstances in which the gifted child can be encouraged to reach optimum development of her talents is the recognition of the role of societal climate and rewards, as well as of family factors (Gensley, 1975).

One special area of productive thinking emphasized in Bulgaria, is the Suggestopaedic Study System (Balevski, 1979), which tries to help the pupil attain a unity between conscious and unconscious states. The teacher creates an environment which liberates the mind through the use of art and aesthetics. Sisk and Zdravchev (1978) have reported on the efforts in Bulgaria to link aesthetics and the sciences through this somewhat philosophical process.

Teacher training

With the advent of specific differential education for the gifted, such as in mathematics and the sciences, and more recent stress on the development of complex thinking skills, the question has arisen how to prepare teachers more effectively for appropriate modifications in their educational practice. During the time in which the problem of what to do with gifted children in the United States was met only with the giving of scholarships for higher education or with extra-school activities, there was little need for a more extensive preparation of teachers. But there is now an increasing call for a clear model, which will prepare teachers to carry out these novel educational procedures (Gold, 1979).

The available world literature is limited in descriptions of special teacher training efforts which would help professionals in their work with gifted children. To some extent, this is due to the fact that many nations are not substantially modifying the system itself, and thus do not feel the need for major shifts in teacher training. The logic of this is—if we continue to move gifted children around in the existing system, for instance by sending them to a special school, then there is no need to change current teacher training. It follows that the countries which are involved in major shifts of outlook for the gifted are also concerned with modifications in training their teachers. Wu-Wu and Schaffer (1981) have reported interest in teacher education in Taiwan which accompanies their special classes. Similarly, Israeli literature has described a need for additional training, particularly in connection with their programmes for the disadvantaged gifted (Butler, 1978; Smilansky, 1978).

A major survey report from Canada (Borthwick *et al.*, 1980) found that there were few educational facilities concerned with the gifted in the initial training of teachers, graduate programmes, or other professional development activities. A national survey in the US (Gallagher *et al.*, 1983) reports similar concerns for shortcomings in teacher preparations as well as a lack of initiative in government agencies and universities in taking charge of that problem. It seems that there is still much to be done in rethinking teacher education to help the gifted (but see Chapter 22).

Minority gifted

Though there is always some diversity of backgrounds within cultures, one group, usually the majority, is often dominant and in control of governmental policies and educational activities. This leaves the other groups, which differ in varying degrees from that majority culture, in a less advantageous or authoritative position. As the need to make maximum use of every child's gifts and talents becomes accepted, more and more attention is being paid to the special abilities of these minority groups, it being generally assumed that the gifted children from the majority culture can more easily be found.

The United States probably has more written material on this topic (see, for example, Gallagher, 1975) than other nations, reflecting the large number of minority groups within its borders and the difficult time that schools have in finding and nurturing outstanding talents in those groups. But there have been many concerted attempts to find these minority youngsters, and many specially designed educational adaptations have been put into practice to allow their talents to emerge and develop most effectively (see Mercer and Lewis, 1981; Chapter 6).

Israel, a nation of many and diverse cultures, has for a long time focused upon attempts to identify and nurture the intellectual talents of minority groups within its borders. Smilansky and Nevo (1975) have described the evaluation of these efforts over a thirty-year period. They identified the pioneer-voluntary stage (pre-1948), the formal equality stage (1948–57), the compensatory education stage (1958–67), the school reform stage (1968–73), and the experimental school stage (1973–75). A follow-up study of disadvantaged gifted children in boarding schools found that they were offered better educational opportunity there than they would have been in the conventional educational system.

Butler-Por (1983; updated in Chapter 17) added some additional data obtained from five different sub-cultural groups within Israel. Despite wide differences in background, the educational goals of the groups appeared to be quite similar. School achievement ranked high with all groups, as did social success. These common aspirations provide the basis for an educational programme whose content can remain similar, but whose manner of delivery may be modified to fit each cultural sub-group. Mari (1981) has described provision to enhance highly creative and talented Arab students in Israel. He found, as did Butler-Por, that cross-cultural experience with Israelis accelerated the process of modernization of Arab children through exposure and first-hand experience, but that it also caused conflict between competing cultures. Arab girls in particular, in interaction with the Israeli culture, tended to move away from their traditionally passive status.

The special need for provision for underprivileged gifted children was outlined by Hitchfield (1973), on the basis of a longitudinal study in Great Britain. Larsson (1981) found that same ambivalence about special help for gifted children to be present in Australia, with its special concerns for the identification and support of Aboriginal children, and others whose talent might be muted or disguised. Larsson believes that the current Australian mood leans towards a rejection of special help for the gifted, based on an: 'egalitarianism which expressed itself in the feelings that children should not be segregated into elites because of gifts they had inherited'. However, there still is a broad range of special options available in Australia, which are being implemented from one state to another.

Talent search

Although it has been taken for granted for many years that individual teachers and local education authorities would search for outstanding mathematicians, musicians, athletes, etc., one of the most popular recent drives in the United States has been to find outstanding talent in a variety of specific fields via organized talent searches (Stanley, 1979). It is also one of the most popular strategies for nations which are concerned to provide the gifted with better educational opportunities, but which have limited resources, as for example in India. It enables children to be identified and subsequently placed in a more advantageous educational environment, whether accelerated into a higher level in the educational sequence, or in a special school or class. The strategy does not involve major changes or modifications in the educational system itself.

The Olympiads held in Eastern European Countries are an example of an attempt to give recognition to fine performers in mathematics and sciences (Lavtentiev, 1975). These Olympiads are mirrored in other Eastern European Countries including Bulgaria (Sisk and Zdravchev, 1978; Angelov, 1979), though they have also become popular in Western Europe. The People's Republic of China has engaged in a mathematics Olympiad, which was used to identify children's strengths and weaknesses (Becker, 1982). Saxena (1976) reported on national and state talent searches in India in the sciences, as well as in athletics. Practically all nations with any substantial economic resources have special programmes and schools for those who display major talents in art and music. Hurwitz (1976) contrasted the differing educational approaches towards art in the United States and Russia, describing how Soviet educators tend to view the arts as an area of pre-professional specialization, while United States educators see it as part of general learning for all.

CONCLUSIONS

On the basis of the articles reviewed here, it seems that despite many cultural differences, educational decision-makers the world over have similar problems and issues to face regarding the education of the gifted. Two major problems have been noted again and again. First, there is the tug-of-war between providing excellent education for a few, as opposed to a comprehensive education for many, and few cultures appear to have solved that problem to their own satisfaction. The result is a continual vacillation in emphasis from one side of the issue to the other, as political fortunes ebb and flow in these nations.

The second issue is the continual struggle between the allocation of resources for long-term educational gains, as opposed to short-range problem-solving. Few would argue that research and development are not extraordinarily valuable tools for improving education, as they have been in agriculture or industry, but investing in such long-range goals means taking limited resources away from immediate service needs. Many nations, faced with an unfavourable balance between available resources and educational needs, find it difficult to withhold resources which could be spent on present needs in favour of an investment in long-term growth and improvement. As social and educational systems become more complex, the need has come about for support systems or mechanisms to undergird the services provided by the educational system. In the end, it is this failure to provide an infrastructure to create the basic conditions for systematic improvement and growth, which is one of the most powerful inhibiting factors to continued improvement in this and other educational fields. The necessary elements of such an infrastructure are fairly well understood, even now, and are outlined below.

Research

We need a continuous flow of research knowledge to provide us with detailed information about gifted learners, in order to help us design more effective education to meet their needs.

Development

We need to develop a systematic organization of knowledge in such a way as to allow new knowledge to be continually incorporated into it. This great resource would then be available to special school curricula, so that gifted learners would have access to the latest in available scientific and cultural information.

Leadership training

Special attention should be paid to those professionals who, through effective performance, have established themselves as the leaders of the next generation in the field of gifted education. These leaders should be provided with special learning opportunities in universities and other training centres, so that they will be able to use and pass on to others the latest in current educational knowledge.

Demonstration

There is a need for emphasis on demonstration—the display of exemplary educational provision and practices—to assist the transfer of the best of current practices from a school system in one community to that in another. This change process, by which schools modify current practice, is one of the more complex tasks to be achieved. It is certain that major local adaptations must be expected in moving even the best of practices from one place to another, since the local educational provision is often shaped by the needs and concerns of the local citizenry, regardless of the particular structure of education systems in that culture.

Dissemination

There is a need for a central agency or agencies at the national, state, or provincial level which has as its prime purpose the movement of materials and ideas from one place to another. The rapidly expanding sets of instructional materials and knowledge need to be moved to the teacher or other professionals in the fastest way possible. This can only be done in a clearing house process, whereby means for storage and dissemination are available to serve a large region.

Advocacy

Finally, there probably needs to be some mechanism for advocacy at the professional and citizen level to encourage educational decision-makers to offer workable educational provision for the gifted.

While each of these infrastructure components may be shaped in different ways by the differing levels of technological sophistication, availability of financial resources, and the values and preferences of cultures, they have already shown their usefulness in maximizing the chances of quality education for the gifted. Future advancement may well depend upon how thoroughly they are put into practice everywhere.

REFERENCES

Angelov, T. (1979). The socially organised system for identification of talents. In *Gifted Children: Reaching their Potential* (ed. J. J. Gallagher). Kollek, Jerusalem, Israel, pp. 105–109.

Balevski, P. (1979). The suggestopaedic study system. In *Gifted Children: Reaching their Potential* (ed. J. J. Gallagher). Kollek, Jerusalem, Israel, pp. 110–118.

Becker, J. (1982). 1979 National middle-school mathematics Olympiads in the People's Republic of China. *Mathematics Teacher*, 75, pp. 161–169.

Berezina, G., and Foteyeva, A. (1972). Educational work and extracurricular educational establishments. In *Education in the USSR* (ed. N. Kugin), Moscow Progress Publishers, Moscow.

Bitan, D. (1976). In *Gifted Children: Looking to their Future* (eds. J. Gibson and P. Chenells). Anchor Press, Tiptree, Essex, pp. 322–327.

Bloom, B. S. (1956). *Taxonomy of Educational Objectives: The Classification of Educational Goals*. McKay, New York.

Borthwick, B., Dow, I., Levesque, D., and Banks, R. (1980). *The Gifted and Talented Students in Canada*. The Canadian Education Associates, Toronto, Ontario.

Brickman, W. (1979). Educational provisions for the gifted and talented in other countries. In *The Gifted and the Talented* (ed. A. Passow). University of Chicago Press, 78th Yearbook, NSSE, Chicago, pp. 308–330.

Bridges, S. (1975). *Gifted Children and the Millfield Experiment*. Pitman Publishing Company, London.

Brooks, R. (1972). *Bright Delinquents: The Story of a Unique School*. Fernhill House, New York.

Butler, N. (1976). Israel's first experiment in special classes for gifted children within regular schools. In *Gifted Children: Looking to their Future* (eds. J. Gibson and P. Chenells). The Anchor Press, Tiptree, Essex, pp. 169–181.

Butler, N. (1978). Training teachers toward responsibility in future education. *EDRS*, EC 111787.

Butler, S. (1981). The talented child in the People's Republic of China. In *Face to Face with Giftedness*. (eds B. Shore, F. Gagné, S. Larivée, R. Tali, and R. Tremblay). First Yearbook, The World Council for Gifted and Talented Children, Trillium Press, New York, pp. 271–289.

Butler-Por, N. (1983). Giftedness across cultures. In *Face to Face with Giftedness*. (eds B. Shore, F. Gagné, S. Larivée, R. Tali, and R. Tremblay). First Yearbook,

The World Council for Gifted and Talented Children, Trillium Press, New York, pp. 250–270.

Chiba, A. (1981). Japan's programmes for gifted and talented children. In *Gifted Children: Challenging their Potential* (ed. A. Kramer), Trillium Press, New York, pp. 112–116.

DES (Department of Education and Science) (1967). *Children and Their Primary Schools: A Report of the Central Advisory Council For Education.* HMSO, London.

Dunstan, J. (1978). *Paths to Excellence and the Soviet School.* NFER, Windsor.

Dunstan, J. (1983). Attitudes to provision for gifted children: The case of the U.S.S.R. In *Face to Face with Giftedness.* (eds B. Shore, F. Gagné, S. Larivée, R. Tali, and R. Tremblay), First Yearbook, The World Council for Gifted and Talented Children. Trillium Press, New York, pp. 290–327.

Flack, C., and Flack, D. (1979). England's clever children. *G/C/T*, **6**, 44-48, 63-64.

Freeman, J. (1976). Developmental influences on children's perception. *Educational Research*, **19**, 69–75.

Gallagher, J. J. (1975). *Teaching the Gifted Child.* Allyn and Bacon, Boston.

Gallagher, J. J. (1979). Issues in education for the gifted. In *The Gifted and the Talented: Their Education and Development*, 1979 (ed. A. H. Passow). The University of Chicago Press (Seventy-eighth Yearbook of the National Society for the Study of Education, Part I), Chicago.

Gallagher, J. J. (1982). A plan for catalytic support for gifted education in the 1980's. *Elementary School Journal*, **82**, 180–184.

Gallagher, J. J., Weiss, P., Oglesby, K., and Thomas, T. (1983). *The Status of Education for Gifted Students in the United States: An examination of needs, practices and policies.* N/S Leadership Training Institute, Los Angeles.

Gardner, D. (Chairman) (1983). *A Nation at Risk.* The National Commission on Excellence in Education, Washington, DC.

Gensley, J. (1975). The most academically talented students in the World. *Gifted Child Quarterly*, **19**, 185–188.

Gold, M. (1979). Teachers and mentors. In *The Gifted and Talented: Their Education and Development* (ed. A. Passow). University of Chicago Press, Chicago, Illinois, pp. 272–288.

Guilford, J. (1972). *The Nature of Human Intelligence.* McGraw Hill, New York.

Hitchfield, E. (1973). *In Search of Promise: A Long Term Natural Study of Able Children and their Families.* Humanities Press, Atlantic Highlands, New Jersey.

Hopkinson, D. (1978). *The Education of Gifted Children.* Woburn Press, Totowa, New Jersey.

Hurwitz, A. (1976). The US and USSR: Two attitudes towards the gifted in art. *Gifted Child Quarterly*, **20**, 458–465.

Husén, T. (1974). *Talent, Equality and Meritocracy: Availability and Utilization of Talent.* Nyhoff, The Hague.

Khatena, J. (1977). The gifted child in the US and abroad. *Gifted Child Quarterly*, **20**, 372–386.

Kramer, A. (Ed.) (1981). *Gifted Children: Challenging their Potential.* Trillium Press, New York.

Kuo, W. (1981). Special classes for the gifted and talented: A review of research in the republic of China. *EDRS*, EC 141536.

Landau, E. (1976). Children ask questions about the future of mankind. In *Gifted Children: Looking to their Future* (eds J. Gibson and P. Chenells). Latimer, London.

Landau, E. (1979). The young persons institute for the promotion of science. In *Gifted Children: Reaching their Potential* (ed. J. J. Gallagher). Kollek, Jerusalem, Israel, pp. 105–109.

Larsson, Y. (1981). *Provision for the Education of Gifted and Talented Children in Australia*. Occasional Paper 13, Department of Education, University of Sydney, Sydney.

Lavtentiev, M. (1975). A school for young mathematicians in Siberia. *Prospects: Quarterly Review of Education*, **5**, 153–158.

Lett, W. (1976). Australia. In *Gifted Children: Looking to their Future* (eds J. Gibson and P. Chenells). Anchor Press, Tiptree, Essex. pp. 285–288.

MacKinnon, F. (1973). Saskatchewan notes about the gifted. *Kootenay Center for the Gifted Journal*, **1**, 11–13.

MacLean, J. (1976). Canada. In *Gifted Children: Looking to their Future* (eds J. Gibson and P. Chenells). Anchor Press, Tiptree, Essex, pp. 292–294.

Mari, S. (1981). The highly creative and talented among Arabs in Israel. In *Gifted Children: Challenging their Potential* (ed. A. Kramer). Trillium Press, New York, pp. 289–295.

Marjoram, D. (1979). The gifted child in the comprehensive school. In *Gifted Children: Reaching their Potential* (ed. J. J. Gallagher). Kollek, Jerusalem, Israel, pp. 85–104.

Meeker, M. (1969). *The Structure of Intellect: Its Interpretation and Uses*. Charles Merrill, Columbus, Ohio.

Meeker, M. (1983). The teaching of intelligence in Japan, America, Canada, and Venezuela. *Gifted International*, **1**, 67–78.

Mercer, J., and Lewis, J. (1981). Using the system of multicultural pluralistic assessment to identify the gifted minority child. In *Balancing the Scale for the Disadvantaged Gifted* (ed. I. Sato). National/State Leadership Training Institute on the Gifted and Talented, Los Angeles, California, pp. 59–66.

Milgram, R. (1979). Gifted children in Israel: theory, practice and research. *EDRS*, EC 122053.

Milgram, R., and Milgram, N. (1976a). Creative thinking and creative performance in Israeli students. *Journal of Educational Psychology*, **68**, pp. 255–259.

Milgram, R., and Milgram, N. (1976b). Selfconcept as a function of intelligence and creativity in gifted Israeli children. *Psychology in the Schools*, **13**, 91–96.

Mitra, S. *et al.* (1968). *Identification of Talent in Elementary and Secondary Schools*. US Office of Education, Washington, DC.

Morton, M. (1972). *The Arts and the Soviet Child: The Esthetic Education of Children in the USSR*. Free Press, New York.

Passow, A. (1979). A look around and a look ahead. In *The Gifted and the Talented* (ed. A. Passow). National Society for the Study of Education, Chicago, pp. 439–456.

Passow, A. (1983). A universal view of gifted and talented programmes. Paper presented at the Fifth World Conference on Gifted and Talented Children, Manila, Philippines.

Pirozzo, R. (1981). Programmes for gifted and talented children. *Australian Journal of Remedial Education*, **13**, 22–26.

Plaza, E. (1979). Programme for gifted and talented children in Venezuela. In *Gifted Children: Reaching their Potential* (ed. J. J. Gallagher). Kollek, Jerusalem, Israel, pp. 162–169.

Povey, R. (1980). *Educating the Gifted Child*. Harper and Row, London.

Raina, M. (1979). Research developments in giftedness and creativity in India. In

Gifted Children: Reaching their Potential (ed. J. J. Gallagher), Kollek, Jerusalem, Israel, pp. 307–332.

Rossillon, V., and Castillon du Perron, M. (1983). A French approach to education for gifted children. In *Face to Face with Giftedness.* (eds B. Shore, F. Gagné, S. Larivée, R. Tali, and R. Tremblay), First Yearbook, The World Council for Gifted and Talented Children, Trillium Press, New York, pp. 460-481.

Saxena, K. (1976). India. In *Gifted Children: Looking to their Future* (eds J. Gibson and P. Chenells). Anchor Press, Tiptree, Essex, pp. 311–314.

Schultze, W., and Fuhr, C. (1973). *Dos Schulwesen in der Bundesrepublik Deutschland* (3rd edn). Beltz, Weinheim.

Sisk, D., and Zdravchev, L. (1978). Conversations about G/C/T youth. *G/C/T,* **1**, 3, 12–16.

Smilansky, M. (1978). The culturally disadvantaged gifted youth. *G/C/T,* **1**, 3–5, 44–46.

Smilansky, M., and Nevo, D. (1975). A longitudinal study of the gifted disadvantaged. *Educational Forum,* **39**, 273–294.

Stanley, J. (1979). The study and facilitation of talent for mathematics. In *The Gifted and Talented: Their Education and Development* (ed. A. Passow). University of Chicago Press, Chicago, Illinois, pp. 169–185.

Stevens, A. (1980). *Clever Children in Comprehensive Schools.* Harper and Row, New York.

Terrassier, J. (1976). France. In *Gifted Children: Looking to their Future* (eds J. Gibson and P. Chenells). Anchor Press, Tiptree, Essex, pp. 303–307.

Terrassier, J. (1981). The negative Pygmalion effect. In *Gifted Children: Challenging Their Potential* (ed. A. Kramer). Trillium Press, New York, pp. 82–84.

Torrance, E. (1979). Unique needs of the creative child and adult. In *The Gifted and Talented: Their Education and Development* (ed. A. Passow). University of Chicago Press, NSSE 78th Yearbook, Chicago, Illinois, pp. 352–371.

Torrance, E. (1980). Lessons about giftedness and creativity from a nation of 115 million overachievers. *Gifted Child Quarterly,* **24**, 10–14.

Urban, K. (1982). *Hochbegabte Kinder.* Schindele Verlag, Heidelberg.

Vernon, P. (1977). *Psychology and Education of Gifted Children.* Westview Press, Boulder, Colorado.

Wu-Wu, T., and Schaffer, E. (1981). Gifted and talented education in the Republic of China. *EDRS,* EC 141530.

Zhivkova, L. (1979). Harmony and beauty in the infinite spiral circle of development. *Gifted and Talented Education,* **1**, 9–26.

The Psychology of Gifted Children
Edited by Joan Freeman
©1985, John Wiley & Sons, Ltd.

CHAPTER 20

Attitudes Towards the Education of the Gifted

KLAUS K. URBAN

A slowly rising crescendo of voices has become audible amongst West German politicians, psychologists, and educationalists in recent years, calling for consideration of the needs, problems, and interests of the gifted, and an appropriate education for them (Glotz, 1980; Granzow, 1980; Urban 1980a,b, 1982; Wagner, 1981; Weinschenk, 1979a,c; Wissenschaftsrat, 1981). Although it is still sadly neglected in both theory and practice, provision for the gifted has become a matter of great controversy; often engendering heated discussion of positive or negative attitudes.

This is especially true for the emotive concept of 'elitism', which is so tied up with the philosophy of our relatively young democracy and the terrible memories of the thirties and forties (Dichgans, 1979; Elite, 1982; Ermert, 1982; Glotz, 1979; Kreklau, 1979; Roth, 1981; Weinschenk, 1979b; Wellmann, 1981; Woelke, 1978, 1979). The anti-elitist arguments often refer to 'equality of opportunities'—a term which has been one of the key words during the reform of the educational system in the sixties and seventies—which implied that, regardless of their cultural and socio-economic background or individual abilities, it would promote better and higher standards, so that all children could become 'gifted'. This hopeful environmentalist stance in the nature-nurture controversy, can, however, be practically misplaced in the form of a move towards equalization at a lower common level, which neglects the uniqueness of each child.

The opinions of the people who participate in an educational system are vitally important, since parents', teachers', and children's attitudes towards

351

it have been found to be directly related to the way it is put into practice (Taylor and Holley, 1975; Bennett, 1976). This is especially true today with regard to the gifted, as earlier ideas about their education are becoming more publicly visible, not only in terms of its practicability, but also in comparison with provision for other exceptional children. Monitored attitudes, both of those who are directly involved with the education of the gifted and the public, are influential factors in the construction of acceptable long- and short-term strategies, which will in turn influence the opinions of others, including politicians. It is hoped that the study presented here may be a first step towards forming a broad and well-founded evaluation of the way it is perceived.

ATTITUDE STUDIES

Descriptions of studies which have evaluated attitudes or opinions in this field are rare in the international literature, though there have been two in England. Freeman (1979) devised and gave the head-teachers of sixty-three primary and secondary schools a questionnaire on their attitudes to gifted education. She found that they were not generally in favour of special material provision for the gifted, and mostly felt they could accommodate the children's needs within the context of a child-centred education in their non-specialist schools.

Tilsley (1981) investigated the attitudes to special provision, especially for the gifted, of 182 secondary teachers, who were reasonably representative of the British teaching population, though not directly involved in gifted education. He identified the following attitude factors, i.e. their beliefs and feelings about, (a) the adequacy of the existing system for gifted children, (b) the consequences for the country of neglecting the gifted, (c) the justice of allocating material resources for the benefit of a privileged potential elite, (d) the justice of giving time and attention to the gifted, (e) the importance of the environment in determining achievement of the gifted child's potential.

The sample teachers were generally found to be in favour of giving extra tuition to gifted children, but only if it were to be offered in terms of enrichment within the regular school. The more positive their general educational attitudes, the more positive their approval of specific provision, and the greater the number of specific forms of provision they considered to be warranted for the gifted. They only seemed to associate the notion of elitism with the allocation of material resources, and even on this matter, on average their attitudes were significantly positive.

Other studies have dealt with parents' and children's ($N = 105$) perceptions, and the impacts of special provision for the gifted (Mira, 1979); classes for highly gifted children (Butler and Butler, 1979); and the attitudes of gifted pupils ($N = 593$), their parents ($N = 331$) and teachers ($N = 58$)

towards programmes which were being provided by the Ministry of Education and Culture in Israel (Burg, 1981). Unfortunately, as there is no special provision for the gifted in West Germany, none of the results of these studies could be used directly for comparison with this present investigation. There is, however, a broad range of specialized school services for children with various types of handicaps, e.g. speech disabled, the hearing disabled, those with specific learning difficulties, the emotionally disturbed, the mentally retarded, the blind, the physically handicapped, etc., which permits the consideration of the education of the gifted within the whole educational context. This is important if it is to be integrated with similar concerns for the education of all children.

THE INVESTIGATION

The West German ministries of education have designated a selective, 'tripartite' system of education from the fifth or seventh grade onwards, as suitable for the needs of most children (Urban, 1983). To tap attitudes towards this system, and potential provision for gifted children, a questionnaire was developed. It was piloted on the basis of an initial hypothetical classification of partially overlapping educational concerns (Urban, 1981) as follows, (a) handicaps and special education, (b) individualization in education, (c) integration vs segregation, (d) gifted children and education, (e) identification, (f) speech disablement.

The complete questionnaire was made up of two different parts, as described below. Both parts were given to a sample of 260 people including teachers—T ($N = 124$) and students at a teachers' college ($N = 136$). A short form of the first part, with eight items (2, 3, 4, 6, 9, 12, 14, 15) and the whole of the second part were given to 118 parents of children aged eleven to thirteen attending a normal public school (fifth and sixth grades—P1, and to thirty-eight parents whose fourteen and fifteen year-old children attended a selective Gymnasium (seventh and eighth grades)—P2. An additional set of ratings was provided by eighteen gifted pupils of seventeen and eighteen years old (eleventh and twelfth grades), who attended the first (and only) two gifted classes at a private Gymnasium in the Federal Republic.

The first part

The resulting sixteen statements were rated by each respondent on a five-point scale as to agreement: '1' meant fully correct or total agreement, '5' meant false or total rejection. They were as follows:

1. Working with handicapped children, it is important to identify and to further their capabilities.

2. Children are so individually different that they should not be taught together in classes organized by age.
3. Unlike less-intelligent children, gifted children do not need special attention in education and learning.
4. Segregation in special schools does not help handicapped children in any way.
5. The earlier you identify children's disorders and handicaps, the better you may be able to help them.
6. An integrated school education of all children, with both handicapped and non-handicapped together, best fits the needs and aims of a democratic system of education.
7. Both theoretical and practical endeavours towards the special education of the gifted improve education and teaching in general.
8. Children with impaired speech need more help than children with normal speech.
9. Every child needs an education in school which is formulated to his individual needs, abilities, and interests.
10. Too early identification of gifted children can be detrimental for them.
11. The normal school handicaps children.
12. Like the special schools for less-intelligent children, there should be schools for highly intelligent ones also.
13. If 'special education' means an education which is orientated towards comparable aims for all children, yet works in a highly individualized way, then 'normal' teaching should mean 'special education' also.
14. An integrated education of all children together—handicapped or not—would fit the needs of children best.
15. Gifted children should be encouraged in a special way within regular schools.
16. Children who cannot be taught adequately in regular schools—assuming that good conditions are provided—can be labelled as handicapped.

The second part

This consisted of the fifteen educational aims (EAs), shown below. The terms used were relatively abstract, with a high level of generalization; referring to attitudes and personality traits, as well as to abilities in cognition and thinking. They were to be rated as to their relevance to three groups of pupils: normal, handicapped, and gifted—the problems of dealing with stereotypes were appreciated. It was assumed that they were all more or less acceptable and relevant, but that they received different weights and rank positions for the different groups of pupils: '1' meant 'of high relevance', '5' 'of none or minimal relevance'. The educational aims were as follows:

1. Independence (INDEP).
2. Creativity (CREAT).
3. Social adjustment (SOCAD).
4. Cognitive flexibility (COGFL).
5. Sense of responsibility (SRESP).
6. Tolerance (TOLER).
7. Autonomy of thinking (AUTTH).
8. Diligence (DILIG).
9. Ability for decision making (ABIDM).
10. Trustworthiness (TRUST).
11. Political consciousness (POLCO).
12. Orderliness (ORDER).
13. Ability for peace making or settling disputes (ABIPM).
14. Contentment (CONTE).
15. Ambition (AMBIT).

RESULTS AND EVALUATION

It is not possible here to describe and discuss the results as a whole, but attention will be focused on the relationship of gifted education with 'general education'.

The factorial structure of the statements

The factors resulting from analysis of the statement ratings by the teachers and pupils were largely in correspondence with the original hypothetical categories. They are presented in Table 20.1.

A four-factor solution seemed to fit best.
Factor I was labelled 'individualization'.
Factor II contained the questions on integration–segregation.
Factor III was on special (gifted) education.
Factor IV was on the implications of regular schooling.

The factor analysis did not isolate attitudes towards any special 'types' of children, such as handicapped or gifted, which was in accord with the author's original hope of combining specific concerns for these children with those of the general educational system and its context.

Assessment of statements by parents

The statements for the parents were concerned with individualization and integration versus segregation in gifted education. As Table 20.2 shows, the

TABLE 20.1   Factor analytic solution of statements based on assessments by the teachers and students, the item numbers are in rank order of loadings on each factor, the items which loaded the highest being underlined. Common variance = 67.3 per cent

Factor I	Factor II	Factor III	Factor IV
9 0.87	6 0.69	1 0.74	11 0.78
14 0.72	12 0.68	5 0.63	16 0.56
2 0.66	4 0.61	10 0.59	3 0.43
3 0.64	15 0.58	7 0.51	
13 0.50	16 0.48	8 0.47	
15 0.49			
8 0.48			

ratings for both groups (P1 and P2) were scattered over the whole scale (except for item 9).

Responses indicated that parents did not consider segregation to be essential for gifted children (items 2, 3, 4, 6, 12) though most of them were strongly convinced that it did help handicapped children (item 4). In spite of parental disagreement about the need for individualized assessment within an integrated school system, especially with regard to its democratic aspects (item 6), there was nevertheless broad agreement on the need for education tailored for individuals in school (item 9). The groups of parents differed a little, but not significantly ($p = 0.05$) (items 2, 3, 4, and 6) seeming to reflect their experiences of school with their children, and their prevailing relationship with schools.

Unlike the eleven to thirteen year-old children of group P1, who were given 'comprehensive' education, the fourteen year-olds of P2 were taught at the Gymnasium at a relatively high achievement level, within a fairly homogeneous grouping. It was understandable that the P1 group of parents of middle- to low-achieving children in main subjects (German, maths, English, environmental sciences) felt the greater desire to break down the rigid age-graded educational system (item 2). But the P2 parents were keener than the P1 on special education for gifted children (item 3), which implies some segregation of the children (item 4). Accordingly, the P2 agreement was high on individualization (item 9), though moderate on special schools for the gifted (item 12), and there was a relatively stronger rejection of integration (item 14). The results of statement 15 seemed to depend on whether parents had stressed the term 'furthered in a special way' or 'within regular

TABLE 20.2   Frequencies of statement ratings for parents and teacher and students

	Ratings					$\bar{x}$	Mode
	1	2	3	4	5		
Item 2							
P 1	11	13	33	31	11	3,14	3
P 2	8	6	30	46	10	3,44	4
T/S	37	39	11	11	1	2,01	2
Item 3							
P 1	9	34	16	34	7	2,96	2+4
P 2	5	18	10	55	12	3,51	4
T/S	6	11	7	24	52	4,20	5
Item 4							
P 1	5	8	10	29	49	4,11	5
P 2	—	—	12	25	63	4,50	5
T	18	25	4	46	7	3,04	4
S	16	61	3	19	—	2,26	2
Item 6							
P 1	31	3	14	49	2	2,89	4
P 2	12	10	41	32	5	3,18	3
T/S	67	26	6	1	—	1,43	1
Item 9							
P 1	60	28	2	10	—	1,62	1
P 2	65	23	5	7	—	1,54	1
T/S	68	25	1	6	—	1,45	1
Item 12							
P 1	11	22	42	14	11	2,92	3
P2	13	16	48	20	3	2,84	3
T/S	5	9	10	28	48	4,06	5
Item 14							
P 1	3	6	55	21	15	3,39	3
P 2	3	4	21	48	24	3,86	4
T/S	48	36	12	1	1	1,71	1
Item 15							
P 1	9	3	48	24	16	3,35	3
P 2	26	13	20	15	26	3,02	1+5
T/S	33	32	15	14	6	2,26	1

schools', which in accordance with previous results some P2 parents would be expected to refuse; this may explain the two discrepant modes of 1 and 5.

Teachers' and students' ratings of statements

There was only one significant difference between the students' and the teachers' responses to the statements (item 4, $p = 0.05$), which allowed

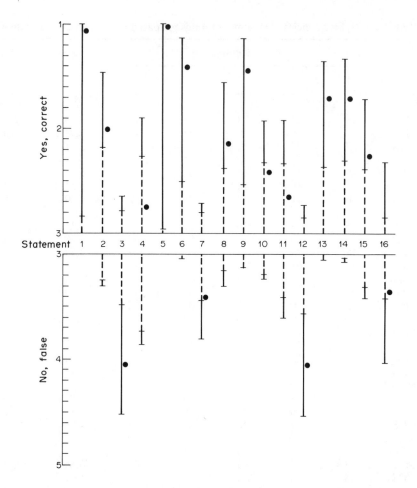

FIGURE 20.1 Distribution of responses to the statements. Above the number 3 on the vertical axis, scores of 2 are indicated by a dotted line, and scores of 1 by an unbroken line. Below 3, scores of 4 are denoted by a dotted line, and scores of 5 by an unbroken line. The length of a column refers to the percentage of the ratings (3 is omitted), and the thick full-stop indicates the mean of the 1–5 rating

them to be considered together. Figure 20.1 illustrates the distribution of agreement and rejection for each statement.

The highest level of agreement was for the identification of handicaps (items 1 and 5), and similarly the two strongest reactions about gifted education both dealt with the question of special provision (items 3 and 12). The teacher's scores were somewhat contradictory, for though 76 per cent believed that gifted children do need special attention, the same proportion were against special schools. This was possibly affected by the non-existence of any special schools and type of education for the gifted, which could not therefore be seen to be transferable for the benefit of normal education. The general feeling was that gifted children should be catered for within normal schools (items 7 and 15) (as Freeman and Tilsley had also found). There was, however, a high consensus of approval for highly individualized school education (items 2 and 9) with full integration (6 and 14), a condition which seems unlikely to be fulfilled in the near future.

The slight differences between the teachers' and the students' responses may have reflected their age differences and style of education. Like the teachers, 70 per cent of the students agreed with the provision of special education for gifted children (items 3, 4, and 15), but unlike them 53 per cent approved of segregation, though they were unsure of the benefits. The students appeared to be in rather more of a dilemma than the teachers about the theory and practice of individual tuition and integrated education—probably due to both their lack of practical experience and the flame of their yet undiminished idealism.

Gifted pupils' ratings

A small group of approximately seventeen-year-olds who were attending special full-time classes at a selctive boarding school, also assessed the statements. They disagreed significantly with the parent groups about integration (items 6 and 15), supporting special provision for the gifted (3, 6, 12, 14, 15), though their concern for individually tailored education was less positive than that of any other groups of the respondents.

Rating of the educational aims (EAs)

All the respondents rated the fifteen EAs as to their importance for the three different ability groups of children. However, as there were no statistically significant differences between the groups, their results were examined together, and are described in Figure 20.2.

A small number of raters, particularly teachers and students, described their educational priorities as the same for children of all abilities, and ranked them at 1. Though parents were more varied in their opinions, the gifted students were very concerned about different EAs for children of different ability. Table 20.3 gives more statistical information about the relationship between the orders in which the EAs were rated by the different groups of raters.

Most of these correlations were highly significant ($p = 0.01$) and all were positive and significantly different from 0. Thus, in spite of the different weightings of the EAs for the different ability groups, their rank-order was not seriously affected.

	All EAs rated as equally important ("1")	Ratings for the handicapped agree with those for the normal children			Ratings for the gifted agree with those for the normal children		
		Fully	Except for 1, 2, or 3 EAs	Only in part or no	Fully	Except for 1, 2, or 3 EAs	Only in part or no
Teachers	12	60	19	21	63	16	21
Pupils	11	77	12	11	80	17	3
Parents (P 1)	3	41	26	36	28	27	45
Parents (P2)	2	26	15	61	20	24	56
Gifted pupils	7	12	23	65	15	21	64

FIGURE 20.2 Agreements of EA ratings, between EAs and between child ability groups. Numbers in percentages

TABLE 20.3 Correlations between rank orders of weighted EAs for teachers and students, parents and gifted pupils

	N/H	N/G	H/G
1) teachers/students	0.97**	0.96**	0.91**
2) parents (P1+P2)	0.72**	0.46*	0.67**
3) gifted pupils	0.81**	0.84**	0.61*

* 0.05 per cent significant; ** 0.01 per cent significant.

Table 20.4 shows that the ranked EA-orders for gifted children had the highest correspondence among the combined raters ($r = 0.71$ to $r = 0.77$). This is the first outstanding indication of the possibility that attitudes towards the education of the gifted are relatively more convergent than those for the handicapped and for normal children. A correlation analysis of all the data provided further evidence that the majority of the coefficients was found to be significant and/or positive, again demonstrating a convergence of educational aims for the gifted.

TABLE 20.4 Correlations between rank orders of weighted EAs by teachers and students, parents and gifted pupils for each group of children

	(3) Gifted students as to			(2) Parents as to		
	N	H	G	N	H	G
(1) Teachers/students as to	0.84**	0.56*	0.76**	0.39	0.56*	0.77**
(2) Parents P1+P2 as to	0.30	0.33	0.71**			

* 0.05 per cent significant; ** 0.01 per cent significant.

FACTORIAL STRUCTURE OF THE EDUCATIONAL AIMS

A factor analysis was calculated with the data from the teacher and pupil raters for each ability group of children. Three factors emerged for the normal children, four for the handicapped, and two for the gifted (Tables 20.5 to 20.7).

TABLE 20.5 Factor analysis of EAs: student and teacher ratings for normal children

Factor I		Factor II		Factor III	
0.79	ABIDM	0.89	DILIG	0.81	CREAT
0.78	TRUST	0.86	ORDER	0.74	COGFL
0.76	INDEP	0.78	AMBIT	0.63	TOLER
0.67	ABIPM	0.60	SOCAD	0.51	AUTTH
0.61	AUTTH	0.45	TRUST	0.50	INDEP
0.56	TOLER			0.48	ABIPM
0.55	CONTE				
0.54	SRESP				
0.46	POLCO				

Common variance = 69.5 per cent

The make-up of the more important factor of EAs for gifted children (52 per cent variance) suggested a mature personality with a marked self-identity, free from external domination, strongly dialectical (between individual and social competences), combined with social responsibility; and all under the influence of a generalized giftedness. The second factor, which had a great similarity with those of the other groups, contained traits which

TABLE 20.6   Factor analysis of EAs: student and teacher ratings for handicapped children

Factor I		Factor II		Factor III		Factor IV	
0.85	ORDER	0.90	INDEP	0.81	TOLER	0.87	POLCO
0.81	DILIG	0.66	CREAT	0.76	SRESP	0.58	ABIPM
0.75	SOCAD	0.59	CONTE	0.60	COGFL	0.54	AUTTH
0.73	AMBIT	0.59	ABIDM	0.51	AUTTH	0.45	INDEP
0.50	TRUST	0.53	ABIPM				
0.46	CONTE	0.49	TRUST				

Common variance = 72.9 per cent

TABLE 20.7   Factor analysis of EAs: student and teacher ratings for gifted children

Factor I		Factor II	
0.91	INDEP	0.88	DILIG
0.85	TOLER	0.85	ORDER
0.81	ABIDM	0.71	AMBIT
0.78	AUTTH	0.63	SOCAD
0.76	CREAT	0.56	TRUST
0.75	COGFL	0.51	SRESP
0.74	ABIPM		
0.69	SRESP		
0.66	TRUST		
0.61	CONTE		
0.58	POLCO		

Common variance = 66.2 per cent

could be described as old-fashioned, traditional educational aims. For the gifted (at 14 per cent variance), just as for the normal group (at 19.5 per cent variance), they played a relatively moderate part; but this was not the case for the handicapped group, where they constituted the main factor (at 38 per cent variance). The more differentiated factor structure for the handicapped seemed to represent their more complex and difficult situation. Those four factors relating to the handicapped could readily be named by the respective first and highest loading variable of each factor: orderliness, independence, tolerance, and political consciousness. Unfortunately, the distribution and constellation of variables within the factor structure for the normal group could not be interpreted clearly.

CONCLUSIONS

There was a relatively high concurrence of opinions and attitudes about educational aims for all children by all the respondents in this study—particularly for their independence—though there was some variation towards children of different abilities. This was shown in the statements referring to integration versus segregation of exceptional children, the teachers being the keenest on integration, and the gifted pupils least. The overall majority, however, approved of the idea that children should not be separated from each other because of their exceptional abilities, but attend the same schools. It was not so much that the children were seen as having different needs, but rather that the ways and means by which these needs were to be met were seen as different.

The respondents' disinclination to isolate specific educational pointers for the gifted may have been due to some extent to the activities of those who have been concerned for the gifted. In trying to direct the attention of teachers and others towards the concept of giftedness, they have run the risk of 'equalizing' these children with a label where the individuality of a child can become subsumed under the umbrella term of gifted. This survey may have identified some of the attitudinal aspects towards children labelled as 'gifted'. Though there was no expressed dislike of them, there was some apparent caution and reserve among the raters, possibly due to lack of information and a poor understanding of the children's situation.

But the discrepancy between the highly desired, individualized approach to education, and its realization in the schools was clearly identified. This is especially so within the rigid selective system in West Germany, where such a change would imply both micro- and macro-alterations in many areas of education, such as teachers' self-understanding, curriculum, general school procedures, the overall organization of schools, and the attitudes of administrators. It would also involve grappling with the basic contradiction within the teaching process—that of the 'internal' realization of self-determination, brought about by 'external' (i.e. teaching) forces (Homburg, 1978).

Such an integration would, however, promote the highest educational ideals of constructive and critical tolerance of people and ideas in the form of an 'operating trait' for all children (Holzkamp and Schurig, 1973), rather than their passive acceptance of the status quo. There is hope for some influence for change, however, through recent discoveries within developmental psychology, which are placing increasing emphasis on the uniqueness of the interactions between an individual and his circumstances. In these more personal terms, problems can be estimated by the balance of the relationship between each child's autonomy and independence—an interpretation which is different from the traditional concept, in that it includes exceptional children.

The raters' very positive attitudes towards the provision of education tailored to each individual's needs, abilities, and interests is more than merely lip-service to an ideal; it offers a basis of popular support to both educators and politicians. Since individualized education applies equally to all children, and cannot therefore be termed 'elitist', it is more likely to be put into practice, and could thereby provide access to an improved understanding of the many and varied needs of gifted children and their education. So-called special education is in fact normal education, and that which is appropriate for normal individuals, is indeed special (Homburg, 1978). Thus, all children can benefit from educational developments, whether designed for special children or not, and gifted education is assuredly for the advantage of all children in a reciprocal, supplementary educational system.

REFERENCES

Bennett, N. (1976). *Teaching Styles and Pupil Progress*. Open Books, London.

Burg, B. (1981). Special programs for the gifted in Israel: a study of attitudes. Presentation at 4th World Conference on Gifted and Talented Children, Montreal, Canada.

Butler, N., and Butler, R. (1979). 'Parents' and children's perception of special classes for highly gifted children. In *Gifted Children: Reaching Their Potential* (ed. J. Gallagher). Kollek, Jerusalem, pp. 223–245.

Dichgans, H. (1979). Die Leistungselite braucht intensive Förderung. *Die Welt*, **142**, 21 June.

Elite–Zukunftsorientierung in der Demokratie (1982). 19. Kolloqium der Walter-Raymond-Stiftung, 9–11 March 1981, Bachem, Köln.

Ermert, K. (Ed.) (1982). *Eliteförderung und Demokratie: Sollen, können, dürfen deutsche Hochschulen Eliten bilden?* Loccumer Protokolle 15/81, Evang. Akademie, Rehburg-Loccum.

Freeman, J. (1979). *Gifted Children: Their Identification and Development in a Social Context.* MTP Press, Lancaster and University Park Press, Baltimore.

Glotz, P. (1979). Eliteförderung—was heisst das?. *Mitteilungen des Hochschulverbandes*, **27**, 262–264.

Glotz, P. (1980). Elite fördern, heisst nicht Extrawürste braten. *Hochschulpolitische Informationen*, **13**.

Granzow, H. (1980). Gleiche Chancen für alle und Förderungen besonderer Begabungen ist kein Widerspruch. *Informationen Bildung/Wissenschaft*, 7/78.

Holzkamp, K., and Schurig, V. (1973). Zur Einführung. In *Probleme der Entwicklung des Psychischen* (ed. A. N. Leontjews), Fischer Athenäum, Frankfurt.

Homburg, G. (1978). *Die Pädagogik der Sprachbehinderten.* Schindele, Rheinstetten.

Kreklau, C. (1979). Hochbegabtenförderung—ein Beitrag zur Elitenbildung. In

Berichte zur Bildungspolitik 1979/80 des Instituts der deutschen Wirtschaft (eds. U. Göbel and W. Schlaffke). Deutscher Instituts-Verlag, Köln, pp. 149–180.

Mira, H. (1979). Creative behavior of gifted children from a disadvantaged social background. *GATE (Gifted and Talented Education)*, 1, 93–96.

Mira, H. (1982). Probleme der Hochbegabung und ihrer Förderung bei Kindern aus einem benachteiligenden sozio-ökonomischen Milieu. In *Hochbegabte Kinder* (ed. K. K. Urban). Schindele, Heidelberg, pp. 224–228.

Roth, H. (1981). Kinderstars halten selten, was sie versprechen. Eliteschulen. *Erziehung und Wissenschaft*, 33, 12, 6–12.

Taylor, P. H., and Holley, B. (1975). A study of the emphasis given by teachers of different age groups to aims in primary education. In *Aims, Influence and Change in the Primary School-Curriculum* (ed. P. H. Taylor), NFER, Slough.

Tilsley, P. J. (1981). Attitudes and opinions on gifted children and their education. In *Gifted Children: Challenging their Potential* (ed. A. H. Kramer). Trillium, New York, pp. 129–135.

Urban, K. K. (1980a). Hochbegabung—(k)ein Problem. *Pädagogische Welt*, 34, 52–54.

Urban, K. K. (1980b). Hochbegabte Kinder—eine Herausforderung. *Bildung und Erziehung*, 33, 526–535.

Urban, K. K. (1981). A comparison of educational attitudes to and opinions of the education of 'normal', handicapped, and gifted children. Paper presented at the 4th World Conference on Gifted and Talented Children, Montreal, Canada.

Urban, K. K. (Ed.) (1982a). *Hochbegabte Kinder: Psychologische, pädagogische, psychiatrische und soziologische Aspekte*. Schindele, Heidelberg.

Urban, K. K. (1982b). Ansichten und Einstellungen von Lehrern und Eltern zu schulischer Erziehung und Erziehungszielen bei 'normalen', behinderten und hochbegabten Kindern. *Vierteljahresschrift für Heilpädagogik und ihre Nachbargebiete (VHN)*, 51, 6.

Urban, K. K. (1985). On the situation of gifted children and youth in the Federal Republic of Germany. In *The Gifted Globe* (eds. N. Maier and K. K. Urban). Trillium, New York.

Wagner, H. (1981). Wer fördert die Hochbegabten: Zur Situation in Deutschland. *Die Welt*, 3 December.

Weinschenk, K. (1979a). Der Hochbegabte—eine deutsche Un-Person?. *Sonderpädagogik*, 9, 42–44.

Weinschenk, K. (1979b). Heilpädagogische 'Elite'—Trimmung?—Ein Denkanstoss zur Förderung pädagogen-leistungsbeeinträchtigter Hochbegabter. *Vierteljahresschrift für Heilpädagogik und ihre Nachbargebiete (VHN)*, 48, 1, 25–36.

Weinschenk, K. (1979c). Re-Habilitation der Hochbegabten? Ein pädagogisches Dilemma. *Zeitschrift für Heilpädagogik*, 30, 198–206.

Wellman, B. (1981). Elite-Zukunftsorientierung in der Demokratie. *Der Arbeitgeber*, 7, 351–353.

Wissenschaftsrat (Ed.) (1981). *Empfehlungen zur Förderung besonders Befähigter*, Berlin.

Woelke, G. (1978). *Eliteschulen. Kommt die Demokratie ohne Eliten aus?*, Deutscher Instituts-Verlag, Köln.

Woelke, G. (1980). *Eliten in der Bundesrepublik Deutschland. Zur Rückkehr eines Begriffs*, Deutscher Instituts-Verlag, Köln.

The Psychology of Gifted Children
Edited by Joan Freeman
©1985, John Wiley & Sons, Ltd.

CHAPTER 21

Vocational Problems

JAMES R. DELISLE

It may seem odd to reflect upon my clearly successful school experience as replete with gaps and blind spots, yet not once in twelve years of expensive schooling did I speak to either a guidance counsellor or any of my excellent teachers about my future career. Because I was seen to be gifted, my prospects were assured—or at least assumed—though I now realize that they owed less to conscious direction and more to luck and stamina, during my haphazard and awkward progress. The first of my five successive colleges, for example, was chosen by a catalogue description of the campus, which promised tall trees, open land and old classroom buildings. I have discussed my 'college selection saga' with teachers, parents, youngsters, and counsellors and learned that I was not unique; it happens still—this haphazard selection—which is the reason for this chapter.

In recent years career education for all pupils has expanded in the United States. Bolstered by the philosophical and financial support of private foundations and various US state and federal agencies, even young children have been introduced to the world of work. Where these early exposure programmes exist, guest lectures by 'community helpers' such as firemen, policewomen, and wild-life managers have become the mainstay. For older pupils, filmstrips and wall charts often accompany field trips to a dairy farm or 'high-tech' showplace, to explain the multitude of options awaiting those who work hard. Secondary schools usually integrate other components also, such as work-study programmes and summertime apprenticeships with practising professionals, which meet with varying degrees of success.

However, this influx of monies and momentum has done little to convince teachers that occupational awareness is anything more than a temporary diversion from the basics of a school curriculum. Though few educators would argue with the definition of career education in schools as being 'the total effort of public education and the community to help all individuals become familiar with the values of a work-oriented society' (Hoyt *et al.*, 1974), many would add 'Please don't expect me to give up either my students or my free time for instruction in that!'

For gifted and talented learners, the problems of career awareness and selection are compounded by a stereotype that if the children are bright they will make it on their own. In fact, data exist which indicate that career guidance is the most over-looked element in the education of gifted youth. Over twenty years of research by Marshall Sanborn (1979) at the Research and Guidance Laboratory of the University of Wisconsin (USA) has given evidence that vocational guidance for the gifted is poor. Similarly, longitudinal follow-up of 1000 high school pupils, identified as gifted for Project TALENT, has revealed that the most blatant curricular omission made in secondary schools is career guidance: 'Students bemoan the fact that they either have not been counselled, or have not been counselled well' (Gordon, 1978). In an evaluation survey of a community-based, career-education programme for gifted and talented adolescents, Colson (1980) has shown that career counselling is at best incomplete, and not one (0 per cent) of the survey's respondents rated their school counselling service as preparing them for future career choices.

The unique vocational problems of high-ability pupils will be described here, and interventions suggested for a comprehensive career-guidance programme. The chapter ends with some suggested future avenues for vocational guidance of the gifted and talented.

VOCATIONAL PROBLEMS OF THE GIFTED AND TALENTED

Multipotentiality

In my early years, I had a very real liking for school; teachers seemed fair and human, the subjects they taught made sense, and my performance reflected this satisfaction. With such success and with good role models, it was perhaps natural that I should choose education as my life career. However, I was also interested in other possibilities, such as medicine, and the outdoors, for I liked the quiet and green woods of a soft New Hampshire summer: maybe a career in forestry. Not only was I interested in an array of potential occupations, but I would probably have succeeded in any one of them. This lack of one area to stand out in—this multipotentiality (Sanborn, 1979)—was a problem masquerading for me as a 'world of opportunity', and selecting among these various choices was a decision that (I thought) I shared with few.

In the words of one pupil: 'Nothing is so simple for me that I can do a perfect job without effort, but nothing is so hard that I cannot do it. This is why I find it so difficult to decide my place in the future' (Hoyt and Hebeler, 1974).

Although not all bright youth share the challenge presented by multi-potentiality, the 'problem' is not uncommon. Sanborn et al. (1971) discovered patterns of multiple interests and aptitudes among superior pupils in Wisconsin schools, while Khatena (1982) noted the complications which arise when the gifted attempt to select one career from many viable alternatives. Perrone et al. (1979) saw the clash between numerous interests and goals among multi-potential students as being a conflict of various internal and external needs and motivations. Recognizing multipotentiality as the 'mixed blessing' it can sometimes be is a start towards understanding the complexity of vocational choices confronting the gifted and talented.

Self and other expectations

The possession of multipotentiality makes it easy to disappoint others, for whatever career is selected, someone will claim that 'you could have done more', which at times can be transformed into 'you could have been more'. What follows then, is a lowered self-image (Delisle, 1981). The gifted themselves tend to agree with this observation: 'At some point, you will probably tell yourself that you have no talent. Your mind will vacillate between believing you are a genius and believing that you are a failure. Neither being true, you may become extremely depressed or confused and your opinion of yourself will begin to break down' (American Association for Gifted Children, 1978).

These expectations from both self and others, and the conflicting interpretations which result, can have negative effects on the career and personal developments of bright youngsters, so that a child can, for example:

1. Become a 'paralysed perfectionist', unwilling to pursue any new interest or potential interest unless success is guaranteed (Whitmore, 1980).
2. Adopt a fear of the future, unsure if s/he can adequately meet the faraway goals set by others (Witt and Grotberg, 1970).
3. Learn to under-achieve, or opt to become 'first worst' instead of 'first best' (Delisle, 1982).
4. Select a career prematurely and undertake advanced training that is, in the end, of little or no direct benefit to his/her ultimate career selection (Colson, 1980).

5. Select a career to satisfy the wishes or needs of others in deference to his/her own system of interests and values (Rodenstein *et al.*, 1977).

In the words of that sage philosopher, Charlie Brown: 'There is no heavier burden than a great potential.' With gifted or talented youth, for whom expectations are set (and set high) by self and others, the benefit of high abilities is sometimes dominated by the excess baggage of inferiority or by the belief that 'my best' is not good enough.

Investment in others' expectations

Although some current rhetoric extols the merits of giftedness across disciplines—gifted mechanics, for example, or talented plumbers—the career tendency for bright youngsters remains, as always, towards professional occupations (Herr and Watanabe, 1977). These careers necessitate long periods of advanced training or schooling preceding entrance into the workaday worlds of doctors, lawyers or college professors, and with these prerequisites, come an array of investments and sacrifices which the gifted are expected to make.

The most obvious investment is financial, due to the long years of study and poorly paid further years of training, and although the financial benefits to be reaped from professional training may eventually provide compensation, the proverbial 'light at the end of the tunnel', can seem quite dim. A second investment is that of time, for while the preprofessional is cloistered in academe for up to ten years following secondary-school education, ex-classmates may be well entrenched in careers. Then, there is the investment of self—the postponement of marriage and family until security is assured. All of these affect the individual's appraisals of present and future self-worth.

Conformity

Bright children are aware from an early age of the social and intellectual divisions between themselves and many of their agemates (Freeman, 1979). From the tedious ritual of sandbox play to the intentional neglect of odious homework assignments, children with high abilities often acquiesce to the mundane so as to be thought of as 'regular', and they often regard conformity as a means to that end. Hollingworth (1942) called it 'suffering fools gladly', i.e. tolerating the boredom brought about in playing life by the unwritten but well-understood rules of group consensus.

Combined with multi-potentials and others' expectations, conformity can play a significant role in the career selection and preparation of bright youth. This may occur when:

1. Despite obvious multipotentials, the range of vocational choices is perceived as being limited to a select few, narrowing the alternatives s/he is 'permitted' to consider (Herr and Watanabe, 1978).
2. Peer pressure to conform results in suffering from an embarrassment of riches, whereby the gifted disguise or downplay particular talents or abilities (Johnson, 1980).
3. There is no adult who can serve as a role model for a real world counterpart, in securing guidance towards an appropriate career (Zaffran and Colangelo, 1977).
4. Creative talents, no matter how outstanding, are waved aside, the youngster being directed towards more intellectual occupations, and obliged to disregard aspirations to pursue such nebulous careers as those of an artist, musician, or actor (Wrenn, 1962).
5. The bright youth is counselled that occupational choice is pre-ordained by sex (Callahan, 1979).

The passive suffering of fools, with regard to career selection, can result in the gifted young adult finding himself inextricably entrenched in a vocation which has never interested him. However, extensive investments of time, money, and training have already been made. Starting over again would be costly, cumbersome, and embarrassing, so, the bright adult remains stuck in a fur-lined rut, materially satisfied, but intellectually and emotionally stifled.

INNOVATIONS AND INTERVENTIONS IN THE PRIMARY-SCHOOL CLASSROOM

There are innovations and interventions which could be used to make career selections less haphazard, more meaningful, and in the end personally fulfilling for gifted and talented youth.

We have become a world of specialists. Medicine is now sub-divided into more divisions than the human body has bones; computer technology is no longer generic — we have programmers and processors, data analysts and software technicians — even trash collection in the USA has become complex, as 'garbologists' train us to separate our waste paper from our more solid refuse. Thus we become ever more selective in our job descriptions. In this world of increasingly intricate expertise, where do school personnel direct their career education efforts? How do we plan for a future when we find it difficult to keep pace with even our present technological and scientific advances? Can we prepare our brightest young people for jobs which, at this time, do not even exist? The answers (not necessarily in proper order) are — yes — by using the human resources readily available to us, and with an eye towards inculcating into our pupils the methods and strategies of dealing with change.

It might be expected that for gifted pupils of elementary-school age, exposure to the many arenas of specific vocations would offer a fine introduction
to career guidance. But the occasional classroom visit by professionals such
as Arthur Architect or Ethel Electrician is not enough.

For example, relive with me this scenario as a teacher. A guest geologist
has arrived in class, ready to share with the ten-year-olds her interests and
knowledge. She has brought samples—quartz, mica, and glitter-rock 'with a
name this long'—and explains how to distinguish one from the next. One
child asks if the rocks are valuable, another queries their origins, a third
wants to know why rocks are hard. Good questions to be sure, and Ms.
Geologist is impressed by the pupils' responsiveness and good behavior.
Then she leaves. All the class write thank you notes, illustrated with 'my
favourite rock', and to save postage, they are mailed in a single pouch.

A splendid day, perhaps, but if the objective was career awareness, it has
failed. Although the class was exposed to a geologist (a valuable learning
opportunity), they were intrigued more with the by-product and end-result
of geology—rocks—than with the processes of either finding or digging for
them. The geologist has been effectively divorced from her vocation, and has
instead provided a three-dimensional show-and-tell. Instead, why not ask
the geologist about her training—earth science, chemistry, mathematics—
and the fields which are open to those who wish to study rocks? Why not
ask how her interests began, and who encouraged this career? Why not be
personal, and ask if it was difficult in college for a 'girl' to be digging for
rocks like a 'man'? That is career awareness in all its nuances and sidelights;
it provides the insights that cannot be found in multicolour text-books, which
distinguish sedimentary from metamorphic specimens.

There are many other ways in which a teacher can create real career
awareness in the gifted.

1. Begin the school year by a thorough review of the local Yellow Pages.
   Discover vocations which seem funny (like Rubber Consultants) or
   suspicious (like Exodontists), or just plain interesting (like beach pollution controllers), and then let your fingers do the walking as you or
   your pupils get in touch with the people listed, to arrange an interview
   or lecture.
2. Gather together a cross-section of parents who (with prior notice)
   would be willing to come in to school to discuss their jobs, debate
   the need for higher education in them, and respond to children's questions.
3. Involve pupils in small-group investigations of various general topics, for which both human and written resources are needed as references. For example, one group may decide to probe questions which
   have no firm answers (religious, philosophical, and scientific realms, in

particular) while another attempts to unravel oddities such as 'Why doesn't snow melt white?' or 'Why are my fingers always wrinkled after I take a bath?' Make the searches game-like.

4. Review current local newspapers; find the newsmakers and ask why they are notable. What have they done or are they doing that keeps them in the public's mind and eye? Arrange a squad of classroom journalists to visit and interview a particularly controversial character (of which every community has at least one!).

5. Invite community members into your classroom to serve as models for pupils about to embark upon new ideas. For example, a stockbroker visited one classroom in my community to advise twelve pupils, who had pooled their allowances and savings, how to speculate on Wall Street. The visiting broker suggested several options, both safe and high-risk, placed the children's order (two shares of Apple, Inc.) and then reported back on dividends and losses. **NB**: Though the initiative must come from the school, local community members, such as journalists and artists, are much more available and accessible than we sometimes believe, and I have never had to pay for the services of a classroom visitor or mentor.

6. Arrange for children to 'shadow' their parents for one full work day. Whether dad toils as a labourer or mum is a nuclear physicist, each can teach their child(ren) about their world of work. This face-front exposure can enlighten pupils more in one day than a full term of filmloops on 'Employment in the "90's" '.

7. Encourage group or classroom projects that deal in commodities, such as lunchtime snack sales; a monthly, by subscription, newspaper, or an after school film festival. Such business ventures, replete with deadlines, budgets, inventories, and divisions of labour, provide an excellent proving ground for would-be entrepreneurs.

8. Think in terms of your pupils' futures. Jobs that exist at present may not be there in 1995, and jobs that can now only be imagined will be commonplace when today's ten-year-olds turn thirty. Statisticians and futurists have tried to distinguish the work force of today from that of fifteen years from now. Read *The Third Wave* by Alvin Toffler (1980), *Future Facts* by Stephen Rosen (1976), or the *Occupational Outlook Handbook* (US Government Printing Office) and help the youngsters to distill this information into both some predictable and improbable outcomes.

It would be as unreasonable to assert that these recommendations offer a complete complement of vocational education programming for the pupil in school, as it would be to claim that only the gifted would benefit from them. However, introducing the community into the classroom, and the active acquaintance of children with the worlds of work are preventive strategies, designed to introduce youngsters to the possibilities that exist in real life.

SECONDARY-SCHOOL OPTIONS

Most secondary-school curricula lack relevant career education for the bright adolescent (Gordon, 1978). Further, what appears 'relevant' for one teenager might be construed as 'a waste of time' by another. Thus, a rigidly structured career-education programme will not suffice for all pupils, and some flexible options towards career education of the gifted and talented must be adopted. Several suggestions are listed below.

COMMUNITY INVOLVEMENT

'A variety of outside opportunities allows us to decide better what we will choose as a career and how to relate what happens in the school year to one's life choices ... to feel worthy, we need to know we can do something well' (American Association for Gifted Children, 1978).

Work experience for the gifted and talented is often considered as a frill. Perhaps we need a new label; we certainly need a new outlook. In an effort to expose the gifted to the array of careers which are available, or which can be manipulated into being, teachers can adapt their pupils' experiences into a version of the old-fashioned apprenticeships, now known as mentorships. For example, if a pupil is interested in architecture, he could contact a local building firm to check the availability of on-site, regularly scheduled visits with a staff designer; if another wants to explore veterinary medicine, she could volunteer at a local animal hospital or clinic. The goals of mentorships —to have a total learning experience and to be ready to try, experiment, and explore (Runions, 1980)—are generalizable to all professions.

Make use of the expertise of people who have lived the profession they decided to enter. Invite psychologists, dentists, writers, artists, photographers, and farmers into your classroom; have each review the pride and salary that results from a full day's work, and have each mention alternative professions that were neglected or by-passed in deference to his or her chosen fields. Prior to this face-front disclosure, have your students read excerpts from Studs Terkel's **Working**, a book which explores each vocation, from merchant to record producer, from a first-person vantage.

Investigate careers in the visual, physical, or performing arts that are often considered to be 'avocations'. Question professionals in these fields as to what options exist for making a career out of acting, dancing, writing, or gymnastics. Also, discuss the frustrations (intellectual, emotional, financial) that occur in a career that depends on others' support.

Visit a courtroom, travel agency, radio station or anywhere else which you and your pupils have never investigated. Explore the intricacies of each environ and decide upon benefits and flaws of the occupations of people who fill the roles established in these settings.

CURRICULUM

Offer in-school mini-courses in areas seldom covered by the general curriculum, such as genetic engineering, nuclear power, existentialism, Dante' and Milton, motivation theory, Balalaika, elements of college life, pottery of the Ming Dynasty. Prey on the seldom-used expertise of local craftsmen, legends, curators, or resident teachers who presently moniter study halls. Explore community college or university provision, which (with some effort and organization) can sometimes be made available to talented secondary school pupils.

Make use of available and respected curricular options, such as Model United Nations forums or regional debate squads to enhance the pretraining of skills and interests.

COUNSELLING

Start early enough for counselling to be preventive. However adequate the school curriculum, vocational training for the gifted and talented is incomplete unless accompanied by a preventive counselling scheme on what it means to be gifted or talented. For example, discuss multipotentialities from a personal perspective, and review the internal and external clashes that exist in attempting to select one career when many are possible. Discover the source of multi-potentiality—'Who says I have talents?'—and relate the feelings of pride, inadequacy, or confusion that accompany such labelling. Refer, too, to your own life and to the lives of visiting speakers, mentors, or literary characters for whom multipotentials present an array of difficult choices.

In reviewing self and other expectations, tie in the duality of 'push vs pull'. 'Pushing' is an externally based pressure to perform more, often implying that present levels are not good enough. 'Pulling' is an active choice to pursue an interest due to a personal quest for knowledge, or to dissatisfaction with the status quo. To perform in response to a 'push' is reflexive, and sometimes based on guilt; to perform (or not perform) for self-set reasons ('pulling') is an independent decision.

When speaking of conformity with bright adolescents, the key is honest example. Refer to real lives—yours and theirs—and an incident or two in each that deals point blank with the consequences of conforming (or not conforming). Relate conformity to career selection, and review the acceptability of not declaring a major field of study until after college has begun. Then, review the individual comfort levels of particular professions, and examine whether personal aspirations mesh with those of parents and counsellors. If so, fine; if not, what comes next? Follow these discussions with a review of the investments—financial, personal, temporal—which co-exist with professional training. Through it all, listen for concerns or answers given by rote, dissect the obvious, and pinpoint specific generalities.

A FOCUS ON THE FUTURE

The main purpose of this chapter has been to acquaint the reader with specific vocational concerns of the gifted, and to suggest interventions for dealing with these issues in a school setting. The strategies offered are intended to be preventive rather than remedial, based on the belief that career selection is best made when vocational possibilities are examined before entrance into the work force.

This developmental approach to career education was pointed out by Herr (1976), who chose several areas of concern for future study.

1. Are there ideal careers for the gifted and talented, or is it more effective to recognize that bright pupils may create their own careers, and therefore do not need direction in this regard?
2. Can career guidance refrain from becoming another form of subtle pressure for the gifted and talented to fulfill societal expectations, rather than to exploit their personal needs?
3. How can career guidance assist parents in recognizing the wide range of vocational options open to their bright children, especially for those families from poor or disadvantaged backgrounds, or for the families where a gifted child's career has been 'pre-ordained'?
4. How can teachers and other school personnel be convinced of the necessity of out-of-school apprenticeships for the brightest pupils?

Career education of the gifted and talented is a challenging task, and one which will continue to flourish in our ever-shrinking yet more complex world. To stand by and watch bright pupils register confusion or awe at the possibilities which lie ahead, without ourselves providing input and direction, is to practise neglect—at best benign and at worst harmful. Instead, more ways must be found of making sure our options for gifted and talented children include early, face-front, and frequent exposure to the multitude of challenges which await their future lives. And in this treasure hunt for the career, the college or the sure road to happiness, it is as well to remember that fool's gold can shine as brilliantly as the real thing.

REFERENCES

American Association for Gifted Children (1978). *On Being Gifted.* Walker, New York.

Callahan, C. M. (1979). The gifted and talented woman. In *The Gifted and The Talented* (ed. A. Harry Passow). University of Chicago, Chicago. pp. 401–423.

Colson, S. (1980). The evaluation of a community-based career education program for gifted and talented students as an administrative model for an alternative program. *Gifted Child Quarterly,* **24**, 101–106.

Delisle, J. R. (1981). The me I see: self-images of the gifted child. *Teaching Gifted Children,* July/August, 7–10.

Delisle, J. R. (1982). Learning to underachieve. *Roeper Review,* **4**, 16–18.

Freeman, J. (1979). *Gifted Children: their Identification and Development in a Social Context.* MTP Press, Lancaster and University Park Press, Baltimore.

Gordon, E. W. (1978). How guidance can help in the development of lives and careers. In *Perspectives on Improving Education: Project Talent's Young Adults Look Back* (ed. J. C. Flanagan). Praeger, New York, pp. 47–56.

Herr, E. L. (1976). Career education for the gifted and talented: some observations. *Peabody Journal of Education,* **53**, 98–103.

Herr, E. L., and Watanabe, A. (1978). Counseling the gifted about career development. In *New Voices in Counseling the Gifted* (eds. Nicholas Colangelo and Ronald T. Zaffran). Kendall-Hunt, Dubuque, Iowa, pp. 251–263.

Hollingworth, L. S. (1942). *Children above 180 I.Q..* World Book Company, Yonkers-on-Hudson, New York.

Hoyt, K. B., and Hebeler, J. R. (1974). *Career Education for Gifted and Talented Students.* Olympus, Salt Lake City.

Hoyt, K. B., Evans, R. N., Mackin, E., and Mangum, G. L. (1974). *Career Education: What It Is and How To Do It.* Olympus, Salt Lake City.

Johnson, T. (1980). *Concerns of the Gifted.* Unpublished research report, University of Connecticut, Storrs, Connecticut.

Khatena, J. (1982). *Educational Psychology of the Gifted.* Wiley, New York.

Perrone, P. A., Karshner, W. W., and Male, R. A. (1979). *Career Development of Talented Persons.* Unpublished manuscript, Guidance Institute for Talented Students, University of Wisconsin, Madison.

Rodenstein, J., Pflegler, L. R., and Colangelo, N. (1977). Career development of gifted women. *Gifted Child Quarterly,* **21**, 340–358.

Rosen, S. (1976). *Future Facts: A Forecast of the World as We Will Know It Before the End of the Century.* Simon and Schuster, New York.

Runions, T. (1980). The Mentor Academy Program: Educating the gifted/talented for the '80's. *Gifted Child Quarterly,* **24**, 152–157.

Sanborn, M .P. (1979). Counseling and guidance needs of the gifted and talented. In *The Gifted and the Talented* (ed. A. Harry Passow). University of Chicago, Chicago. pp. 424-438.

Sanborn, M. P., Pulvino, C. J., and Wunderlin, R. F. (1971). *Research Reports: Superior Students in Wisconsin High Schools.* University of Wisconsin, Madison.

Terkel, S. (1972). *Working.* Avon, New York.

Toffler, A. (1980). *The Third Wave.* Morrow, New York.

Whitmore, J. R. (1980). *Giftedness, Conflict and Underachievement.* Allyn and Bacon, Boston.

Witt, P. A., and Grotberg, E.H. (1970). *Helping the Gifted Child,* Science Research Associates, Chicago.

Wrenn, C. G. (1962). *The Counselor in a Changing World.* American Personnel and
  Guidance Association, Washington, DC.
Zaffran, R. T., and Colangelo, N. (1977). Counseling with gifted and talented stu-
  dents. *Gifted Child Quarterly,* **21**, 305–320.

The Psychology of Gifted Children
Edited by Joan Freeman
©1985, John Wiley & Sons, Ltd.

CHAPTER 22

Creative Questioning for the Future

ERIKA LANDAU

As both an educator and a psychotherapist—a re-educator—I see the purpose of education not only as an academic preparation for life, but as facilitating the development of open-minded, creative attitudes to knowledge. Although it has a genetic base, giftedness is a phenotypic phenomenon, strongly influenced in its promotion or inhibition by the environment. However, this does not work on a passive individual; each one plays an effective and dynamic role in the actualization of his own potential (Block and Dworkin, 1976; Bronfenbrenner, 1979). In my psychotherapeutic work with gifted adults who have lost their way emotionally, and lost faith in their potentials, I have often been able to help them realize, accept, and alter the part they have been playing in its rejection (Landau, 1973).

Many of my patients and pupils have shown emotional as well as intellectual growth in their increasing ability to ask questions. It is through the formulation and reformulation of questions, and with help towards finding their own answers, that both groups become better able to develop their own individual forms of constructive thinking. Questioning pushes an individual's present knowledge to its limits so that he has to think again, thus challenging his potential, and the greater the potential, the more powerful the challenge must be to be effective. It is important, though, to teach children to ask questions which are not based only on passively accepted knowledge, but which are dynamic and future-orientated, for they will help to close the gap between what is studied by the child today, and what will be needed by the adult in many years time.

By encouraging questions, we can help keep children's natural curiosity alive, stimulate their imagination and sense of adventure, and at the same

379

time keep the learning process enjoyable. Once children enjoy learning, they become more involved in the subject, and venture to ask more questions; all of which leads to its continuing enjoyment and progress. Though obviously we cannot assist children with knowledge of the future, we can help them acquire the mental means to deal with it more effectively.

A QUESTIONING APPROACH TO CREATIVITY

From years of investigation into aspects of creativity and questioning, Getzels (1979) has concluded that: 'finding and formulating a problem is an important aspect in creative performance in art as in science. Indeed the orientation toward problems may be the essential difference between the scientist and the technician, the artist and the copyist'—creative success depending not only on craftsmanship, but on the quality of the problems he 'finds'.

Writing about the lack of research on problem-posing, which he calls 'the problem of the problem', Getzels (1982) described three essential classes of problem situation. The first, the 'presented problem' is the kind which a teacher often gives a pupil, having a clear format and an answer, such as in geometry. The second, the 'discovered problem' is investigated by the discoverer, and is unlikely to have a known formulation or solution, such as when Roentgen, instead of merely accepting that the photographic plate had fogged up, as others had done before him, asked 'why?'. This was a self-initiated question which led to the discovery of the X-ray and to a revolution in atomic science. Thirdly, there is the 'created problem', such as when the scientist conceives of the problem of investigating the nature of light, or the artist creates a still-life where no such problem or juxtaposition existed before. In these last two situations, the formulating of the problem is an addition to knowledge, and thus a discovery in its own right (Polanyi, 1958; Henlé, 1971).

OVERCOMING BARRIERS TO CREATIVITY

Creative thinking comes into action in every situation in which the individual is confronted with a problem to be solved (Borkowski, 1978; Noppe, 1980; Perkins, 1981). It calls for sensitive awareness and sufficient mental flexibility for new problems to be reseen in terms of what has already been experienced—a process which involves some relearning. But this process is not linear and causal, as in a closed system; it is more a feed-back of inter-relationships. Piaget (1971) described it as the child's structuring of complex and flexible mental 'schemata', during which he positively constructs his own reality, rather than merely absorbing information. Investigating problem-posing in the cognitive domain, Arlin (1974, in Getzels 1982) found that those who found the most problems were using formal operational thought processes and were divergent thinkers.

This structuring is, however, only part of the process. The newly recognized set of perceptual relationships has then to be made unfamiliar again, though in a different way. This is by means of two questions about comparisons of the relationships of old to new knowledge—those of 'sameness' and 'difference' (Gordon, 1961; Bohm, 1968).

It is through the association or 'coding' of new with past events that the outer world becomes significant to the individual, i.e. we learn by generalizing about both old and new tasks (Bruner, 1970). As this depends on sequential intelligent behaviour by the learner through the discernment of attributes, it might be supposed that superior purposive intelligent behaviour might enhance the discernment of attributes, and thus the subsequent formation of concepts. But even at the higher levels of intelligence, this procedure can be severely inhibited, especially in its creative aspects, by the acceptance of predigested categories, such as those given scholastically or in social mores. As a result, that members of the same school or culture will show a tendency to 'code' in a like manner. To be original, thinkers have to reach beyond the bounds of learned coding and to create their personal coding languages, which are both innovative and distinctive. Thinking can then become increasingly creative, as new relationships are discovered between different aspects of knowledge. It is at its most effective when the experience and relationships from different disciplines can be harnessed to work together on specific problems to be solved. The personal recognition, reorganization and expansion of categories of data and ideas are vital parts of creative thinking, particularly in the forming of new dimensions of concepts (Leonard, 1969; Wallach, 1971; Austin, 1978; Nisbett and Wilson, 1979).

INDIVIDUAL DIFFERENCES

The emergence of broader, inter-disciplinary forms of classification is conditional, however, upon certain features of the thinker. Creativity is not measurable by cognitive measures alone, emotion and personality being implicit in both its appreciation and production. Getzels and Csikszentmihalyi (1976), investigating 179 (86 male and 93 female) fine-art students, found that cognitive measures did not distinguish them from other students, but that the future artists possessed distinctive traits on three values and six of Cattell's personality factors. They had higher aesthetic and lower social and economic values, and were more aloof, introspective, alienated, imaginative, self-sufficient and experimental in outlook. In addition, each sex had traits which are culturally associated with the opposite sex, and they appeared to posses a fuller spectrum of human feelings and emotions than other individuals of the same age and sex.

Recently, Getzels and Smilansky (1983) looked at 122 secondary school pupils' responses to a questionnaire which was designed to evoke the content of school problems, and measured their intellectual characteristics—intelligence, academic aptitude, and divergence. For all ability levels, the primary problem was of teachers' uncaring attitudes, but there was a significant relationship between the pupils of high intelligence and their ability to formulate problems at a pluralistic, rather than at an egocentric level. They concluded that 'in order to pose problems in a complex way, one must possess the ability to think abstractly and see the problematic situation from multiple points of view ... and such children's interpersonal problems would be of a higher quality than those which only take the problem poser's point of view'. This evidence supports Abroms' conclusions (Chapter 11) of the superior levels of social cognition of the gifted.

There is a conflict between the two natural tendencies in man—either to open up the world or to seek the security of a closed world of familiar perspective. Every educational process is a departure to a more open world than that originally conceived at the point of departure. According to Carl Rogers (1959), the atmosphere which facilitates the growth of the creative process is one of security and of the freedom to be oneself—thus to make use of inherent ability. A creative thinker has to be sufficiently self-confident to take risks if he is to glean the widest variety of knowledge, for the unknown is always threatening. Jung (1964) called this 'deep and suspicious fear of novelty ... misoneism'. He described how 'just as the "primitives" manifest all the reactions of the wild animal against untoward events ... "civilised" man reacts to new ideas, erecting psychological barriers to protect himself from the shock of facing something new'. The creative person must have considerable courage, keep hold of his ideas, be able to tolerate ambiguity, defer judgement until he feels ready, and resist being undermined by the criticism and potential rejection of others. The mental freedom brought about by security permits honest perceptual experiences, which are relatively free from coding and stereotyping, and which increase awareness; this combination of sound feelings of self-worth and freedom of thought is a potentially fertile creative combination. The courage needed to stand alone with your own problem, and the openness to break into new fields of exploration for fresh insight, are as necessary as the gift itself (May, 1975).

The less confident convergent thinker, however, is most likely from the start, to accept only those data which seem to fit in with a socially acceptable, and safer way of thinking, and will question little of what he perceives (Crutchfield, 1962; Shallcross, 1981). If the norm is to be a conformist, even the creative pupil will be easily satisfied, and as Getzels and Jackson (1962) describe it, he will supress his creative talent in order to be accepted by society. This is not to deny the value of the acquisition of conformist knowledge in creative thought, since there is ample evidence that access to a sizable body of information is essential if an individual is to have the base from which he can think divergently (Guilford, 1967; Ferguson and Ferguson, 1981; Stanley, 1980). The processes of divergent thinking act to expand those of the convergent processes into wider conceptual frameworks, which in turn effect the formation of new creative questions. One of the existential gains of asking questions about the future is that it helps children to confront the anxiety implicit in open-ended searching, and which has to be accepted as a part of the self in order for it to continue. Children often modify this anxiety, by making the unfamiliar familiar, using strategies of analogy. With their growing emotional strength, they can develop the skills to cope with themselves and to play their part in society.

STYLES OF CREATIVE QUESTIONING

There is a quality of playfulness in the search for basic elements in ideas, enjoying their contradictions, and rearranging them into experimental combinations (Winnicott, 1971; Landau, 1974; Chapter 5). Apart from statistical difficulties, absence of this freedom to play with ideas was considered to be one reason why the study of creative ability in American private-school children by Getzels and Jackson (1962), when replicated in Scotland by Hasan and Butcher (1966), not only failed to confirm the Americans' distinctions between the children's intelligence and creativity, but failed to reveal the 'outstanding humourous responses' described for the creative American children. Unfortunately, methods of education and social upbringing were not included in either study. Others have also failed to make a distinction between creativity and intelligence, finding them not mutually exclusive (Wallach and Kogan, 1965), but it may be supposed that the combination of high intelligence and high creativity in children would produce worthwhile products, given the child's ability to exercise intellectual control and play in a child-like way. Einstein delighted in his research, once writing that if he had regarded it as work, he would never have succeeded (Einstein and Infield, 1938). In respect of language learning, Buescher (1979) described the benefits of playful learning as increased scores on intelligence subtests, indices of sequential memory, originality in thinking, problem-solving tasks, and verbal communication.

The spirit of playful enquiry helps the creatively gifted person to avoid taking himself too seriously, for humour provides that vital flexibility to look at failure from another angle and with a smile. Zorba the Greek could laugh admiringly at the monumental breakdown of his intensely wrought plan and construction, dance away his disappointment, and ... start another project.

Conflicts of subjectivity and objectivity are particularly acute in creative work—conflicts which bring into question the apparent paradoxes of using imagination in science, or logic in art, and the accidentality of creative work in both areas. To be successful, the creative individual has to be able to use imagination and logic in juggling with both aspects. Though he has to be able to immerse himself personally, he still has to step back objectively from time to time, and see how it is integrated into the whole—to examine and improve his endeavour within its context. This dichotomy between analysis and intuition can, however, be exaggerated. Since the creative process normally involves more than one insight, the proof or product requires many insights along the way, and often a personality which is prepared to rework the same problem over and over, until a satisfactory conclusion is reached.

It is probably the creative person's ability to question the most ordinary things, as though he were seeing them for the first time, which allows him to perceive with greater clarity than other people, and which has often earned him the reputation of prophecy. Hieronymus Bosch, Chirico, Michael Faraday, H. G. Wells, Picasso, and Linus Pauling are just a few of the eminent creative people who have had predictive powers attributed to them, though none would ever have claimed them. Each creative person has to ask those simple, open-minded questions which are so often anticipatory. He does not merely ask why it is so, or what we know about the problem, but 'What is the purpose?', 'What do we want to achieve?' and he has the courage to ask 'What will happen if?'

DEVELOPING GIFTED CHILDREN'S CREATIVE THINKING

The primary educational aim of the Young Person's Institute for the Promotion of Art and Science in Tel Aviv is to develop creative attitudes in gifted pupils aged five to fifteen. They come after school because we believe they need to be with a variety of children for their emotional adjustment, but at the same time, they need the opportunity to use their special talents in an extracurricular situation. Our thinking courses are a form of enrichment focusing on questioning, which is the basis for the other 180 courses offered in all fields of sciences and arts for over 3000 gifted and talented children. The courses usually last a semester each, though some continue at the twelve to fourteen-year-old level. For example, there are fourteen levels in mathematics, eleven in biology, and eight in creative writing, which range from jokes to journalism. There are also summer 'Creative Activity Months'. The children are recommended by teachers, by psychological services, and by their parents; sometimes the children ask themselves, because their friends come. We also work with parents and provide refresher courses for teachers.

The children are assessed in groups on verbal and non-verbal intelligence tests, and their admission point is equivalent to about 140 on the Weschler scale. For follow-up purposes, they are also tested with creativity, anxiety, autonomy, motivation, and self-image tests. However, rather than relying solely on a rigid IQ point, we increase flexibility with an individual interview. In its sixteen years of existence, the Institute has interviewed over 5000 children and their parents, and from the descriptions of them, we have developed an attribute list, which we now use as our interview questionnaire. Children from underprivileged, culturally deprived surroundings, with family or psychological problems, or with former achievements or special talents, are accepted even if their IQs are not at 140 or more. No child is debarred for financial reasons.

We work on the understanding that all learning has both specific and general aspects. The specific aspects refer to a particular area, and cannot be transferred, but the general ones, which develop during up-bringing and education into an attitude, a pattern of thinking and acting, can be applied in any field—including the creative attitude. Education for creativity is considered to stimulate talents which already exist, and in our provision, we believe that we are helping children to actualize all their gifts and talents.

We began in 1972 by inviting fifty boys and girls, aged between nine and fifteen, of different cultural backgrounds, to meet together (Landau, 1976). Of these, thirty had high measured intelligence and twelve average intelligence. They were each asked to construct a questionnaire of twenty questions on the future of mankind, and as we were concerned that they would give their own opinions, they made them up on the spot.

THE QUESTIONNAIRES

We were surprised by the wide spread of the children's interests in nearly all areas of life; man with himself, man with society, man and his environment, man and his inventions, his needs, his feelings, his fears, and his hopes. They asked questions about the continuance of life, and also about the quality of life we could expect; about the kind of inventions men will discover, and also about whether these would make the world better and more pleasant to live in.

We did find some differences in the responses, according to the ages, cultural backgrounds, and intellectual levels of the children. The younger (nine to eleven year-olds) and the more culturally deprived children asked more general questions which were not particularly relevant to their lives. They looked forward to more gadgets in the future, and theirs were the wildest science-fiction fantasies. The responses of the older (twelve to fifteen year-olds), and the better-informed gifted children were, however, more personal, of longer range, more pessimistic, and more anxious. They were concerned, for example, with the future role of the family and of males and females;

would there be enough fresh air to breathe? The gifted children asked many questions about individual responsibility for their own and mankind's fate, such as, 'Will man be able to meet his needs without imposing himself on society?' 'Will there be control over aggression, with the purpose of avoiding wars, or will man invent gadgets which will fight his wars for him?' 'Will a substitute for oil be invented, not only to lessen Arab pressure but also to lessen pollution?' As early as 1972, these children were asking what would happen if a certain group controlled the energy sources of the world. Above all, they were concerned that present-day adults should know what they were doing to the environment.

The gifted had more anxiety than the average-ability children. For example, where the latter were keen on money-making machines, the former asked such questions as whether the destruction of mankind would be instant; how the third world war would end; or cures for inflation (an Israeli speciality). However, it seemed that even in this initial making of a questionnaire, the conceptual and verbal formulation of their anxieties helped them to come to terms and cope with them a little, for as the questions progressed, they became more hopeful of solutions. For example, an early anxiety expressed in the question 'Will there be the destruction of the human race?' turned into a search for alternatives in a later question, 'Will psychology and science find ways to control evil in man?' Their questions also became more constructive: 'Will man learn how to control his impulses?', 'Will man learn how to avoid mistakes? In the final questions about how to learn and teach responsibility towards oneself and towards mankind, we could see a certain relaxation of tension as the children coped with their anxiety.

Our conclusions from the collection of these questions was that children do think about the future; their world is not one of seeking instant gratification, and their thoughts are often clearer and brighter than adults' in their naivite'. They also have a certain clarity in their natural spontaneous way of questioning, which made us adults nostalgic for the innocence we had lost.

We have devised many exercises at the Institute for challenging children to ask questions about their life today, their social involvement, and their ideas on the future, some of which are described briefly below.

Definitions

As a form of mental strengthening for the children, the course starts with some difficult definitions, such as the broad concept of curiosity, openness, flexibility, imagination, surprise, and sense of humour (Landau, 1976, 1981). Then, they are asked to consider the function and value of these attributes and of their opposites. For example, in answer to the question 'What is play?' a child might answer 'Something to enjoy'. The opposite construct to play might then be boredom. One nine-year-old answered this question with 'Sleep. When I'm awake, I play'. And 'What about school?' we asked. 'Children's play' was the answer. Here, we can see the outgoing, adventurous thinking of a bright, challenged child. The same courage could be seen in their responses, when we asked the children 'Under what kind of teacher would you like to learn?' They mostly rejected the proffered answers of 'understanding', 'warm', 'not demanding' and 'gives freedom to work alone' in favour of different and challenging new ideas, such as 'happy'.

Imagination

We said to the children, 'Let us try and imagine the world we shall inhabit in thirty years' time, the houses, food, clothes, transport, communication, leisure, work, family life, etc.!' After each child had thought of his own response alone, we worked on the possibilities together. Here are some of their ideas.

One child saw a house of the future as a self-sufficient unity, but there had to be a channel to his friend's house. Another saw houses with all-electronic devices, built in the air. Another thought that food would consist only of pills, coated with a delicious tasty substance, a kind of bubble-gum to exercise the lips and keep the mouth flexible. There would not be much use for the mouth, because there would not be a lot of talking; communication would be either through television, body movement, or brain waves.

There would be no need for transport because the destination would come upon wish, when and where the need arose. Goods would be sent by underground tubes. Some spoke about the problem of space; living in closed mansions would eliminate bacteria and infection. Eating programmed food in pills would prevent illness. People would live forever, and there would be no space for them.

Family life would be very close because everyone would be at home, working or learning; yet it might be boring and lonely because everybody would be in different parts of the house. The house would become a kind of tribe accommodation, in order to give the feeling of belonging, keeping together. Personal privacy would be very much respected because of limited space; there would be more need for giving and receiving love.

Work would be done mostly by computers and robots; man would only programme it. The kind of jobs that we know today such as postmen, bus drivers, bakers, shopkeepers, shoemakers would cease to exist, or would be done as hobbies by men and women, to actualize their creative potentials. There would be no policemen, because order and control would be kept by the 'EYE', which would see everything, or by the accepted code of behaviour within the tribe-family.

Comparisons

To foster the gifted child's creative, combinatory skills, we have devised exercises which involve comparative, paradoxical, or analogous problems. For example, when an eleven-year-old was asked to compare a phenomenon of life today with that of 100 and 50 years ago, and then to compare it with life 10 and 50 years hence, he chose to compare religion and education. 'A hundred years ago', he said 'many people were religious and very few were educated. Today, they are about equal. Ten years from now, there will be more educated people and less religious people. And in fifty years, there will be ... a new religion'.

Another response to that question was, '100 years ago, man invented the machine to help him be more free for other tasks, widening the range of his activities. Today, the machine does the work of man in a better and quicker way. In ten years from now, the machine will think for man, and in fifty years, the machine will rule over man'. Another answered, 'A hundred years ago, man dressed in order to keep warm, to cover himself. Fifty years ago, man showed his status by the clothes he wore. Today, man emphasises his equality by wearing jeans, clothes for poor and rich. Ten years from now, he will try to show his individuality by his own way of dressing, and fifty years from now, man will dress to impress or pacify the beings on another planet.' These are some of the many responses that we have recorded on our courses at the Institute. They are the original, creative products of the children, at a time when science-fiction was not yet popular in Israel. It is only since the beginning of the 1980s that Popeye has given way to science-fiction on Israeli television.

When I asked a gifted ten-year-old how she had gained most of her knowledge, she replied, 'By asking questions.' I asked a gifted ten-year-old boy what he considered to be the opposite to a question, and he answered, 'My teacher'; I wanted to know why, and he said it was because 'she never questions anything, she just states facts'. Then I asked a third gifted child of the same age to tell me what a question was, and she replied, 'Something that makes you learn, that makes you be in communication with the world.'

As our dominant procedure at the Institute is in the task of creative education, teaching is through questions, and we hope that the outlook it engenders also provides the children with the tools to cope with the problems of the future, so that in this positive way, their future will appear to them to be in some part their own responsibility. The missing bits of their limited knowledge can always be filled in by tuition with what we know of the past, but the questions the children ask are always the products of their own life experiences, and must be seen in that context (Langer, 1978; Rubin and Pepler, 1980; Albert, 1982). By giving the children the opportunity to question the future, we aim to give them the means to work with their imaginative, cognitive, and affective abilities.

CREATIVE THINKING IN SCHOOL

During many long discussions with artists and scientists, I have become aware of their shared problems in creative work, and many of the strategies they have evolved to cope with them. For both groups, the compartmentalized approach to knowledge and thought in their conventional school education sometimes proved to be less of a help than a handicap to their creative thinking, which they had to overcome. Even as pupils, they had to search for ideas and inspiration in areas usually regarded as outside the recognized disciplines—something which Medawar (1969) described as a feature of his own professional scientific life. Abraham Maslow (1962) has described the scholastic problem succinctly: 'When the only tool you have is a hammer, it is tempting to treat everything as if it were a nail', though in fact, every teacher has many other readily available tools and more open-ended approaches to knowledge.

Creativity is based on high intelligence; probably from about IQ 120. It is by means of stimulating questions that the subject matter is brought to consciousness, encouraging further discovery, while direction-giving questions open the doors to creative development (Bannister and Fransella, 1971; Czikszentmihalyi 1978; Czikszentmihalyi and Beattie, 1979). The experience of many educationalists has shown that the teaching of a questioning approach enhances children's curiosity. The most frequent style of teaching in schools, whereby the teacher tells the children what they have to absorb, and they are consequently examined on the effects of the teaching by means of achievement tests, merely encourages more convergent thinking. This method of teaching is most suited to the conservation of information acquired over generations, and is least likely to contribute a novel link in the further continuance of learning (Landau, 1979).

Translated into practical terms, a teacher would be advised to take up an approach to the teaching of a new skill or idea, which encourages questioning in the learner even in its introductory stages, before she moves on to its more complex aspects. This should be accompanied by exercises or imagery, which the teacher judges to be as closely allied to the child's ability as possible. When both teacher and pupil feel they are ready to move on, then the more complex, abstract, or symbolic aspects of the subjects can be tackled, still keeping the questioning approach.

A particular benefit of the questioning, open-ended style of teacher guidance, as distinct from the old didactic presentation of information, is the possibility of bringing the pupil's latent fears of failing to understand, or doubts about the rightness of his own approach to the problem, into a perspective with which he can cope (Cautela and McCullough, 1978; Wine, 1980; Meichenbaum, et al., 1980; Posner and Rothbart, 1981). The child is encouraged to proceed at his own level of competence, whether in depth or detail. With gentle encouragement, he is able to accept that his lack of total understanding today is quite alright, and that it is better to ask questions about what mystifies him, for in that way it can serve as a challenge and as a basis for what is to be understood tomorrow (Landau, 1976).

By teaching children how to ask questions, we are teaching them how to 'fish' for knowledge and experience, nicely illustrated by an old Chinese story. A beggar once asked a fisherman to relieve his terrible hunger by giving him a fish to eat. The old fisherman refused him and instead, offered to teach him how to fish, explaining that if he provided a fish for the beggar to eat today, he would be hungry again tomorrow, but if he taught him how to fish now, he would never be hungry again. It is not only technology which the world needs to secure our future, but ability to see the problems and produce creative solutions.

REFERENCES

Albert, R. S. (1982). *Genius and Eminence: the Social Psychology of Creativity and Exceptional Achievement.* Pergamon Press, Oxford.

Austin, J. H. (1978). *Chase, Chance and Creativity, the Lucky Art of Novelty.* Columbia University Press, New York.

Bannister, D., and Fransella, F. (1971).*Enquiring Man.* Penguin, London.

Block, N. J., and Dworkin, G. (1976). I.Q. heritability and inequality. In *I.Q. Controversy* (eds N. J. Block and G. Dworkin. Pantheon Books, USA.

Bohm, D. (1968). On Creativity. *Leonardo,* **1.** 137–149.

Borkowski, J. G. (1978). Research tactics in complex learning, memory and cognition. In *Experimental Psychology: Research Tactics and their Applications* (eds D. C. Anderson and J. G. Borkowski), Scott-Foresman, Glenview, Illinois.

Bronfenbrenner, U. (1979). *The Ecology of Human Development; Experiments by Nature and Design.* Harvard University Press, Cambridge, Massachusetts.

Bruner, S. J. (1970). Some theories on instruction. In *Readings in Educational Psychology* (ed. E. Stones) Methuen, London.

Buescher, T. (1979). Language as play: a case for playfulness in language arts for gifted children. *Language Arts,* **56**NI, 16–20.

Cautela, J., and McCullough, L. (1978). Covert condition: a learning-theory perspective on imagery. In *The Power of Human Imagination. New Methods in Psychotherapy* (eds K. S. Pope and J. L. Singer). Plenum Press, New York.

Crutchfield, R. S. (1962). Conformity and creative thinking. In *Contemporary Approaches to Creative Thinking* (eds H. E. Gruber, J. Terell and A. Wetheimer). Atherton Press, New York.

Csikszentmihalyi, M. (1978). Attention and the holistic approach to behaviour. In *The Stream of Consciousness: Scientific Investigations into the Flow of Human Experience* (eds K. S. Pope and J. L. Singer). Plenum Press, New York.

Csikszentmihalyi, M., and Beattie, O. (1979). Life themes; a theoretical and empirical explanation of their origins and effects. *Journal of Humanistic Psychology,* **19.** 45–63.

Einstein, A., and Infeld, L. (1938). *The Evolution of Physics* Simon and Schuster, New York.

Ferguson, S., and Ferguson, S. D. (1981). *Intercom: Readings in Organisational Communication.* Hayden, New Jersey.

Getzels, J. W. (1979). From art student to fine artist: potential, problem finding and performance. In *The Gifted and Talented: their Education and Development, The 78th Yearbook of the National Society for the Study of Education* (ed. H. Passow). University of Chicago Press, Chicago.

Getzels, J. W. (1982). The problem of the problem. In *New Directions for Methodology of Social and Behavioural Science: Question Framing and Response Consistency* (ed. R. Hogarth). Jossey-Bass, San Francisco.

Getzels, J. W., and Csikszentmihalyi, M. (1976). *The Creative Vision: A Longitudinal Study of Problem Finding in Art.* Wiley, New York.

Getzels, J. W., and Jackson, P. (1962). *Creativity and Intelligence.* Wiley, New York.

Getzels, J. W., and Smilansky J. (1983). Individual differences in pupil perceptions of school problems. In *Br. J. Educ. Psychol.,* **53**, 307–316.

Gordon, W. J. J. (1961). *Synectics: the Development of Creative Capacity.* Harper and Row, New York.

Guilford, J. P. (1967). Some new views of creativity. In *Theories and Dates in Psychology* (ed. J. Helson). Van Nostrand, Princeton.

Hasan, P., and Butcher, H. J. (1966). Creativity and intelligence, a partial replication with Scottish children of Getzels and Jackson's study. *Brit. J. Psychol.,* **57**, 129–135.

Henlé, M. (1971). The snail beneath the shell. *Abraxas,* **1**, 119–133.

Jung, C. G. (1964). Approaching the unconscious. In *Man and his Symbols* (ed. C. G. Jung). Aldus Books, London.

Landau, E. (1969). *Psychologie der Kreativitaet.* Ernst Reinhardt Verlag, Muenchen-Basel.

Landau, E. (1973). The Creative Approach to Psychotherapy. *American Journal for Psychotherapy,* XXVII, 566–598.

Landau, E. (1974). My game is life, or educational games in personality development. *Forum for Human Dialogue on Important Contemporary Issues and Problems and on the Future of Man,* **6**, 76–78.

Landau, E. (1976). The questions children ask. *Futures,* **8**, 154–162.

Landau, E. (1979). The Young Persons' Institute for the Promotion of Art and Science, Tel-Aviv. In *Gifted Children Reaching their Potential* (ed. J. Gallagher), Kollek, Jerusalem.

Landau, E. (1981). The profile of the gifted child. In *Gifted Children Challenging their Potential; New Perspectives and Alternatives* (ed. A. H. Kramer), Trillium Press, New York.

Langer, E. (1978). Rethinking the role of thought in social interactions. In *New Directions in Attribution Research,* Vol. 2 (eds J. Harvey, W. Ickes, and R. Kidd). Erlbaum, Hillsdale, New Jersey.

Leonard, G. B. (1969). *Education and Ecstasy.* Delta, New York.

Maslow, A. (1962). *Towards a Psychology of being.* Van Nostrand, New York.

May, R. (1975). *The Courage to Create.* Norton, New York.

May, R. (1977). *The Meaning of Anxiety.* Norton, New York.

Medawar, P. N. (1969). *Induction and Intuition in Scientific Thought.* Methuen, London.

Meichenbaum, D., Henshaw, D., and Himel, N. (1980). Coping with stress as a problem-solving process. In *Achievement Stress and Anxiety* (eds W. Krohne and L. Laux). Hemisphere, Washington, DC.

Nisbett, R., and Wilson, T. (1979). Telling more than we can know. Verbal reports on mental processes. *Psychological Review*, **84**, 613–624.

Noppe, L. D. (1980). Creative thinking. In *Encyclopaedia of Clinical Assessment*, Vol. 2 (ed. R. H. Woody). Jossey-Bass, San Francisco.

Perkins, D. N. (1981). *The Mind's Best Work; a New Psychology of Creative Thinking*. Harvard University Press, USA.

Piaget, J. (1971). *Structuralism*. Routledge and Kegan Paul, London.

Polanyi, M. (1958). *Personal Knowledge*. University of Chicago Press, Chicago.

Posner M. I., and Rothbart, M. K. (1981). The development of attentional mechanisms. In *Nebraska Symposium on Motivation* (eds J. H. Flowers and H. E. Howe), University of Nebraska Press, Lincoln.

Rogers, C. R. (1959). Towards a theory of creativity. In *Creativity and its Cultivation* (ed. H. Anderson), Harper, New York.

Rubin, K. H., and Pepler, D. J. (1980). The relationship of child's play to social-cognitive development. In *Friendship and Social Relations in Children* (eds H. Foot, T. Chapman and J. Smith), Wiley, London.

Shallcross, D. J. (1981). *Teaching Creative Behaviour*. Prentice Hall, New Jersey.

Stanley, J. C. (1980). The intellectually talented child. *Educational Researcher*, **9**, 8–12.

Wallach, M. A. (1971). The Intelligence/Creativity Distinction. *General Learning Press*, New York.

Wallach, W. C., and Kogan, N. (1965). *Modes of Thinking in Young Children: a Study of the Creativity–Intelligence Distinction*. Holt Reinhart and Winston, New York.

Wine, J. (1980). Cognitive-attentional theory of test anxiety. In *Test Anxiety: Theory, Research and Applications* (ed. I. Sarason), Erlbaum, New Jersey.

Winnicott, D. W. (1971). *Playing and Reality*. Tavistock, London.

Author Index

Subject Index